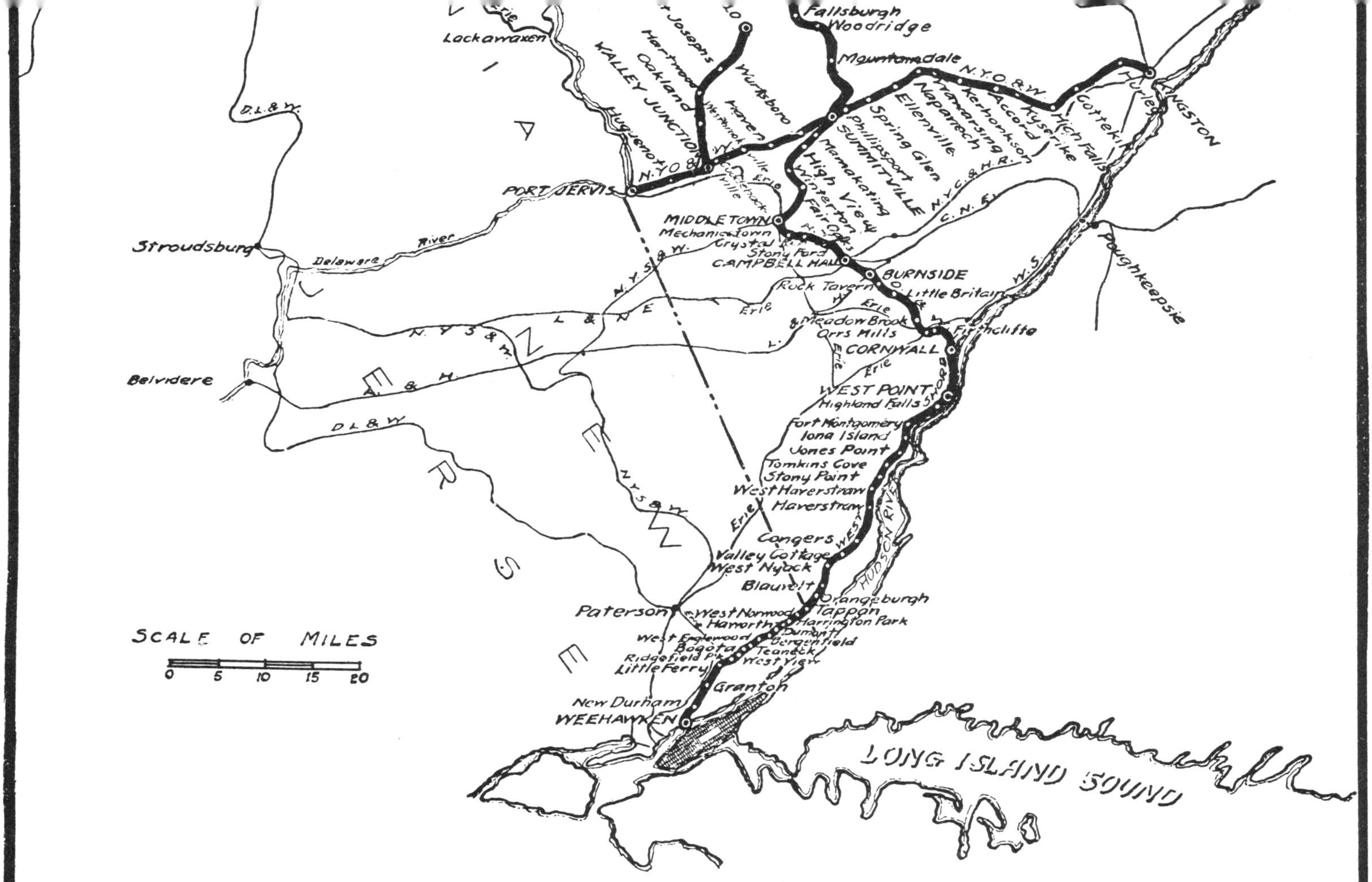

NEW YORK, ONTARIO & WESTERN RAILWAY.

Courtesy of Russ Colegrove

The New York, Ontario & Western Railway and the Dairy Industry in Central New York State

Milk Cans, Mixed Trains and Motor Cars

by
Robert E. Mohowski

Featuring the artwork of
Carl A. Ohlson

Garrigues House, Publishers
P. O. Box 400   Laurys Station, PA 18059

OPPOSITE TITLE PAGE: Soft, measured exhaust puffs leave the 308's stack while it moves over the O&W's upper Maywood (Sidney Center) trestle in 1947. Clanking rods, whining generator and clanging of the fireman's coal scoop accompany the passage. This will prove to be the locomotive's final year of service and its assignment to the milk train during that time will be ever less frequent.
The demise of the transportation system that had radically altererd conceptions of space and time, that redefined the possibilities and opportunites presented by the natural resources of the counties which the O&W served, would not be far behind the steam locomotive in passing from the region. Within a decade the screeching wheels, raucous whistles and horns, plumes of smoke and steam, growling diesels and the friendly waves of train crews would be only memories.

It is difficult, if not impossible, for railroad historians to think of a railroad without a geographic context. Every train, locomotive, or right-of-way appears against or within a natural or man-made environment. Inspired by a photograph taken by A. V. Neusser, artist Carl Ohlson—employing pen and ink technique—has put together those elements that have defined and characterized the major facets of the O&W's personality as contained in the 70-odd miles of the railroad covered in this book. Ohlson gives us a visual "fix" on what follows in word and photograph.
Happily, the Maywood depot and the wing retaining wall of the trestle can still be seen today in Sidney Center, N.Y., almost 40 years after the railrod closed. The foresight and dedicated efforts of a community historical society has preserved what had been a center of the community's existence. It holds many memories for an older generation and is a key to understanding the past while providing a sense of continuity for those of the present and those to come. —R.M.

The New York, Ontario & Western Railway and the Dairy Industry in Central New York State:
Milk Cans, Mixed Trains and Motor Cars

Copyright © 1995 by Robert E. Mohowski

First Edition
First Printing

Published by:
Garrigues House, Publishers
P. O. Box 400
Laurys Station, Pa 18059

All rights reserved.
No part of this book may be reproduced in any manner
without written permission from the publisher, with the
exception of brief quotations embodied in reviews or articles.

Manufactured in the United States of America

Library of Congress Cataloging-in-Publication Data

Mohowski, Robert E. 1941-
    The New York, Ontario & Western Railway and the dairy industry in
central New York State : milk cans, mixed trains, and motor cars   / by
Robert E. Mohowski : featuring the artwork of Carl A. Ohlson. — 1st
ed.
       p.   cm.
    Includes bibliographical references and index.
    ISBN 0-9620844-6-8
    1. New York, Ontario, and Western Railway Co. 2. Dairying—New
York (State)   3. Railroads—New York (State)   I. Title.
TF25.N728M65   1995
385'.54'0974—dc20   95-17349
                                                            CIP

For Pat, Dan and Dave Mohowski
and for
Kyle and Ryan Ohlson

Foreword

There is no escaping the New York, Ontario & Western—not that I would want to. For 30 years I spent part of almost every summer near its tracks. For another 20 years, by which time the road had gone out of business, I lived in O&W territory.

It turned out that I had cousins working for the O&W, including the last superintendent of motive power, Guy Bennett. It turned out that the bridge engineer Albert Lucius and his family, neighbors of my grandparents in Brooklyn, had visited our family's summer place while he was building the steel bridge at Preston Park on the Scranton Division. A great-aunt of mine gave Lucius' daughter Florence her first art lesson, and Florence eventually married the sculptor Jo Davidson.

Bicycle-train trips I made as a boy to Middletown, Scranton and New Berlin all involved the O&W. The train home in the last case was the O&W from Walton. One morning I cycled to Preston Park and saw two trains all day, a diesel-powered through freight and the steam-powered way freight. Helping to keep that day alive after 50 years is an experience that came on the way over. As I topped a familiar hill, something unfamiliar ran across and down the road ahead. It was my first sight of a fox in the wild.

The O&W was like the wildlife, fleeting and elusive. When I took my first O&W photograph, in 1944—a Y-class Mountain type leading a freight through Preston Park at twilight—the engine pushing on the rear in near-darkness was a Lackawanna Mikado. No railroad in the O&W's region passed through wilder country. Its steam whistles were the most lonesome I have ever heard.

Now I live in South Carolina, and there's still no escaping the O&W. An early look around revealed that a nearby short line in Georgia, the Hartwell Railway, was harboring an old O&W 44-ton diesel. Then there's the matter of Isaac W. Fowler, a former O&W official and a cousin of O&W President Thomas P. Fowler. Isaac Fowler ran short lines in South Carolina in the 1890's, including what is now our local Norfolk Southern branch. He found a wife in our town and spent his last years here; by special dispensation he belonged to a local Masonic lodge and also kept his lodge membership in Middletown. All of this was news to a neighbor of mine, an old O&W buff who is a grandson of Thomas P. Fowler and a member of the church in whose yard his grandfather's cousin lies at rest.

There is a lot more to the O&W than private experience. It pervades history, local and beyond. The closing of the road awakened many of us to coming changes in the rail industry. One can foresee only growing interest in a railroad that ran across the state of New York, and vanished at a stroke. Small wonder that there has been for 50 years now a historical organization bent on preserving every detail of the failed company that was the largest American rail abandonment ever.

The work of saving the record becomes harder each year. Robert Mohowski was an early editor of the O&W Society's journal and has spent many days studying the O&W and hiking its abandoned grades. He is well-liked by a large circle of friends. This is his first book. It has been researched and written with care and devotion and in the best tradition of the historian.

William S. Young
Aiken, South Carolina
January, 1993

Contents

Foreword vi

Introduction ix

Prologue: The Milk Trains 3

Chapter 1: The Dairy Farmers and the Creameries 19

Chapter 2: The New York, Ontario and Western's Milk Traffic 39

Chapter 3: The O&W's Wooden Milk Cars 71

Chapter 4: The Milk Tank Cars 83

Chapter 5: Bulk Tank Containers on Flatcars 99

Chapter 6: Delhi and the Delhi Branch 113

Chapter 7: Walton 151

Chapter 8: Walton to Northfield 175

Chapter 9: The *Zig* Zag and Northfield Tunnel 185

Chapter 10: Merrickville to Sidney 199

Chapter 11: Sidney 229

Chapter 12: Sidney to New Berlin Junction 261

Chapter 13: The New Berlin Branch 269

Chapter 14: The Wharton Valley Railway 291

Chapter 15: The Unadilla Valley Railway 305

Chapter 16: The Gas-Mechanical and Gas-Electric Cars 321

Addenda 334

Bibliography 349

Index 352

The whistle of the locomotive penetrates my woods summer and winter, sounding like the scream of a hawk sailing over some farmer's yard, informing me that many restless city merchants are arriving within the circle of the town, or adventurous country traders from the other side. As they come under one horizon, they shout their warning to get off the track to the other. heard sometimes through the circles of two towns. Here come your groceries, country; your rations, countrymen! Nor is there any man so independent on his farm that he can say them nay. And here's your pay for them! screams the countryman's whistle; timber like long battering-rams going twenty miles an hour against the city's walls, and chairs enough to seat all the weary and heavy-laden that dwell within them. With such large and lumbering civility the country hands a chair to the city. All the Indian huckleberry hills are stripped, all the cranberry meadows are raked into the city. Up comes the cotton, down goes the woven cloth; up comes the silk, down goes the woolen; up come the books, but down goes the wit that writes them.

—Henry David Thoreau
Walden

Introduction

It was the Lehigh & Hudson River Railway (L&HR) that introduced me to the New York, Ontario & Western. The L&HR was celebrating its Centennial Year in 1960 and sponsored an excursion that ran in two sections on June 4th of that year. The trains first ran north out of Warwick, N.Y., to cover the 20 miles to Maybrook, the L&HR's northern terminus. I had managed to find a place on the crowded rear vestibule of the second section, from which a rolling schematic of the L&HR's route was observed. In due time, we crossed a right-of-way that held vestiges of a railroad. The crossing diamond was gone, but a few lengths of deeply rusted rails extended at right angles and in both directions from the L&HR's roadbed. An interchange track was still intact in the southeast quadrant of the former junction. Within the triangle formed by roadbed and tracks were stacks of rails and signal masts.

"What was that?" I asked of no one in particular on the crowded platform.

"The O&W," came a flat reply. (Later, I would learn that my informant was Ray W. Brown, a dedicated O&W historian and contributor to this book.)

A vague remembrance of those initials drifted across my memory. The piles of rail and empty ties gave such a strong visual substance to the initials N.Y.O.&W., that 30 years later the desolate scene is still vivid. Shortly after that I discovered William F. Helmer's book, *O&W*, and so began my long fascination with a railroad that died in 1957.

What is this magnetic appeal that makes one dig through dusty papers or search out antique shops on the back roads near the O&W's right-of-way in hopes of finding hardware, postcards, or rusty shards of an extinct transportation system? Why such reverence for the recollections of an elderly gentleman whose gnarled fingers rasped the stubby throttle of a gray and yellow FT, or a man whose work place was a ramshackle station that was rattled by the north country's winter blizzards and crashing summer thunderstorms?

In the February, 1981, issue of *Trains,* Ken Kreitner wrote that it is the fascination with death that draws us back repeatedly to the remnants of the line ("Lament for an Old Woman," Trains, February 1981). It may well be. But I also believe there is an element in our national consciousness that makes us root for an underdog and perpetuate romanticized lost causes. Certainly no one this side of the analyst's couch has come forward with a better reason. Some of us will forever poke in foundation holes and dig in the kitchen middens of both the recent and distant past to attempt to satisfy some insatiable desire to know more about a subject we will never know firsthand. There we are while fellow enthusiasts photograph the latest diesels from General Electric with a train of modern container cars. We have our ways and they have theirs.

Paraphrasing Psalms 137: 1, Lucius Beebe, in one of his books on the Colorado narrow gauge lines, had this to say about those of our fraternity who wander the abandoned three-foot gauge rights-of-way in Colorado and, with ineffable sadness, mourn their loss: "By the waters of Gunnison [River] they sat them down and wept." (Lucius Beebe and Charles Clegg, *Narrow Gauge in the Rockies* Berkeley: Howell North, 1958). If you will substitute the Beaverkill, the East Branch, or the Chenango River for us O&W faithful, you may better understand. I can truly say, however, that I saw no tears. We were too busy examining the bridge piers and measuring retaining walls.

It has been popular for some historians to express the view that the New York, Ontario & Western Railway should never have been built. The twenty years of bankruptcy from 1937 to abandonment in 1957 and the stigma of failure that bankruptcy and abandonment imply have overshadowed an earlier history and made such a casual viewpoint popular. It has been convenient for many to accept this idea and dismiss the road as just one more in a long line of overly optimistic railway enterprises, many of which could not even pay monthly wages, let alone their fixed charges. I don't believe it is that simple.

It is true that the great hopes for Oswego to become a major trading center of the lower Great Lakes never materialized, that the route took little traffic away from the Erie and the New York Central, and that the costs of building, operating, and maintaining its rugged profile took a large bite out of income. There is no question that the road could have been better located and that some of its early promoters seem to have been fast buck artists who used political office and played upon the naivete of New York's rural population to accomplish their own ends. However, it was also a time of great national faith and a business ethic that operated differently from that of the present—although some may see similarities. There was a national feeling of optimism despite several earlier business depressions and the recent Civil War. Even though a number of enterprises had failed, there existed a direction if not an ultimate goal that we of the present day may not understand, since we do not seem to have one. The sense of wonder and faith in scientific advancement that came from the Enlightenment was still strong.

Events and institutions of the past will never be completely understood because their formative context is gone. The O&W did not drop from the sky and drape itself over the landscape; it was a product of the age. Two cultural critics of the period give us contrasting opinions on the new transportation.

Ralph Waldo Emerson, who possessed something of the Jeffersonian belief in nature and the agrarian ideal, saw that America's vast spaces required technology to bind all parts into a cultural whole. Distance had to be overcome. Social intercourse would create a national identity, and it had to occur over distances of 20 miles as well as 2000. "Railroad iron was a magician's rod, in its power to evoke the sleeping energies of land and water." This was a qualified affirmation because he did warn that technology could be bent to selfish aims that were separate from moral values and that such a trend would subvert the whole nation.

Nathaniel Hawthorne saw no positive value in the transportation system and in Mr. Smooth-it-away of *The Celestial Railroad* he created the archetype of the latter nineteenth century railroad promoter and business manipulator. He saw the railroad as upsetting traditional arrangements, destroying beliefs and value systems. We were deluded by the railroads; they were not the road to heaven but rather the road to hell. They destroyed the pastoral landscape, created industrial filth, compromised our beliefs, and speeded up life so we had less time for thoughtful contemplation and simple innocent pleasures. Many pulpits echoed his word, but Emersonian optimism carried the day.

It is probably true that the great efforts expended to keep the O&W alive in its entirety after 1945 were a waste of time and money. A good case for scrap-

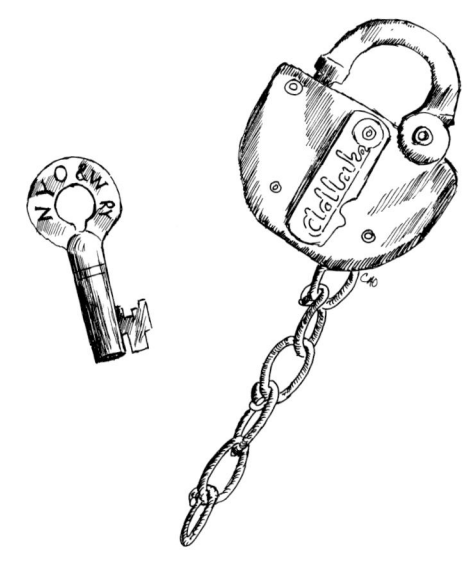

ping the road during the latter part of the depression might also be made.

Between 1890 and 1937, however, the NYO&W was a highly useful agency of transportation. It paid taxes and dividends (almost $20,000,000 went to the controlling New Haven during the first quarter of this century), provided meaningful and dignified employment for thousands of people, and was most certainly an agent in the industrial, commercial, and agricultural development of the United States in general and New York State in particular. During its successful years it maintained a first-class property by the liberal spending of surplus earnings on physical improvements and modern equipment. Many of its administrative officers and operating managers were talented, innovative men who were respected in the rail industry and contributed to its advancement.

To look back from the closing decade of the twentieth century and say that the O&W would have no purpose in this day and age is quite correct. It is equally true to say the same of the Delaware & Hudson Canal or Butterfield's Overland Stage Company. However, if the three transportation systems are placed in correct historical context, I believe they all appear as business enterprises of definite purpose and important links in the commercial-transportation complexes of their day.

Local business was one of the main purposes of the line. In this category I include originating and terminating traffic to and from off-line points. While local traffic did not develop rapidly enough to save the New York & Oswego Midland, it did reach adequate levels to support the O&W. Coal, milk, and passengers became the railroad's reasons for existence. Those who will take the time to review the annual reports and seek out the figures for on-line business will be quite surprised. The traffic flowing to, from, and between towns was easily twice the tonnage and dollar income of bridge traffic for many years. Trade and travel were much more local in nature than they are today.

The changes in the way this country carries on its commercial activity, i.e., from local to national to global scale, are mirrored in its rail systems. Some had particular advantages and could adapt and others could not or did not. It simply is not economical for a local freight to drop off a car of feed or pick up a half-dozen cans of milk at the depot and has not been for many years. The O&W outlived its usefulness, but it took many people a long time to understand that fact.

The reader may ask why a particular 70 miles of the New York, Ontario & Western were chosen for coverage in this book. William Helmer's *O&W* gave a fine general description of the railroad and Manville Wakefield's *To The Mountains by Rail* covered the Southern Division passenger service and its connection with the resort hotels. The O&W Society's two earlier books, *The Scranton Division* and *The Wood Chemical Industry in the Delaware Valley,* dealt with the coal business and wood chemical plants along the railroad. One can see that there is both a topical and geographic tendency to head northward in the writing of O&W history. This tied in nicely with my own love of rural Delaware County, the valley of the Unadilla River, and the connection of both regions with the dairy industry. It is my hope that someone in the near future will throw the switch at New Berlin Junction for the main line and take us, in whole or in part, to the shore of Lake Ontario, as well as up the northern branches.

While this book concentrates on the 70 route miles between Delhi and Edmeston, I have considered any milk or milk related business anywhere on the railroad fair subject for inclusion as I have indicated in this book's title.

Geographically, the O&W route can best be described as running in a northwest-southeast direction, but for operating purposes, company officials decided to make it a north-south railroad. Thus reference to direction on the main line is done in the same manner in the text. On both the New Berlin and Delhi branches, movement away from the junction is northward and toward the junction is southward. The Scranton Division presents an interesting circumstance. Originally movement from Cadosia to Scranton was considered southbound and Scranton to Cadosia was northbound. Between 1940 and 1946 this was reversed. This would make a through freight northbound for an entire run from Maybrook to Mayfield and make for uniformity in issuing train orders and other operational directives. I have used this latter definition of direction for a small section of chapter two where the Scranton Division is mentioned.

The reader is cautioned that there may be discrepancies between the track maps and the printed word regarding track arrangements in a number of locations. Documents and records were frequently not dated or recording procedures were inconsistent in detail from one time period to another. There were also reports from different departments on the same subject that did not agree. While it is true that railroads left a paper trail, and that stacks of correspondence exist over seemingly trivial matters, many items of greater historical interest to us of the present day were lightly treated.

Records relating to all aspects of the railway have been scattered far and wide, and I have tried, so far as was consistent with time and financial considerations, to locate and draw upon these records. The largest such file belongs to this book's sponsoring organization, The Ontario & Western Historical Society, and was heavily used. I have no doubt that additional records and information will surface in the future to clarify—or correct—this and earlier efforts concerned with O&W history. Knowing this, it has been most difficult to stop research and commit these words to the typesetter. Whenever I left an individual, library, or museum, the host's parting words always included mention of another individual, library, or museum that should be visited.

In those communities and villages where telegraph operators or agents were established, the station call letters are given. I have also added the milepost numbers for each station. These generally occur only at the first mention of the location. Some places, such as Sages Corners on the New Berlin branch, were only flag stops and may have had a mere cinder platform for passenger convenience. This may tend to confuse the rail historian, since it is still referred to as a station by the railroad although it had no agent to conduct business at the site. Related to this are stations such as Colchester on the Delhi branch and South Unadilla on the main line. One would look in vain for a cluster of homes in the vicinity of these two stations. Here the railroad served a very scattered population, but one that was adequate to provide a business base for the O&W.

It might also help if one understands the New York State definition of a town. The state's counties are divided into geopolitical units called towns. Within many of these towns are villages of the same name: Sidney, Walton, and Hamden are examples. The O&W had stations in all these villages, as well as locations such as Youngs, which was within the bounds of the town of Sidney. Youngs did not have a local government, but was considered a village as far as the railroad was concerned. I have tried to be consistent with the state's definition.

An addenda has been added to provide additional information on certain subjects to give them greater depth and clarification.

I am well aware that the O&W, in its corporate title, was called a railway. This may have come about because of, or in deference to, the British money that help to resurrect the old Midland. However it became awkward to speak of a railway in one sentence and use railroad generically in referring to the O&W or another company in the next. I hope the use of railroad for all will not be an affront to those loyal to the O&W.

Much to my surprise, I found that there is a host of individuals who are very interested in the many aspects of the dairy business. They collect memorabilia in the same manner that the rail enthusiast collects lanterns, tickets, and books for his favorite route. Tony Knipp, an Orange County resident with a keen appreciation of his area's agricultural history, is among that group and provided sources to answer hundreds of questions about cows, farmers, milk. and their connection to railroad transportation.

Many of the photos used herein existed as postcards in individual collections. The value of many of these cards has reached such a point that some of the owners were reluctant to trust them to the mail or even allow them out of the house. In such cases, a copy negative was made using a Minolta SRT 101 camera with close-up filters and Kodak Tech-Pan film. Virtually all of these copy negatives were made by Carl Ohlson and frequently under less than ideal conditions. He not only did a superb job on the dust jacket cover and with the pen and ink sketches within the following pages, but his photographic talents made available many rare and irreplaceable photos that could otherwise not have been used. Carl was also an excellent traveling companion whose conversation and insights made the miles of travel pass quickly and profitably. His enthusiasm and support for the project, as well as his quick grasp of the value and significance of bits of information, will, I'm sure, make this effort more enjoyable to the reader. It must be mentioned that many cards and photos appeared in more than one collection and in such cases we chose the sharpest image for use and, when known, the original photographer was given credit.

A good deal of time was spent discussing an appropriate title for this book since there are several separate but closely related elements here. These include a technical view of dairy farming, milk cars, milk transportation, a specific geographic region containing the towns located on some 15% of the O&W's route mileage, and the self-propelled rail cars. A more comprehensive title would have been *The N.Y.O.&W. and the Dairy Business Covering Primarily, but Not Limited to: The Main Line Between Walton and Sidney and the Delhi and New Berlin Branches and Including Coverage of all Villages on the Above Lines as well as the Rail Cars Owned by the O&W and an Explanation of the Various Types of Cars Used to Transport Milk,* an unworkable and awkward title to say the least! While I am less than ecstatic with the title selected, it came the closest to satisfying those involved in the book's production.

Chapters 15 and 16 were included for the following reasons. The Unadilla Valley Railway was one of the few short-line connections the O&W had, and it became more important after it was purchased by the Salzberg interests. Our concern in the UV increases after its 1941 purchase of the O&W's New Berlin branch. Its closer relationship with the O&W, its purchase and use of O&W locomotives and equipment, and the integration of certain operations could liken the UV to being a piece of the true cross. For further reading on this engrossing line, I refer you to Fred Pugh's *Days Along the Buckwheat & Dandelion,* listed in the bibliography.

The motor cars of the last chapter have been endowed by the passage of time with almost as much of a hazy and mystical aura as enjoyed by steam locomotives. With something like the strange, romanticized reverence with which some view the Great Depression or the dark days of past wars, the sputtering and frequently unreliable machines have been forgiven their sins and at least permitted, if not welcomed, into warm memories. New information and photographs have come to light recently, and since the cars ran over much of the route mileage covered in this volume, I wanted to include them. I also readily confess to an avid fascination with the diesel locomotive's ancestors and the ingenious technology that put internal combustion on flanged wheels.

I have enjoyed a special affiliation with Carsten's Publications and owner Hal Carstens for almost 30 years and appreciate the occasional opportunity he and his editors have given me to get on a soapbox and share my discoveries on selected rail-related subjects. It was, and continues to be, an opportunity to meet people of similar interests and to increase my fund of railroad knowledge. A large part of the material on milk cars originally came from articles in *Railroad Model Craftsman*, a project in which I was deeply involved and from which Hal has kindly allowed me to extract information for use here. In addition, an excellent file of General American Car Company builder's photographs in the company collection was made available to me.

Very special help came from four individuals. Jon Schaub provided additional high-quality photo service and offered technical suggestions. Bill Calaroso (Cal's Classics) has been very generous in providing custom-printed photographs from his large collection. Fred Arone and John Martin (Depot Attic) have kindly permitted the use of many rare photos that have come into their possession.

William S. Young has long been a favorite railroad author and editor. I have admired his careful research, literary skills, and elegant presentations. I am honored to have had him write the foreword, read the text and offer suggestions. Carleton Frost, a colleague in the teaching profession, has read the text and made suggestions in matters of grammatical form and use. Chris Kostenko patiently taught me necessary computer skills and gave needed advice to improve my writing productivity. (I have not yet made a lamp out of my typewriter, per his suggestion.) Karl Zimmermann, a good friend and author of many fine books and numerous travel and railroad articles, created the layouts. Chuck Yungkurth contributed several graphs and plans. To the best of my knowledge, his two car plans have never before been done for the rail historian-model builder. Finally, warm thanks are extended to Paul & Eileen Kuehner of Garrigues House. Doug Lilly and Lance Metz were correct. They are both pleasant people to work with.

The introduction must end here because I see the flagman has hung the marker lamps on No. 9's hind end. Up ahead of the empty milk cars, the pop valves of the 308 are sputtering and the engineer is looking back from the cab. If you plan to make Walton today you had better get aboard before the conductor waves him a highball. I hope you have a pleasant trip.

Robert E. Mohowski
Franklin Lakes, New Jersey
December 12, 1994

Acknowledgements

Susan Ackerman (New Berlin Public Library)
Richard Arrandale
Fred Arone (Depot Attic)
Mr. & Mrs. Willian Baird
Gerald M. Best
Dan Biernacki
John Biffano
Don Bishop
Borden's Inc.
Lou Boselli
Charles A. Brown
Raymond W. Brown
Aldelbert Button
Joe Bux
Bill Caloroso
Lee P. Campbell
Dennis Carpenter
Cannon Free Library (Delhi)
Harold H. Carstens (Carstens Publications)
Peter Chaplin (Sealtest)
Clyde Conrow
Chenango County Historical Society
Marv Cohen
Robert F. Collins
Chris D'Amato (Carstens Publications)
Gerald N. D'Aurora
Harold Deal
Mr. & Mrs. Dave Dexheimer
D. Diver Collection, Cornell University
Bill Drake
Harold Dumond
Doug Ellison (Adirondack Scenic Railroad)
Robert F. Harding
Edmeston Historical Society
Historical Society of Middletown and the Wallkill Precinct

Mary Fargo
Mrs. M.. Fennessey
John Forni
Marfield Foster
Harold S. Fredericks
Bud Friend
Frisbee Library & Museum (Delhi)
Lawrence Gifford
Ms. Sybil Glanville
Ted Gleichmann, Jr.
Gene Graffouliere
Gurnsey Library (Norwich)
Bob Haines
Steve Hansen
Russ Hallock
Henry A. Harter
Peter Hasler
Dr. William F. Helmer
Mike Holdridge
K. Elizabeth Howe
Richard Howe
Mrs. Phyllis Howes
Emily Hoyt
John & Sue Hudson
Vernon Kelly
Mrs. Wannita Kilmer
Sterling O. Kimball
Tony Knipp
Walter Kierzkowski
John C. LaRue
Fred Lewis (General Road Foreman of Engines, NYO&W)
Robert Lewis (*Railway Age*)
Merritt Lloyd
Jim Loudon (Leatherstocking Railway Historical Society)

Gary Madden
Charles Magness
John Martin (Depot Attic)
Tom Matthews
Ivan Mauer
Frank Mozzarella (operator, NYO&W)
John E. Moffat
Pat, Daniel R. & David P. Mohowski
Mr. & Mrs. Edward Mohowski
Elwin & Mabel Mumford (engineer, NYO&W)
Dan Myers
New York Central Historical Society
A. V. Neusser
Robert Nonemacher (Edmeston Historical Society)
Ogden Free Library (Walton)
Leslie O'Reilly
Mr. & Mrs. Louis Parisi
Bob Pastorkey
John Pavelchak
Albert Peake (*Walton Reporter*)
Bob Pennisi (Railroad Avenue Enterprises)
Pennsylvania Historical Society
John Pickett
Fred Pugh
J. R. Quinn
Rusty Recordon
Sam Reeder
Mr. & Mrs. Richard Reit
Mr. & Mrs. George Rich
Walter Rich
Rick Rickenbach
William Rinn
Dr. C. R. Roberts (President, ret., Sheffield Farms)
Jon Schaub Studio

William C. Schaumburg (Carstens Publications)
William Schriever
Allan Seebach
George Shamus
Jim Shaughnessy
Sidney Historical Society
Dr. Dave Simon
Wilmer Sipple
Wayne Sittner
Bruce V. Snow (Dairylea)
Bernie Stafford (Sheffield Farms)
Richard Stoving
Steve Swirsky
Richard Taylor
Clarence Tharp
Herb Thieme
Bruce Tracy (Leatherstocking Railway Historical Society)
Tom Travers
John L. Treen
Herb Trice
Walton Historical Society
Washington University (St. Louis, Mo.)
Bob Wyer
Dr. Wayne Tremper
Unadilla Valley Historical Society
George Votava
Ed Weber
West Monroe Historical Society
Tom Woltman
John H. White (Smithsonian Institute)
Dennis G. Williams
Dr. Raymond Wood
William S. Young
Chuck Yungkurth
Karl Zimmermann

Engine 405, semi-streamlined for 'Mountaineer Limited' service, is about to head south on a hazy humid summer day. Behind the tank is a milk car loaded with 6000 gallons of New York state milk bound for metropolitan markets. A 4-8-2 of the Y-2 class sits on the next track in this circa-1940 view at Cadosia. Judging from the height of the condensation of the tenders, both locomotives have been under the water standpipe recently. O&W SOCIETY COLLECTION.

Prologue: The Milk Trains

The Milk Train Doesn't Stop Here Anymore

Play by Tennessee Williams

We are here, you and I, because we like trains. Beyond that each component part of railroading holds its own special fascination and draws its own devotees. We have managed to divide ourselves into camps of locomotive rivet-counters, compilers of Pullman car names and data, station and structure artists and draftsmen, plotters of train movements and operational details, and even a limited number who enjoy the analysis of financial statistics—and that's only part of the spectrum. The common bond is quite apparent; however, when we gather for the monthly rail-club meeting or when we stand on a hill and watch a westbound leave the yard and accelerate to main line speed all understand and find satisfaction in the generalities if not every specific.

As we look at the photographs in this section, let's imagine ourselves sitting on the Railway Express wagon in a rural upstate New York village, or wandering along the O&W's main track, looking into the terminals and picking up a feel for the sound, sights, and smells of milk-train activity—getting the big picture, as newsmen say.

After our final view of an F3-powered No. 10 disappearing around a distant curve, its red marker lamps fading into the dusk, we will delve into the specifics—the history, the cars, and the communities that were part of getting milk to market on the O&W.

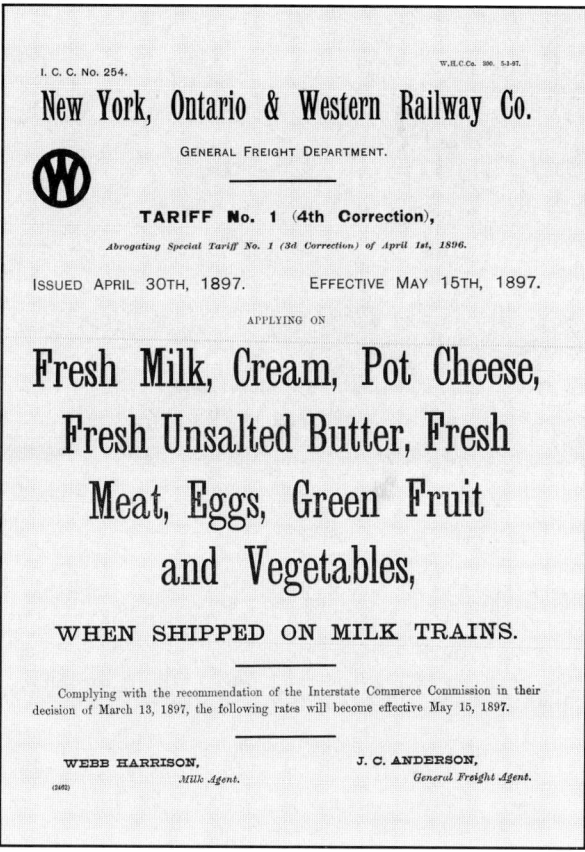

RIGHT: Scranton Division milk arrives in Cadosia behind a 4-4-0. It may be switched into the consist of the southbound train waiting at the depot. Cadosia did not have a creamery but local can shipments moved in small quantities from the depot. Track construction at the right shows that this junction yard was being enlarged in this pre-1900 photograph. O&W SOCIETY COLLECTION.

LEFT: Train 10 is in the siding at Munnsville on a run in 1893 with fireman John Murphy in the cab. The first car still has its original open platforms in this view taken by the train's engineer, William Harding. Harding ran the first trip of the milk train north of Sidney and continued on the job through to July 4, 1903. ROBERT F. HARDING COLLECTION.

LEFT: Built by the Brooks Locomotive Works, No. 77 does switching work at the Valley Mills creamery. The 77 had been rebuilt in 1903 at the Rome Machine Works and, with other members of the G class, was frequently assigned to milk trains. JOE BUX COLLECTION.

BELOW: High above the Stockbridge Valley, a 4-4-0 and its milk train race south from Munnsville. The O&W had several stations along the valley which provided many other types of agricultural carloads along with milk. This train originated at Oneida, some ten miles to the north. O&W SOCIETY COLLECTION.

The quintessential elements of the O&W—single track, cinder fill, a high trestle, a milk train and rural scenery—are all present in these two scenes. In the 1900-era picture at right, at least ten cars of milk and a passenger car trail the locomotive across the famed Lyon Brook Bridge, near Oxford, N.Y. The train in the photograph below has made a special stop at the same location to allow a carload of rail enthusiasts a rare picture opportunity. RIGHT: JOE BUX COLLECTION. BELOW: HERB HEIT COLLECTION.

Coupled to the 241's tender is one of the ex-freight refrigerator cars bought for milk service. Air signal lines would have been a necessity for these cars but passenger-type brake systems and steam lines probably were not. Roofwalks and grab irons were required to reach both ice hatches and the hand brake. CAL'S CLASSICS.

8

FACING PAGE, TOP: On October 11, 1935, a westbound passenger train makes the Liberty station stop. The Dairymen's League had a plant here but the 50-foot GPEX car on the head end is destined for delivery farther north. Three miles of hill are ahead before engine 244 will top the grade at Young's Gap. ROBERT G. LEWIS PHOTOGRAPH.

FACING PAGE. BOTTOM: Train 2. with two milk cars and engine 407. traverses the numerous curves on one of the most remote sections of the railroad. Leaving the valley of the West Branch of the Delaware River above Rock Rift, N.Y. No. 2 will crest the ridge at Apex and roll south along Cadosia Creek to its junction with the East Branch of the Delaware at Cadosia. COURTESY OF RAILROAD AVE. ENTERPRISES.

ABOVE: While the Ontario Express makes a local stop, the engine crew is busy. The fireman is back on the tender deck controlling the high volume flow of water into the tender and the engineer primes the injector to put some of that water into the boiler. Milk crates await the arrival of a following train which will have the older milk cars. CAL's CLASSICS.

ABOVE: A seven-car 'Mountaineer Limited,' train 37, has arrived at Middletown where the station stop conveniently allows for a change to a larger locomotive. The car inspector is behind the tender cutting the 226 from the train. One of the Y-class, 'light 400's' (so named to distinguish them from the heavier Y-2's of the same wheel arrangement), is probably around Wisner Ave. waiting to back down on February 4, 1940. GEORGE VOTAVIA.

LEFT: W-class 2-8-0's frequently handled trains 9 and 10 over the main line. They were usually found north of Cadosia because they were not restricted by the Northfield Tunnel's clearances. Here is the 323 northbound at Cadosia. AUTHOR'S COLLECTION.

The Railroadians of America, one of the earlier rail enthusiast groups, arranged to have two extra coaches put on train 10 out of Oneida on April 10, 1941. Stops at Eaton (left) and Randallsville (below) provided photography opportunities. The tracks in the foreground of the left picture originally led to Rome and Utica and later became part of the Pecksport Loop. The train sits on the original mainline that went through to Hamilton. TWO PHOTOGRAPHS: PAUL PRESCOTT.

LEFT: What appears to be the longest milk train in this book leaves Summitville in 1947. Steam power is on the point of No. 9 but in a year's time the O&W will be fully dieselized. Trains 9 and 10 no longer carried revenue passengers, but the combine on the rear provided deadheading employees with an additional train between home and work. BOB LORENZ.

BELOW: An engineer wearing a sports cap brings the 401 past the locomotive service facilities at Middletown. Two styles of General American milk tank cars are on the head end of this southbound train. O&W SOCIETY COLLECTION.

BELOW: Milk cars were usually carried on the head end to avoid backing a long string of cars into a siding for a setout or a pickup. Here is a southbound local at Hamilton with an early bulk tank style car which will be relayed south at Randallsville or Norwich. CAL'S CLASSICS.

ABOVE: Cold air condenses the exhausted steam of a Y-class bound up the grade between Walton and Cadosia. The steam cloud shadows the short train which will next stop at Apex. CAL'S CLASSICS.

RIGHT: The U.S. Mail as well as a variety of package and express freight will be loaded on the rear cars of a long southbound milk train arriving at East Branch, N.Y. The Delaware & Northern's gas-electric car waits for connecting passengers before leaving for Arkville. CAL'S CLASSICS.

The way freight for Mayfield stretches around the curve and back into Cadosia yard. Milk cars in a train of greasy black tank cars and gritty coal hoppers may appear somewhat incongruous, but the way freight was nothing if not democratic. It delivered to industries big and small, carload freight or LCL (less-than-carload), and sanitary food stuffs or toxic chemicals. A green combine on the rear carries the conductor and flagman and perhaps a third crewman to handle the express. ROBERT F. COLLINS PHOTOGRAPH, DAN MYERS COLLECTION.

ABOVE LEFT: A very lengthy train No. 9, loaded with head end business and milk cars returning for loads, rolls north at Firthcliff on March 23, 1946. The 408 is on the upgrade here where the O&W turns inland from the Hudson River and picks up its own route leading to Lake Ontario. JOE BUX COLLECTION.

ABOVE RIGHT: The misty morning of October 14, 1944, finds train No. 1 at Middletown with a seven-car consist of milk empties and passengers for upstate destinations. COURTESY OF JOE BUX AND DEPOT ATTIC.

RIGHT: The ubiquitous 245, eventually one of the road's last active camelbacks, leads a five-car train at Middletown. An Osgood-Bradley steel combine is coupled behind the milk car. The steel combines and coaches were sold during the war, after which the railroad would depend upon its fleet of wooden coaches and leased steel cars to convey passengers. CAL'S CLASSICS.

ABOVE: Smokey volumes of locomotive exhaust and accompanying plumes of steam would soon be gone from the O&W about the time this diesel-powered northbound arrived at Cadosia. Silhouettes holding the elements of steam generation—coal and water—pierce the skyline at the small junction community in the late 1940's. CAL'S CLASSICS.

RIGHT: In the late 1940's, the O&W accommodated a few rail enthusiast groups that requested fan trips on regularly operated trains. A wooden car or two on the end of the train was perfectly satisfactory and the crew was happy for some diversion from the regular routine. The riders of the above combine will have the opportunity to watch the placement of two empty milk cars on the upper end of the Scranton Division. CAL'S CLASSICS.

Maintenance of the GPEX car seems lacking, the double track is gone, and the standpipe is a superfluous lineside fixture. It is as much the decline of an industry as of a single railroad that is represented in this circa-1950 scene. O&W SOCIETY COLLECTION.

Chapter 1: The Dairy Farmers and the Creameries

If a farmer could bring in four or five cans a day, he was doing quite well. Usually it was less than that. It was all hand milking, you know, and we had to get the milk down to the creamery at a certain time. There was a feed and supply store across from the creamery, and we would pick up necessary items on the way home. Back in those days farmers helped each other out, and there was more neighborliness. We didn't have all the machines or the money like today.

William Baird, sixth-generation farmer, Warwick, N.Y. (conversations with the author)

An historical subject can be better understood if the researcher goes back in time to understand the events preceding it. In a similar sense, readers might gain a better understanding of the railroads' relationship with the milk business if we trace it back from the railroad siding, through the creamery, to the dairy that provided this important food and its associated products for our use. The details that follow were fairly typical of a New York State dairyman and his local creamery during the New York, Ontario & Western's peak years of milk traffic—the first three decades of this century.

Most farmers did not have herds of 40 or more cows that are necessary for a profitable operation today. Ten cows or fewer would have been more typical for the family farm of the period. Cows would be milked morning and evening at an average rate of six cows per hour when milking was done by hand. The evening milk had to be cooled quickly and kept at a temperature below 50 degrees Fahrenheit by order of the creamery. At higher temperatures, harmful bacteria grow rapidly in raw milk. Some creameries required a temperature as low as 40 degrees Fahrenheit. To cool the milk to this temperature prior to the days of electrical refrigeration, a farmer might have used a spring if the water was cold enough. A small building was built over the spring and the cold water flowed among the cans in a stone-lined pit. Another method was placing the cans in a vat of ice water. The vat might be a tight, wooden box or a concrete pit built into the floor of a separate room attached to the barn. Ice that had been purchased from the creamery's icehouse that morning would be chopped and put into the water. Some farmers had ice ponds and their own icehouses where they stored a season's supply. The cans from the evening milking would remain in the cold water through the night. The morning milk did not have to be cooled, but it had to be put in separate cans and not mixed with the previous evening's cold milk. Both sets of cans were then put into the wagon or truck for delivery to the creamery before the morning cutoff time, a fixed hour before the morning train was due. Sometimes the cans were covered with a quilted jacket to provide insulation. Three or four cans would be a typical delivery, but it was not unusual for a farmer to bring in only a single can. However, in the flush months when the cows had

FACING PAGE: Black and white Holsteins browse in a Delaware County, N.Y., pasture where the thick green grass is the result of an ample water supply and good soil. These and other natural advantages gave many New York counties an edge for successful dairy farming. AUTHOR'S PHOTOGRAPH.

ABOVE: A spring house, usually of stone or masonry construction, was used to cool and store fresh milk on the farm before it went to the creamery. Thick walls and a shady location were additional features that were incorporated into the planning and building of these structures. The farm wife could also use them to store butter, cheese and other perishable foods. BELOW: In the winter, cows were usually kept in barns, and the farms appear bleak, brown and barren when there was no snow cover. Muddy spring thaws and greening pastures mark calving time and the flush months of highest milk production. This farm is located in Orange County near the drowned lands where rich soil was created by an ancient swamp. AUTHOR'S PHOTOGRAPHS.

calved in the spring, they produced more milk and the price paid to the farmer was lower.

The collection point for milk in the country had several names. It was known as a creamery, milk receiving station, shipping depot or milk plant. Within these pages it will be referred to as a creamery since that seems to have been the most common reference along the O&W. There were also cheese factories, condenseries, and bottling plants that could receive milk directly. They could be owned and operated by local people, a farmers' cooperative or a large dairy company such as Borden's or the Dairymen's League. The O&W also built and leased creameries at many locations along the line.

There were three requirements for a good creamery location. It had to be near an ample supply of good water, had to have adequate drainage for disposal of waste water, and had to be near a large number of cows to insure an adequate supply of milk. None of these were especially difficult to find given the many excellent dairy farming regions of New York State. In fact, the dairy farmers had determined the sites earlier by their need for adequate water for animals and crops.

The creamery workday began well before dawn. The furnace grates had to be shaken and a layer of coal spread over the fire. Steam and hot water were needed in great quantity for cleaning milk cans, holding tanks, pipes, and fittings through which the milk would pass. Some of the pumps were steam powered, although gravity flow was used where possible, explaining the multilevel design of many creameries. Shortly after sunrise, the first farmers would arrive. An efficient creamery was usually arranged so that the milk cans came in one side of the building, and cooled, processed city bound milk went out the other. The raw milk from the farm, in separate evening and morning cans, would be placed on a conveyor of rollers that ran along an outside wall and entered the building via a small door that was slightly taller than can height. Creamery men subjected each can to a number of tests and proce-

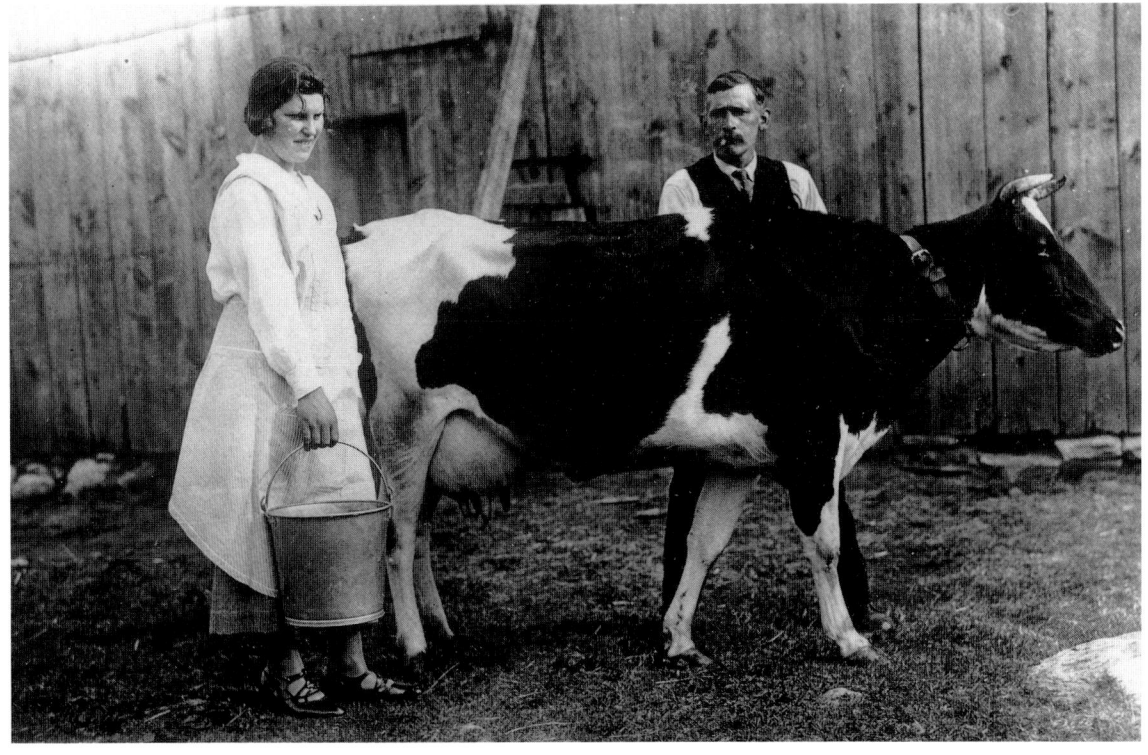

Good old Bessie or Daisy (perhaps Elsie?) appears clean, healthy and under the firm care of her owner. The clean apron and pail clearly imply the role of milkmaid for the young lady who may be the farmer's wife or daughter. In the days prior to mechanical aids, hand-milking of even a modest herd required hired help or a large family with all members taking on chores. COURTESY OF JON SCHAUB.

dures that would determine the quality and quantity of the raw milk.

The most simple test was the sniffing of can lids for unusual odors. Cows that had grazed on wild onions or other undesirable plants tended to taint their milk and make it unfit for retail use. Temperature and sediment checks were next and then the milk would be filtered through a clarifier to remove hair, dust and other impurities. It would then go into a weighing tank. At some point samples were taken and checked in a small lab for butterfat content and bacteria count. Payment was made upon a formula that included percentage of butterfat and weight, with a check issued to each farmer monthly. Volume by cubic or common liquid measure was not considered. The milk would leave the weighing tank and enter a cooling system. Prior to rural electrification, the cooling was done by pouring the milk into clean creamery-owned cans that were submersed in ice water vats or tanks. These vats would be much larger than those found on the farm, and there might be several of them in a creamery. However, by the 1920's some of the creameries had converted to electrical appliances and cooling systems.

Many facilities had a cream separator to remove the cream from the raw milk. Later, some cream would be added to milk sold for regular consumption. Other dairy products that originated at creameries were butter, buttermilk, cheese, evaporated and skim milk, ice cream, and sour cream. Special processing for these products usually took place in plants equipped to manufacture and package whatever particular byproduct was desirable.

If inspection at the creamery determined the milk to be unacceptable, it would be red-tagged and the problem discussed with the farmer. Depending upon the degree of the problem, the rejected milk would be used for dairy products other than fluid milk, fed to farm animals or dumped.

After the cans had been emptied, they continued along the conveyor to a can washing station where the cleaning was done by hand with a scrub brush or semiautomatically by a machine. The latter method was preferred because of the higher temperature of the water and the use of live steam for final sterilizing. After drying, the lids were attached and the cans passed out of the building via another conveyor and were claimed by the owner. Cans were identified by letters and/or numbers that had been applied by their owner. The farmer might also pick up a large block of ice to take home for cooling of the evening milk. Frequently there were lines of farmers waiting to deliver their milk, but those who got to the creamery early enough might be heading homeward within ten minutes of his delivery.

ABOVE: Inverted milk cans and lids sit on the platform of an O&W creamery. In a time of less stringent sanitation standards, the outdoor privy was very close to the creamery. Frequently the foreman or other workers lived on the second floor of the building. State and local health codes eventually put an end to both practices. O&W SOCIETY COLLECTION. BELOW: The Crystal Run, N.Y., creamery was connected to an adjoining icehouse at its left via a sheltered passageway. O&W COLLECTION COURTESY OF DEPOT ATTIC. TOP AND MIDDLE RIGHT: In June of 1911, an icehouse was under construction south of the Kenwood, N.Y., creamery. Through the narrow doors, large blocks of ice were slid into the creamery for the milk cooling vats. It appears that the existing structure was simply a collecting point since the lack of a smokestack meant limited or no processing capability. BOTTOM RIGHT: The high switchstand at the Morrisville creamery provided approaching enginemen with an early indication of the alignment of the crossover at left. This September, 1911, view shows that the plant volume is almost at the car load stage and the building may soon require enlarging. THREE PHOTOGRAPHS: DENNIS CARPENTER COLLECTION.

TOP: Clark's creamery at Campbell Hall, N.Y., was similar in design to the nearby Crystal Run creamery. O&W COLLECTION COURTESY OF DEPOT ATTIC. BOTTOM: This view shows the receiving side of Clark's creamery with the O&W curving off to the north. Farmers would drive into the portico and unload their milk prior to the days of the roller conveyor and small can doors. WAYNE SITTNER COLLECTION.

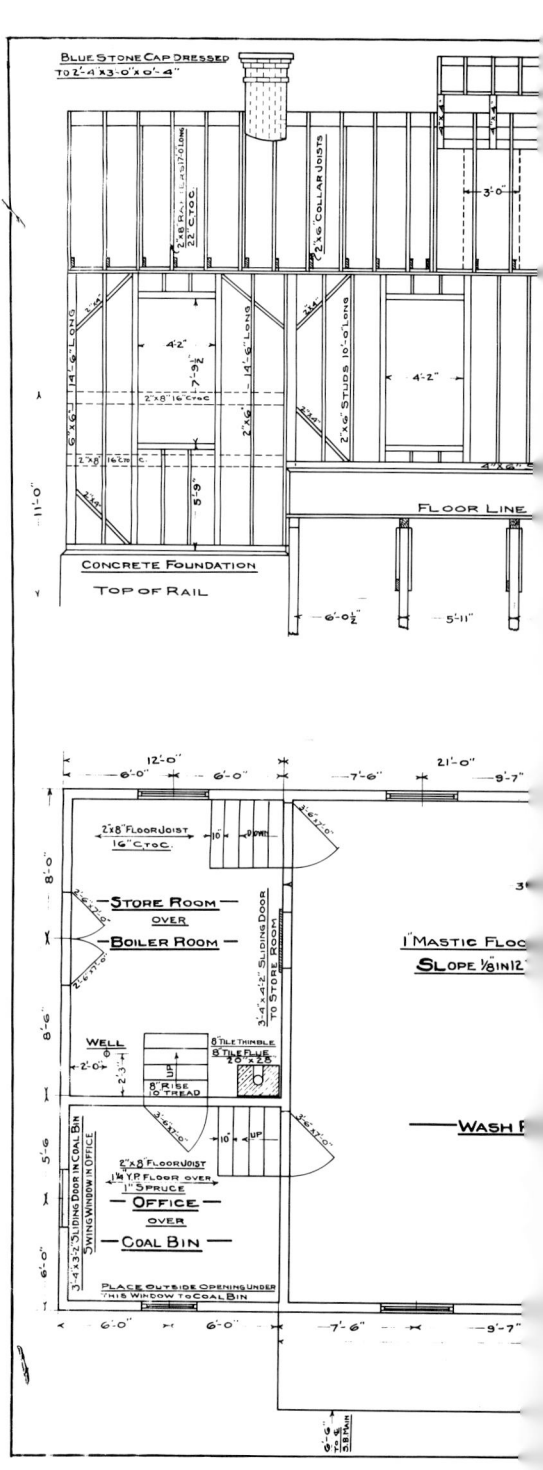

ABOVE: Prior to 1900, a limited number of creameries shipped bottled milk. In this unspecified New York state creamery, workers bottle, cap and crate milk. The wooden cases would be loaded into milk cars and iced for the trip to metropolitan markets. O&W SOCIETY COLLECTION. RIGHT: The plans for the creamery at Winterton carried approval signatures of the chief inspector of New York City's Board of Health, the O&W's chief engineer, and the milk agent. An icehouse sat next to its north side. O&W SOCIETY COLLECTION.

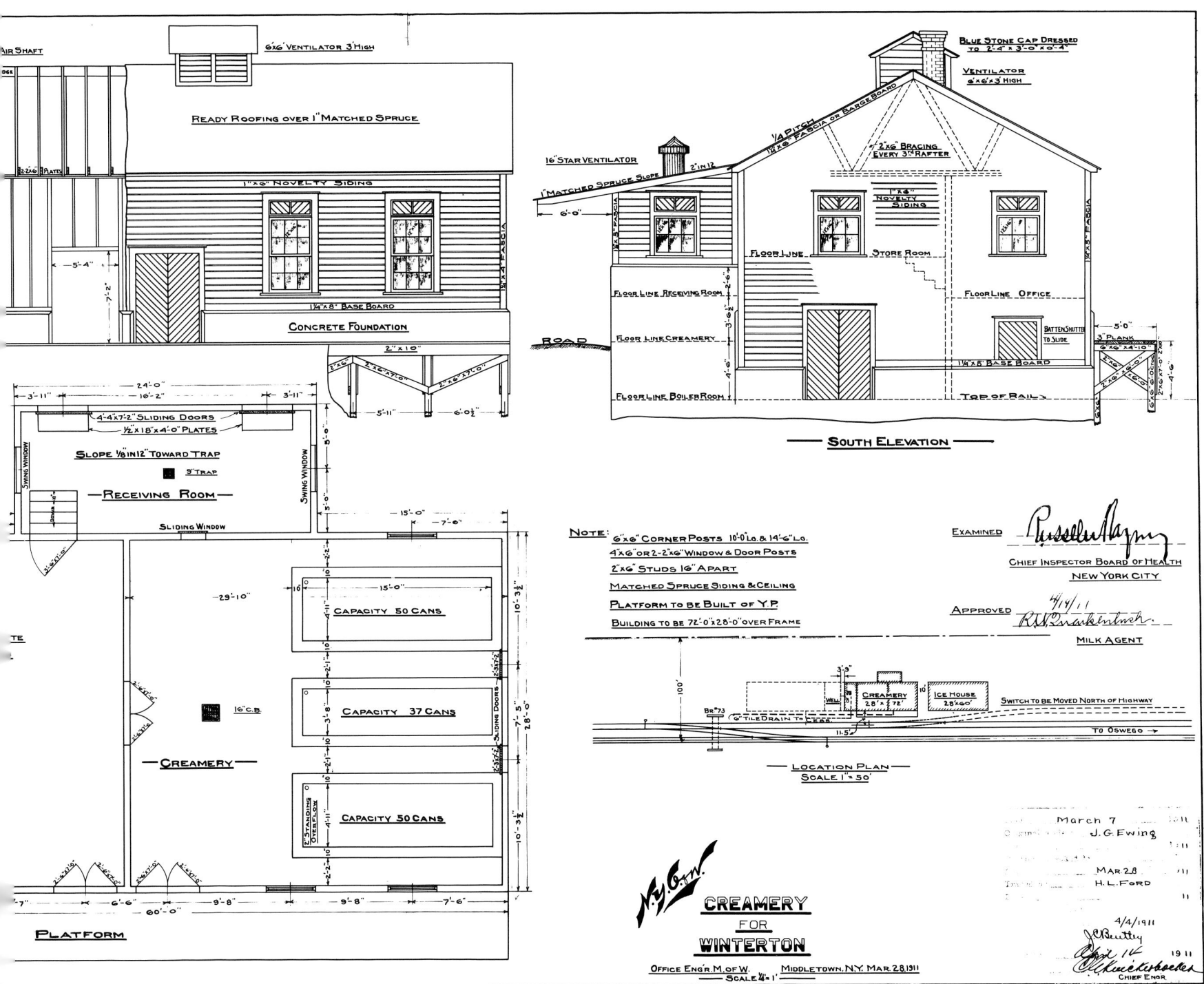

ABOVE: Earlville, N.Y., had at least two creameries served by the O&W. This cupola-topped building was one although it appears to be abandoned or was serving another use at the time of this photograph. The coal hoppers and converyor at the ice storage end of the building support the theory. JOHN MOFFAT COLLECTION. TOP RIGHT: Standard Dairy of New York City owned this plant in Sherburne-Four Corners, N.Y. As adults, several decades later, the two children in the scene may have witnessed the first milk shipment to utilize portable tanks and flatcars. It was the Hohneker's receiving plant, in this little village, that made the shipment. MARY S. FARGO COLLECTION, COURTESY OF RICHARD REIT AND LEE CAMPBELL. MIDDLE RIGHT: Munns (later Munnsville), N.Y., creamery is viewed from the boilerhouse end. The arrival of the southbound milk train must have caused furious activity since the small platform provided little space for can storage. BOTTOM RIGHT: A new icehouse and an extension were additions to the Valley Mills creamery. The concrete foundation under the addition was better suited to the damp environment of a creamery. If this creamery was not shipping in carload quantity, it might have been after the enlargement. TWO PHOTOGRAPHS: DENNIS CARPENTER COLLECTION.

TOP: Because of the greater complexity of their processing, condenseries were much larger than creameries. Borden's established this rail-served facility in Earlville, N.Y. The cupolas were not merely decorative but also allowed dampness and summer heat to escape. Ventilators in the icehouse also allowed damp air to escape. O&W SOCIETY COLLECTION. BOTTOM: Most of the business from the Borden's plant at Norwich, N.Y., is said to have been shipped over the Delaware, Lackawanna & Western. This view from the Lackawanna side shows coal hoppers that may latter have rolled into the facility to fuel its boilers. The O&W served the plant from the opposite side. Part of the main structure is in use today as a supermarket warehouse. JOE BUX COLLECTION.

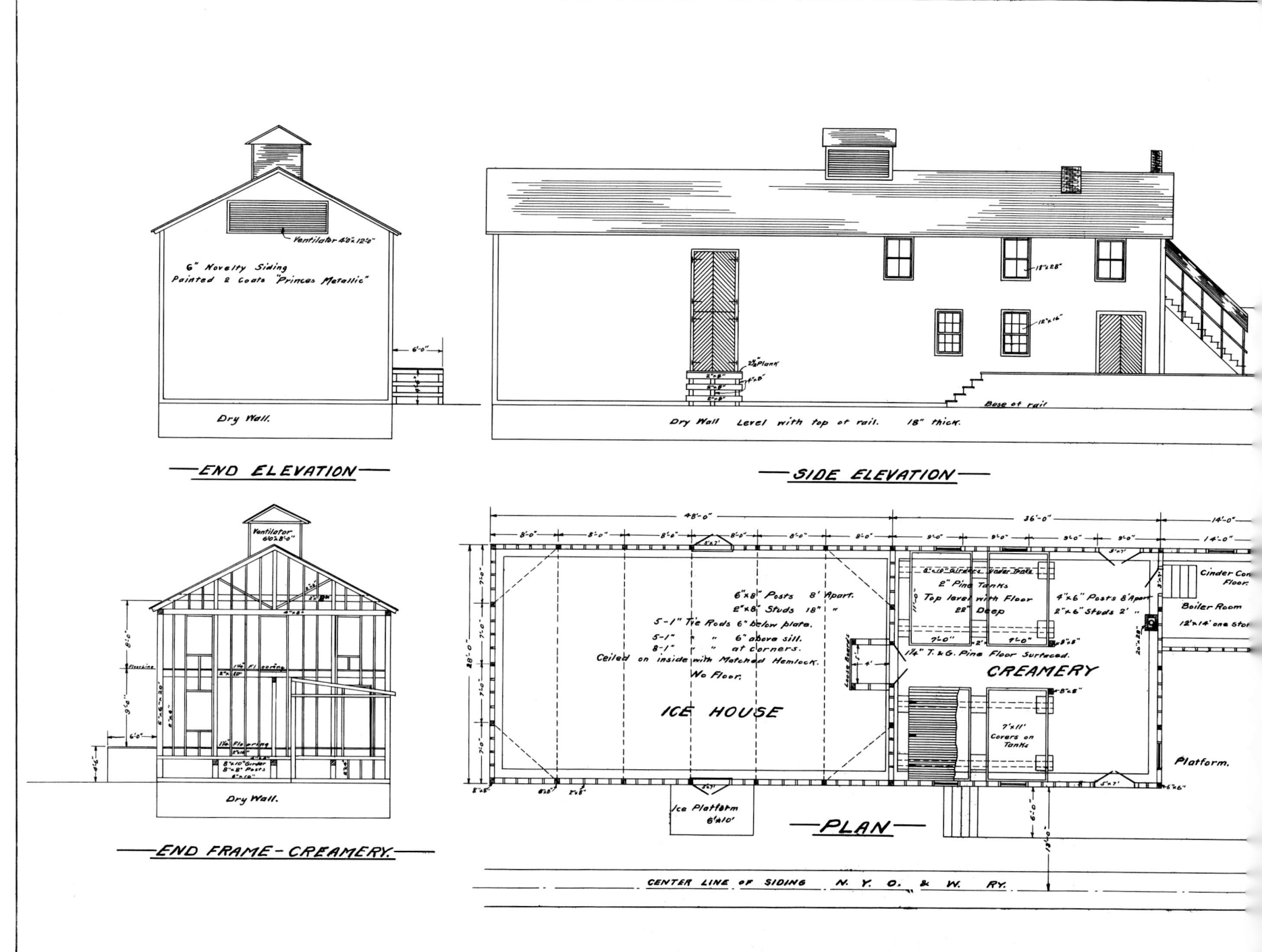

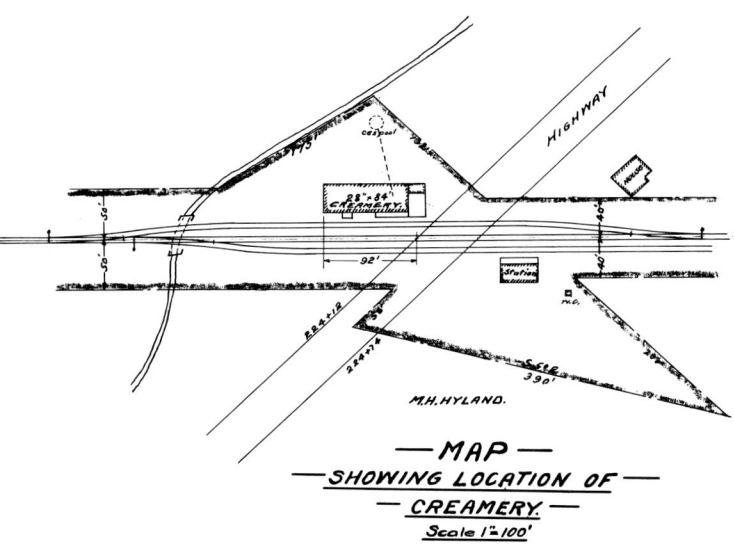

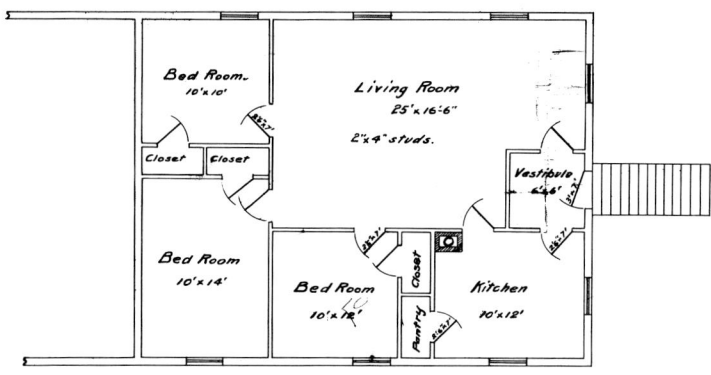

State Bridge, N.Y., had a creamery that was diagonally across from its depot and was served by its own siding. It was built by the railroad in 1903. O&W SOCIETY COLLECTION.

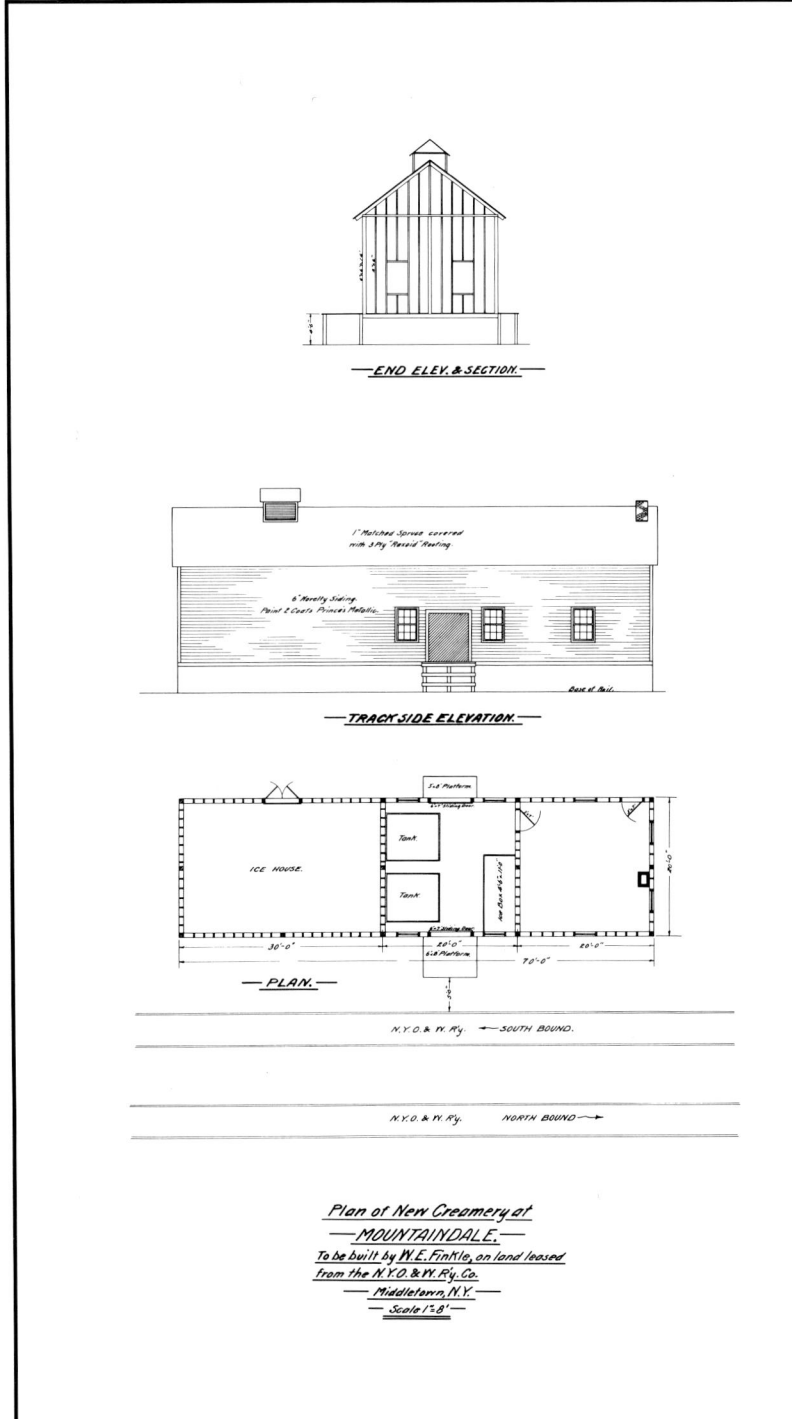

LEFT: The Mountaindale creamery was a study in simplicity. It was built on land owned by the railroad but operated independently. O&W SOCIETY COLLECTION. ABOVE: This view of Smyrna, N.Y., shows a typical trackside scene in a rural community. McDermott's Dairy, at the right, processes and ships enough milk to require a full car for each day's production. Since the door is open and the section crew is moving out of the siding, a train may have recently placed the car for loading. JOHN MOFFAT COLLECTION. BELOW: The McDermott plant had an unusually sturdy boiler room of stone construction and it was very logical to put the steam plant at one end of the creamery with the icehouse at the other. Note the line of wagons with their covered milk cans awaiting a turn to unload. MARY S. FARGO COLLECTION, COURTESY OF RICHARD REIT AND LEE CAMPBELL.

RIGHT: Similar to the condensed milk plants, dry milk plants such as this one in Pennelville, N.Y., also used a great deal of heat to produce their products. The milk requirements for daily production can be judged from the number of cans on the platform. Since the final product did not require refrigeration it is being loaded into a boxcar in the background. O&W SOCIETY COLLECTION.

Depending upon the degree of sanitation practiced on the farm, butterfat content and bacteria count, milk was graded A or B. The grade A milk was produced under very strict sanitation and required more work and care on the part of the farmer to produce, but he was also paid more for his product. Certified milk was another premium quality product. This milk had the certification or endorsement of a doctor or public health official as to its purity and high quality. Grade B milk was the less expensive standard product produced in quantity under less stringent regulations, and was used to produce cheese and other solid dairy foods. Although it was still safe, grade B had a higher bacteria count.

Because of the steam and hot water, creameries were very humid. Winter operations could be cold and damp. Workers wearing rubber aprons and gloves had to accept even greater dampness in the summer. The moisture and heat were conducive to bacteria growth, especially in warm weather. This in turn meant plenty of soap and strong disinfectants after each day's operations. It is not surprising to see that the creameries built after 1900 made use of concrete floors and ceramic tile walls that could better withstand the constant moisture and cleaning agents.

A notable feature of many country creameries was the boiler room with its tall smokestack. A wisp of soft-coal smoke and steam from a number of pipes on the roof trailed downwind. A pile of coal sat outside the boiler room door. If the operation was large enough, like the Borden's condensery at New Berlin, the coal would come in by the carload and a trestle or wheeled conveyor was used for unloading.

Most of the procedures mentioned were basic to virtually all creameries and were typical of the processing that was done to milk before shipment to consuming areas for bottling and distribution. However, a few creameries such as the Borden's facility above Pittsfield on the Wharton Valley line did produce bottled milk at a country plant. After 1920, pasteurization was required and was usually done at the bottling end of the operation. By that time many of the small creameries were gone. The motor age required fewer collection points since farmers could travel farther to consolidated, more efficient creamery facilities. With a few exceptions, such as the Borden's Pittsfield facility, very little work, other than collecting and shipping, was done near the source of the milk. The city and suburban plants did all the processing, which included the more complex tasks of pasteurizing and homogenization.

Today's dairy farmers are required to have large bulk holding and cooling facilities. Tank trucks generally appear every other day and take the milk directly to large city plants that have consolidated country and city functions under one roof. Modern motor trucks, headed for metropolitan markets, cross the weed-grown railroad rights-of-way and speed by the abandoned concrete platforms of the old country creameries.

There is one other facet of the O&W's milk business that was very important prior to 1900 and the advent of electrical refrigeration. This was the condensation of milk. Gail Borden, whose name was to be associated with dairy foods for the next century, invented the condensing process in 1856. After modest success, Borden found it difficult to supply

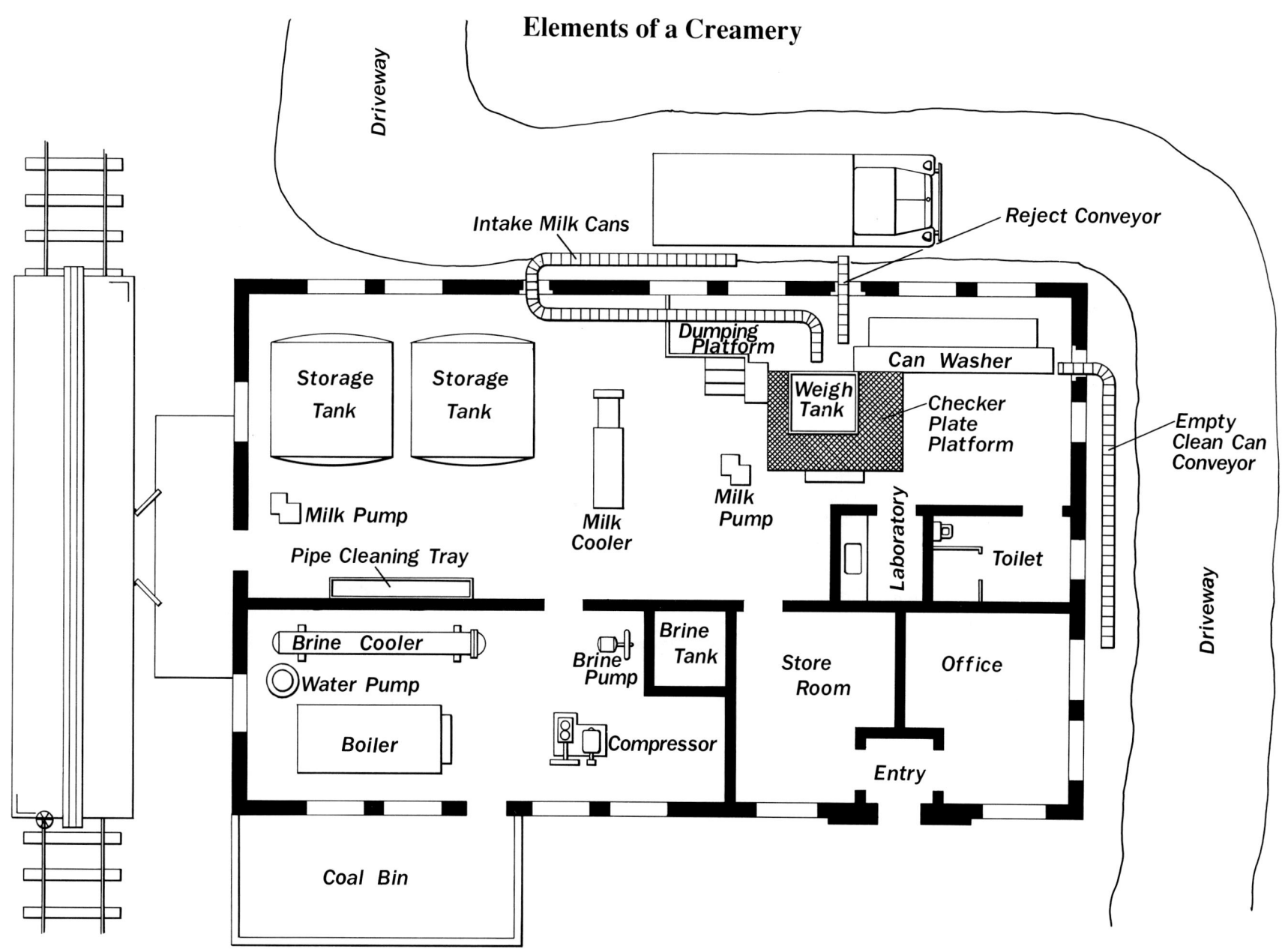

enough milk for Union troops during the Civil War. The process required fairly large and sometimes rambling structures in which 60 percent of the water in whole milk was evaporated by heat applied to milk in vacuum tanks. The thicker milk was then canned, sealed, and immediately sterilized by heat. Sugar was added during the process to aid in preservation. Evaporated milk was developed in the 1880s and did not require sugar for preservation. Both types were canned and shipped to worldwide markets. Milk in this form did not require refrigeration and could be shipped more conveniently. Like today's orange juice, it could easily be reconstituted to its original form at the place of consumption.

Condenseries received raw milk and performed the initial processing in the same manner as did creameries. However, the evaporating procedure required greater amounts of heat and this demanded a larger supply of coal. Since both milk and fuel were required in larger quantities, there was more business for the railroad. One would expect that the canned milk could have been shipped in boxcars if it were protected from freezing. Photographs from the earlier period, though, show only wooden milk cars on condensery sidings, and these appear with doors open, presumably to dry out the damp interior that was the result of earlier can milk loads.

LEFT: Creameries were basically collection and storage points for milk brought in from surrounding farms. Later they performed tests to measure quality as well as quantity and did some of the required processing for market. Motor transport and better roads permitted consolidation of creamery facilities and eliminated the need for creameries in every farming community. The floor plan here shows an arrangement for a plant that shipped by rail in the period from the mid-1930s through the 1950s. Many such plants added truck bays and abandoned rail service. *DRAWING BY CHUCK YUNGKURTH.*

ABOVE: A farmer could bring one can or dozens of cans by horse and wagon, station wagon, car or truck. A snowy morning in Orange County finds dairymen waiting at Bordens' Burnside creamery. *TOM MATTHEWS COLLECTION.*

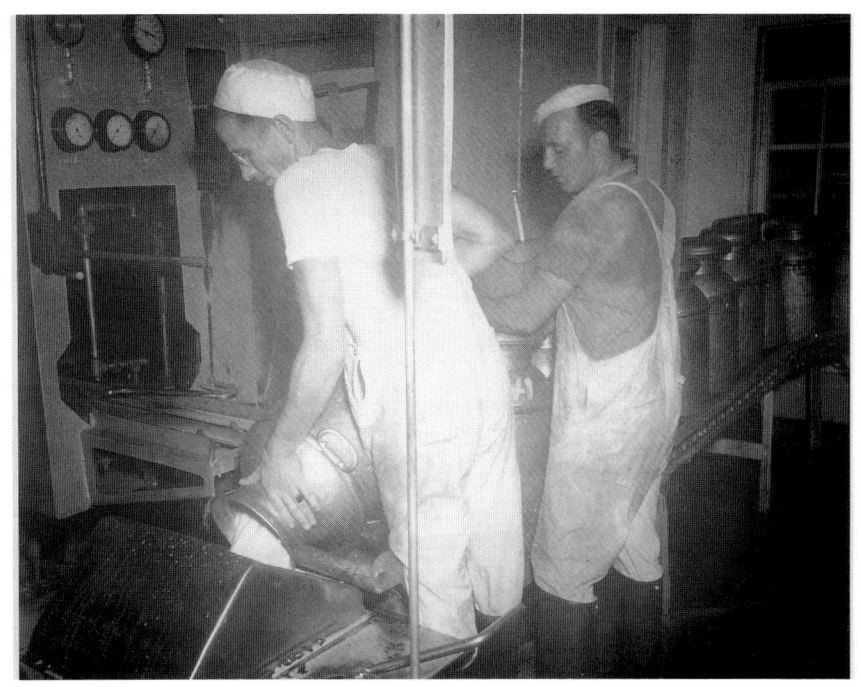

LEFT TO RIGHT, TOP: In the predawn darkness, a creamery worker checks the temperature of arriving milk to be sure it meets the company standard. This was the first of several quality checks on the arriving milk. TOM MATTHEWS COLLECTION. Samples of milk from the cans at the right are being placed in bottles for lab testing. By the 1930s, most creameries had a small lab and personnel trained to perform a few simple tests. NEXT: Incoming milk is being dumped into a weighing tank and the cans will then go to the can washer at the left. TWO PHOTOGRAPHS: ERIE LACKAWANNA HISTORICAL SOCIETY COLLECTION, COURTESY OF DAN BIERNACKI. All pipes, coolers, tanks and pumps had to be cleaned daily. Inspections were frequent and rigid, and were conducted by both company and public health authorities. Cooled milk was stored in the tanks until transferred to milk tank cars or trucks for shipment to city processing and bottling plants. RICHARD REIT COLLECTION. LEFT TO RIGHT, BOTTOM: The cans and lids are being matched after passing through the washer and dryer. Note the hammer being used by the man at the right. RICHARD REIT COLLECTION. Scrubbing, mopping and wiping was a large part of the creamery workers' day. Chlorinated and phosphate-loaded detergents created water pollution that was accepted at the time as part of the business. TOM MATTHEWS COLLECTION. A farmer loads his clean, dry cans for the return trip home from a creamery in Owego, N.Y., while behind the conveyor, another farmer unloads full cans. The clean cans exited the creamery over a roller conveyor. The farmers recognize their cans by their markings. The elapsed time from delivery to departure was approximately 15 minutes. ERIE LACKAWANNA HISTORICAL SOCIETY COLLECTION, COURTESY OF DAN BIERNACKI.

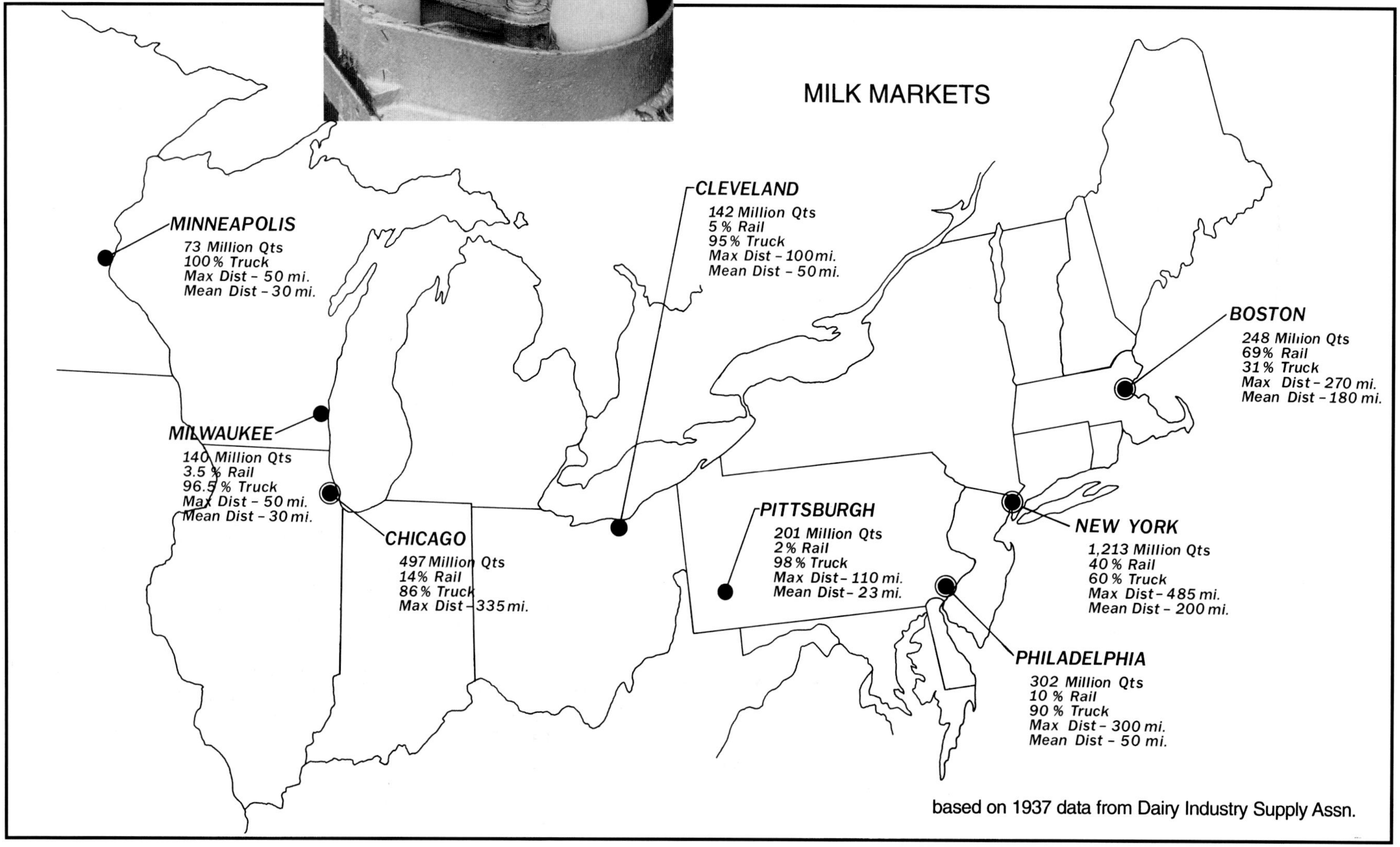

The longer established Northeastern cities, with their extensive suburbs and their higher surrounding land values, generally had to reach out farther to gain a milk supply. Rail service had the advantage over other forms of transportation in bringing milk from a distance and it was not until the late 1960s that tank trucks finally took all the business. DATA SUPPLIED BY TOM TRAVERS, DRAWING BY CHUCK YUNGKURTH. INSET: Before the age of plastic and paper milk containers, all milk was bottled. Borden's "Golden Crest," a premium grade product, is being capped and sealed for delivery. Today, most of the initial and final processing and bottling has moved to city plants. TOM MATTHEWS COLLECTION.

MILK MARKETS

MINNEAPOLIS
73 Million Qts
100% Truck
Max Dist – 50 mi.
Mean Dist – 30 mi.

CLEVELAND
142 Million Qts
5 % Rail
95% Truck
Max Dist – 100 mi.
Mean Dist – 50 mi.

BOSTON
248 Million Qts
69% Rail
31% Truck
Max Dist – 270 mi.
Mean Dist – 180 mi.

MILWAUKEE
140 Million Qts
3.5 % Rail
96.5% Truck
Max Dist – 50 mi.
Mean Dist – 30 mi.

CHICAGO
497 Million Qts
14% Rail
86% Truck
Max Dist – 335 mi.

PITTSBURGH
201 Million Qts
2% Rail
98% Truck
Max Dist – 110 mi.
Mean Dist – 23 mi.

NEW YORK
1,213 Million Qts
40 % Rail
60% Truck
Max Dist – 485 mi.
Mean Dist – 200 mi.

PHILADELPHIA
302 Million Qts
10 % Rail
90% Truck
Max Dist – 300 mi.
Mean Dist – 50 mi.

based on 1937 data from Dairy Industry Supply Assn.

Similar to many empty rights-of-way in the region, these abandoned Orange County, N.Y., dairy farms are left to the ravages of time and season. There is little doubt that people now out number cows in Orange County as developers turn pastures into sub-divisions. Increasing land values, higher taxes, increased costs of feed and veterinary care as well as the decline in consumption and prices paid for milk have caused many dairymen to leave a life-long occupation. AUTHOR'S PHOTOGRAPHS.

The O&W was enjoying prosperous times according to this scene at Rock Tavern, N.Y., and the signs of prosperity are everywhere. The double track is well-maintained, the team track is full, and a new creamery is taking form. Milk will be delivered to the small room at the right, cooled in the vats at the near end, and shipped out through doors in the left wall. O&W SOCIETY COLLECTION.

Chapter 2: The New York, Ontario & Western's Milk Traffic

The city dweller, beyond a hazy notion that milk is in some way associated with a farmer and a cow, for the most part remains ignorant of the enormous effort and planning involved in the delivery of the milk bottle at his door.

S. Kip Farrington, Jr., *Railroading From the Rear End*

The New York & Oswego Midland (NY&OM or OM) was incorporated in 1866, and by 1873 the line was completed between Oswego, N.Y. and Jersey City, N.J. Well before that it was clear that railroads would replace canals, stages, and freight wagons in the continuing evolution of long-distance transportation. It was also becoming clear that the steel highways would figure dramatically in creating business opportunities and a higher quality of life for many people. Grains, meat, fruits and vegetables, building materials, ice, fuel, minerals, textiles, manufactured goods, and machinery were available quicker, fresher, cheaper, and in larger quantities. The improved access and new demands created money-making opportunities in transporting and selling these commodities. An examination of the milk business demonstrates that, in the production and transportation of a basic food long considered essential to healthy life, the railroads did keep at least a part of the promise they implied for improved life.

The transportation of milk is a good example of the railroads' usefulness and success as referred to in the introduction. The milk business started out on a small scale under the NY&OM. Its careful development contributed significantly to the growth and development of several upstate counties in New York and to the profit columns of the company's books. During a 50-year period the railroad would rise to a leadership position in the New York City milk market, and it would bring a number of innovations to the technology of the milk-hauling railroads.

Although some individuals believe the NY&OM was the first railroad to handle milk shipments, this was not the case. In fact, the New York, Ontario & Western, successor to the Midland, published a booklet in 1902 which clearly credits a neighboring railroad with the first shipment of milk. Mr. Thaddeus Selleck, a contractor working for the New York & Erie (NY&E), the predecessor of the Erie, originated the idea of shipping milk by rail. While supervising a pile-driving gang in the vicinity of Chester, Orange County, N.Y., Selleck noted the quality of the local milk and saw its superiority to milk produced in New York City from cows that were fed brewery and distillery waste grains. Although some country milk was reaching the city from Long Island and other near environs, no one believed that the product could be transported the 50 miles from Orange County without suffering from heat and the churning action of the bouncing cars. The farmers near Chester were satisfied with the trade they had established in the production of butter, and they consequently scoffed at Selleck and his idea in the same manner that has greeted most visionaries since the dawn of time.

Once the NY&E was in operation between Piermont, N.Y., and Chester, Selleck was made station agent at the latter location. This placed him in a position to promote his earlier idea of shipping local milk to New York City. After arranging for a receiving station in the city, he was able to persuade a local farmer to make an experimental shipment in the spring of 1842. If not the first then this is believed to be one of the first shipments of milk by rail to NewYork City. The milk was carried in wooden containers and the total shipment was said to be 240 quarts. This does seem to be an unusually large amount for an experimental shipment, but the results were successful. The greatest concern was not in selling the milk but in proving that it could arrive at its destination without souring. An interesting and labor-saving part of the shipping arrangement was the placement of the loaded milk containers on four-wheel trucks which could be rolled into the cars. At Piermont, these trucks were transferred to the city bound steamboat. (This procedure is amazingly similar to a transportation system developed a century later and discussed in Chapter 5.)

The farmer received two cents per quart, which, because of larger volume, was more profitable than making and selling butter for 15 cents a pound. The Orange County milk proved extremely popular, and in time the Orange County Milk Association was established and purchased the business from Selleck. It is likely that the association was some sort of cooperative arrangement with members sharing costs and profits. Certainly the association could promote a more formal exchange of ideas and procedures.

One problem to be addressed was that of milk spoilage during hot weather and transit delays. The difficulty was solved in the fall of 1842 by Jacob Vail, a farmer of Goshen, N.Y. He made a coil of lead pipe which was placed in a wooden barrel packed with ice. Warm, fresh milk was allowed to run down through the coil which absorbed the animal heat. Other farmers were soon cooling their milk with ice or placing the containers in cold spring water. Each year new ideas and developments improved the collection, storage, and transportation of the product to keep pace with the increasing demand.

At some point a change was made from the conical, wooden containers to metal cans that were more durable, easier to clean, and quicker to transfer heat from the contents to the cooling water tank. How the earlier, porous wood churns were cleaned to keep them from souring and spoiling the contents is a mystery. The common 40-quart cans that were to become such a part of the rural scene were developed in several stages.

A variety of shapes and sizes was created over the years with certain designs finding wider acceptance than others. Part of this was the result of tinkering by local tinsmiths who had the ease and practicality of assembly foremost in mind. Another factor that influenced can size was that the milk from three or four cows would fill a 40-quart can. Since the average farmer had fewer than ten cows, two or three 40-quart cans were relatively convenient to handle each day. Larger herds of dairy cattle would appear later as mechanical milking aids and improved farming technology made them possible. Weight was another consideration in determining can size. Forty quarts of milk weigh approximately 85 pounds, and although the cans could be rolled along their bottom rims, they were just short of being too awkward for an average man to handle.

From these beginnings, it can be seen that the groundwork for milk shipping was fairly well in place by the time the NY&OM came into existence. The New York & Erie, with prompting by Selleck, managed to get the business started, and 30 years of experience and refinement were available upon which the NY&OM could draw. DeWitt C. Littlejohn and other promoters of the NY&OM were clearly aware of the NY&E's successful and lucrative milk business. Frequent reference was made by railroad promoters to that road's income from the traffic with the expectation that the proposed NY&OM would do as well.

In 1871, about two years before the NY&OM route was completed across New York State, the railroad made its first milk shipment. The milk containers were loaded at Bloomingburg, N.Y., and were shipped to Middletown on a passenger train. The milk would likely have been placed in a baggage car or perhaps a freight car added to the train. After the 8-mile run to Middletown, the milk was turned over to the NY&E to reach New York City. After the Middletown, Unionville & Water Gap (MU&WG) and the New Jersey Midland (NJM) were completed, the NY&OM milk went to Jersey City via these affiliated lines. In May of 1877, milk shipments began at Liberty, 30 miles north of Bloomingburg, where a farmer named A. J. Bennett sent three cans to market. Combine car 101 was assigned to the train for the purpose.

A year later the milk territory was extended to Livingston Manor, N.Y., and in January of 1880, the New York, Ontario & Western emerged from the bankrupt New York & Oswego Midland. The continuing growth of the milk traffic was a very encouraging sign for the new investors.

Now under the NYO&W, the milk business was extended to Walton, in Delaware County, on April 25, 1881, with a connecting service to Delhi. Delaware County would prove to be prime milk territory and fully the equal of Orange County in terms of dairy production. A year later, the new milk terminus was Sidney, N.Y., 21 miles further north. In June, 1883, the milk train began operating over the new trackage of the New York, West Shore & Buffalo (West Shore) from Middletown, N.Y., to Weehawken, N.J., via Cornwall, N.Y. The West Shore route was 24 hours faster than the circuitous route via the MU&WG and the NJM. In January, 1888, a Sunday milk train was put on the New Berlin branch. This might have been an extension of the main line run that originated at Sidney during the week. A milk train on the New Berlin line had been proposed in 1883, but farmers were not yet convinced that the business was worth their effort. With the leasing of the Wharton Valley Railway, the New Berlin branch was extended to Edmeston, N.Y., and in November of 1889, a milk run was established between that point and Sidney. Norwich, N.Y., became the next northern point for originating milk in 1891, and a connecting service from the New Berlin branch met the main line train at Sidney. That same year marked the introduction of a milk train to the Scranton Division.

Up to this time, a flat rate had been charged per

each can of milk the railroad handled. When the Interstate Commerce Commission was established in 1887, certain farmers objected to the 32-cent per can flat rate. The ICC appeal resulted in graduated rates that ranged from 23 cents for distances up to 40 miles, to 32 cents for haulage of more than 190 miles. The railroad's fear of reduced earnings proved groundless and the milk business continued to increase.

Three major developments in the railroad's milk business occurred in 1892. The regular milk run, now *the long milk,* was extended to Oneida, N.Y., and a second main line milk train *the short milk,* was begun at Livingston Manor. Finally, milk pickup service was provided on the Utica Division by branch trains 1 and 2. In December of 1900, the short milk was extended to Sidney.

Additional milk may have been brought down from points farther north on the main line, and this business may have gone into the consist that left Oneida every day as Milk Train 10. Some milk that originated north of Oneida went to creameries or processing plants in Fulton, Oswego, and other on-line communities in the two northernmost counties served by the NYO&W. It is also possible that some of this milk was interchanged to the old Rome, Watertown & Ogdensburg (RW&O) at Central Square, Fulton or Oswego. The RW&O became part of the New York Central (NYC) in 1891.

There was a wide variety in train schedules, numbers, and operations during the years that the business flourished. Addendum A provides a framework for understanding the train movements. These operations were constantly modified to meet changing service requirements.

Into the first two decades of this century, the O&W was still meeting the steadily increasing production of the upstate farmers. The opening of the Ellenville & Kingston Railroad in 1902 brought immediate rewards to the NYO&W, which had financed its construction. New milk traffic began to flow down to the main-line connection at Summitville, N.Y., via a number of passenger trains and local freights.

In addition to all the on-line milk it carried, the railroad received milk from the Unadilla Valley Railway (UV) at New Berlin and the Port Jervis, Monticello & New York Railroad (PJM&NY) north of Port Jervis. When the PJM&NY made a connection with O&W in 1889, it listed three milk cars on its roster, which gives a good idea of the traffic volume. The PJM&NY became part of the O&W in 1900. The Central New England (CNE) brought

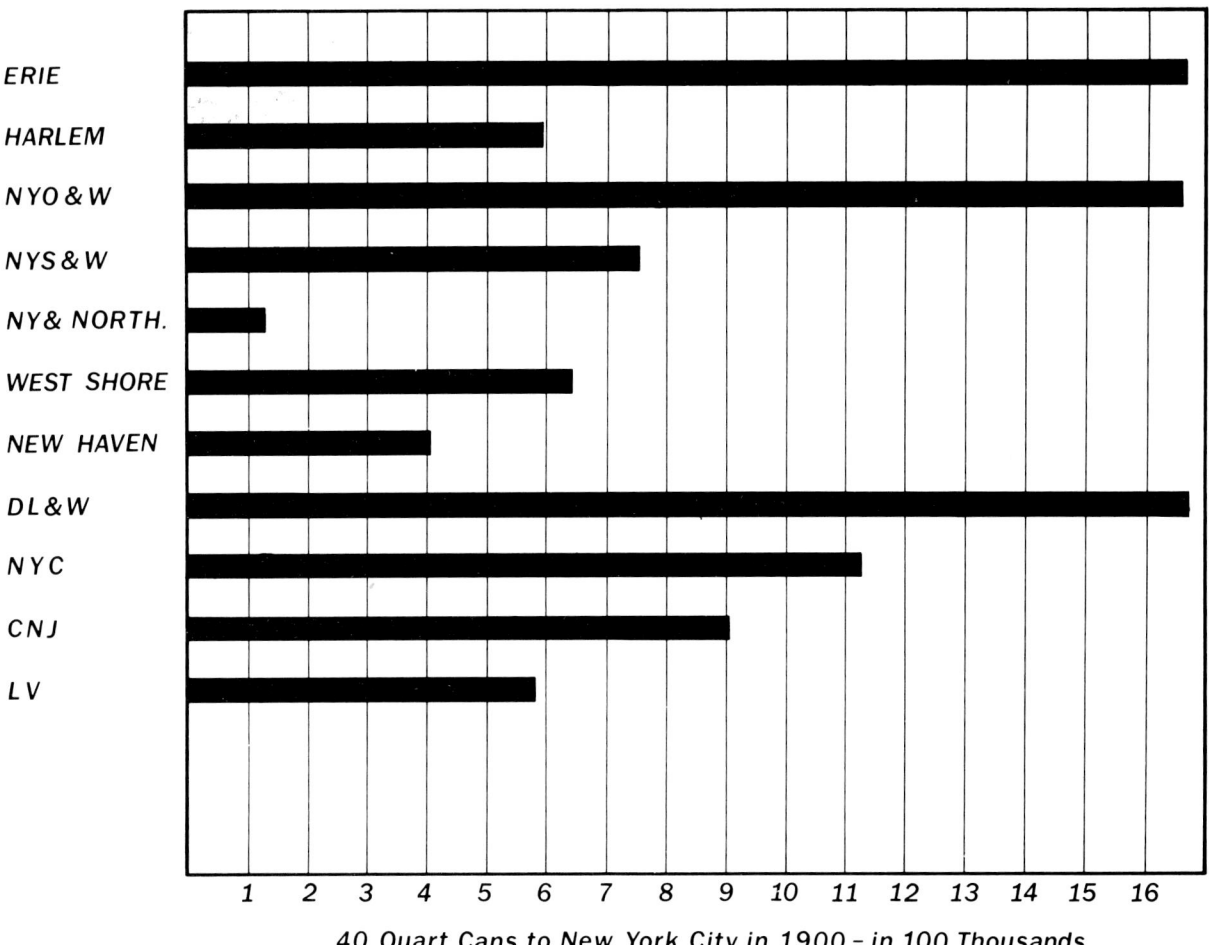

It can be seen from the graph that the O&W was close to being the number one carrier of milk to New York City in 1900. By 1902 the O&W had captured first place but later lost the lead to the New York Central. At this time some milk was also coming down the Hudson River by steamer and a small amount was also being handled by express companies. GRAPH BY CHUCK YUNGKURTH, BASED ON O&W DATA.

New York, Ontario & Western Railway Co.

GENERAL FREIGHT OFFICE,

No. 24 STATE STREET, Cor. BRIDGE.

CIRCULAR No. 101.

NEW YORK, December 26th, 1883.

To All Concerned:

On and after Monday, January 14th, the Milk Train of this Company will run to the new terminus at Weehawken, instead of Jersey City, as heretofore.

Ferries, for the accommodation of milk wagons, have been established to 42d and Desbrosses Sts., New York.

The train will arrive at Weehawken at 11.20 P. M., and ferry-boats will leave New York from foot of 42d and Desbrosses Sts. at 10.30 P. M., running every thirty minutes up to 2.30 A. M. Boats will leave Weehawken every thirty minutes up to 2.30 A. M. On this date also, all milk from the Ulster and Delaware and Wallkill Valley R. R. will be taken to Weehawken.

Yours respectfully,

Approved: J. C. ANDERSON,
General Freight Agent.
W. P. ROBINSON,
Traffic Manager.

Two milk cans show the railroad and station identification system used on the O&W. The railroad's milk station list indicates that "8D" is Hawley and "9D" is Hamden. TWO PHOTOGRAPHS: CARL OHLSON AND GEORGE SHAMMAS. Note the following details on this list: suffix letters "M.B." in the left column stand for Middletown branch, which was the original designation of the Cornwall-Middletown route. In the middle column, Bloomingburgh, the first place to ship milk on the railroad was assigned identification number 1. The "D" suffix in column three was used for Delhi branch locations. LIST FROM NYWS&B and NYO&W JOINT TIMETABLE NO. 2 DATED JUNE 25, 1883, COURTESY OF WALTER KIERZKOWSKI.

milk to the O&W at Campbell Hall. After 1906, the Delaware & Eastern, later the Delaware & Northern (D&N), brought milk down to East Branch, N.Y. There was also a time in the 1880's when milk came south from the Ulster & Delaware (U&D) and the Wallkill Valley Railroads via Kingston & Campbell Hall.

All of the loaded southbound milk trains had their northbound counterparts that distributed the empty cans and cars to their originating terminals. To

LIST OF MILK STATIONS.

STATIONS.	Distances from Weehawk'n	Station Letters for Milk.	STATIONS.	Distances from Middletown	Station Letters for Milk.	STATIONS.	Distances from Middletown	Station Letters for Milk.
Middletown	77	77 M.B.	Sands	1	7	Rockland	58	58
Tryon's Cross'g	75	75 M.B.	Crawford Junc.	3	6	Cook's Falls	63	63
Mechanicstown	74	74 M.B.	Fair Oaks	5	5	Trout Brook	70	70
Ireland	72	72 M.B.	Purdy's	6	4	East Branch	73	73
Stony Ford	70	70 M.B.	Lockwood's	7	3	Fish's Eddy	76	76
Clark's	69	69 M.B.	Winterton	8	2	Hancock	82	82
Campbell Hall	68	68 M.B.	Bloomingburgh	10	1	Griffis' Switch	84	84
McBride's	67	67 M.B.	Wurtsboro'	12	A	Keery's	85	85
Otter	66	66 M.B.	Summitville	15	B	Rock Rift	94	94
Burnside	65	65 M.B.	Phillipsport	16	C	Beers' Switch	97	98
Rock Tavern	64	64 M.B.	Mountain Dale	23	D	Walton	102	102
Clinton	63	63 M.B.	Dugall's	24	D½	Marvins'	103	1D
Little Britain	62	62 M.B.	Centreville	27	E	Colchester	105	4D
Genung's	61	61 M.B.	Thompson	29	E½	Hawley's	109	8D
Denniston's	59	59 M.B.	Fallsburgh	30	F	Hamden	111	9D
Meadow Brook	57	57 M.B.	Conklin's	31	F½	De Lancey	113	11D
Montana	55	55 M.B.	Hurley	33	G	Frazer's	115	13D
			Gardner's	35	G½	Peake's Creek	116	14D
			Parliman's	36	H½	Delhi	119	17D
			Strongtown	37	I	North Walton	109	109
			Liberty Falls	39	J	Merrickville	112	112
			Gerow's	40	J½	Franklin	114	114
			Liberty	41	K	Sidney Centre	117	117
			Parksville	46	L	Southwick's	119	119
			McGrath's	47	La	Young's	120	120
			Finkle's	49	M	Gillett's	124	124
			Livingston Manor	51	SM	Frye's	124½	124½
						Sidney	125	125

In addition to railroad and station identification, this can displays another feature. Soft solder was flowed onto the lid and on it the farmer's name, "John Logan," was stamped. Heavier stamping below pressed "DeLancey Del Co NY" into the metal. GEORGE S. SHAMMAS COLLECTION.

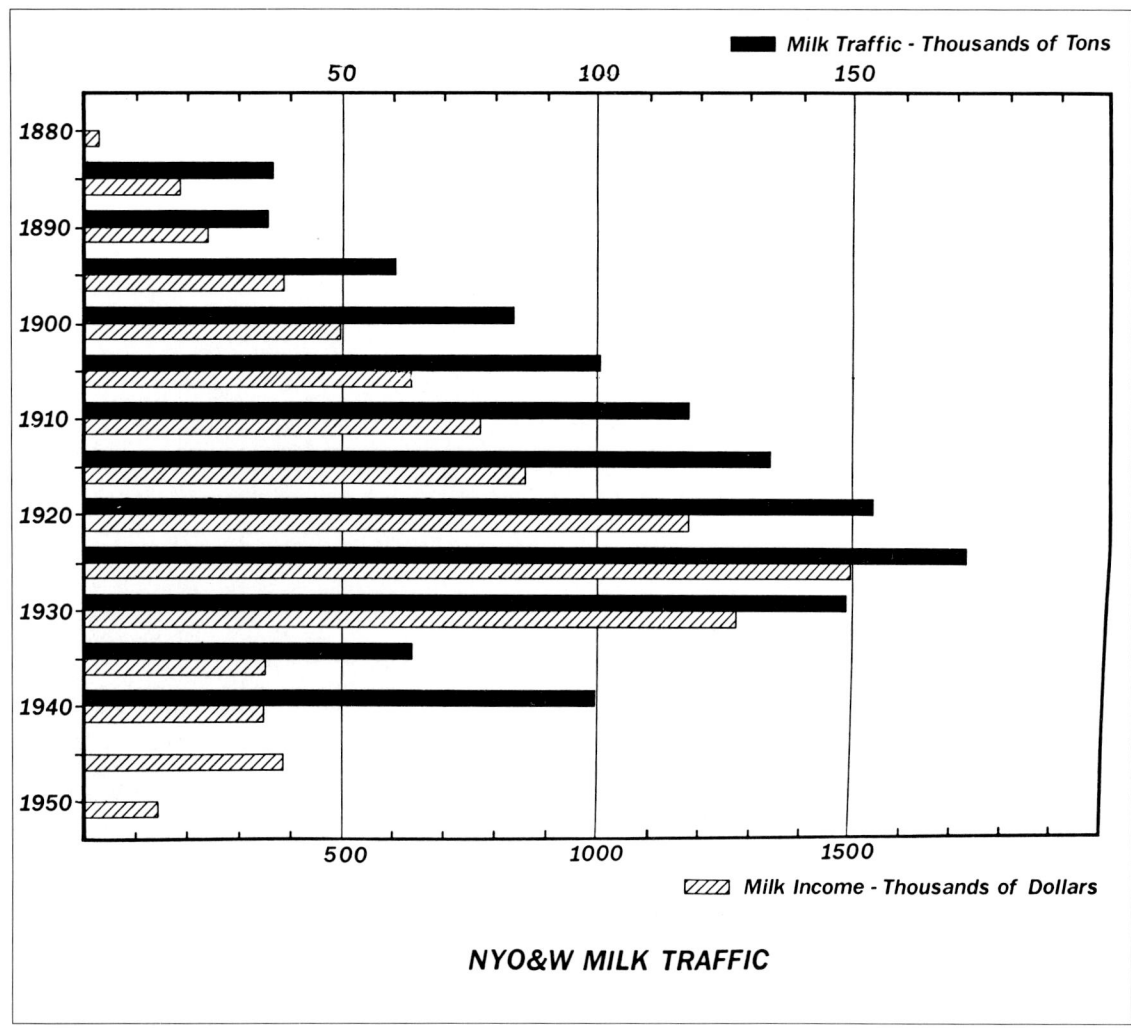

NYO&W MILK TRAFFIC

ensure proper return of empty cans to their home terminals a code system was formulated which used combinations of copper or tin letters, numerals, and O&W logos that were soldered to the cans and lids. Train crews, milk messengers, and creamery workers could easily identify the ownership and destination of the empty cans.

Milk trains had special operating rights that were listed in the Employees' Timetable. The main line and some of the branch milk trains were allowed to make all ordinary stops. These stops were not to exceed three minutes at all regular milk stations. Unless there was a first class train following, a flagman did not have to protect the rear until his train was 20 minutes late. All second class and extra trains following within 30 minutes of the time of the milk trains were to approach all milk stations slowly and with the train under full control, expecting to find a milk train occupying the main track. In July of 1890 and again in February of 1901 milk trains were hit by following trains due to poor flagging protection. In the latter wreck, a passenger and an employee were killed. Several of the railroad's high officials were injured on April 26, 1907, when an inspection train smashed into the rear of a milk train at Parker, N.Y. It is likely that there were other such accidents and close calls involving milk trains.

A place where the flagging rules definitely had to be carefully observed was Burnside, N.Y. A mile-long siding was constructed here in the late 1890's to reach a creamery-icehouse complex at Burnside Pond. This complex was built by Anglo-Swiss Milk Company which was later bought by Borden's. Crews picking up loads and setting out empties had to leave the hind cars of their trains on the main when the engine backed down the long siding to work at the plant. A similar situation existed at Mt. Upton, N.Y., on the New Berlin branch, where creamery facilities were located on a long siding that extended some distance from the main track.

From the very early days of the milk business, the railroad encouraged farmers to enter the dairy field. Many roads, including the O&W and possibly the NY&OM before it, guaranteed to take back, at the farmer's cost price, the milk cans they had purchased, if they chose to abandon the business. In cooperation with state agricultural services and colleges, demonstration cars and dairy displays were brought to local communities by rail to promote better farming practices. The O&W's policy was clearly stated in the company's annual report for June, 1896:

> The policy of your company has been to offer the best facilities to the farmers and creamerymen adjacent to its main line and branches ... Facilities have been afforded at nearly every available point on the line for shipping, and at several places creameries have been erected and leased to responsible tenants ...

There were 77 creameries on the railroad in 1896, 19 of them being built and owned by the O&W. In 1911, this ownership increased to about 40. Re-

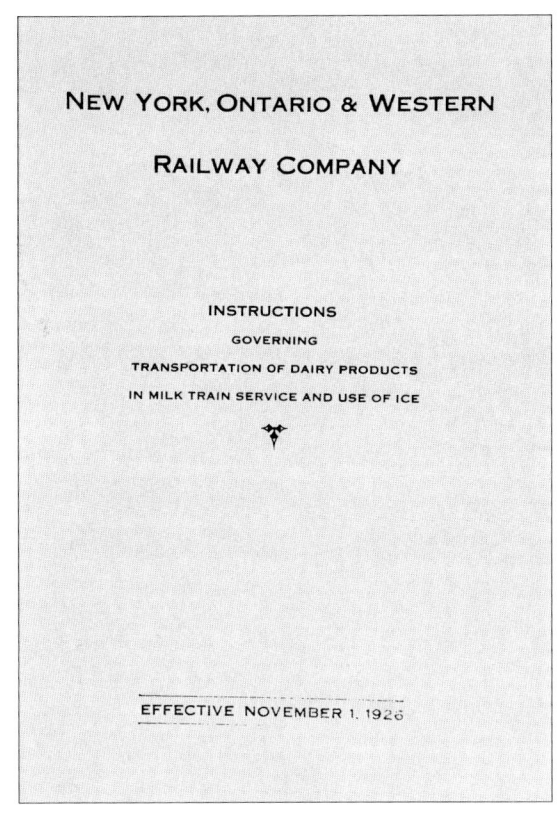

ABOVE: The milk business generated scores of missives and instructional booklets dealing with the efficient and timely handling of the traffic. AUTHOR'S COLLECTION. TOP RIGHT: In addition to bluestone, wood chemicals, and tourists, Cooks Falls, N.Y., also provided the O&W with milk business. It was handled in this creamery-icehouse combination south of the station and opposite the bend in the Beaverkill. O&W SOCIETY COLLECTION. RIGHT: Four cooling vats are still visible in the old concrete base of the Cooks Falls creamery. Those curious enough to spend some time in the area may also find a steel bridge, the stone base of a water tank, a station and a section house. AUTHOR'S PHOTOGRAPH.

ABOVE: On the flatlands of the north country, the Bernhard's, N.Y., (Bernhard's Bay) creamery served the farmers of Oswego County. In spite of harsh winters, many of the state's northern counties were rated as prime dairy country by New York's Department of Agriculture (possibly due to abundant snowfall). An empty 1000-series milk car has its doors open to dry out before another trip. EMILY HOYT COLLECTION, COURTESY OF EVA REYMORE AND GENE GRAFFOULIERE.

LEFT: Hinged wooden lids covered the ice-water cooling vats in the Bernhards' Creamery. Note the lack of any lifting devices to lower or raise the cans. It is possible that a portable, wheeled device might have been used although none of the creamerymen interviewed recalled such an aid. DENNIS CARPENTER COLLECTION.

ABOVE: The Eaton, N.Y., creamery was under construction in this scene. A boiler sits on the ground at the left of the building although at this point of completion, one would expect the boiler to have been installed. Wooden planking in the right foreground is part of the station platform, and the white post was used for hanging a train order or flag stop signal. DENNIS CARPENTER COLLECTION. OVERLEAF: Plans for the creamery include details for the cooling vats which show a depth of 24 inches. This was equal to can height, which was standardized at a nominal 24 inches including the lid. Displacement of water by the cans had to be considered when filling the vat. Not shown is the gentle slope of the floor to a corner of the vat. A drain ran from this corner to the creamery's central drainage system. No doubt spilled milk did get into the water at times. This vat could hold 96 cans. O&W SOCIETY COLLECTION.

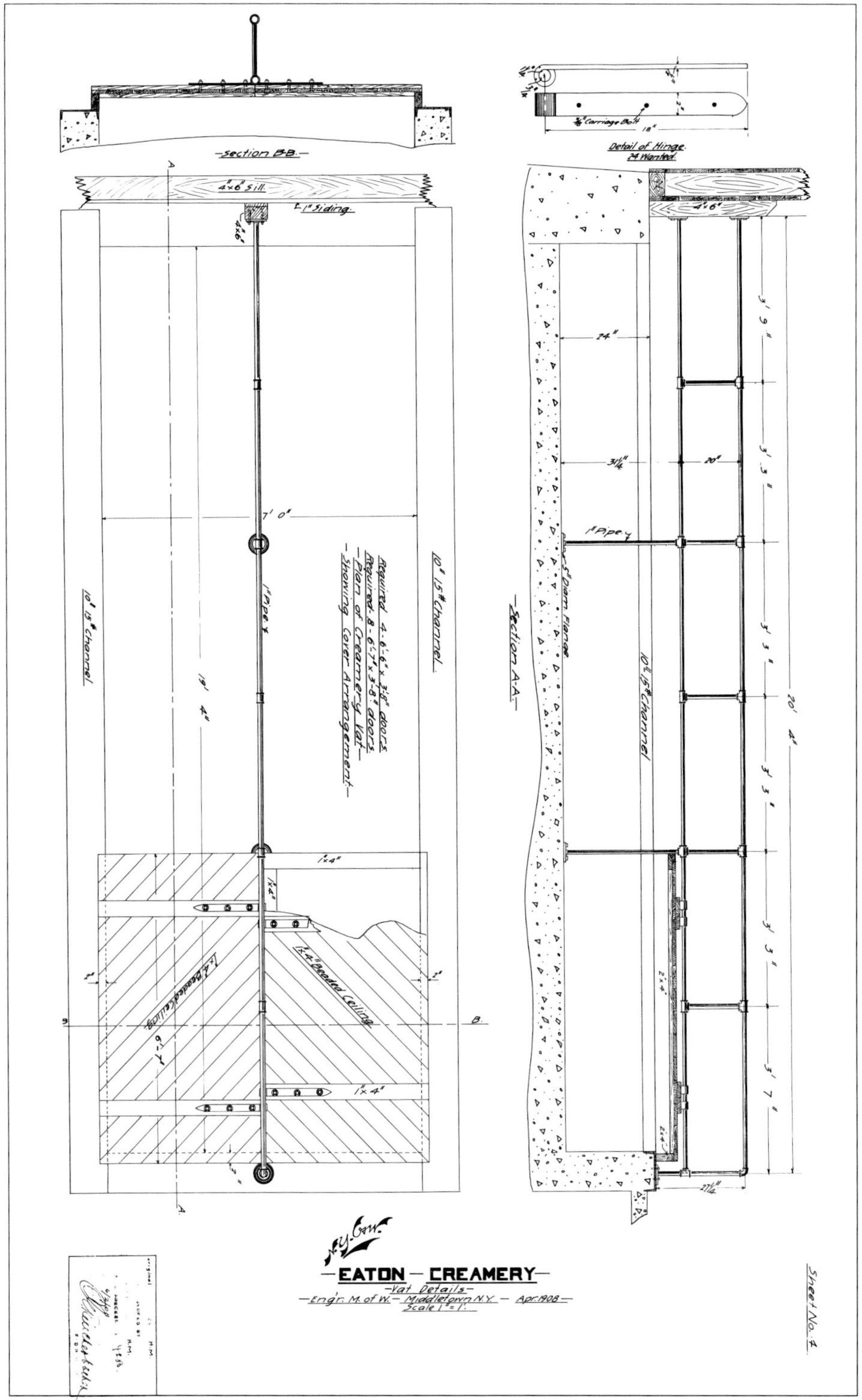
Section B-B.
Detail of Hinge.
24 Wanted.
3/8" Carriage Bolt
4"x6" Sill
1" Siding
4"x6"
24"
20"
1" Pipe
7' 0"
19' 4"
20' 4"
10" 15# Channel
Section A-A
Required 4-6'-6"x3'-8" doors
Required 8-6'-7"x3'-8" doors
Plan of Creamery Vat
Showing Cover Arrangement
1"x4"
1"x4" Beaded Ceiling
27 1/4"
EATON — CREAMERY
Vat Details
Engr. M. of W. – Middletown N.Y. – Apr. 1908
Scale 1"=1'.
Sheet No. 4

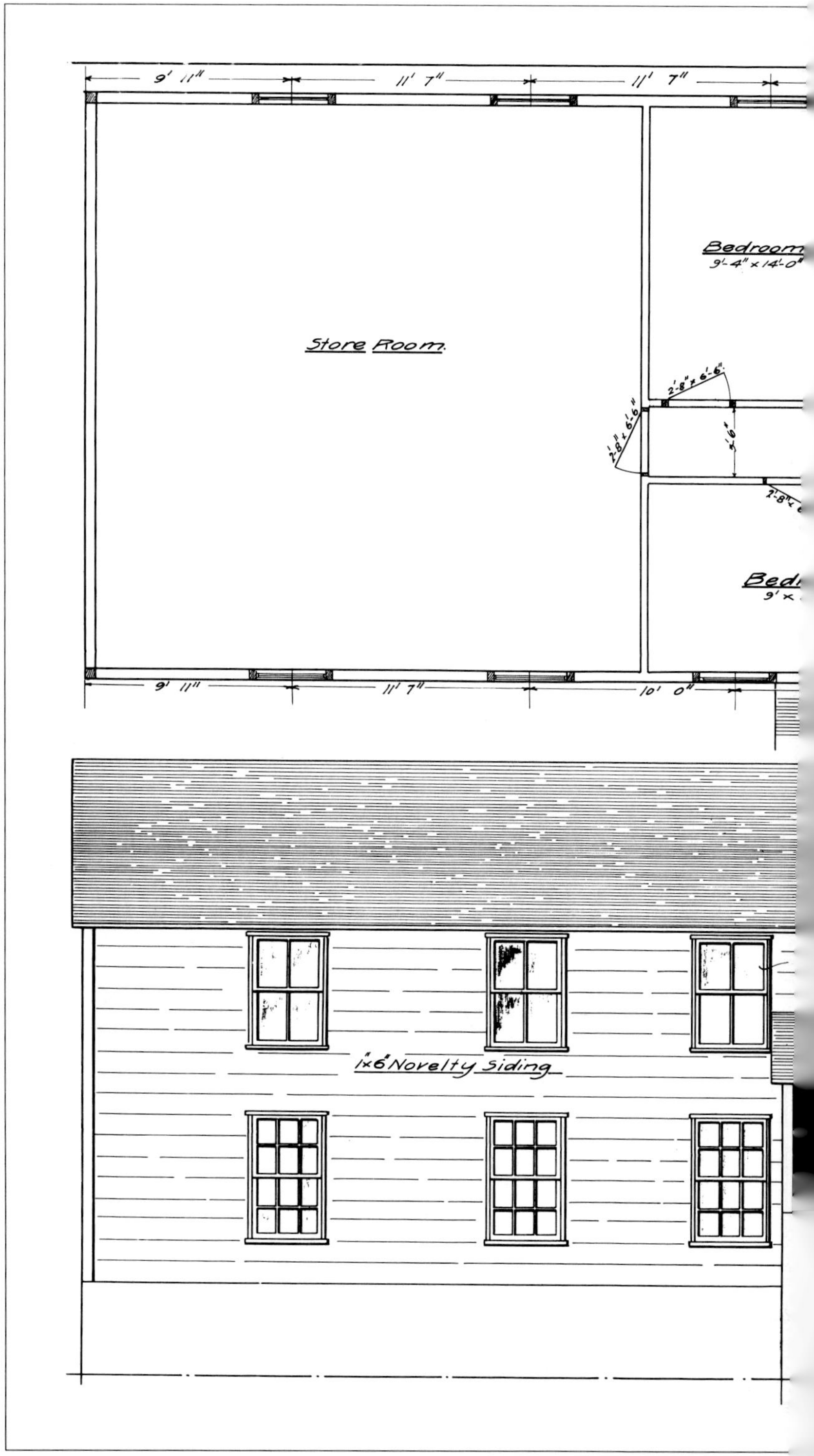
9' 11"
11' 7"
10' 0"
Store Room.
Bedroom
9'-4"x14'-0"
2'-8"x6'-6"
3'-6"
1"x6" Novelty Siding

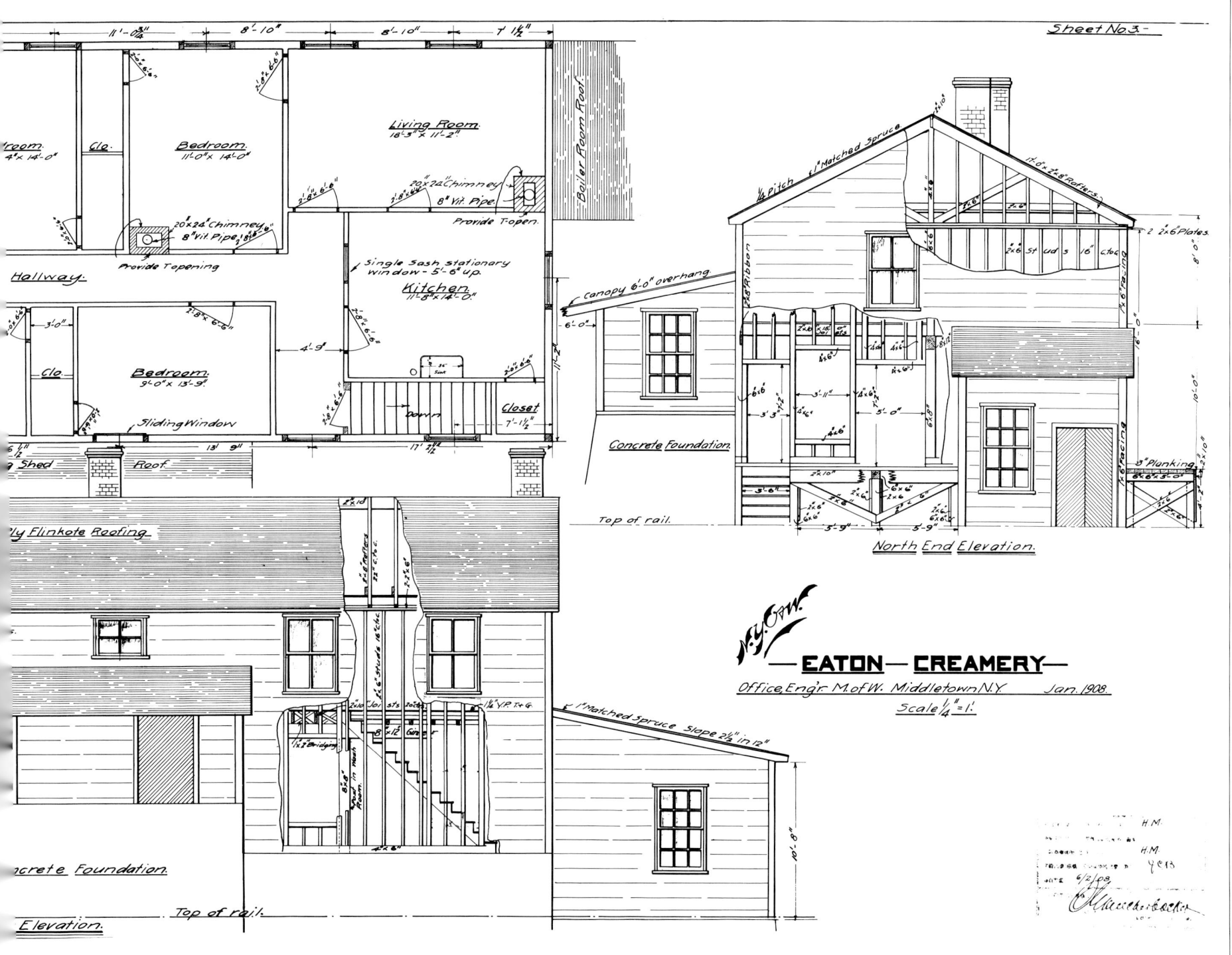

TOP LEFT: The Preston Park, Pa., creamery was conveniently located next to the depot and saved the agent and creamery foreman many steps in the transacting of business. The far end of the building is an icehouse. JOHN PAVELCHAK COLLECTION. TOP RIGHT: The Central Square, N.Y., creamery was located near the present day Route 11 and Railroad St. Two farm wagons are about to unload a day's milk production which will shortly appear on the platform at the left. Some milk may have been interchanged to the Rome, Watertown & Ogdensburg which crossed the O&W at this point. EMILY HOYT COLLECTION, COURTESY OF EVA REYMORE AND GENE GRAFFOULIERE. BOTTOM LEFT: Approximately 30 miles from the end of the line at Oswego, the community of West Monroe, N.Y., had a combination freight and passenger station and a combination creamery-icehouse. The main track is to the right with its important mail crane by which the town forwarded and received its daily communication. MARFIELD FOSTER PHOTOGRAPH, COURTESY OF WEST MONROE HISTORICAL SOCIETY.

Constructed in the early years of this century, the creamery at Munnsville, N.Y., was part of a small commercial complex near the O&W station in that community. Those having business with the railroad had to drive up the steep hill from town. SAM REEDER COLLECTION.

BELOW: Circumstances sometimes required the construction of an open or sheltered platform, such as this, to encourage local farmers to produce milk and use rail transportation. It may have been that there was no creamery or depot nearby from which to ship. COURTESY OF MARV COHEN.

ABOVE: Not all the milk was picked up at creameries. Some milk stops were simple platforms, while others were roofed or enclosed shelters. The open structure at the right was located at a rural crossing in Oxford, N.Y., and the closed shelter at the left served an unidentified village on the Southern Division. The Hebrew writing on the store suggests a Sullivan County, N.Y., location. TWO PHOTOGRAPHS, WAYNE SITTNER COLLECTION.

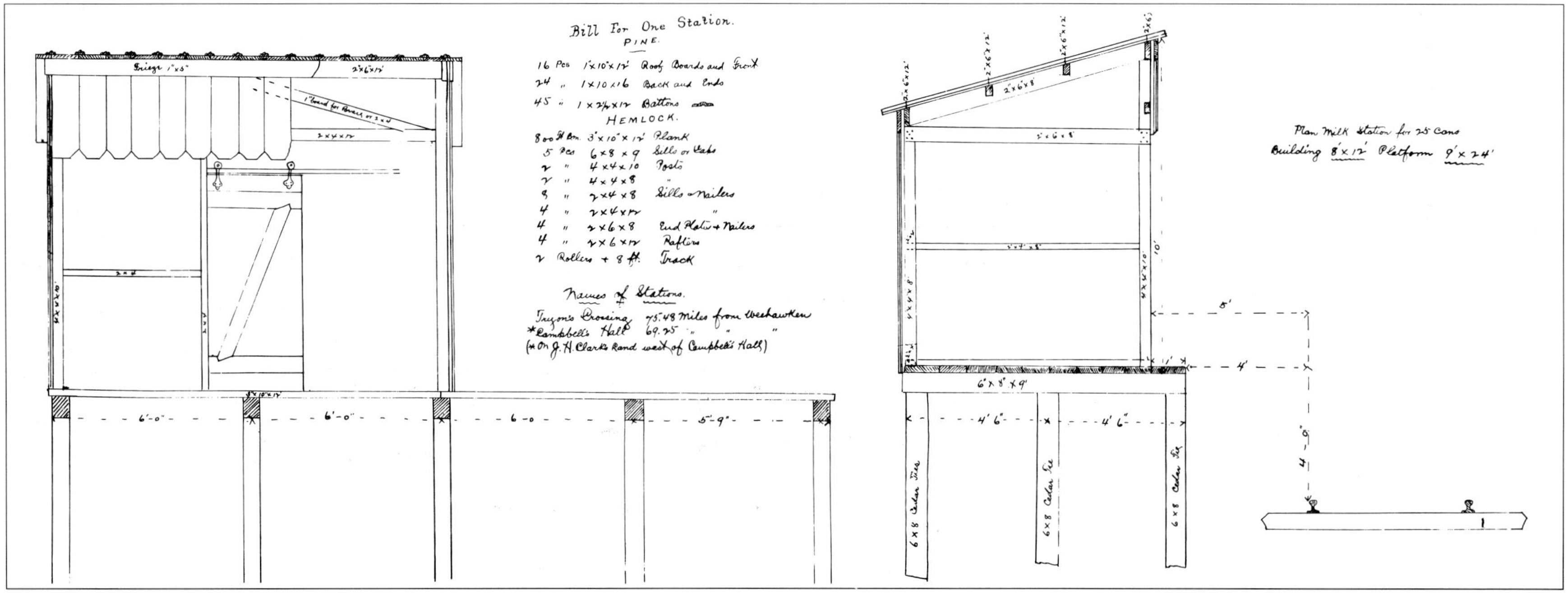

buildings, enlargements, and complete replacements of earlier structures make it difficult to determine an exact number.

Wooden platforms for can loading were located at a great many rural crossings where volume did not justify more expensive arrangements. Photographs and limited written information indicate that most of these small structures were roofed for elementary protection from the sun and weather. Farmers using such structures had to remember train schedules so as not to bring the milk too early and have it suffer the effects of heat or cold. By 1910, the construction of creameries and simple platforms had essentially ended. The milk business then entered a phase of consolidation through mergers and takeovers by larger companies. Many of the smaller, less efficient operations found themselves unable to compete and were forced to close. It is likely that the O&W began to sell its own creameries during this period to local operators who in turn were later bought out by larger companies. These changes did not seem to have a negative impact on the railroad, for the revenues and tonnage of O&W milk would continue to grow into the 1920's.

The greatest part of the O&W's milk business went to Weehawken, N.J. By 1916 this terminal had five platforms for unloading milk cars, and four of them were used by the O&W. A total of 46 cars could be placed for unloading, and a force of 18 men was employed for this purpose. The terminal was modified through the years to accommodate the variety and number of cans and bulk cars that arrived daily. There were complaints from customers that they frequently had to wait for their cars to be unloaded because of the crowded facility. It does not appear that the O&W delivered directly to any consignee at the Weehawken end of the operation. This necessity of transshipment for final delivery created a big disadvantage for the railroad that became increasingly evident in the 1930's and 1940's.

Mr. Richard Howe, whose father was the O&W station agent at Pleasant Mount, Pa., gives us some insight into an agent's responsibilities regarding the milk business. He recalled the following:

The Cadosia operator would have to be notified by telegraph about the quantity of milk and the car numbers that would be shipped from the Dairymen's League creamery. This plant was located near the station, and they generally shipped one or two cars each day. Cadosia needed this information so that the consist of train No. 2 could be planned. The freight charges on milk shipments averaged $3000 per month from Pleasant Mount during the late 1930's, so this business required close attention. One detail was that the empty milk tank cars had to be properly placed to make the pipe connections for loading. On more than one occasion, when main line train connections were missed and the way freight did not bring the cars, my father made a 10:00 P.M. visit to the station and waited for freight train BO-1 to see that the crew placed the cars properly. Each morning, especially in bad weather, the agent anxiously watched the incoming milk trucks go by the station on the way to the creamery. Two of the drivers were notorious for tardiness and the creamery superintendent would not release the

Milk picked up at this covered platform at Starlight, Pa., was not bound for the New York metropolitan area since the platform is on the Scranton-bound track. Lakewood had creameries that did processing as did Carbondale, Scranton and other towns on the Scranton Division, so milk from this location could well have been transported toward the coal mining region. O&W SOCIETY COLLECTION.

The Dairymen's League facility at Pleasant Mount, Pa., stood across from the O&W depot. Behind the plant, the Scranton Division tracks climbed geographically north to Poyntelle, Pa., and then dropped downgrade to cross the West Branch of the Delaware River at Hancock, N.Y. The plant relied on a local freight for set-outs and pick-ups before switching to trucks. In fact, the facility outlasted the railroad by a decade or more. K. ELIZABETH HOWE PHOTOGRAPHS.

tank car bill of lading until all the milk loads were in. Late shipments meant holding the way freight, missing the passenger train connections at Cadosia and incurring the wrath of railroad superintendent Fred Hawk. However leaving the milk cars behind was unthinkable. If necessary, the way freight was held, and trains 1 and 2 were delayed. Mr. Hawk got another ulcer and the agent a reprimand. Today's people in all businesses would recognize this as a classic customer service problem with internal conflict.

In addition to the League milk out of Pleasant Mount, Sheffield Farms loaded a car at Lakewood, Pa. This car made a connection at Cadosia with train No. 1 for delivery to Sheffield's Walton plant. This made it urgent to get the Scranton Division way freight into Cadosia before the arrival of train No. 1, around 12:30 P.M. A delay to this train would shorten its turnaround time at Walton and make its southbound trip, as No. 2, late in starting out. Conductor Jack Collins thus exhorted his crew to hustle along. If the way freight were late, arriving after 4:00 P.M. because of a delayed No. 2, another problem arose. Switching the League car would require occupancy of the southbound track and might necessitate stopping through freight SU-1 on the grade. Holding the northbound track might delay train BL-1, which was also undesirable. Usually the way freight had a long string of empty hoppers for the Northwest Coal Company, too long to clear the station switch. Locating the symbol freights via railroad phone was not possible due to earlier austerity measures that eliminated the agent-operators at Forest City and Poyntelle. Quick calls were made to friendly store owners in Forest City and Poyntelle to determine whether the symbol freights had passed. Then a quick conference with the crew led to a decision to either back over to the southbound track and let BL-1 go by, or to hold position and let SU-1 pass. If a train had to be delayed it would probably have been BL-1

NEW YORK, ONTARIO AND WESTERN RAILWAY COMPANY

Norwich, N.Y. April 20, 1940.

Train Dispatchers:

We are receiving full tank of milk from Jetter Dairy Company, Solsville, in addition to tank car from Dairymens League at that station.

In order to hold this business it will be necessary to place the empty cars early as possible. If can not get SU 1 started by 5.15 A.M. it will be necessary to send an extra out with the milkcars and they can run to Canal Branc and leave there with the express car to do milk and express work south.

Yours truly,

[signature]

Assistant Superintendent.

---

because it was headed down grade and would have an easier time getting started. In any event flagmen would have gone out earlier to protect their trains.

The company went to great lengths to get the milk through. There was an instance during a severe snow storm in the 1930's when the plow train brought in the milk. During the 1946 railroad strike, a supervisory train crew handled the milk.

After dropping the milk car and picking up any empty freight cars, the less-than-carload freight and perhaps some company supplies were unloaded from an ancient, wooden O&W boxcar in the way freight consist. Planks extended from the freight platform to the car door, and the aging hand truck carried the packages. Finally, combine car 121 paused in front of the station, one or two express parcels were unloaded, and the train departed for Mayfield Yard.

By the 1930's or possibly earlier, the O&W became aware of motor truck competition for the milk business. At first these trucks must have been viewed as a curiosity, but this soon gave way to alarm as the dairy industry accepted and supported this new mode of transportation. Correspondence between O&W officials and officers of other railroads expressed a constant concern with trucks cutting into the milk business. Rates were adjusted to meet the competition, but the rail industry's cumbersome, time-consuming, and fractious system of formulating and adjusting rates worked against it. To set or change rates, the railroad had to present its case to the Trunk Line Association, where regional members such as the Erie, Pennsylvania, Lehigh Valley, Delaware, Lackawanna & Western, and Delaware & Hudson could veto the proposal for reasons of their own. They had this power even though the proposed rate covered a single line's haul. In addition to this, rates had to be approved by the Interstate Commerce Commission, or the New York Public Service Commission if an intrastate haul was involved. At times, it was a seesaw battle with one form of transport taking it away from the other and then losing it again as rates were readjusted.

A big advantage that the truckers had was that their rates and services covered door-to-door movement. When the O&W moved milk to Weehawken, it still had to be transferred to the dairy company's city plant. This meant the additional cost and time of a ferryboat trip if the plant was east of the Hudson River. Jetter Dairy of Bronx, N.Y., told the railroad that it had been approached by several trucking companies who indicated that they could move that company's milk at the same rate that the O&W charged, but would take it from country creamery directly to the city processing plant.

Although the time advantage that the truckers had was small—where it existed at all—it constantly became greater as roads and vehicles were improved. After 1927, Hudson River bridges and tunnel crossings significantly improved the truckers' time into the city. By 1940 the O&W's agricultural agent reported that there were seven to nine trucking

Form still followed function in what was essentially the final evolution of the country creamery. Borden's last plant at Burnside, N.Y., constructed in the 1940's, employed modern materials and some aspects of Art Deco architecture. It was strictly a truck-served plant and with the abandonment of the earlier buildings, the O&W no longer needed its long siding to reach the business. TOM MATTHEWS COLLECTION.

firms competing with the railroad for milk traffic. The railroad did try to find a solution to the problem, with one of the most promising being the ideas of Benjamin Fitch and his portable containers (Chapter 5). There was also an attempt to interest the dairy trucking industry in handling the short haul and leaving the longer part of the line haul to the railroad. This involved a scheme to make Middletown the facility where milk would be transferred from rail car to tank trucks for final delivery. World War II restrictions on gasoline, tires, and parts slowed down trucking inroads into the milk market. Less than a decade remained, however, before the advantages of high-way transportation tipped the balance completely in favor of motor trucks, and the O&W was out of the milk business forever. The last car of milk was shipped from Lakewood, Pa., in 1952.

An adjunct to the milk business and one that represented significant income to the railroad was the harvesting, shipping, and storing of ice. Each year, fewer people can recall the time before electrical refrigeration, when ice wagons and trucks, icehouses, and icemen were so much a part of the daily scene. Many creameries were located near lakes and ponds where ice could be gathered relatively easily and stored for year-round use. Others had to rely on some method of transportation to bring it in from a distance. In those days there was probably less danger of industrial pollution and almost any clear body of water near the right of way could have been the end point of a spur or short branch. The beginning and length of the ice-gathering season and the quantity of ice cut depended upon the severity and length of the winter season and thus varied from year to year. The ice had to be at least a foot thick to safely hold the workers and equipment as well as to make harvesting worth the effort. Old-timers said that a heavy snow on top of a few inches of early ice could substantially reduce the season's harvest. When this happened, holes might be bored through the ice to allow water to overflow the surface. In very cold weather, this water would freeze quickly and add to the thickness of the ice field. Several days of clear, freezing weather were considered ideal conditions and made clear, dense, thick ice. In a typical winter, January and February were the best months, since the temperatures were usually the lowest and the time between cuttings would not be long. The colder temperatures also meant that the runways and chutes would retain icy surfaces for easier handling, and water on the blocks would freeze quickly when they were pulled from the lake or pond.

Organized work crews would clear away snow, determine thickness, mark out the lines, and then cut and convey large grids or floats of over 200 cakes of ice. The floats were pushed or pulled to an open channel that led to the icehouse or railroad cars. Sometimes this work was done at night with the workers moonlighting in the true sense. Horses and manpower were the primary energy sources until well after World War I, although gas-powered saws and outboard motorboats came into use during the second decade. The boats replaced some of the manpower used in moving the floats of ice through channels. The large grids would then be cut into blocks and removed from the water. Mechanical devices would shave or plane the blocks to standard sizes before they reached the icehouse.

Planing also removed surface impurities. Pikes were used to move the blocks in the water and through slippery passageways. Where horses were

The Scranton Division right-of-way curves southward in this scene from the Lakewood, Pa., station in 1989. Across the way the Dairymen's League plant, still retaining its blue and white scheme, may have been the last active milk shipper on the O&W since company records indicate the final carload came from this point. The other possibility was a Sheffield Farms plant that was geographically south of this scene. AUTHOR'S PHOTOGRAPH.

ABOVE: Borden's great icehouse at Burnside, N.Y., held thousands of tons of ice harvested from Smith's Pond in the foreground. Two railroad cars—possibly O&W milk cars—sit under the conveyor near the end of the mile-long spur. After their original use ended, some icehouses held on to a tenuous existence as mushroom farms. The dark, damp interiors were well suited for that purpose. TOP RIGHT: (facing page) The construction of the giant building with four vertical rows of doors and its elevator extending down to the pond, is near completion. TWO PHOTOGRAPHS: MIDDLETOWN AND WALLKILL PRECINCT HISTORICAL SOCIETY, ELLIOT MCLURE COLLECTION, COURTESY OF DENNIS CARPENTER.

LEFT: Men and teams pause momentarily on Smith's Pond while cutting ice. Note the straight edge to open water on the left side. Horses used in this work frequently wore a choke rope that had to be quickly pulled to keep the horse from taking water into its lungs if it fell in. In view of this icehouse's capacity, a cold winter must have provided plenty of work. DENNIS CARPENTER COLLECTION.

LEFT: Ice cakes can be seen ascending the elevator; the scaffolding has been raised to the top row of doors. A particularly long and hard winter has permitted several cuttings and the house is filled to maximum capacity. MIDDLETOWN AND WALLKILL PRECINCT HISTORICAL SOCIETY, ELLIOT MCLURE COLLECTION, COURTESY OF DENNIS CARPENTER.

FACING PAGE: This excellent series of photographs shows the details and operations of the O&W's icehouse at Fargo, N.Y. Fargo was on the Pecksport Loop with the icehouse located on Leland Pond. The first view (top left) was taken from the top to the ice conveyor and looks out over the pond. The second view (top right) shows the conveyor system taking cakes of ice up to the house with the steam power plant to the left. In the third scene (bottom right), a continuous chain moves the blocks into position for loading into boxcars which will take the ice to other locations on the railroad. The final scene (bottom left) shows workmen operating the mechanism to raise or lower the platform. FOUR PHOTOGRAPHS: DENNIS CARPENTER COLLECTION.

RIGHT AND BELOW: Another large Borden's icehouse was located in Walton, behind the condensery that was opposite the O&W station. A point gang, posed on the scaffold, serves as a good scale comparison. TWO PHOTOGRAPHS: WILLIAM SCHRIVER COLLECTION.

New York, Ontario and Western Railway.

ICE CAR SERVICE

To SCRANTON, and PHILADELPHIA, PA.

Commencing June 10th, this Company will establish a semi-weekly service for shipments of Butter, Cheese, Eggs, etc., between points on this line, Scranton and Philadelphia, Pa., on the following schedule:

TUESDAYS and SATURDAYS

Lv. DELHI	11.00 a.m.	
" HAMDEN	11 20	"
" SIDNEY	9.30	"
" SO. UNADILLA	9.35	"
" MAYWOOD	10.10	"
" FRANKLIN	10.30	"
" WALTON	12.45 p.m.	
Ar. SCRANTON	7.00	"
" PHILADELPHIA	6.00 a.m.	

J. C. ANDERSON,
General Freight Agent.

H. H. PURDY,
Special Agent,
UTICA, N. Y.

ABOVE: A refrigerated service operated in conjunction with the Jersey Central and Reading Railroads was advertised in this notice. The car(s) traveled the O&W to Scranton where they were interchanged to the Jersey Central. The Central delivered them to the Reading at Bethlehem, Pa. The service seems to have been aimed toward produce and dairy products other than milk. O&W SOCIETY COLLECTION.

Pray's Patent Ice Plows

Four Tooth Plow. Price $16.50

The Teeth are adjustable and can easily be taken off, sharpened and put on to cut as before. They are firmly fastened with bolts in slots, admitting movement up and down. They are locked to their places with bolts running up through beams and flanges on upper part of teeth. The plow is made very strong, and is thoroughly braced. The points of the teeth are tempered and made very sharp. Care should be taken to keep the shoes on when not in use. If a tooth should become broken, it can be replaced at a small cost.

The Four-Tooth Plow is designed for a cheap ice plow for farmers and dairymen. It will cut 15 to 30 tons an hour, cutting the ice blocks of uniform size, saving much labor when packing.

The teeth cut seven and one-quarter inches deep, and each tooth should cut one-quarter inch. The plow will then run smooth, do good work, and give satisfaction. The sizes cut are 16, 19, 23½ and 27 inches. The adjustment of the teeth are all properly marked at each tooth and runner. The plows leave our factory properly adjusted and require no changing.

TOP LEFT: Specialized tools were developed for the ice cutting and ice handling tasks. Power tools were eventually developed and in some places, ice continued to be used for home refrigeration into the 1950's. BELOW LEFT: A rare interior view shows ice being stacked inside the ice house. TWO PHOTOGRAPHS, HAROLD FREDERICKS COLLECTION. THIS PAGE AND OVERLEAF: Horse-drawn plows and ice-handling tools were manufactured by many companies, each extolling the virtues of its own designs. Many such tools still lie at the bottom of ice ponds. HAGLEY MUSEUM COLLECTION.

JOHN DORSCH & SONS . . . ICE PLOWS . . . MILWAUKEE, WIS.

Eight Tooth Plow.   Price $30.00

This is the fastest ice cutting plow on the market today and is especially adapted for those putting up large quantities of ice. Will cut any depth from four to ten inches. It is also especially recommended where the time is short for harvest, since it cuts just twice as fast as our regular four-tooth plow. It frequently occurs that the time is very short in which to gather in the ice harvest, and in such cases the eight-tooth answers the purpose better than any other plow made. The eight-tooth wood frame plow was in big demand last season. The capacity is from 40 to 80 tons an hour. It cuts one inch on each side, or equal to two inches on a single row or furrow. It cuts the same size cakes as the six-tooth plow.

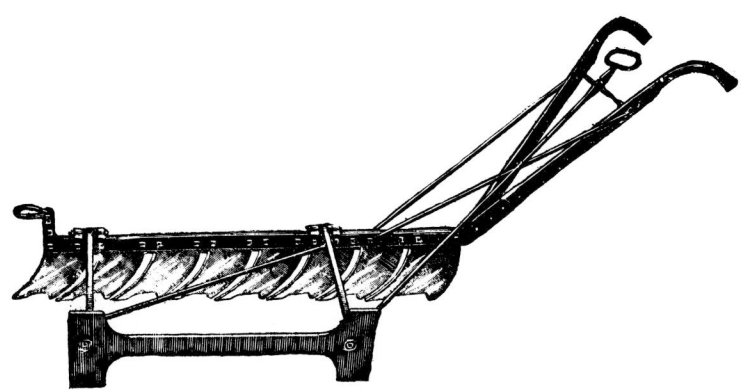

Swing Guide Swing.

Prices:
No. 1—Marker, with swing guide, - - - 58.00
No. 7—Six-inch, with 22-inch swing guide, - 50.50
No. 8—Eight-inch, with 22-inch swing guide, - 56.50
No. 12—Nine-inch, with 22-inch swing guide, - 59.50
No. 9 -Ten-inch, with 22-inch swing guide, - 61.50
No. 10 - Twelve-inch, with 22-inch swing guide, 66.50
No 21—Swing guide for 22-inch only, - - 9.50

Eight Tooth Plow.

Prices:
No. 2—Six-inch, 8 teeth, - 42.00
No. 3—Eight-inch, 7 teeth, - 48.00
No. 11—Nine-inch, 7 teeth, - 51.00
No. 4—Ten-inch, 6 teeth, - 53.00
No 5—Twelve-inch, 5 teeth, - 58.00
No. 6—Fourteen-inch, 5 teeth, - 65.00

No. 39—Breaking Off Bar, each $3.25.

Length 4 feet 8 inches. Made with a broad blunt blade on one end. supplied with ears on which to bear the foot in breaking off sheets or floats of ice. The other end is a chisel and convenient for many purposes.

No. 44—Chisel Bar, each $3.25.

Blade 4½x10½ inches; length 4 feet 7 inches. Made with wide blade, beveled on one side, used mostly in getting ice out of the ice house.

No. 45—Packing Chisel, each $3.25.

Blade 5x10½ inches; length 4 feet 9 inches. The blade is same as the chisel bar, but has a wooden handle. A light. convenient bar for packing ice.

No. 2 and 4 Splitting Fork.

No. 31—2-tine, ring handle, length 4 feet 10½ inches, each $4.25.
No. 4—2-tine, knob handle, length 4 feet 7¼ inches, each $4.60.

Our Splitting Forks are made with long steel tines, tapered so as to give great welding power in the grooves without shelling the ice.

No. 64—House Bar, each $2.50.
Weight 12 lbs; length 4 feet; width 4¼ inches.

No. 38—Calking Bar, each $2.50.
Blade 4¾x17 inches; length 4 feet 9 inches. This bar is used to calk the ends of grooves on the field of ice, and on the floats before they are detached, with the chips made in grooving, in order to prevent the water from running in.

No. 32—Lynn Splitting Bar, each $3.25.
One tine, 3 inches wide. Made with a solid steel tine or blade. This is preferred by some to the splitting fork for barring off, especially when the grooves have become frozen.

No. 1 Fork Bar   No. 34—Length 4 feet 6 inches.   **Each $4.60.**

No. 2 Fork Bar.   No. 35—Length 4 feet 9 inches.   **Each $4.60.**

No. 3 Fork Bar.   No. 36—Length 4 feet 9 inches.   **Each $4.00.**

No. 184—Ice Shave, each 50c.
With ferrule handle, total length 10 inches; blades 4½x2¾ inches.
  No. 200—Socket Shave, length 14 inches, $1.50
  No. 200a—Ferrule Shave, length 14 inches, 1.00
  No. 201—Loop snaped handle, length 14 in., per doz. 5.00
  No. 202—Loop shaped handle, length 18 in., per doz. 6.50

Ice Saws.
  No. 29—Ice Saw, 4 feet, complete $4.50
  No. 30—Ice Saw, 4½ feet, complete 5 00
  No. 31—Ice Saw, 5 feet, complete 5.50
  No. 32—Ice Saw, 5½ feet, complete 6.50

As the result of long and careful attention devoted to the perfecting of Ice Saws, we have the best cutting Ice Saws for pond, house and wagon use.

Ice Tongs.

Hollow Handle.   Wood Handle.   New York.   Philadelphia.   Cincinnati.

No. 162 New York—13-inch span, per dozen $13.00
                 15-inch span, per dozen 14.00
                 17-inch span, per dozen 15.00
                 24-inch span, per dozen 17.00
No 164 Philadelphia—14-inch span, per dozen 15.00
                 17-inch span, per dozen 18.00
                 24-inch span, per dozen 21.00
             Heavy Loading, per dozen 24.00

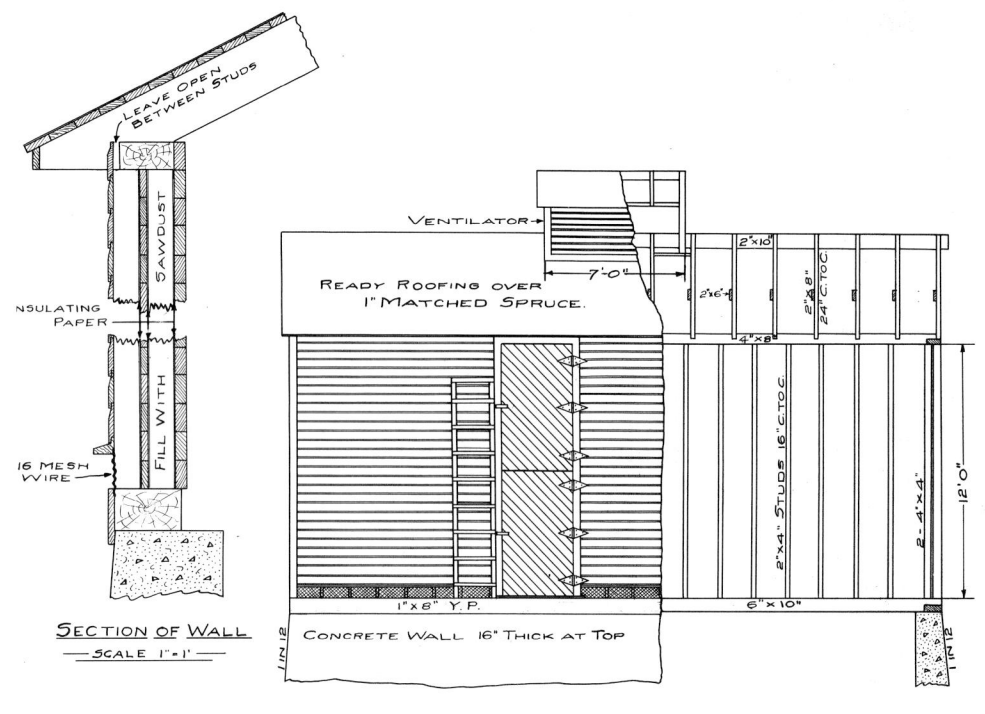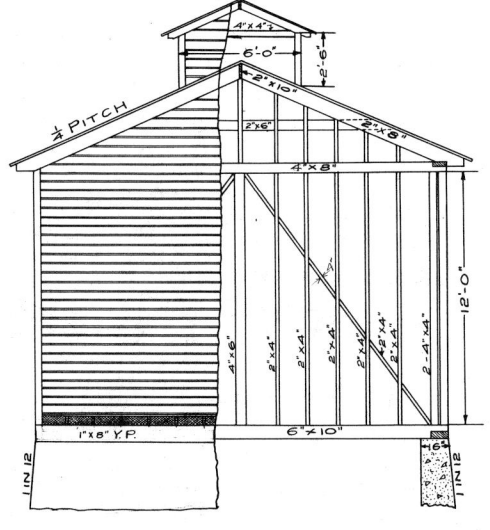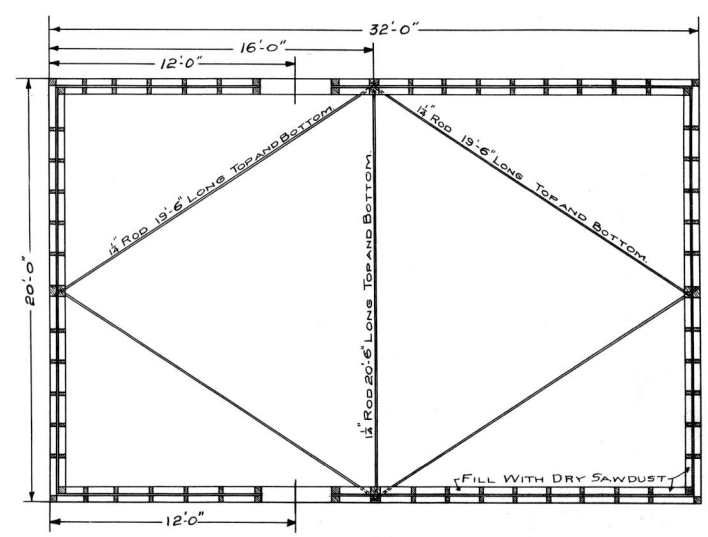

4"x4" Posts at Corners
4"x6" Posts at Tie Rods
4"x4" Posts at Doors
2"x4" Studs 16" C. to C.
2"x8" Rafters 24" C. to C.
6"x10" Sill
4"x8" Plate
2"x10" Ridge
1" Matched Spruce Between Studs
Inside Lined with 1⅛" Matched Hemlock
Insulating Paper Both Sides of Studs.
1"x6" Novelty Siding

N.Y.C.␣
—ICE HOUSE—
—MIDDLETOWN YARD—
Office Eng'r M of W. Middletown N.Y. Oct. 1910
Scale ¼"=1'

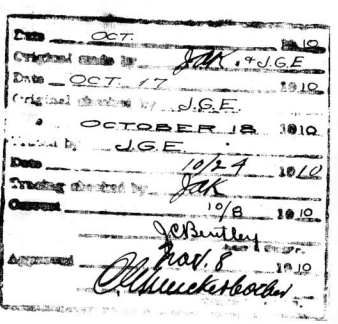

ABOVE: Framing of the Munnsville, N.Y., icehouse is almost complete, and the application of spruce and hemlock planks to exterior and interior walls will be the next step of construction. Iron or steel tie-rods strengthen the frame. The completed structure held roughly 1000 tons of ice. SAM REEDER COLLECTION. TOP RIGHT: Many railroad yards had large icehouses for servicing freight refrigerator cars. The O&W had a big facility at Norwich, N.Y., that served the company needs. This included refrigerator cars assigned to the Northern Division vegetable traffic and the milk loads that originated on the upper end of the railroad. STERLING KIMBALL COLLECTION. BOTTOM RIGHT: A loaded icehouse would seem an unlikely candidate for a fire, yet several of them met just such an end. Their great size and height usually made them the tallest structures in the area and they presented a higher risk for being struck by lightning. After a spectacular blaze, they might leave an equally spectacular mountin of ice as in this photograph. The cause of this particular fire, somewhere in Delaware County, N.Y., is unknown. The hundreds of tons of ice may take more than a year to melt. WILLIAM SCHRIVER COLLECTION.

FACING PAGE: All of the O&W's larger yards seem to have had several of these structures. This one, with a capacity of approximately 6700 cubic feet, was one of the smaller icehouses on the property. O&W SOCIETY COLLECTION.

used, a special harness was required so that several blocks could be moved along the passageways and up the icehouse elevators.

The larger icehouses used an elevator or conveyor system to store the ice in layers. The system resembled a scaffold arrangement that was several stories tall. An ingenious system of switches, pulleys and inclined planes was used to route the blocks to the required level of the icehouse. As in the harvesting phase, electricity and gas engines replaced horsepower in lifting the blocks. Once in the icehouse, salt hay and sawdust were used to keep the layers apart and the blocks from freezing together. Salt hay would not freeze to the ice and it was preferred to sawdust; however, it was more expensive. An air gap was kept all around the ice, and a final layer of salt hay insulated the stack.

Virtually all of the icehouses built by the railroads were of frame construction and many were very large. Some contained more than 40,000 tons of ice after a good season. Many creameries had attached icehouses for convenience. These were usually not as large as those which stood alone. One that was well-constructed had double walls with sawdust insulation between the walls, and melt loss could be kept to 30 percent or less throughout the year. To reflect the sun's heat, the structures were painted a light color, usually white or light gray. A vertical row of doors was a sure clue to the building's purpose. There were no windows, but some type of ventilator arrangement would sit along the roof peak to carry off dampness, since humid air would hasten melting. The exterior elevator and its framework would be permanently attached to one wall. The level of stored ice inside could be determined by which door was open and the height to which the elevator was operating. The ice blocks could weigh as much as 300 pounds; but smaller, standard sizes were available. Wet slippery surfaces and the weight of the blocks posed constant danger to those involved in their handling. Crushing injuries were

the most common hazard. Yet, despite the dangers, there were some compensations. Summer employees worked in cool surroundings, and there was ice for their drinks.

The commercial ice purveyors who supplied homes and businesses used the same methods to gather a supply for city and town use. All those concerned with the business tried to do most, if not all, of the shipping during the winter season to minimize melt loss in transit and storage handling. Ice was very profitable freight for the railroads, and cars were specifically assigned to the service. It appears that most of this business originated and terminated on line.

Older refrigerator cars and milk cars of lower capacity found second service lives. Usually the traffic was limited to home road routings and the cars did not require all the latest appliances as required for interchange cars. Since most of the business moved during cold weather, regular boxcars might be used with some hay provided for insulation and separation of the blocks. An old, well-weathered freight refrigerator car, water slowly dripping through the floor, was a standard fixture in many rail yards. This was where a supply of ice was kept for the caboose cooler and the locomotive water jug. It was a regular stop for brakemen and firemen preparing for a run.

FACING PAGE: A large icehouse still stood at Monticello, N.Y., on September 1, 1939, although it may no longer have been in use. Extras south 246 and 251 are taking summer camp children home at the end of the season. A. V. NEUSSER PHOTOGRAPH

Two sidings extended from the main track of the Rome, N.Y., branch served three icehouses in what was a reasonably typical community arrangement of structures and track. Three oil companies also got their deliveries of kerosene and gasoline from the same sidings according to this 1925 map. O&W SOCIETY COLLECTION.

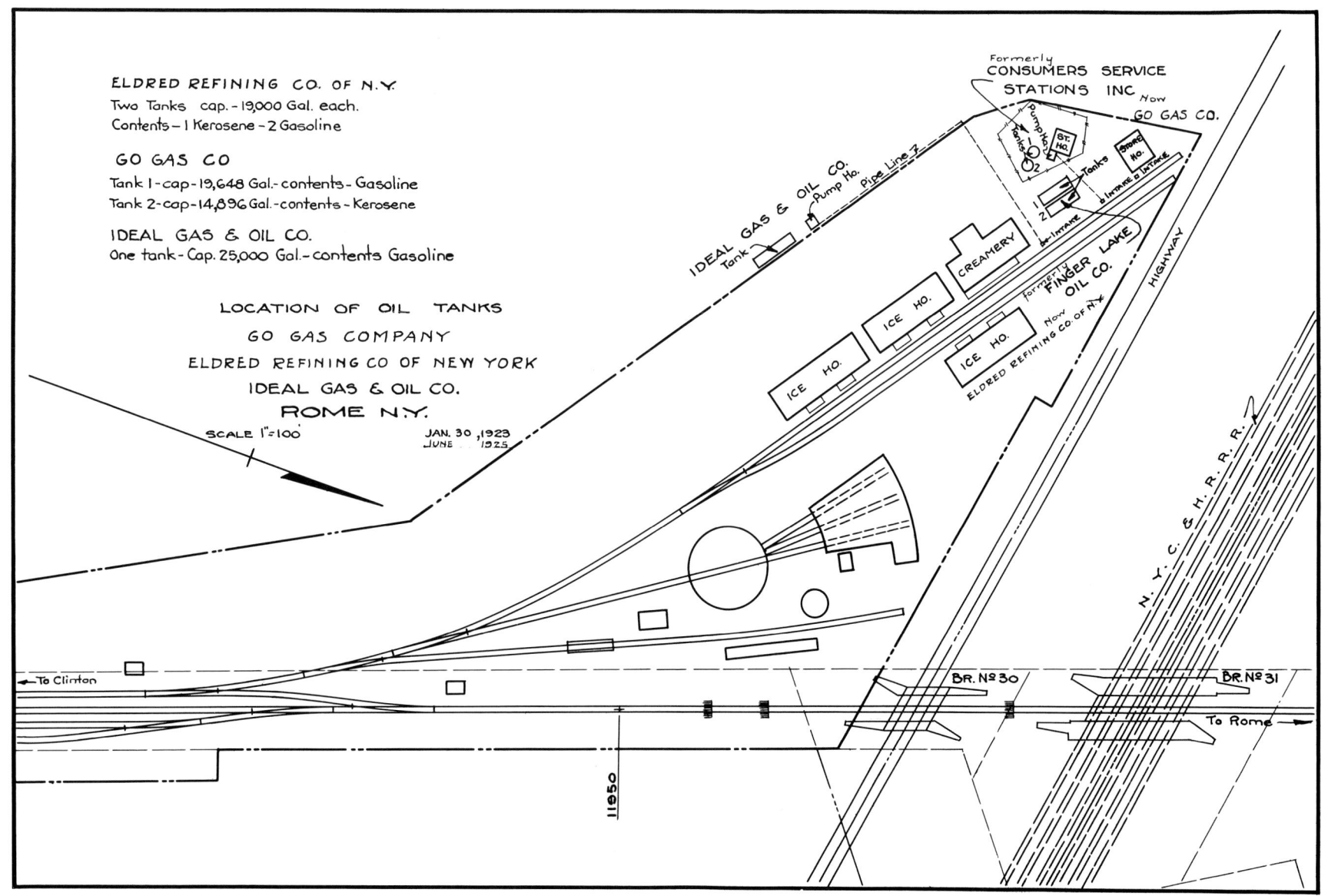

Chapter 3: The O&W's Wooden Milk Cars

21 milk cars have had Westinghouse brakes changed from old to new automatic. 38 milk cars have been equipped with Westinghouse train air signals, also with vertical plane couplers, replacing ordinary Miller couplers.

NYO&W 1895 Annual Report

When the first shipment of milk came down the New York & Oswego Midland in 1871, it is unlikely that it was in cars specifically designed for the business. Though more than one neighboring railroad was handling milk in cars built for the purpose and the NY&OM management was hopeful of a profitable new revenue source, it would not have been prudent to build special cars on speculation. A boxcar, baggage or combine car with some minor changes could have adequately filled the need for the short eight-mile-haul from Bloomingburg to Middletown. At some later point, profits, or at least a reasonable expectation of a profitable milk operation, prompted the NY&OM to build up a modest roster of nine milk cars. Then, with the 1880 reorganization of the NY&OM into the New York, Ontario & Western, all rolling stock and property were transferred to the new owner.

Although photographs showing NY&OM milk cars have not surfaced, some idea of their appearance can be drawn from looking at the cars operating over neighboring roads during the decade that the Midland company existed. Milk cars of that period had arched or duck-billed clerestory roofs. A few had the peaked freight roof. Virtually all had end doors and end platforms to allow brakemen to walk through the entire train in the era before air brakes were standard equipment. The platforms also provided a safe position from which the brakes could be operated. Vertical wooden sheathing covered sides and ends. Wooden underframes were strengthened by truss rods that also stiffened the body. Passenger-type trucks were used with these cars. They had a longer wheelbase and heavier side frame members than those used under freight cars. These longer, heavier trucks provided greater stability for faster passenger train speeds.

Unlike the freight or long-distance refrigerator car, milk cars generally did not have ice bunkers at the ends. However, there were exceptions to this among the NYO&W milk cars. The creamery kept the can milk cold prior to the arrival of the train. As soon as the cans were loaded, chopped ice was spread over the tops of the cans to keep the milk at a safe temperature during transit This provided adequate refrigeration since the shipments seldom, if ever, required a full day to travel from country station to city market. This was certainly true on the O&W. The company issued a booklet of regulations covering the milk traffic and it stipulated that 25

OPPOSITE PAGE: Reduced to an object of passing curiosity, milk car 1034 sits in the weeds just north of Middletown station. The well-preserved lettering and the lack of a mid-car sag belie years of heavy service and hundreds of passages through Middletown when only car inspectors gave the 1034 a second glance. At this late 1940's date, the car still had a tight roof and secure doors, and was used for storage of company records. HAL CARSTENS PHOTOGRAPH.

ABOVE: The 6046 sits on a track reserved for cars needing shop attention. The Fox trucks, designed in England and manufactured under license in the U.S., were frequently found under the O&W's milk cars. They later fell from favor and were replaced by more conventional designs. O&W SOCIETY COLLECTION. BELOW: In 1938, when car 1008 was photographed, the use of can-carrying cars had already begun to diminish and the railroad was selective in determining which cars were to remain in revenue use. The general appearance of this car might indicate its retention in active service. The small lettering in the lower right corner gave the car's light weight and date of weighing at AV (Middletown). GERALD M. BEST PHOTOGRAPH.

pounds of ice per can and 15 pounds per case of milk and cream should be used under most conditions. This was to be increased if the weather was warmer than usual.

The early milk cars on most railroads were 30 to 35 feet in length. The general shape and appearance of these cars would evolve through the years and finally appear as the heavy 50-foot express refrigerator cars that became so much a part of later passenger train consists. However, the visual differences between some milk cars and express refrigerator cars was so minor that it was often hard to tell the two apart.

At least five of the NY&OM cars may have been built by the New Haven Car Works in 1874. The others might have been a second order or copies built by the Middletown Shops while the line was still known as the NY&OM. Undoubtedly the design and features of these early cars influenced those built by the NYO&W. In 1882, Middletown turned out the first four milk cars for the O&W fleet. Over the next 18 years similar ones would continue to be constructed in groups of four or five. In 1899, eight new cars were completed, followed by a dozen more in 1900 for a total of 66 cars in service at that time. Some of the earlier ones, including the OM originals, had already been back through the shop for rebuilding. More than twenty years of constant dampness and demanding service required the replacement of many wooden parts, application of new canvas on the roof, and several repaintings.

Rebuilding began in 1885 and continued through 1911, incorporating such changes as removing the end platforms, increasing the length of the OM cars, adding buffers and double hinged doors, installing new draft gear and Fox trucks, and equipping some with steam lines for train heating. Later improvements included steel bolsters, larger and stronger truss rods, and slack adjusters. In 1914, three baggage and postal cars were converted into milk cars.

In 1917, Middletown built the last nine archroofed cars for a grand total of 113 standard milk cars. The need for such a large roster was shortlived, although the 1920's proved the most lucrative years for the milk business. However, 1925 saw the first retirements of the standard milk cars.

The final revenue service version of the Middletown-built milk car had a length of 45 feet. The underframe apparently remained wood. Steel plates protected the sheathing on both sides of the doors. Wolfe trucks and trucks from retired passenger cars became common as the Fox trucks became obsolete. A vertical brake staff was located at one end along with a retainer valve. The light weight of a car was 41,000 pounds with a weight capacity of 60,000 pounds and a volume of 1869 cubic feet. An ice hatch clearly shows on the roof of some of the cars, indicating an ice bunker at one end. No information has been found to explain why some had this feature. Perhaps this was a characteristic of earlier cars built at a time when more cooling was thought necessary.

In regular service, the cars were a dark green color that matched the coach or Pullman green so typical of wooden coaches and sleepers. Lettering was a dark yellow or imitation gold color. Prior to December 1899, O&W passenger equipment was painted maroon, and the milk cars may have carried the same color. Before 1920, these cars were numbered in the 6000 series. At some point after that date, they were renumbered 1001 through 1113.

In 1929 and 1930, 55 freight refrigerators were transferred to milk service. These reefers were built in 1912 and might have been a group purchased second-hand early in the 1920's to haul fruits and vegetables from Northern Division agricultural areas. They were numbered in the 1200 series. They were 40 feet long and had wooden superstructures and, with two exceptions, steel underframes. This transfer created an all-time high of 154 units in the milk car column of the rolling stock roster,

The 1200-series cars are something of an enigma. Like their longer, arch roofed roster mates, they were used for can shipments. However, without color photographs, it is difficult to positively identify their paint scheme. A close scrutiny of photographs with a magnifying glass does show that they had the same style of lettering as the 1000-series cars. This included the NYO&W initials on the left side and the word "Milk" on the right. The car number was located on both sides of the doors and below the other lettering. Their shorter length limited them to a lower capacity, and this may well have contributed to an earlier retirement for the class. A 1937 report recommended their retirement due to bent center sills and need of underbody reinforcement.

Partially reflecting the precipitous drop in milk tonnage, 1937 and 1939 saw 34 and 58 milk cars respectively retired from the roster. Only eight wooden cars were left by 1945, and the last one was retired in 1950. Some O&W veterans believed that after 1945, those remaining were used for company service. Through the 1940's and 1950's, a number of them, unfit for movement, sat on rusty trucks on equally rusty sidings along the railroad. At least one was reported to have been painted in the maintenance-of-way red and used in ice service.

Can-shipment cars from other roads did appear on the O&W when creamery production exceeded car supply or other conditions required them. Records from the Delhi station show that D&H, NYC, and

Primarily intended to carry milk in cans, the O&W's cars could also handle bottled milk and cases of evaporated milk. The latter did not require icing. The doors might be open to permit drying of the interior since water from melting ice and milk spillage could create unhealthy conditions in the cars—especially in summer weather. CHUCK YUNGKURTH COLLECTION.

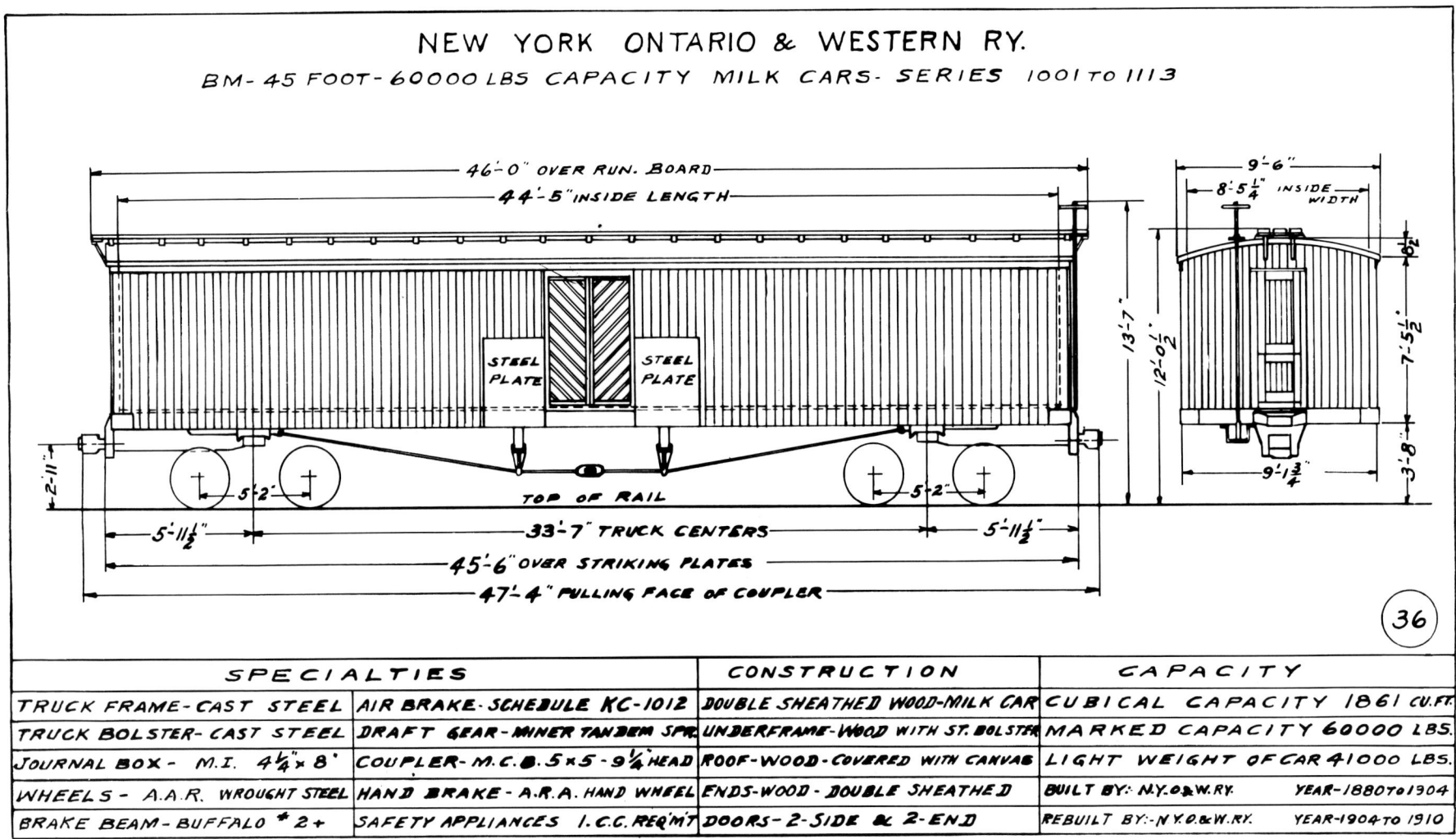

Railroads usually had equipment diagrams drawn for all their revenue rolling stock and locomotives. Sometimes a single diagram sufficed for all classes and sub-classes of particular rolling stock. A number of key dimensions and specific fittings, construction features, and appliances were listed in these diagrams. Beyond that, the degree of detail varied considerably from one road to another. All of the O&W's 1001-1113 cars were covered by this diagram. O&W SOCIETY COLLECTION.

The general similarity of milk car designs is illustrated by these three cars of railroads that served nearby areas and connected with the O&W. LEFT: New York, Susquehanna & Western 820 had a peaked roof and appears to be equipped with link-and-pin couplers. The 820 was built by Jackson & Sharp in 1892—a suspiciously late date for such couplers. GEORGE VOTAVA COLLECTION. TOP LEFT: Lehigh Valley 94053 was of more recent construction and is very close in appearance to the O&W's 1000-series cars. Like the O&W, the Lehigh Valley seemed to make a major changeover to bulk shipping and relegated the can cars to company ice service. CLARENCE THARP PHOTOGRAPH: CHUCK YUNKGURTH COLLECTION. TOP RIGHT: DL&W's 1700-series cars were shorter but otherwise similar. CHUCK YUNGKURTH COLLECTION.

W. & H. 350. 3-13-95.

New York, Ontario & Western R'y Co.

Statement of Equipment.

REVISED APRIL 1st, 1895.

FREIGHT.

KIND	NUMBERS	INSIDE DIMENSIONS Length	Width	Height	CAPACITY	No.
Flat..........	1 to 499	28 29 31 34			28000 & 40000	30
"	500 " 700	31 ft.			40000	17
"	701 " 726	34 "			40000	2
"	750 " 755	34 "			60000	
Box..........	2001 " 2249	27 " 6 in.	7 ft. 9 in.	6 ft.	28000 & 40000	214
" (Lumber).	2250 " 2299	33 " ½ "	7 " 11 "	6 " 4 in.	40000	48
"	2300 " 2425	27 " 2 "	7 " 8 "	6 " 2 "	28000 & 40000	109
"	2477 " 2510	27 " 8 "	8 " ½ "	6 " 1 "	28000 & 40000	28
" (ONTARIO DESPATCH)....	2550 " 2699	33 " ½ "	7 " 11 "	6 " 4 "	40000	141
"	2700 " 2702	33 " 10½ "	7 " 10 "	6 " 6 "	60000	3
Stock........	4001 " 4064	33 " 2 "	8 "	6 " 9½ "	40000	63
Gondola......	4400 " 4409	31 " 4½ "	8 " 3 "	2 " 8½ "	40000	10
"	4414 "	31 " 4½ "	8 " 3 "	2 " 8½ "	40000	1
"	4410 " 4413	31 " 10½ "	7 " 10½ "	2 "	60000	4
"	4415 " 4443	31 " 10½ "	7 " 10½ "	2 "	60000	28
"	4501 " 5100	26 " 7 "	7 " 10 "	1 " 7 "	24000 28000&40000	188
"	5101 " 5399	23 " 5½ "	7 " 7 "	3 " 3 "	40000	290
"	5400 " 5550	23 " 7 "	7 " 7 "	4 "	40000	148
Milk..........	6001 " 6017	40 "				17
"	6018 " 6038	45 "				21
Ref. Pass. Trucks...	6501 " 6504	33 " ¾ "	7 " 10½ "	7 " 3½ "	50000	4
" Frt. " ...	6526 " 6531	33 " ¾ "	7 " 10½ "	7 " 3½ "	50000	6
Hay...........	9001 " 9081	33 " ¾ "	8 " ¾ "	7 " 6⅛ "	40000	73
Charcoal......	9100 " 9104	33 " 7½ "	8 " 7⅝ "	7 " 6½ "	40000	4
Gondola......	10001 " 11500	25 " 6 "	7 " 6½ "	4 "	60000	3850 (with next row)
"	11501 " 13856	27 " 3 "	8 "	4 "	60000	
Caboose, 8 wh.	8002 8004 8005					6 (with next row)
" "	8008 8010 8011					
" 4 "	8101 to 8149					48
Tool Cars.....	01 02 002					6 (with next row)
" "	03 04 05					
Derricks......	D1 D2 D3 D4					4
Snow Plows...	1 3 7 8 9					5
					Total,	5837

PASSENGER.

NUMBERS.	No.
Coaches, 2d Class, 1 to 20	18
" 1st " 21 to 68	48
" 1st " 69 to 74 (Vestibule)	6
" 1st " 201 to 206	6
" 31, 32, 55, 56 are reclining chair cars.	
Coach and Baggage 100 101 102 103 104 105 106 108	19 (with next three rows)
109 110 112 114 115 301 302 303	
Baggage, Mail and Smoker 107 111	
Baggage and Chair Smoker 113	
Express 151 152 155 159 166 167 169	23 (with next two rows)
Baggage 153 154 157 161 170 172 173 174 501	
Baggage and Mail 156 158 160 162 163 401 402	
Total	120

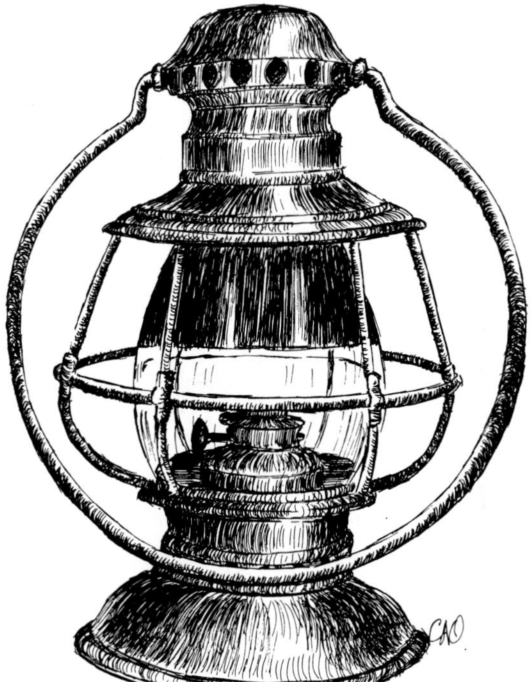

The first page of an 1895 listing of rolling stock shows that the O&W had 38 milk cars and numbered them 6001 to 6038. At a later date these cars were renumbered into the 1000 series. O&W SOCIETY COLLECTION.

LEFT: A rare view of the roof of a 1000-series car was provided by the milk train accident of May 29, 1929, near Livingston Manor, N.Y. Car 1025 was one of a group that had a single ice hatch. WALTER KIERZKOWSKI COLLECTION. LOWER LEFT: The September 23, 1908, milk train wreck at Rock Rift, N.Y., shows a car without roof hatches. Fox trucks are visible in the foreground debris and cases of empty quart milk bottles have spilled from the torn car at the right. At least one of these cars will be struck from the roster and its salvaged parts used for future construction or repair. WILMER SIPPLE COLLECTION. BELOW: Sometime in the 1920's or 1930's, an O&W train came to an abrupt halt at Summitville, N.Y. Milk car 1239 seems to have survived the experience and its open door may indicate that its perishable cargo had been removed. The lighter colored rectangular on the car side was probably applied when the car was reassigned and renumbered for milk service. O&W SOCIETY COLLECTION.

Converted from freight refrigerators, the enigmatic 1200-series cars still pose a number of questions—the first one being their ancestry. A reasonable supposition is that they were a group of 50 cars that were purchased from Union Refrigerator Line in 1923. RAY BROWN COLLECTION.

Numerous small details are visible in this close-up view of the 6082 prior to its renumbering. Unlike the 6082, most of the wooden cars had steel plates protecting only the bottom half of the sides at the doors. The hinges that permitted the door to swing inward are visible and the railing below the door opening supported the loading ramp that sat on each creamery platform. WALTER RICH COLLECTION.

RIGHT: After a few years of demanding service, the milk cars developed characteristic sags or humps depending upon the tension of their truss rods. Replacement parts, repairs and patching also aided in giving cars slightly different appearances in spite of the essential uniformity of the design. Engine 273 waits at Walton, N.Y., while mail is exchanged and express packages are checked. The water crane seems in alignment with the tender; so, with one skillful stop, the engineer may have accommodated several functions. DR. WILLIAM HELMER COLLECTION. BOTTOM: A class L 0-6-0 sits at Norwich, N.Y., possibly waiting for the southbound milk train to which it will add car 1206. The two-story station and Northern Division office building stands behind the locomotive. BILL DRAKE COLLECTION.

B&M cars were used on that branch during World War II. These cars were used for interline shipments. It would be reasonable to expect that O&W cars were leased to other roads as well. In 1941, during a period of wide fluctuation in milk traffic levels due to rate changes in response to truck competition and because it had retired many of its own cars, the railroad had to lease cars from Fruit Growers Express Company. They were fitted with air signal lines at Norwich shops for use in passenger train service and were to handle business for Breakstone Brothers in Walton. They proved unsatisfactory because the O&W's carload rates were for 250 cans and these cars held 224 cans. As a result, the company considered contracting North American Car Company for larger capacity cars and may actually have done so.

The large decrease in the number of wooden milk cars in the 1930's was due to a combination of circumstances. A sharp decline in the O&W's share of the milk business was a major factor. Another was the increasingly wider acceptance of the milk tank cars and the bulk milk containers on flatcars.

During its travels under load, every revenue-producing car was accompanied by a waybill which was similar to this shipping order. It listed the car's number, owning railroad, and information relating to the contents. The shipper, consignee, and any other pertinent data were also listed. This order was for O&W 1035 traveling between Mt. Upton and Weehawken with Dairymen's League cream and cheese. JOHN MOFFAT COLLECTION.

This latter development coincided with the advanced age of the railroad's truss rod and wooden underframe cars. Finally, there was the shift to motor transport that eventually took all of the business from the railroads. By 1940, photographic evidence indicates that very little can milk was being shipped on the O&W. The advantages of bulk shipping seemed to have gained great acceptance among the milk producers along the O&W; thus the need for the wooden can cars dropped significantly. However, the neighboring Lehigh Valley (LV) and the DL&W continued to handle can milk and use wooden cars for the purpose. The Erie's purchase of 100 new, 40-foot steel cars for can shipments in the 1930's points out one of the incongruities of both the railroad and the milk business.

A good indicator of the O&W's almost exclusive use of bulk transport cars for milk after 1940 is the familiar circular tender logo. This emblem began replacing initials on locomotive tenders in the late 1930's or early 1940's. It is a rare photograph that shows wooden railroad-owned can-milk cars behind a steam tender with the O&W emblem. It is extremely doubtful that any of the wooden cars ever ran behind the EMD diesels that began to arrive in 1945.

TOP RIGHT: Two ancient veterans of milk and mixed train service sit at the north end of Middletown, N.Y., station. Because of bankruptcy procedures, a great deal of paperwork had to be completed before any equipment was scrapped. COLLECTION OF RAILROAD AVENUE ENTERPRISES, COURTESY OF BOB PENNISI. BOTTOM: Sway-backed and neglected, the 1023 sat at Port Jervis, N.Y., in 1952 with each season's sun, rain and ice adding to the car's decrepitude. The mile post to the right reads 115 at this extremity of the Port Jervis branch. EDWARD WEBER PHOTOGRAPH.

GARE 779 is believed to represent the most common milk tank car design used on the O&W. This paint scheme, of blue and white, must also have been a common sight on the railroad since the Dairymen's League was a big shipper in O&W territory. COLLECTION OF CARSTENS PUBLICATIONS.

Chapter 4: The Milk Tank Cars

The eight tank refrigerator cars received from you have been in service three months and to date have shown themselves entirely satisfactory, both in design and construction. We desire at the same time, to commend you for the service which your company has given us with them.

Letter to General American Car Company from the Dairymen's League, January 26, 1926

The first bulk shipment of milk in a tank has been attributed to several dairies and railroads. Taking credit for the earliest is one W.A. Graustein for a shipment from Bellows Falls, Vt., to Boston over the Boston & Maine in 1903. Details of the car or its ownership were not reported. In 1910 the B&M had two cars, each with a single tank, in regular service on the Bellows Falls run. In 1920, the Whiting Milk Company of Boston employed a milk tank car for shipments between Johnsonville, N.Y., and Boston, also via the B&M. A year later, the Harmony Creamery Company was operating a milk tank car between West Farrington, Ohio and Pittsburgh, Pa., and exhibited the car at a National Dairy Show. In this same time period the Baltimore & Ohio was considering the installation of two tanks in a baggage car for milk service, but it is not known if the plan was carried out. All of these early efforts were technological stepping stones that led to an important and historic decision by the Wieland Dairy Company. In 1922 Wieland agreed to employ three glass-lined milk tank cars in regular service between its country receiving plants in Wisconsin and processing facilities in Chicago.

The unique cars were built and owned by the General American Car Company of Chicago. This firm had a respected name in car construction and its cars 1X-3X showed a flair for innovation as well. The "X" suffix attached to the car numbers might have indicated an experimental model, since the glass-lined tanks were a revolutionary feature. These tanks were provided by the Elyria Enameled Products Company of Elyria, Ohio. While the cars certainly were a departure from conventional practice, externally they looked quite familiar. Ice bunkers, with their roof hatches and platforms, were considered requisite appliances as were arch bar trucks, type K brakes, and conventional access through hinged doors. It would be interesting to know if General American worked with Wieland Dairy or if it proceeded on its own and sold the idea to Wieland.

The advantages gained in labor savings, sanitary handling, and time were obvious and strong motivators for milk shippers to convert from cans to bulk shipment. Coupled with electrical refrigeration and motor trucks, the milk tank cars allowed for greater efficiency in milk transportation. Yet, despite all their advantages, the milk tank cars would never totally supplant the 40-quart can. As previously mentioned, virtually all milk shippers along the NYO&W seem to have switched over to bulk transport methods after 1940, while in the next valley can cars still served the creameries on another railroad.

Wieland Dairy's success with the General American cars was given a great deal of coverage in both

ABOVE: In March, 1922, General American Car Co., built three cars, including the IX, for Wieland Dairy Co. of Chicago. This was the prototype, or the first successful prototype, for the bulk tank car. Arch bar trucks and the lack of various passenger service appliances indicated that the car would travel in freight service. Once the concept had proved successful, the design was modified for both freight and passenger train use. LEFT: General American Car Co. built the wooden bulk tank cars at its East Chicago shop. Here the tanks are in place but have yet to receive additional layers of insulation. Steel bands held the tanks in a bed of asphalt-like material. The design and engineering concepts proved sound and the cars' durability exceeded the company's expectations. FACING PAGE: GPEX 1933 is believed to have been numbered for the year in which it was built. It might have been painted in this manner for publicity purposes and possibly to promote the recent formation of the General American Pfaudler Corporation. TWO PHOTOGRAPHS: COLLECTION OF CARSTENS PUBLICATIONS.

the dairy and railroad trade publications. About the time that this information was being digested and evaluated by the rail industry, General American Car Company drew on the information gained from the Wieland cars and developed a production design with further innovations and a more distinctive appearance. In an article in the March, 1986, issue of *Railroad Model Craftsman,* rail historian Chuck Yungkurth tells the story of these cars:

Soon after the first milk tank cars with standard freight-car body designs were put into service, General American designed an entirely new car body to meet the unique problems of installing two 3000-gallon glass-lined tanks inside a closed car. The new cars were intended for movement in passenger trains, so they had short-wheelbase passenger-type trucks, train signal and heating lines, buffer plates and passenger train brake equipment.

The most obvious feature of many of the new cars was the one-piece, patented, removable roof. The installation of the tanks could thus be done after the car body was finished, and the roof could easily be removed should one of the large tanks have to be replaced or taken out for repairs. The walls of the car and the insulation of the roof did not have to be disturbed. Cars with the removable roof can easily be identified by the two lifting lugs on each side at the edge of the roof. The milk tanks apparently proved to be quite reliable and the roof was seldom removed. The lift-off feature was not part of later General American cars.

Another external feature of these General American cars was a small sliding door above the side entry doors. This opening was used for the loading hose. To keep the car interior as sanitary as possible, the entry doors were kept closed at all times except when workers were entering or leaving the cars. On later cars, the traditional outward-swinging doors were replaced by a single small door just large enough for a man to enter. Unloading was done from the bottom tank valves and through a pipe out the door; a tee was put in place to connect the two tanks, which were slightly pitched to facilitate draining.

Besides the valves for filling and emptying, other interior equipment included piping for the brine coils used to cool the car at the creamery, electric lights, and agitation mechanisms to stir the milk within the tanks while the car was sitting at the receiving station. Stirring distributed the butterfat in the milk, kept the temperature of the cooled milk even and prevented the residue of the milk from sticking to the tank walls, thus making cleaning easier. These agitators were electrically powered and plugged in at the creamery during the loading. The doorway vestibule between the tanks was sometimes used for carrying containers of cheese or cream. [Chuck Yungkurth, "To Market by Rail: The Milk Tank Cars," *Railroad Model Craftsman,* March 1986: 85.]

Although General American's first three cars contained enameled tanks provided by the Elyria Enameled Products Company, tanks for the production cars were obtained from the Pfaudler Company. Pfaudler had a long history as a manufacturer of brewery and food-processing equipment. It had its own patented methods for bonding glass to the inside surfaces of steel containers and was finding a big market for its wares due to federal laws that required greater sanitation in commercial food preparation. The tanks were of seamless, one-piece construction and a 3000-gallon capacity gave them the equivalent of 300 40-quart cans. They rested in asphalt beds on the floor of the car, and this provided both insulation and cushioning.

Cars could be equipped with either a stationary milk pump or an air compressor for unloading. The compressed-air system seemed to be more common, probably because it did not require involved cleaning after each use. Only the air filter would have to be checked for cleaning or replacement. A reservoir tank provided water to wash the milk tanks and vestibule area if no other source was available. The

Brightly colored panels and lettering were applied to many of the General American wooden cars. Although built for the same company in the same year, these two cars vary in both hardware, lettering and some minor details. Purchasers and lessees sometimes specified which parts supplier's hardware was to be applied to cars they had ordered.
TWO PHOTOGRAPHS: COLLECTION OF CARSTENS PUBLICATIONS.

brine cooling system was an option that was later dropped. After the cars were in service, tests proved that they could easily keep the milk temperature within required limits during transit. Varieties of motors, lights, switches, and conduits were standard features.

The cars were originally lettered for General American Refrigerator Express (GARE), a subsidiary of General American Car Company. In the lower left corner were the GARE reporting initials and a number. Other lettering and emblems identified the lessor. Many of these lettering schemes were very colorful and helped to advertise the lessee's dairy products. Separate plaques carrying the lettering and emblems were frequently bolted to the car side. Several dairy companies purchased these cars and applied their own reporting marks. Borden's and Sheffield Farms' cars operated over the O&W under both arrangements, and the same may be true of other dairy companies. None of the GARE cars were railroad-owned.

General American Car Company and Pfaudler formed a subsidiary in 1930, called General American-Pfaudler Corporation. The reporting initials GPEX were used from this time on. At about this time GPEX introduced a 50-foot wooden milk car with the potential for higher capacity. This design would be duplicated in quantity to form a large fleet of express refrigerator cars. A major difference between the two types of cars was the presence of end ice-bunkers and roof-loading hatches on the express refrigerator version. As with the shorter, earlier GARE cars, the body color was a dark green with yellow, gold, or white lettering. Some cars had a single 2.5-foot wide door, which might have been a retrofit rather than original equipment. The standard appears to have been a double, outward-hinged door.

In the late 1930's, GPEX began a shift to steel cars. The first of the steel cars are believed to have been rebuilt from the earlier GARE wooden cars. Although all steel cars were of riveted construction,

they presented a very smooth, modern appearance. This was due to the flat ends and the rolled meeting of the roof and sides along the top of the car. Some cars had a similar roll along the bottom edge that hid much of the underbody hardware. Others had a straight or flat bottom edge. Like the wooden GARE cars, these were built in a 40-foot version only. In the mid-1940's the final design from GPEX was introduced, and it was very similar to the rebuilds of the 1930's. Both 40- and 50-foot versions were offered, but cars of the longer design were somewhat scarce and none are believed to have run on the O&W. Steel safety tread roof walks, a new truck design, and a different buffer arrangement distinguished these cars from previous designs. Like the first of the steel cars, they had the rolled roof edge, and all cars of this design had the rolled bottom edge as well. GPEX seems to have retained ownership of these particular cars during their entire period of milk service and would lease but not sell them to the dairy companies. Most of these were old customers by now, having leased the earlier wooden and steel cars of the 1920's and 1930's.

In 1937, lessees were charged $7.00 per day for use of a GPEX car. In addition, there was a 2.5 cent per mile wheelage fee charged to the railroads over

The foreground car, carrying SFCX reporting marks, is part of Train 9 waiting at Randallsville for the passage of a southbound local. Engine 225 is on train 9 and faces an approaching W class 2-8-0 that is sending up a cloud of dense white steam on a cold and dismal day. D. DIVER COLLECTION, CORNELL UNIVERSITY.

MILK FREIGHT COLLECTOR,

WEEHAWKEN, N. J.

R. R. B.

Form MC-24

New York, Ontario & Western Railway Company
RUNNING SLIP FOR MILK CONTAINERS RETURNED

Car O. & W. _901_ (Number) From Weehawken To _Liberty_ (Station) SLIP No. _____ 9-18-1938 (Date)

CONSIGNOR	CONSIGNEE	CANS	CASES	CHECK OF DELIVERY	SIGNED (AGENT OR CONDUCTOR)
League	Tank				

This slip must accompany car through to final destination, and a record made hereon of empty cans or cases delivered. If cars are for one consignee and destination, and are placed on siding without check of contents, notation to that effect should be made hereon. If milk packages are transferred en route, make notation on original slip, showing car number and initial to which transfer is made, correct the slip for car into which transfer is made, showing destination, consignee and number of packages transferred, original car number and shipping point.

Cars 900 and 950 show the two types of door arrangements on the longer GPEX cars. The wider doors made it easier to load boxes of cheese, cans of cream and other dairy products that occasionally moved in LCL lots in bulk cars. The form on the facing page shows that GPEX 901 was in Dairymen's League service out of Liberty, N.Y., in 1938. Assigned cars would move back and forth in 48-hour cycles between country and city for months at a time. Spare cars were substituted when regular cars needed shop attention. TWO PHOTOGRAPHS: COLLECTION OF CARSTENS PUBLICATIONS.

which the cars ran. The wheelage was charged against the daily rental up to the full $7.00, and some cars paid the lessee's rental costs in this manner. These cars did not carry advertising slogans or colorful dairy company emblems as did the earlier designs. A standardized scheme was adopted. The lessee's name was modestly applied on one side of the door and *Milk Tank Cars* on the other. Glossy dark green paint and yellow lettering along with their modern, streamlined appearance portrayed a tasteful image for both the rail and milk business. It is believed that the last milk handled by the O&W in 1952 moved in a GPEX car of this last design.

In June, 1937, the NYO&W reported that it was bringing 14 tank cars of milk into Weehawken. The number and types of these cars varied greatly due to seasonal production and changes in dairy processing locations. The 1930's were especially a time of change as constantly varying rates marked the reaction to truck competition.

During the late 1960's and early 1970's, GPEX began final divestiture of its milk tank cars. The last GPEX milk shipments were made over the B&M in 1972. However, many of the cars were still sound and were used to ship other liquids via freight train. They were well suited for shipments of chemical and food products. In the latter category were wine, vinegar, and brewery products. The Gulf, Mobile & Ohio and the Louisville & Nashville purchased cars for work train service and at least three cars have been preserved in transportation museums. These are the St. Louis Museum of Transport, the Illinois Railway Museum in Union, and the California State Railway Museum in Sacramento, Ca.

Besides General American Car, another company looked into Pfaudler equipment and its early rail applications in the 1920's. This was Merchants Despatch Transportation Corporation (MDT), a car-building affiliate of the New York Central Railroad. Like the Pfaudler, Merchants Despatch was also located in the Rochester area. It is possible that officials of these two companies got together professionally or even socially because of their proximity. Whether this happened at the country club or the chief draftsman's office, MDT developed a design to use Pfaudler tanks and compete with General American for milk business. The car was similar in appearance to the GARE wooden car and had the same capacity, but did not have the removable roof feature. Other prominent recognition features were a higher arch to the roof and a C-channel frame member visible below the side. It appears that all of the MDT cars were fitted with the UB-type brake system found on passenger equipment.

Borden's, which claimed to have been the first to introduce the milk tank car to the New York metropolitan area in 1926, was an early purchaser of cars built to this design. The 1930 combination of General American and Pfaudler may have cut off the supply of glass-lined tanks and associated fittings for MDT. Lack of further development of the design would indicate that MDT did not feel that the market was worth the effort of finding or developing another source of interior equipment. Only 40-foot versions of this car are believed to have been produced. Some of them retained their original appearance and were in service during the 1950's. In spite of this longevity, it definitely seems that the GARE cars were built and used in greater numbers. MDT did try another approach to the milk business that involved piggybacking and is discussed in Addendum B.

LEFT: GPEX 887 was built in 1927 to a design that was more often used for express refrigerator cars. Its capacity was 6000 gallons, the same as the more common but shorter General American cars such as GPEX 746 below. The longer cars were frequently seen on the O&W, usually in service to the Dairymen's League. COLLECTION OF CARSTENS PUBLICATIONS.

FACING PAGE: In the 1930's GPEX began applying steel sheathing to earlier wooden cars and may also have built new, all-steel cars to the configuration of the 544. Several differences appear along the bottom sides of these cars. Nos. 766 and 782 have "flat bottoms" whereas 544 has a channel sill member and 945 displays the rolled bottom edge that was characteristic of the later and final GPEX design. Borden's and Sheffield Farms had adopted the enameled, metal plaques to identify their leased cars while the League used painted lettering. The buffer and wooden roof-walk identify the 544 as being one of the pre-war cars. The marker lamp brackets were found on all cars used in passenger train service and since milk cars were frequently on the hind end, they had to carry the marker lamps. Both the steam and air signal lines were secured by chains when not in use. FIVE PHOTOGRAPHS: COLLECTION OF CARSTENS PUBLICATIONS.

TOP LEFT: The final GPEX design is displayed by the 987. The lettering scheme had been standardized with the lessee's name being the only non-GPEX marking on the car. Evidence suggests that all the post-war cars were equipped with signal lines and steam connections for passenger service. Improved buffers and trucks were two of the most obvious changes from earlier cars. RIGHT: The doors of the steel GPEX cars were a mere two feet in width and hinged to swing inward. A car seal has been applied and the access hatch is closed; the car is ready to move. Smaller doors made for greater carbody strength and kept down the entry of dust, dirt and heat. BELOW: GPEX built at least 40 of these longer cars that approached 50 feet in length. Bowman Dairy, later to become part of Borden's, was one company that leased such cars. They had two 4000-gallon tanks in place of the 3000-gallon tanks in smaller cars. Some of these cars may have rolled over the O&W, but the usual 3/4 or "wedge" photographs make the additional length difficult to see. THREE PHOTOGRAPHS: COLLECTION OF CARSTENS PUBLICATIONS.

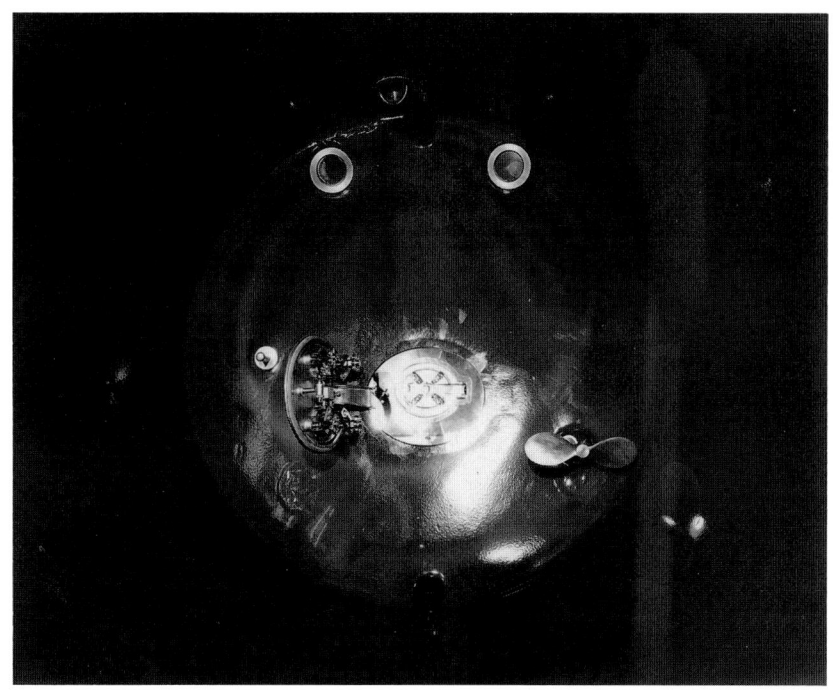

TOP LEFT: In this view we are inside the 3000-gallon tank looking out of the manhole. The manhole of the opposite tank is visible through the oval opening. To the left is a temperature probe and on the right is a propeller to agitate the milk and maintain its uniformity while the car sits at either creamery or city plant. TOP RIGHT: The damp, dank interiors of the can carrying cars would not compare to the cleanliness of the bulk tank cars. The vestibule of this car is lined with stainless steel, which made for easier cleaning. Tanks, pipes and all interior surfaces were cleaned with chlorine detergents after each trip. Loading was done via the pipe entering the top of the tank and unloading through a hose connected to the covered valve at the bottom. The agitator motor and a large drive gear are behind the tear-shaped cover to the left of the manhole. A cleaning drain was located in the low center of the vestibule floor. BOTTOM RIGHT: An electric motor powered the air compressor used to unload the tanks. One of the two inspection windows can be seen at the upper right of the tanks. A thermometer is to the left of the motor shelf. General American claimed that cooled milk could remain in the tanks for 48 hours during normal summer temperatures and gain only one degree of temperature. THREE PHOTOGRAPHS: COLLECTION OF CARSTENS PUBLICATIONS.

Bulk milk cars built by the Merchants Despatch Transportation Co. were slightly taller than their General American counterparts. The opening for the loading hose, above the door, was closed with a plug rather than the sliding plate of the GARE and GPEX cars. Borden's was an early purchaser of the MDT design and later rebuilt the cars to streamlined appearance. The top photograph was taken at the Lackawanna's Hoboken terminal and the bottom view may be an LV terminal. TWO PHOTOGRAPHS: BORDEN'S INC.

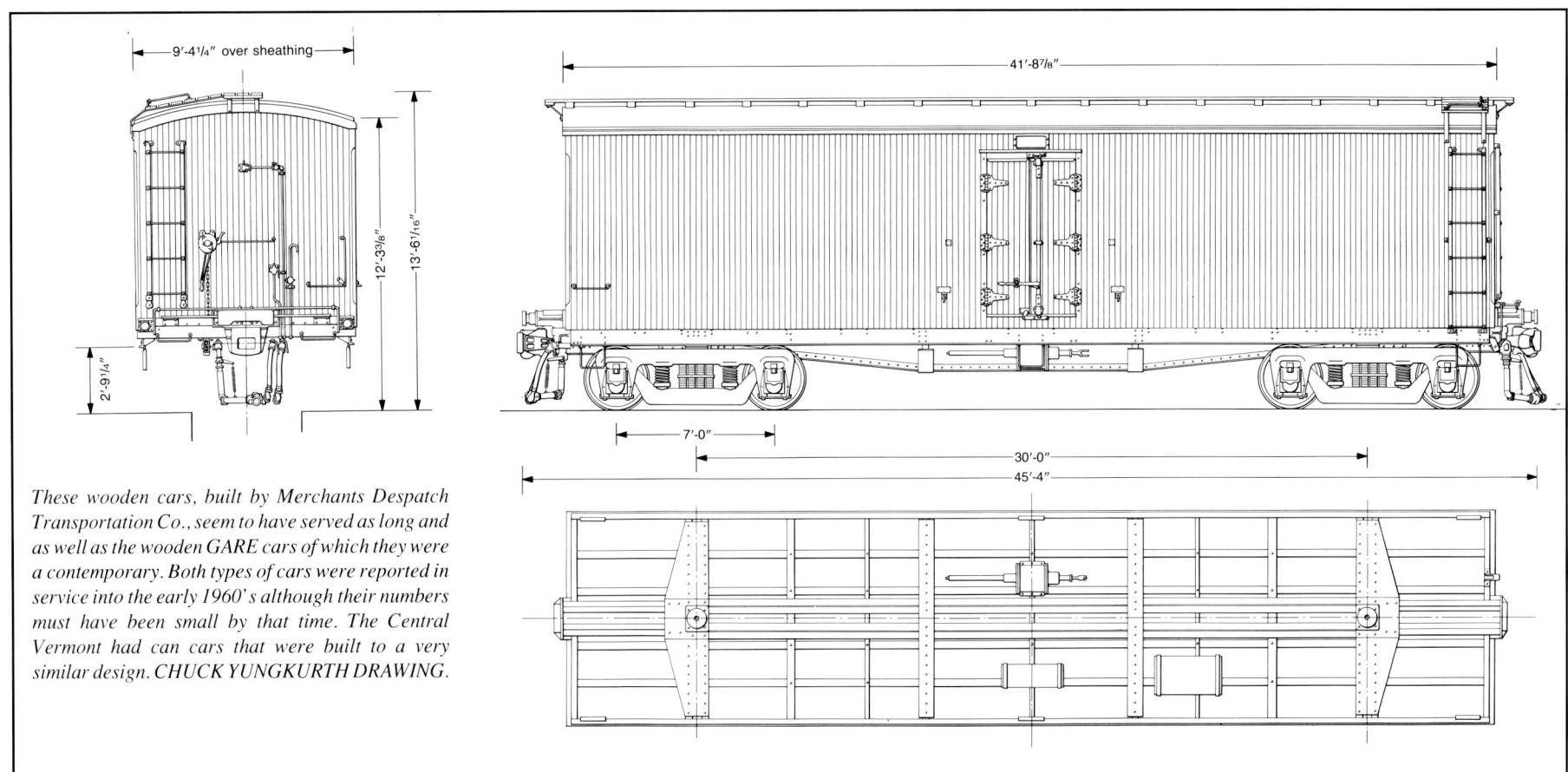

These wooden cars, built by Merchants Despatch Transportation Co., seem to have served as long and as well as the wooden GARE cars of which they were a contemporary. Both types of cars were reported in service into the early 1960's although their numbers must have been small by that time. The Central Vermont had can cars that were built to a very similar design. CHUCK YUNGKURTH DRAWING.

In 1935 or early in 1936, Borden's developed its unique butter dish design (so named because of the car's configuration) by rebuilding some of its wooden milk cars. These rebuilds were the MDT cars that Borden's had purchased in the 1920's. The rebuilding was done in Jersey City, N.J., where Borden's had its own car shop next to the Erie yard. The conversion was done to simplify maintenance and reduce weight. The butter dish cover was made of formed steel with a coating of aluminum fused to the surface. Six inches of cork insulation surrounded the interior tanks and sheet metal. Art Deco fins extended over the ends and top of the car. These were removed during World War II scrap metal drives.

The work was done at about the same time that GPEX was rebuilding the earlier GARE cars with steel superstructures. There is no photographic evidence to show that the rebuilt Borden's cars rolled over the NYO&W, but it is possible. By the late 1930's Borden's was listed as having only one remaining shipping point on the railroad, and this could explain their absence from the line.

A white car body with black or red lettering was the first color scheme applied to the rebuilt cars. This was later changed to a red body with yellow lettering. The final appearance was in silver or aluminum with black lettering. Some were later assigned to Borden's chemical division and had a blue body with white lettering. The Illinois Railway Museum has the one extant car of this design.

There was one major drawback to the use of milk tank cars. Cleaning operations after each trip were usually performed outdoors, and in the northern winters this was a cause of labor-management friction. Processing plant workers made it clear that they preferred tank truck shipments since the trailers could be washed and rinsed in protected truck bays. This issue, along with other factors, most of which favored trucking, helped push the business toward full motor truck transport.

ABOVE: Borden's used the phrase, "Glass Lined Tank Refrigeration Car" on its MDT cars. Their BFPX reporting marks provided Borden's ownership and so the company was free to letter the cars as it wished. GARE and GPEX generally did not include "refrigerator" on their leased cars. Information from an Erie Railroad Company magazine said that the cars were painted bright green with red and black lettering. A protective coat of gloss varnish gave the cars a quality appearance that enhanced the Borden's name. COLLECTION OF BORDEN'S INC.

BELOW: The Pennsylvania Railroad's main line provides the opportunity to compare two types of milk cars that were also used on the O&W. At the left is a General American wooden, bulk tank car and to the right is a Merchant's Despatch car of similar construction. Supplee-Wills-Jones was a Pennsylvania dairy company operating out of Philadelphia and it received milk from stations along the PRR's main line. AUTHOR'S COLLECTION.

THE FIRST *STREAMLINED* MILK TANK CAR

Borden's was the first to introduce the Milk Tank Railroad Car in the New York Metropolitan District—(in 1926). Borden's now take another initial step through its introduction of the Streamline type all-metal Railroad Car—the first in commercial service by any company.

Body Construction

These cars are to be used to speedily transport milk at low temperature from Borden's Country Milk Stations to its City Pasteurizing and Bottling Plants. They are designed to operate in the fastest passenger train runs.

Borden's new streamline tank car is of all-metal construction, yet it actually weighs less than the conventional wooden body car. It has a steel outside shell, with a protective coat of aluminum metal fused to the steel surface by a new process of sprayed-on molten metal. Weight of car: Empty 42 tons; Loaded, 67 tons. Body construction work done in Borden's own Jersey City Car Shop.

Twin Tanks—24,000 quart capacity

Two huge glass-lined tanks like this are set inside the car. Each tank holds 12,000 quarts of milk, and is insulated on the outside with six inches of cork. The milk is pumped into these tanks at the Country Milk Plant at 36° F. The temperature of the milk does not vary more than one degree during transit. No air can reach it, no change takes place in its purity.

Up-to-date transportation methods are as much a part of Borden's system of milk protection as supervision of the herd and double-laboratory control. No step is overlooked that makes for finer, safer milk.

TOP LEFT: The Borden's "butter dish" cars were the most unusual of the bulk tank designs. This photo is believed to show the red scheme with yellow lettering. WAYNE SITTNER COLLECTION. MIDDLE: This car has a silver body with black lettering. BOB PASTORKEY COLLECTION. BOTTOM: BCDX 1006 was a milk tank car reassigned by Borden's to its chemical division and was used to haul "Elmer's Glue." CLARENCE THARP PHOTOGRAPH: COURTESY RAIL DATA SERVICES. ABOVE: This Borden's ad appeared on the back of a DL&W timetable in the 1940's. AUTHOR'S COLLECTION.

Chapter 5: Bulk Tank Containers on Flatcars

Fitch found a special transportation problem in the New York City area that could be solved by better intermodal transit. Each day over 1,000,000 gallons of raw milk were delivered to the dairies of Manhattan for processing. Most of it came in old-fashioned ten-gallon milk cans aboard trucks bound for the nearest railhead. Fitch wanted to send the tanks directly to the farms.

John H. White, *An Early Chapter in Freight Handling, Cincinnati and the Container,* Queen City Heritage Magazine, 1985.

Although we may regard it as a recent idea, freight containerization has been around for a long time. A surprising variety of examples show up in railroad history. Rising costs of labor, more efficient transfer systems, and reduced damage and pilferage claims have supported continuous development of this type of freight handling through the years. In the mid-1930's, the NYO&W became involved in the development of containerization technology through affiliation with a company called Motor Terminals Inc., of Cleveland, Ohio. The president of Motor Terminals, Benjamin F. Fitch, had developed a system for the inter-terminal transfer of rail freight at Cincinnati, Ohio, and it had possibilities for additional rail application. Fitch obtained floor space in the O&W's Middletown Shops in 1935 to take his concept to a new market. Motor Terminals design people and O&W shopmen refined and gave shape to his ideas in the development of a system of great potential. It had four components designed to handle liquid freight, and milk traffic in particular. These components were 2000-gallon portable tanks, specially equipped flatcars, a flatbed motor truck equipped with its own power take-off, and a one-man transfer system that could move the tanks between the truck and railroad car.

The container system had a number of real advantages over the milk tank cars. The portable container was suitable for storage of milk at either the creamery or pasteurization plant. Lifting devices at either the shipping or receiving end could place the container at a level that permitted gravity loading and unloading. This saved the expense of pumps and the required cleaning of pumps and pipes after each use. Some butterfat loss was also avoided. When milk was transferred from a container, some butterfat stuck to the inside surfaces and was lost in the cleaning-waste water. The use of containers eliminated the need for a tank truck to transfer the milk from tank car to processing plant and thus saved cleaning time and expense as well as retaining milk quality. Pumping agitation, a cause of homogenization, and not a desired quality in milk at that time, was also avoided to a large degree.

Additional factors of flexibility were also promoted. Although it was not usually necessary to do so, shippers could change the city delivery point

FACING PAGE: Hohneker Dairy containers arrived at Weehawken milk terminal late in the day. A driver transfers one of the containers, loaded with approximately ten tons of milk, and will deliver it to the plant for processing during the night. The packaged products will be ready for daylight delivery. The flatcar is O&W 3029 which rolled thousands of miles in one of the railroad's more successful traffic solicitation programs. AUTHOR'S COLLECTION.

Benjamin F. Fitch's first intermodal operation involved an interurban line, the Cincinnati, Lawrenceburg & Aurora Railway. In this photograph, the lifting and transfer system can clearly be seen. The container was lettered for Cincinnati Motor Terminals but had CL&A initials as well as a map of the route represented by the wavy line on the container doors. Not surprisingly, the motor truck was built by White Motors, Fitch's former employer. Walter C. White, a member of that family, was Fitch's partner in the Motor Terminals Company. CHARLES MAGNESS, COURTESY OF JOHN H. WHITE, JR.: SMITHSONIAN INSTITUTE.

RIGHT: In these two photographs, Fitch's ideas have taken prototype form and a trial demonstration will be the next step. Flatcar 3068 has had its side sills reinforced to carry three 2000-gallon tanks, the deck has been rebuilt, and an air signal line has been added for passenger service. Weight and data information has yet to be completed and sheet metal skirting will be added to cover the tank cradles. The O&W's first rail motor car, the 801, sits in the background. COURTESY OF NEW YORK CENTRAL SYSTEM HISTORICAL SOCIETY.

more readily than they could with tank cars. Such re-routings to city plants did not have to involve the railroads with their attendant switching and interchange delays. Washing and cleaning of containers, necessary after each load, could be done indoors. This was certainly a factor that pleased laborers who previously had to work outdoors in winter with the tank cars.

The original milk containers had a capacity of 2000 gallons (or 200 cans) with a length of eight feet and an oval cross section. An inner container was constructed of ten-gauge welded stainless steel which was separated by 2.5 inches of cork insulation from the outer shell. This outer cover was fabricated from twelve-gauge steel welded at the seams. A top hatch was used for loading and a valve at the bottom for unloading.

The containers were attached to structural steel cradles which were covered with sheet-metal skirting. A pair of skids or runners was provided on the bottom of the cradle. These would slide or track in two of the eight transverse receiving grooves across the deck of the flatcar. The truck had an arrangement similar to this, but the tracks extended longitudinally for the length of the bed rather than laterally as they did on the flatcar. To transfer the container, the truck was backed against the car side and fastened to it with a pair of coupling links. A chain was connected to the tank cradle and an electric motor driven by the truck's generator pulled the container

HOHNEKER'S DAIRY

SHIPPERS, WHOLESALERS AND RETAILERS

CREAMERY AT
SHERBURNE, FOUR CORNERS
NEW YORK

MAIN OFFICE:
567 THIRTIETH STREET
NORTH BERGEN, N.J.
PALISADE 6-0051

May 31, 1939.

Motor Terminals, Inc.,
420 Lexington Avenue,
New York, N. Y.

Gentlemen,

    Three years ago you stopped at our office to offer us a new system you had developed for transporting milk.

    Naturally we were a little skeptical about trying out a method of transportation that had never been used. Our milk had to travel 240 miles after it left the creamery and one of the main requisites in the milk business is that the milk must reach the pasteurization plant on time.

    We saw great possibilities in your plan and decided to try it. After three years of use, through all sorts of adverse weather conditions our milk has never been lost or delayed.

    We feel that we are using the most superior method of transporting milk in the market to-day and for flexibility and temperature control it can't be beat.

    The reason for this letter is to congratulate you on one of the finest inovations to the milk industry and to thank you for the little visit you paid us three years ago.

Very truly yours,

President
HOHNEKER'S DAIRY, Inc.

---

off the flatcar and onto the truck bed. The transfer procedure required only one-man operation in either direction and could be accomplished in 90 seconds. Initially, three of these containers were loaded onto a flatcar and provided a total capacity equal to most of the milk tank cars. Later variations in car and truck length, container size, and loading systems resulted in cars that could carry up to four containers. This provided a total car capacity of 8000 gallons, a 2000-gallon increase over most milk tank cars.

Fitch took O&W flatcars 3029 and 3034, dating from 1913, and modified the decks for the new service. The load-bearing side sills were strengthened with steel plates. The friction-bearing 40-ton Andrews cast-steel trucks, so commonly applied to other examples of the railroad's rolling stock, supported the cars. Steam and signal lines were applied for passenger service and the cars were placed in use. The system proved very successful and trouble-free and at least one additional flatcar, the 3068, was later converted for the service.

Hohnecker's Dairy Inc., which had a country creamery at Sherburne Four Corners, N.Y., and a processing plant in North Bergen, N.J., was Fitch's first customer. According to railroad correspondence, O&W traffic people knew that Fred Hohneker was *strongly prejudiced* against General

Hohneker's satisfaction with Fitch's system is enthusiastically communicated in this letter to Motor Terminals in 1939. The letter may have been solicited by Motor Terminals as part of a sales campaign to get other shippers interest in the service. General American used this method in the 1920's and sent out advertising booklets with suppport letters from dozens of milk shippers. AUTHOR'S COLLECTION.

American Transportation Company and was a likely candidate for the new system. This proved to be the case. Hohneker's was not only Fitch's first success with the system but also one of the most satisfied customers, and the dairy used the service for many years. At the very least Hohneker's got plenty of free publicity in both the railroad and dairy trade press when the new system was reviewed. Muller Dairies was another Fitch customer on the O&W, and the big three (Borden's, Dairymen's League, and Sheffield Farms; see Addendum C) also endorsed and employed Fitch's system, but not to a great degree on the O&W.

After its 1936 introduction, Fitch continued to develop and improve the system. Container capacity was increased to 2500 gallons and later to 3000 gallons. The larger containers had end vestibules that enclosed filling and discharge pipes, along with valves, agitators, thermometers, coupling wrenches, and a cleaning manhole. Along with the larger tanks came a change in transfer position. Instead of backing up to the flatcar, the truck would park parallel to it and the transfer was made laterally. This system eliminated time loss due to trucks' maneuvering in confined areas such as the narrow driveways between team tracks. The development of these larger containers also involved the O&W to an extent.

In addition to the larger tank containers, a rectangular insulated box was developed that could be used to carry can milk. Eventually such boxes were enlarged to hold 250 forty-quart cans. The original boxes were 20 feet long, 8 feet wide, and 8 feet high and were of welded steel construction. The boxes could be transferred between rail and highway modes by the same method used for the milk containers. In addition, lifting rings permitted the use of a crane for transfer. It appears that the boxes found wide use for traffic other than milk. They were especially well suited for less-than-carload (LCL) shipments and were used widely in this service on the Pennsylvania and New York Central Railroads.

Simplicity of ideas and operation was part of the success of Fitch's system. Both truck and tank were devoid of mechanisms that required high skill-levels for operation or maintenance. Once the tank had been emptied, it was cleaned, sterilized and sealed. This attention was usually sufficient for a full round trip. The truck-flatcar coupling system and the connection between the conveyor chain and milk tank are visible in the lower view. Greased skidways would seem necessary for this system, yet there is no photographic evidence of grease buildup or dirt-catching grease and oil smears on equipment. AUTHOR'S COLLECTION.

Standard Dairy's original plant at Sherburne Four Corners was replaced by this concrete barn-like structure. By merger or purchase, it became Hohneker's Dairy's country plant from which the first portable milk containers were shipped. MARY S. FARGO COLLECTION. COURTESY OF RICHARD REIT AND LEE CAMPBELL.

Fitch-coordinated equipment while National Car supplied and operated the special equipment. The arrangement made FGE's Alexandria, Va., shops available for further development and construction, and Fitch left the O&W's Middletown facility. A fleet of container flatcars, designed specifically for container service, was constructed and given the reporting initials NX. At first glance, these cars simply looked like ordinary flatcars but were equipped with passenger-type trucks, buffers, and signal and steam lines. Collision posts were located at both ends. Load-locking clamps were attached by hinges to the deck. The new cars and the expanded system met with a satisfactory degree of success. In the northeast several milk-hauling lines, notably the B&M, Erie, LV, NYC, PRR, and Rutland, as well as the O&W, were among the roads that handled NX cars. Although all the flatcars in the NX fleet served the same purpose, there were differences in car lengths, number series, and frame details.

The NYO&W sold the two prototype cars to Fitch in 1938 for "$1.00 and other valuable considerations," according to O&W records. It is likely that these two cars became part of National Car's holdings and were leased back to the O&W for continued service. Further changes must have been made to them, since photographs show these cars carrying the larger, heavier tanks in the 1940's. The MTIX cars also went into the National Car fleet.

Unlike the milk tank cars, which had practically eliminated can shipping on the O&W, the containers met with a more limited acceptance. This was partly due to the requirements or limitations of on-line dairy shippers, but the following factors were more likely. Fitch had challenged an industry giant in

A big selling point for Fitch's system was that virtually any 40- to 50-foot flatcar could be converted to the service, and the container size could be modified to suit the requirements of the customer. Much promotional activity was directed toward the producers and shippers of liquid foods, chemicals, and petroleum products in order to bring them in as customers. Sales calls were also made to potential users of the box containers.

In 1939, a 4000-gallon stainless steel tank was developed by Glascote Products Inc. of Cleveland. It had a length of 20 feet and, like the smaller tanks, sat in a sheet-metal-enclosed cradle. It had the more efficient lateral skid rails on the bottom (across the width rather then the length) for rail-to-truck transfer. To handle the larger containers, Motor Terminals worked with the Pennsylvania Railroad to convert a 70-ton steel underframe flatcar for container service. This was done at the PRR's Wilmington, Del., shop. The car was given reporting initials MTIX for Motor Terminals Inc. It had ten transverse rails across the deck and ten locking devices per side to hold two containers in place during transit. It is believed that Motor Terminals eventually operated several of these modified exPRR flatcars.

Instead of a flatbed, straight motor truck, a trailer with a single axle was needed to hold the longer container used with this larger car. A White Motor Company tractor did the highway hauling.

Early in 1940, National Car Company, a subsidiary of Fruit Growers Express Company (FGE), was sufficiently impressed by Fitch's ideas and operation to enter into a partnership with his Motor Terminals, Inc., to form National Fitch Corporation.

National Fitch acted as the leasing agency for

RIGHT: Sometime in the 1940's, I-1 No. 35 is ready to take the milk train north from Norwich. The head car is a descendant of Fitch's original design, and it was fitting that some of the National Car fleet ran on the O&W to continue a service that began in the previous decade. WALTER RICH COLLECTION. BELOW: The railroad station and creamery sat high above the town of Munnsville where the 225 and its train of two milk cars and a combine are about to leave town. The flatcar appears to be one of Fitch's early conversions and the can car is one of the O&W's 1200-series cars. O&W SOCIETY COLLECTION.

Tank holding clamps are in the raised position in this builder's view of NX 1472. This is one of the earlier series of container flats built in Alexandria, Virginia, for National Car Co. Some of the NX cars shared design and construction features with standard freight refrigerator cars of the period. The end and three-quarter views below show that these are basically flatcars fitted for passenger service. The buffer mechanism is the same design that was used earlier on the GARE wooden cars. Car 1472 was part of a group of six cars once assigned to Borden's use. THREE PHOTOGRAPHS: R. L. RECORDON COLLECTION.

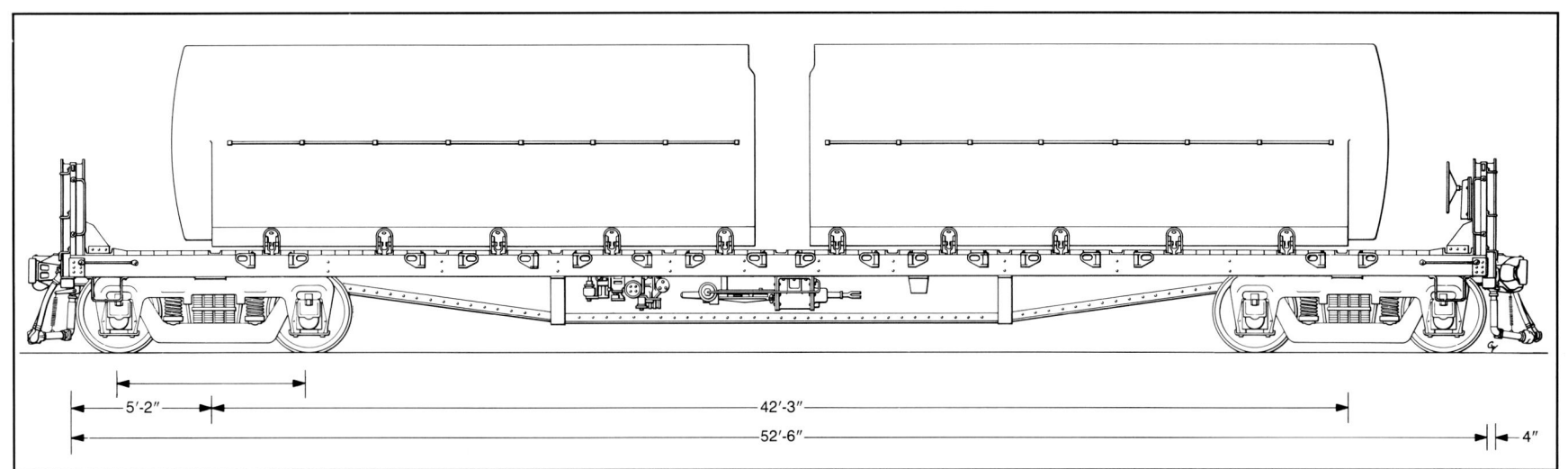

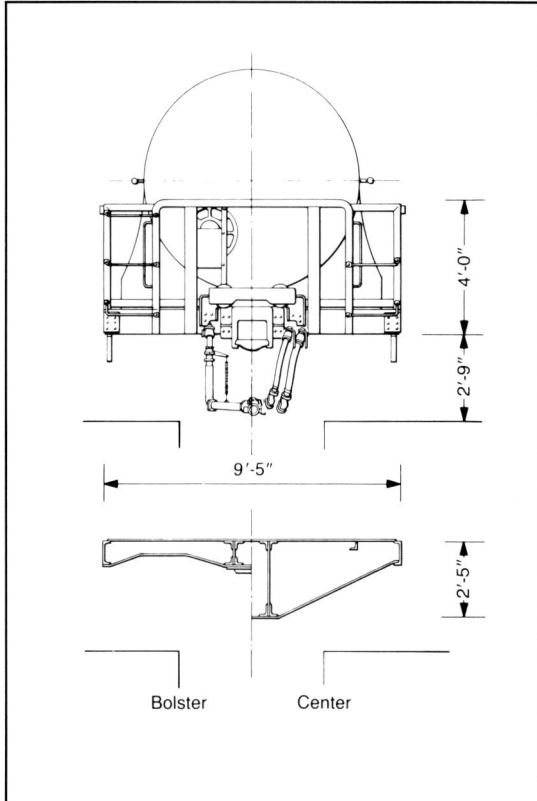

BELOW: An end view shows subtle differences in cross-section and height of two containers. These were leased to or owned by Borden's and are being switched at their Newark, N.J., plant located on the Lackawanna Railroad. A few color photographs of these containers in their latter years of service do exist and they appear surprisingly grimy for equipment used in food service. RAILROAD AVENUE ENTERPRISES, COURTESY OF BOB PENNISI.

From an engineering viewpoint, Fitch's system was quite simple and did not require sophisticated hardware. In fact Fruit Growers Express managed to use an existing refrigerator car underframe design for at least one series of milk container flats. Present day international movement of liquid freight in cylindrical containers via ships, rail and highway follows Fitch's ideas. DRAWINGS BY CHUCK YUNGKURTH.

THIS PAGE: A variety of close-up details is provided by these photographs of NX flats that were stored in Potomac Yard, Alexandria, Virginia. These cars may have been built at the Fruit Growers Express shop located in the same city. FGE also had a construction and repair shop in Indiana Harbor, Indiana. These cars and tanks were no longer in dairy service and may have returned home after final revenue service. Some cars were later sold for use as regular flatcars. FOUR PHOTOGRAPHS: WILLIAM RINN.

ABOVE: The tanks on NX 1464 are of slightly different configurations. Borden's applied individual metal letters and numerals to these containers during the 1940's after using painted markings earlier. The 1464 is of center rather than side sill design. Although flatcars do not lend themselves to elaborate lettering schemes, National Car did vary the placement of the name, reporting marks and required data on car sides. JOHN C. LARUE COLLECTION.

BELOW: Merchant's Despatch put together this ingenious, self-contained system of a special flatcar, turntables and two trailers in 1934. It was designed to recapture milk traffic that had been lost to tank trucks. The Fitch system made its debut shortly after and had a number of advantages over the MDT design. Two of these were lower tare weight and maintenance costs. Fitch's transfer system required only one-man operation where MDT needed two. Some type of fixed or portable ramp must have been necessary to load the trailers. RICHARD STOVING COLLECTION.

An interesting variety of milk cars has arrived at the Erie's Jersey City Terminal. From left to right are a Borden's butter dish car, an NX flat with a single container, a GPEX postwar car assigned to Borden's, two more NX flats and a former GARE wooden car from the 1920's or 1930's. Such combinations of cars must have occurred frequently on the milk-hauling roads. The Borden's butter dish car had a capacity of 6000 gallons. Some sources have erroneously listed this car as having a 12,000-gallon capacity. ERIE LACKAWANNA HISTORICAL SOCIETY COLLECTION: COURTESY OF DAN BIERNACKI.

General American Transportation Corp., which had greater resources to protect its established business. Probably the greatest determinant was the lower wheelage fee paid by railroads for the use of the container cars. They brought in 1.5 cents per mile as opposed to 2.5 cents per mile for the milk tank cars. Although Fitch originally indicated that he was satisfied with the lower fee, it posed a drawback for the equipment lessees. As with the milk tank cars, the railroad allowed the wheelage charges to be applied to the lessee's equipment rental cost. In some cases this fully covered the lessee's daily rent. The one-cent-per-mile difference between the GPEX cars and Fitch's equipment caused quite a few customers to stay with the GPEX tank cars. The wheelage fee for the container flatcars may later have been raised to 2.5 cents, which would have made them more competitive. Another problem was the increasing number of truckers who were getting into the milk transportation business. As the O&W itself noted in 1939, before a milk shipper could avail himself of the rail service, even if its rates were lower, he had to acquire by purchase or long-term lease his own cars or tanks. He also had to buy or hire tank trucks to make the terminal delivery of the rail-hauled milk. Dairy shippers no doubt asked: "Why not have trucks do the line haul as well as terminal delivery?" (Refer to Addendum B for additional information on this point.)

In common with the milk tank cars, the containers represented an innovative approach to holding and regaining some traffic in a special market. Much like the piggyback and container operations of the present day, they offered the flexibility of motor trucks with the efficiency and lower rates of rail transport. Equally important, they allowed the railroads to solicit business that did not have to be located directly on line. It would be interesting to know how vigorously the NYO&W pursued the concept. The fact that Motor Terminals was welcomed in Middletown indicates that new ideas were well received and that the O&W was not afraid to be the first in a unique rail-truck partnership.

This scene shows the Lehigh Valley's milk terminal in Jersey City, N.J., but the same scene occurred in Weehawken with cars delivered by the O&W and the New York Central. The plug-in cord and control box permitted one-man transfer in either direction. The driver or LV car inspector would raise the retaining clamps if this were an empty tank returning to the country. These particular tanks had a capacity of 4000 gallons. AUTHOR'S COLLECTION.

Engine 71, shown here in the days of assigned locomotives, displays the care and touches of individualilty that each crew lavished upon its machine. The sense of ownership was so great that management often had to mediate disputes between shopmen and enginemen over matters of proper maintenance. JOHN AND SUE HUDSON COLLECTION.

Chapter 6: Delhi and the Delhi Branch

The dignified gentleman passenger, a Delaware County native, was none other than the Hon. William B. Ogden, once mayor of the City of Chicago, and a railroad king of the west. He had been president of four or five great western railroads, one of which was the well-known Union Pacific. The 'Midland' or O&W railroad had arrived for the first time in Delhi early in the preceding year, and this may well have been Mr. Ogden's first look at railroading in the county of his youth.

John E. Raitt, *Ruts in the Road*, A Compilation of Articles on Topics of Delaware County History, Vol. I (107).

The upper valley of the West Branch of the Delaware River is a hilly region covered with grassy meadows and wooded slopes where maples and other hardwoods are the dominant vegetation. Small brooks feed the West Branch, which originates farther north from the runoff of the western Catskills. The stream's passage through the Delaware County seat of Delhi splits the village and is wide enough at this location to require a respectable bridge to connect the two parts. Delhi was incorporated in 1821, and because of water power provided by the West Branch, it became a commercial and social center. Earlier, it had become the seat of government when Delaware County was established in 1797 and a courthouse was built the following year. In 1848 the pioneering New York & Erie, following a route along the Delaware River, was completed along the southern edge of the county. Some twenty years later the Albany & Susquehanna (A&S) came down the Susquehanna Valley along the western boundary. The actual presence and further potential of these two railroads in the county gave impetus to many ideas, plans, and schemes. As was typical of every county seat in the state, there was a great deal of interest in a rail connection with the major villages, towns, and cities of New York and the nation. Railroad booster organizations were formed in a number of the state's communities and each prodded the other toward action. Amateur surveyors and promoters hiked many miles of woodland paths as they laid imaginary and real survey stakes along the streams and over the passes between the valleys.

On October 4, 1865, railroad delegates from many upstate New York counties and New York City met in Delhi to arrange the construction of a rail line that would be located between the route of the New York Central to the north and the Erie to the south. This was followed by another convention in New York City in December, and here the New York & Oswego Midland was organized. One faction of promoters at those early meetings favored a line that would reach the Hudson River well to the north of New York City. This can be readily seen in the original formal resolution that made the plans officially public. The eastern or southern end of the railroad was to be directed through Ulster or Sullivan and Orange Counties. However, by the time the articles of association were presented to the State of New York in 1866, the general route had been determined. Article three of the resolution plainly stated that the railroad would terminate "on the Hudson River, opposite the city of New York." This ruled out Ulster County.

Although the first organizational meeting was held in Delhi and bode well for that town's future, the route finally decided upon did not pass through the village. A letter to a local paper later put the blame on the citizens for inadequate stock subscriptions and general lack of spirit during the early planning stages. Mr. John C. Stellwagen researched the OM's proposed alignments and found that south of Sidney, one of the possible surveys would have passed through Delhi.

The plan called for the right-of-way to run from Sidney to Unadilla along the Susquehanna River and parallel to the D&H. The line would then have passed through Franklin and Meredith into Delhi. The rails would then head for Andes and down Tremper Creek to the East Branch of the Delaware River. Turning a few miles to run downstream the railroad then began to ascend to tunnel the mountains and reach Spring Brook. This stream would be followed to the Beaverkill which led to Roscoe. The Midland calculated this route to be 67 miles long with grades averaging 56 feet per mile. No less than six deep crossings of rivers were encountered. These crossings, plus the tunnel, made the route prohibitively expensive and the route via Walton was chosen. [John C. Stellwagen, *The New York & Oswego Midland Railroad Company: The Planning Stages.* Unpublished manuscript, n.d.]

Subsequent surveys and meetings, including those held in New York City, put Delhi at the terminus of a 17-mile branch. Thus the village found itself north of the proposed New York & Oswego Midland, eight miles south of the future Ulster & Delaware (U&D), and some ten miles east of the established Albany & Susquehanna (later the Delaware & Hudson).

The survey of the branch was completed in October, 1868, and the construction contract was given to the company of Cross and Ferguson of Canada. On May 1, 1869, ground was broken near Hamden (HM, M.P. 188.46), on the 17th at Walton (WN, M.P. 179.45), and in mid-June at Delhi (DI, M.P. 196.06). NY&OM directors H.E. Barlett and A.C. Edgerton were present with ceremonial pick, shovel, and wheelbarrow. Those who had pushed the Midland management for this branch raised some of the necessary construction funds, since this was a condition for work to begin. The controversial town bonding bill, passed by the New York legislature in April, 1866, allowed towns to bond themselves for up to 30 percent of their assessed valuation and funds raised by this method financed much of the Oswego Midland's construction. Delaware County raised $660,800 through town bonding, with the Town of Delhi contributing $245,800 and the Town of Hamden, $100,000.

Work halted briefly the following year because of flood damage and at least one riot staged by Irish construction workers. Although it was not written in reference to this particular brawl, the following might be applicable here. The *Hancock Times* quoted the Montrose, Pennsylvania, *Democrat* of October 18, 1871, when that paper wrote these lines:

> The pick and shovel brigade are upon us in 'bloody' earnest, they rank and file through our streets, fill our hotels and saloons, and their arms and equipments are piled mountain high in our depot, and store-houses, and the biggest skeptic in town has been forced to admit that the 'Midland' is surely coming.

Railroad construction was completed to Delhi on January 18, 1872, and within hours after the final length of rail had been spiked in place, President Littlejohn and other company dignitaries arrived for a dinner at Cottrell's Hotel. Shortly after the opening, misfortune struck with the destruction by fire of the depot and a train of new passenger cars. Reconstruction of the depot was quickly accomplished. It was reported that the fare to Walton was initially 70 cents and was later reduced to 50 cents. Perhaps as a result of the financial problems that arose almost immediately after the OM opened, a newspaper article reported that both the Delhi and New Berlin branches were "leased by individual conductors" under an unusual arrangement that lasted about two years. This might have been an attempt to provide service while avoiding tax seizures. The railroad resumed control of both branches in May, 1877.

With the OM in the village, Delhi had its cherished rail link with the world, and there was ample promise of additional routes reaching the village in spite of the Midland's poor financial showing thus far. On April 3, 1866, a railroad called the Rondout & Oswego (R&O) was chartered by Ulster County interests under Thomas Cornell, a steamboat entrepreneur, banker, and congressman of Kingston, N.Y. This road would become the Ulster & Delaware. Cornell was also involved in another plan for a line known as the Delhi & Middletown (D&M) that was chartered in 1871. This route would run eastward, 30 miles from the county seat through Andes, to a connection with the Rondout & Oswego at Dean's Corners near Margaretville, N.Y. (The Middletown in the title was the town in Delaware County and not the city of Middletown in Orange County.) The former contains the communities of Arkville and Margaretville. Although the route would not fulfill its original concept, roadbed in the form of cuts, fills, bridge piers, and graded right-of-way was completed east of Lake Delaware. Much of the work was done in 1871. The panic of 1873 and Cornell's loss of interest brought the project to a dead end. In later years, parts of this construction were used by the Delaware & Eastern, a project in which R.B. Williams, a former New York, Ontario & Western division superintendent, was a moving force. This little company, later the Delaware & Northern, connected with the O&W at East Branch and the U&D at Arkville. It also had a branch to Andes. Plans to extend the main line to Schenectady and the Pennsylvania anthracite fields were never carried out.

In 1871 Cornell's R&O reached Arkville. During that same year, the D&M grading was well under way. In 1872 the R&O became the New York, Kingston & Syracuse and in 1875 it became the Ulster & Delaware. This road had been opened to Stamford by 1872, and a connection with the Albany & Susquehanna at or near Oneonta was in the works. With the R&O active to the east, and the D&M grading in its direction, the county seat of Delaware County must have projected a rosy picture for itself as a railroad center.

If the dream of grandeur died slowly, it got a revival late in the century when Thomas Cornell announced the intention of extending the U&D to Bloomville, a scant eight miles upstream from Delhi. Talks with dairy and businessmen found they were not happy with the rates and services of the New York, Ontario & Western, heir to the Oswego Midland. Originally Cornell had figured his road to go west from Stamford via Harpersfield to Oneonta. No doubt the possibility of a swing to the south caused a flutter in Delhi as once again it saw itself on a mainline. As it turned out, the U&D did not turn south but resumed its westward course after reaching Bloomville, and it finally reached Oneonta in 1900. Although it did not actually touch Delhi, the U&D did offer those shippers located between the village and Bloomville an alternative to the railroad at Delhi. Such close competition could not have made the NYO&W's managers happy.

Yet this was not the end of railroad plans in the

TOP: The Edgerton House, located on Main St., was Delhi's largest hostelry. A number of men sporting the derby hats of the period congregate on the porch, perhaps to discuss the national political campaign proclaimed by the overhead banner. BELOW: A gas station has replaced the Edgerton House and the town name has been painted in large letters on a roof to aid early aviators. TWO VIEWS: WILLIAM SCHRIVER COLLECTION.

Crawford Wagon Works in Delhi was located north of Steel Brook which was bridged by the siding serving the works. A drying kiln to the right rear of the photograph indicates that the company cut its own lumber locally. BUD FRIEND COLLECTION.

Delhi region. Property deeds give credence to a proposed electric interurban line between Delhi and Bloomville. It got no further than the ownership of a few parcels of land. The Delhi & Hudson River, chartered in 1883, was a futile attempt to revive the old Delhi & Middletown. A final effort to connect Delhi and Andes was made in 1898 when a company called the Delaware Valley (also known as the Andes & Delhi) was organized. A switch was reportedly installed in the O&W yard at Delhi and a few lengths of rail were laid to connect with this company before it too faded from the scene. Almost ten miles of roadbed were graded, and a branch was planned to reach Bovina. The careful observer can still find traces of the Delhi & Middletown, Delaware & Eastern, and Andes & Delhi along Route 28 and other locations east of Delhi.

Within their respective time periods, the OM and the O&W management must have had some concern about all the possible competition. A single shipment of 40 tons of butter in 1879 was a fair indication of the success of the dairy business in the Delhi vicinity. This was only part of the 2,570,219 pounds of butter shipped out on the OM that year as reported by the local agent. The next year, John McNaugh, a farmer from Meredith, made the first shipment of milk from Delhi to New York City, and dairymen from Orange County were involved in the establishment of a creamery in Delhi. By 1890, several creameries were operating on the branch. Such traffic acted as an inducement for railroad planners to consider pushing those additional routes toward the Delaware County seat. To the northwest of Delhi, the famous Merridale Farms complex was being created and would soon become internationally recognized for its prize cattle, many of which were shipped via the O&W. The nearby communities of Bloomville and Hobart, located on the U&D, would become important dairy shipping and processing locations, with Sheffield Farms being the dominant company.

Prior to 1900, Delhi had a small collection of manufacturing works. A woolen mill, the Gallant Brothers' silk mill, and the Crawford Wagon Works provided employment and rail business. New York Condensed Milk Company set up a large milk bottling establishment in 1895 and Borden's was reported to have done the same in 1899. However, since Borden's bought the New York Condensed Milk Company in 1899, it might have been the same plant. Along with county offices, a state agricultural college, and a number of small businesses, there was enough work to support a population of 2078 in 1900.

A new station was erected in the late 1890's to replace the second depot, which had been moved uptown for a wagon house. This last station building was sold to the Grange League Federation (GLF) in 1941 for $500 and razed to make way for a new feed mill.

TOP LEFT: Formerly named the "Hackensack," engine 34 is shown here at Delhi in a pre-1900 view. The engine was later sold to the neighboring Cooperstown & Charlotte Railroad in 1900. Engines of this wheel arrangement continued to work branch line runs early in this century after heavier locomotives bumped them from the main line. By 1932, all 4-4-0's were gone from the O&W. ROBERT HARDING COLLECTION, COURTESY OF JOE BUX.
TOP RIGHT: No. 76 displays meticulous care during its assignment to the Delhi and Utica Flyers. Bill Root, Cal Sanford, Bill Foster and Windy Norton knew the locomotive well in their jobs as trainman, engineer, fireman and watchman respectively. ROBERT HARDING COLLECTION, O&W HISTORICAL SOCIETY.

RIGHT: Gravity flow was used to avoid the cost of expensive pumping equipment in a milk plant. Incoming milk arrived at a high elevation and flowed downward to final processing and exit from the building. Such a design also helped in draining off the large amounts of water used in processing and cleaning. This view shows Borden's Delhi plant circa 1910. JOE BUX COLLECTION.

A section of the Delhi & Middletown grade and a stone cattle pass still exist on a farm property in a small valley called "The Bullet Hole" near Andes. No train ran over the right-of-way despite efforts to revive the company. AUTHOR'S PHOTOGRAPH.

South of Delhi, the main business was dairy farming. Receiving stations were built in each community with Frasers (railroad spelling), Delancey, and Hamden having large facilities. An idea of the magnitude of dairy farming in the area can be had from the fact that just one major milk producer, the Dairymen's League, had 43 branches in Delaware County in 1921 with 3038 members owning 46,512 cows.

Just south of the Delhi yard, near M.P. 195.9, a creamery and two stores shared a siding. In the vicinity of M.P. 195.4 another siding served a creamery and store. The switches for most of the single-ended sidings on the branch were at the south end and made for faster pickup of the loaded milk cars. Frasers (M.P. 192.88) was not listed as a station until after 1900. The station was only a flag stop with a siding to serve a store and creamery.

Delancey (DC, M.P. 190.29), also spelled "Delancy" and "DeLancey" by the railroad, was originally named Lansingville and had a siding that served a creamery, ice house, loading dock, and storehouse. A shallow ice pond adjoined the railroad right-of-way across from the depot. In 1910 the railroad put up a new frame station.

The busiest location on the branch, other than the terminal at Delhi, was Hamden (HM, M.P. 188.56). The track was built along the eastside of Main Street for the greater part of a mile. Curbing separated the sidewalk from the track for a distance along the more residential section of Main Street. In such a setting the branch resembled a traction line rather than a steam railroad. Borden's established a plant in 1910 at the south end of the village just across from the station. An independent creamery was located at the north end. Hamden also had a cattle pen, loading dock, and feed and coal dealer plus a few small industries.

Hawleys (railroad spelling) (M.P. 187.20) was a flag stop and had a short siding. At Colchester (M.P. 183.17) a siding on the west side of the main track was used by a creamery and a stone dock. The creamery was built in 1895 and enlarged ten years later. A flag-stop shelter was located at the crossing that led to a covered bridge over the West Branch.

At the northern outskirts of Walton there were two sidings to serve businesses between the first milepost on the branch, 181.00, and the station at Bridge Street. This smaller of the two Walton stations allowed through trains between Delhi and New York City to avoid a backup move to reach the mainline station. However the through service did not last very long. About 650 feet of trestle-work kept the right-of-way out of a marsh south of Bridge Street and took it over East Brook. Another 800 feet of trestle bridged low ground and West Brook. These trestles ranged in height from 8 to 13 feet and by the 1920's the railroad had replaced them with a continuous long fill. The single-track branch then joined the main line via a wye at Delaware Street.

Although the Delhi line did not cross the West Branch, it came very close to a number of covered vehicular bridges that did. Delaware County had many of these historic structures, but only three remain at the time of this writing. One of them, the bridge at Hamden built by Robert Murray of Andes in 1859, adjoins the O&W right-of-way and is still in daily use.

A number of notable events involved the railroad around the turn of the century. In 1888 a new iron bridge arrived via flat car to replace the wooden Sherwood's Bridge. In June 1894, President Grover Cleveland visited relatives in the county via the railroad. Governor Teddy Roosevelt came in 1899 while making a state circuit by rail. The Delhi Soldiers' Monument, made of Vermont marble, came in on three flatcars in 1906 and was assembled

BELOW: Sales promotions, political contests, national holidays, traveling shows, lectures, choral societies, church social societies and a host of similar diversions were the entertainments of decades past. No doubt that age wasn't without its religious zealots who saw the decline of civilizations in several such activities. "Deering" is obviously the cause of this gathering in front of Delhi's American House Hotel. BUD FRIEND COLLECTION. RIGHT: Evening band concerts in the park were another source of enjoyment that could be found within the village borders. These Delhi musicians probably used the O&W to visit other towns in exchange programs that promoted local civic pride and boosterism. WILLIAM SCHRIVER COLLECTION.

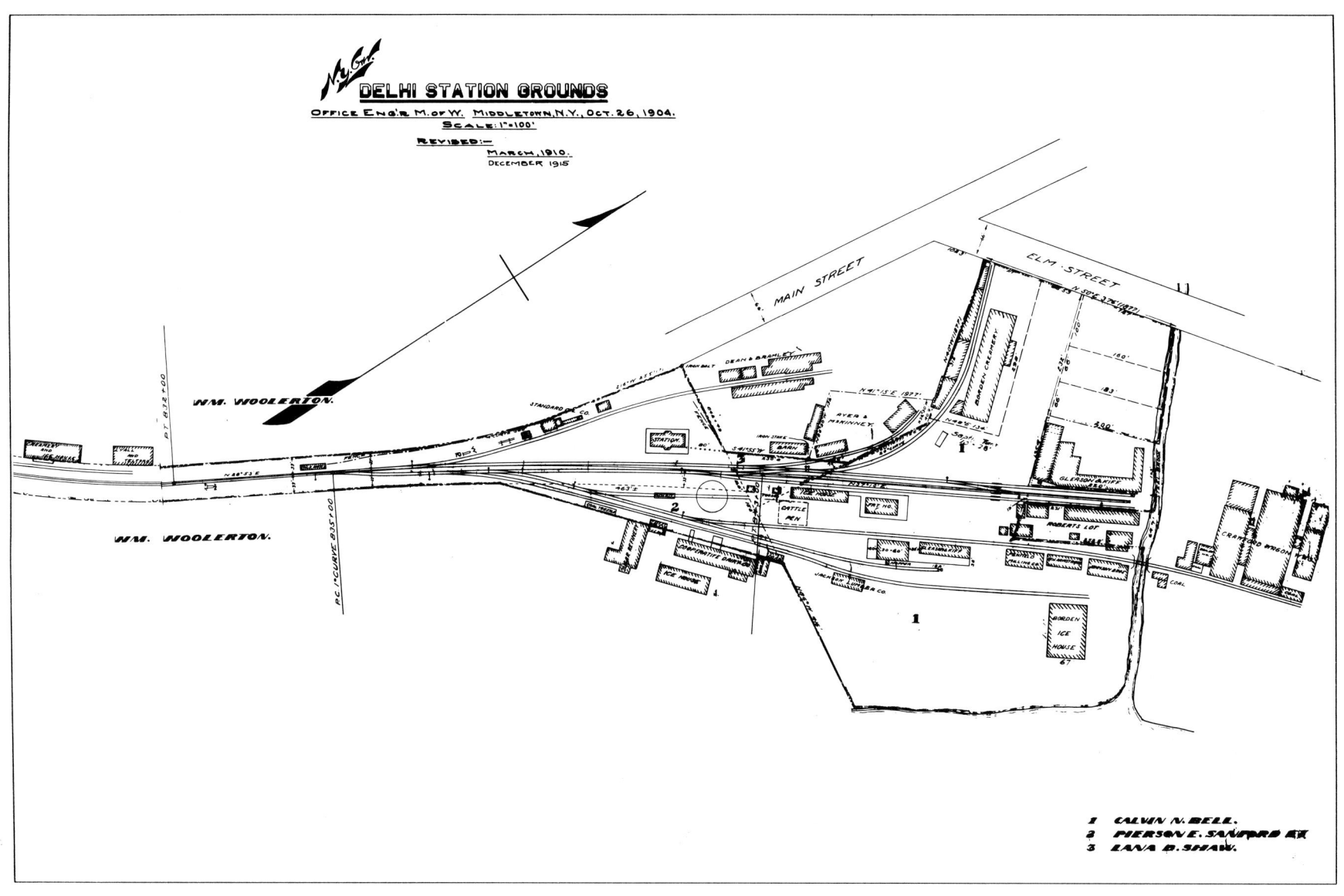

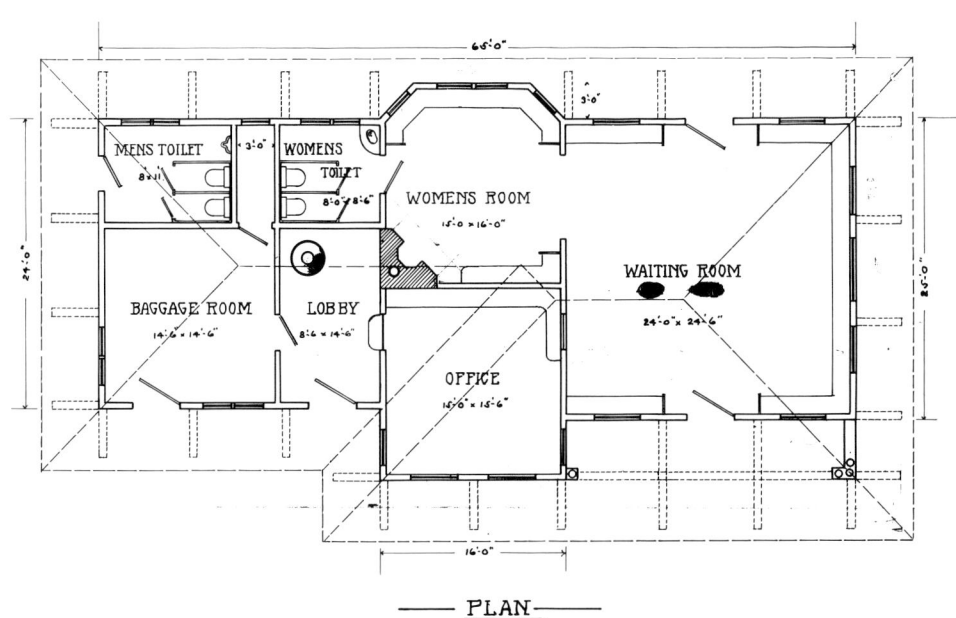

PLAN OF PROPOSED STATION, DELHI, N.Y.

SCALE 1" = 8'

Middletown N.Y. Jan 26/1897

— PLAN —

— FRONT ELEVATION. —

— END ELEVATION. —

ABOVE AND RIGHT: The open-platform, wooden coaches shown in these three pictures (above and opposite page bottom) were heated by coal or wood-burning stoves and were standard on the Delhi and Utica Flyers that ran between the two towns. Later, closed-vestibule, steam-heated cars made the trip more comfortable. As passenger revenues dropped, the more primitive earlier equipment returned and was used until the passenger service was finally abandoned. There are many legendary stories in the railroad literature about animals that met or rode trains on a regular basis. In the photograph at right, the dog on the rear platform with the conductor might have been one of the legendary breed. ABOVE: O&W COLLECTION. FACING PAGE: AUTHOR'S COLLECTION. FAR RIGHT: COURTESY OF JOE BUX AND DEPOT ATTIC.

TOP RIGHT: A daily ritual for the Delhi branch crew was turning the locomotive on the manual turntable in the Delhi yard. The engine had to be correctly spotted to make the job easier for the crew. Too much weight on either end of the table could make the turning difficult and the engineer very unpopular with his crew. Firemen on these double-cab engines, working in the gangway between the engine and tender, had little protection from the extremes of weather but were probably cooler in the summer than they would have been if firing a single-cab locomotive. After turning, the 278 will back to the depot, couple to its train and begin the return trip to Walton. O&W SOCIETY COLLECTION.

THIS PAGE: Three views circa 1910 show the station and grounds at Delhi. At the time, the village had a population of 1700 people and was served by four weekday trains in each direction. JOE BUX COLLECTION.

Pullman cars "Tamarack" and "Scarsdale" have brought these gentlemen to Delhi for what one would suspect to be an agriculturally-related meeting. The state's Agricultural and Technical Institute in the village would figure prominently in such affairs. WALTER RICH COLLECTION.

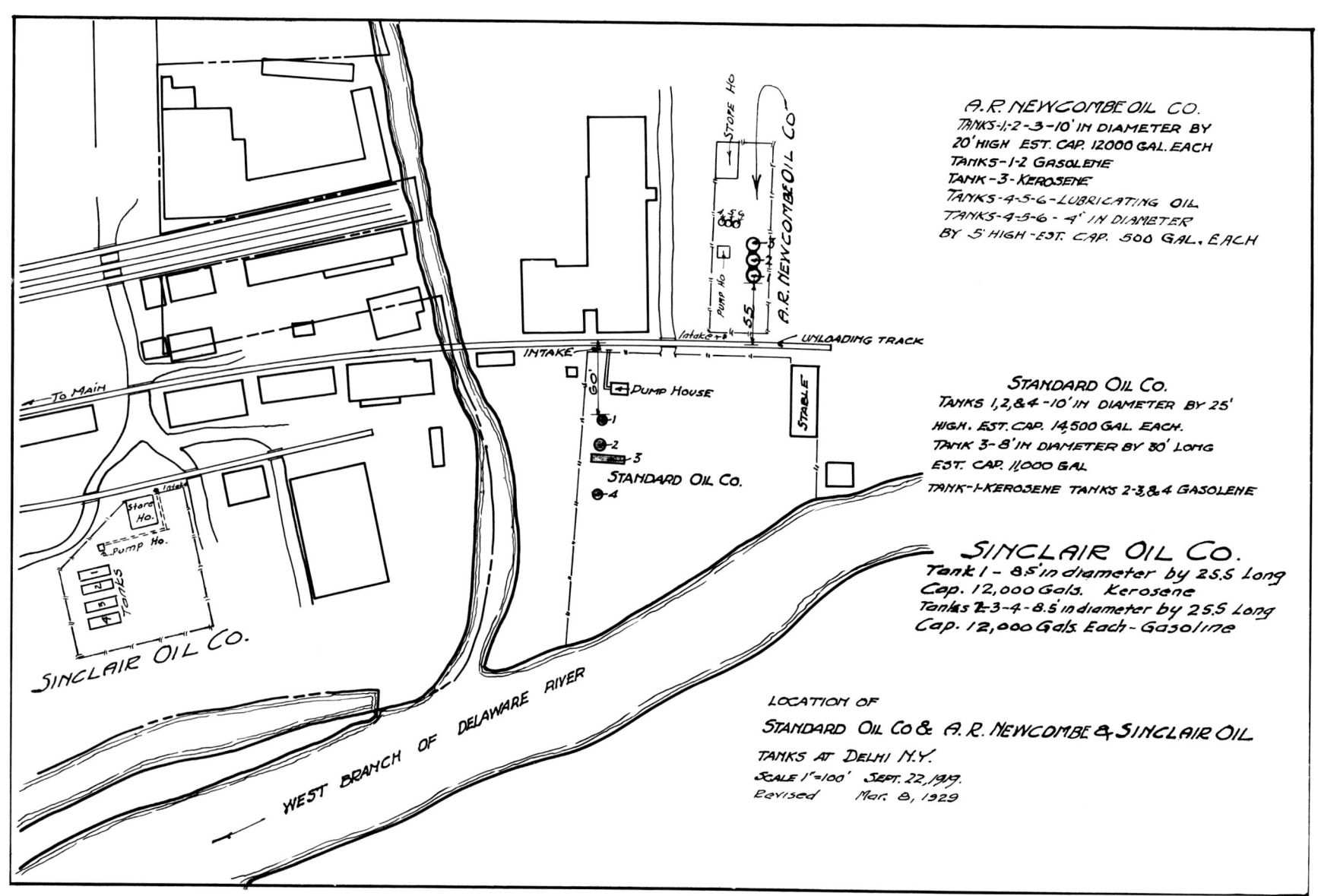

Three oil and gasoline dealers were receiving rail deliveries at the extreme end of the Delhi branch in the 1920's. There was at least one other fuel dealer near the O&W yard complex. Steel Brook, bridged by the siding, is the unnamed stream leading into the West Branch. O&W SOCIETY COLLECTION.

RIGHT: The Dean & Bramley feed and supply complex at the yard at Delhi was serviced by the O&W. By the mid-1960's, the buildings were looking quite decrepit as the farm supply houses consolidated and modernized or went out of business. Part of the modernization included replacing rail service with trucks. BUD FRIEND.

BELOW AND BELOW RIGHT: "Reuse," a word that came into our language in the 1970's, was earlier applied to many O&W buildings when the railroad had no further use for them. Most of these second uses were for purposes of warehousing and storage. The Delhi freight house looked better in the 1968 view at right than in the 1954 photograph at left where evidence of deferred maintenance is so clear. BELOW: COURTESY OF JOE BUX AND DEPOT ATTIC. RIGHT: SOUTH FLORIDA RAIL SALES, JOE BUX COLLECTION.

LEFT: Elms and maples could still be found along Delhi's Main Street in the 1950's. Improved roads meant more cars and less reliance on the branch line that terminated two blocks east and a little south of this location. Passenger service had already been discontinued but there was enough freight business to bring a local into town at least three days per week. AUTHOR'S COLLECTION. BOTTOM: LOWER LEFT: In this aerial view, the campus of the state college is at the lower left and the West Branch of the Delaware flows southward at the right. Between them is the O&W yard. Feed, fuel and agricultural supply houses surround the triangular yard area and mean the branch was essentially a receiving service with few outbound loads. WILLIAM SCHRIVER COLLECTION.

LEFT: The Delaware County Farmers' Co-op was probably the largest dairy plant on the Delhi branch. It closed in 1963. The large boiler house and four conveyors for empty cans give a good idea of the size of the operation. The wooden building across the track was an earlier creamery. This location is just south of Delhi village. BOB WYER PHOTOGRAPH.

BELOW LEFT AND BELOW: Two photographs show the arrival of the Delhi mixed train on an unknown date. In the left view the train is just south of town where engineers had to work steam over the final stretch of main track to get up the hill and into the yard. In the right view, the train has arrived in the yard where two small four-wheel caboose bodies serve as section crew shanties. Others were used as telegraph operator quarters and watchman's shanties. The O&W's switch to larger, four-axle cabooses made the smaller cars surplus. TWO PHOTOGRAPHS: LESLIE O'REILLY COLLECTION.

LEFT: This plant at Frasers is still used to manufacture dairy products. It can no longer be recognized from the nearby road since it was incorporated into a larger structure in later years. In the late 1980's, the complex was operated by the Great American Cheese Co. for the production of yogurt. The railroad tracks are on the opposite side of the building. AUTHOR'S COLLECTION. BOTTOM LEFT: A trackside view of an earlier creamery at Frasers shows brickwork which was unusual for a creamery of this period. The apron-clad worker may be taking a moment from the cleaning chores after having completed the day's processing and shipping. Note the signal flag attached to the shed. BUD FRIEND COLLECTION. BOTTOM RIGHT: A well-dressed farm woman, possibly combining a milk delivery with a shopping trip, loads her cart with empty cans at the same creamery. The delivery ramp appears to have been built up with ashes from the boiler room. BUD FRIEND COLLECTION.

TOP LEFT: The beautiful maple-shaded main street of Delancey led to a covered bridge over the West Branch and on to the O&W depot. The second floor over "Uncle John's Store" housed the village library where, if the library trustees approved, the recent works of Katherine Anne Porter, John Steinbeck and William Faulkner might be found. Local readers might have noted some characteristics of their own rural region in the latter's fictional Yoknapatawpha County, Mississippi. TOP RIGHT: Stewart & Bailey's, as the store had been known in an earlier era before the automobiles had replaced carriages, was a country village emporium that sold clothing and general merchandise in Delancey. A customer could be quite certain of finding an oiled wood floor and a trolley ladder inside. The proprietor might also have the wooden pole device that, to the delight of children, was used to reach and retrieve items from upper shelves. TWO PHOTOGRAPHS: WILLIAM SCHRIVER COLLECTION.

RIGHT: Delancey's covered bridge connected the village with the railroad station. It looked very similar to the one at Hamden just a few miles downstream and might have been built by Robert Murray. The O&W track is off to the right in this view looking downstream. WILLIAM SCHRIVER COLLECTION.

ABOVE: McDermott Dairy Co. once owned this creamery at Delancey but Sheffield Farms is believed to have been the final operator. The railroad ran on the opposite side of the building, behind the wagon at right. AUTHOR'S COLLECTION.

BELOW: This scene is at the same building, standing on the right-of-way looking north toward Delhi. The creamery-icehouse combination is next to the Andes-Delancey Road. Ice was harvested from a shallow pond diagonal to the buildings. FACING PAGE: Trains coming into Hamden from the north passed just beyond the left portal of this covered bridge, shown here in a contemporary photograph. Robert Murray, a Scottish immigrant, designed this bridge to the Long Truss pattern in 1859. Three covered bridges still existed (in 1992) in Delaware County. AUTHOR'S PHOTOGRAPH.

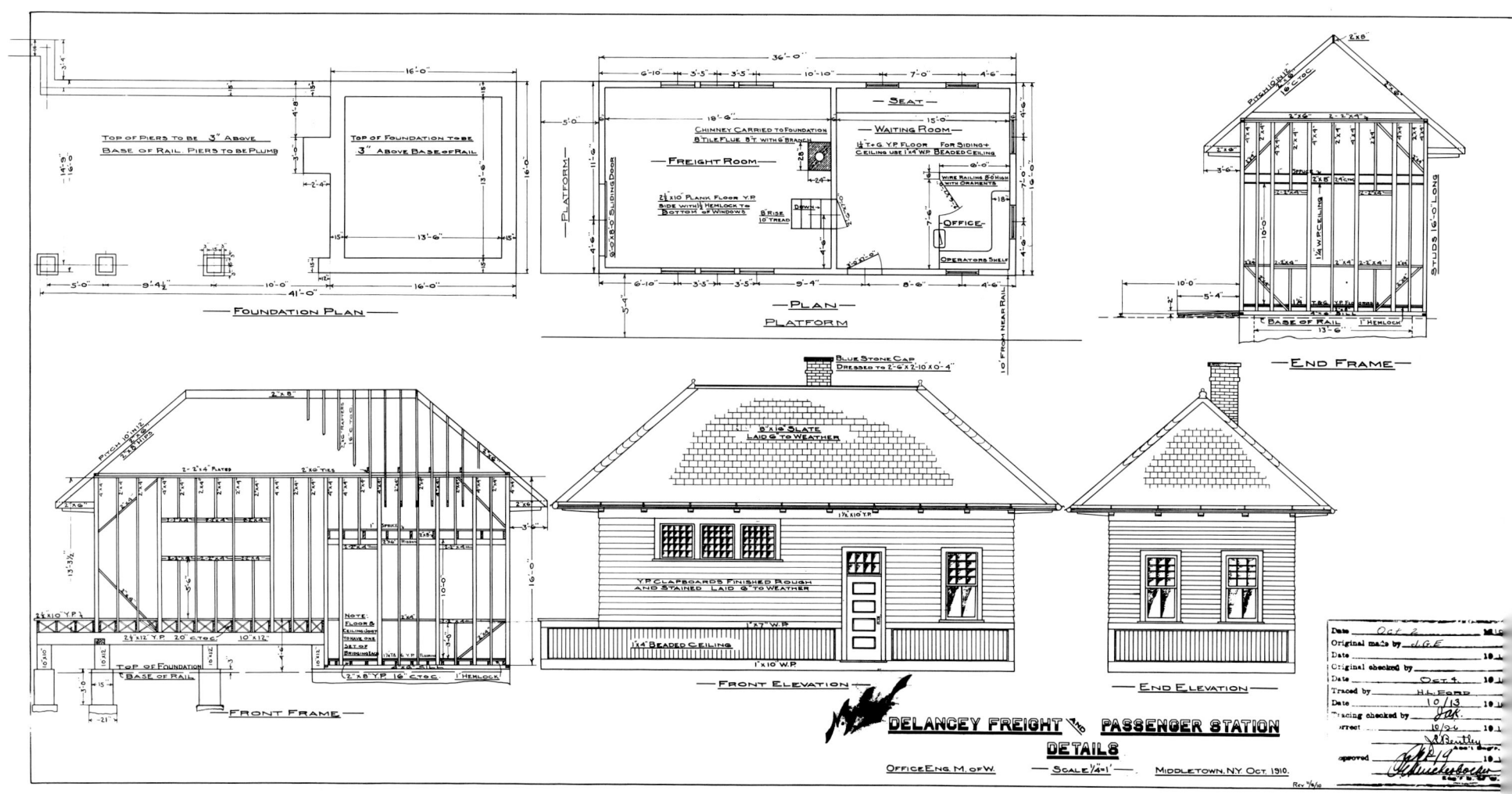

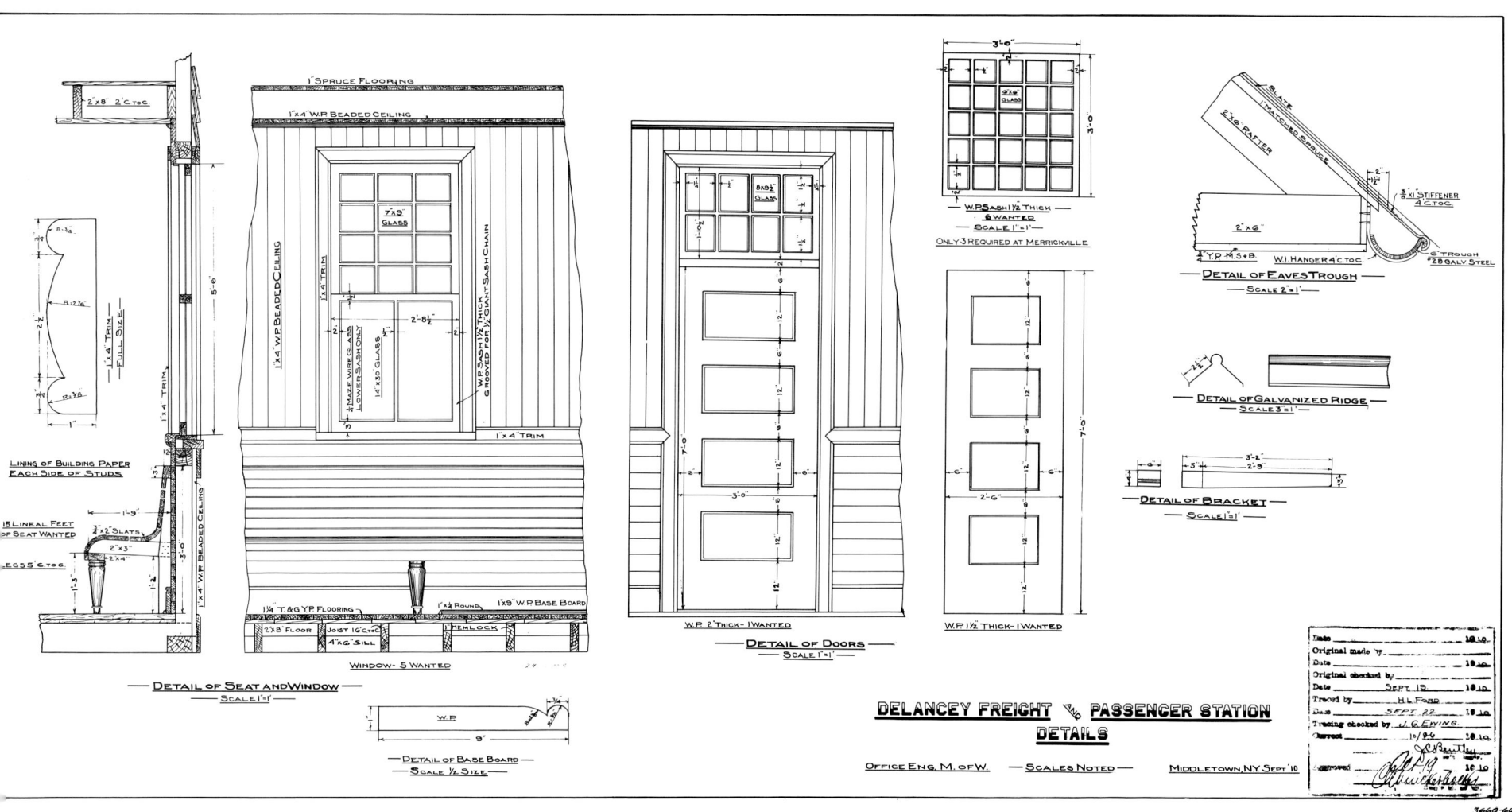

LEFT: A southbound mixed train passes through the village of Hamden in this turn-of-century scene. A camelback 4-4-0, the "jack of all trades" wheel arrangement for many years, was well-suited to the lighter rails and lower traffic densities of secondary lines. Many small merchandise shipments came to rural communities via the baggage car of such mixed trains, as contributor Arthur Mitchell tells us in this chapter. LAWRENCE GIFFORD COLLECTION.

BOTTOM LEFT: The Co-Operative Creamery and a factory at the north end of Hamden were both served by the same siding. The main track appears relatively level for a roadbed that was not ballasted and for ties that were not given proper drainage. Much smaller in physical size and operation that the nearby Borden's plant, the production of the Co-Operative Creamery did not fill a car but the combined output of such small operations provided the O&W with a sizable amount of business. BOTTOM RIGHT: As is evident here, many creameries had one or more additions built to handle increased business. TWO PHOTOGRAPHS: WILLIAM SCHRIVER COLLECTION.

RIGHT: Hamden was served by eight or more trains per day at the time of this photograph. The Hamden Inn is at left and was a short walk from the depot. Teamsters had to be wary of approaching trains since horses might panic at the sight or sound of a nearby steam engine. O&W SOCIETY COLLECTION.

LEFT: The Hamden Inn was a popular hostelry on the route between Walton and Delhi. It was a convenient meeting place and may have figured in matters concerning the planning and construction of the railroad. Front porch loungers had a clear view of the O&W's branch activities in the days when train punctuality was a subject of community concern. WILLIAM SCHRIVER COLLECTION.

ABOVE LEFT: Passenger trains were probably most appreciated during the mud-time of early spring. The thawing earth, melting snow and seasonal rain could make dirt roads such as these, a severe trial for animals, wagons and carriages. Rural self-sufficiency took such conditions into account, and residents realized that county, town or village road departments would eventually smooth the roads again. ABOVE RIGHT: At the Hamden station, around the turn of the century, what is probably an inbound carload of freight or package shipments will be checked against the agent's waybills before the consignees arrive. TWO PHOTOGRAPHS: WILLIAM SCHRIVER COLLECTION.

RIGHT: A half-century later this 1954 scene shows a now weather-beaten Hamden depot that may have been leased to a local business for storage purposes, thus bringing some small rental to the railroad. The track next to the station is gone and freight service on the branch has been greatly reduced. COURTESY OF JOE BUX AND DEPOT ATTIC.

ABOVE: Two views of the Borden's operation at Hamden show a few differences. Most notable is the change in function. In the left view the plant is labeled a "Bottle Milk Station" and in the right it is titled "Condensed Milk Company." Various economic and market demands had dairy companies building, buying or selling facilities through the years as well as revising the functions of plants. Only the front wall remains today and can be seen from Route 10 if one looks east while entering Hamden from the south. O&W SOCIETY COLLECTION.

RIGHT: In the historic tradition of rural service, a northbound train at Hamden has cars to carry milk, mail, baggage, express and passengers while mixed trains and local freights took care of the heavier business. Individual appointments and commercial shipments, the whole of the local economy was based upon the schedule of the railroad, and as Henry David Thoreau had earlier observed of the Fitchburg Railroad: "One well-conducted institution regulates a whole country." O&W SOCIETY COLLECTION.

A half-dozen or more freight cars lie on their sides in a field at Hamden. Damage to the track structure seems light and service was probably resumed in a day or two. The railroad's first efforts will be spent to reopen the line, and then the cars and freight will be salvaged. It appears that the train was southbound. Route 10 is at the left edge of the field. BOB WYER PHOTOGRAPH, WALTER RICH COLLECTION.

branch lines with low passenger volumes and small quantities of mail and express. No doubt each of the four motor cars that the railroad owned took turns working on the branch. They provided a segment of the traveling public with a few more years of train service than would otherwise have been the case. In May 1930, a bus service from Delhi to Sidney via Walton was making two round trips per day and the passenger trains were discontinued. Earlier attempts to substitute buses in 1924 were not successful because they could not meet road conditions and winter weather. For several years travelers had the option of riding the combine at the end of the mixed train that made two daily round trips with the usual exception of Sunday. The late Art Mitchell of Newburgh wrote the following account of a ride on the mixed. It is presented as he wrote it.

at Court House Square. There were numerous circuses, touring entertainers, and lecturers that played in Delhi and offered rural residents more cosmopolitan diversions.

At least three weekday round-trip passenger trains operated on the branch up to World War I. Two of them had through connections for New York City, and there was a time when at least one ran through to the City. After the war, passenger income from the branch was insufficient to operate more than a single passenger train. This was the Delhi Flyer, which departed early in the morning. The train and its opposite number, the Utica Flyer, were first put on in June 1886. Operating under three different numbers, the Flyer covered the 113-mile run to Utica in 4.5 hours. Anyone making a round trip had a few hours to spend in Utica before boarding again around 3:30 PM. The return trip got the passengers back to Delhi by 8:15 PM, where the equipment would remain overnight. Titling the trains *Flyers* may sound like an attempt at humor today, but the circuitous rail route was much faster than any other conveyance in those days.

In the mid-1920's self-propelled motor cars replaced the steam-powered *Flyers*. In company with many other railroads, the O&W was attracted by the reduced maintenance and operating costs of the motor cars. They were particularly well suited to

On a fine August morning in 1945, having come up the previous day via the main line, I had stayed overnight in Walton and with the intention of riding the Delhi train, I proceeded to the station.

I purchased a round-trip ticket; the agent gravely date-stamped it and with the same gravity informed me that the departure time shown on the timetable was abstract, as the train would leave only after completing switching operations. It was rarely that it left at 9:15 AM.

This gave me ample opportunity to observe the train which was chugging about in the discharge of its duties. The vintage wooden combine car which dignified the title *mixed*, was sidetracked during switching. It was tuscan red with open

TOP: A road came down from the present Route 10, out of sight at the left of the picture, passed a creamery, crossed the Delhi branch, and went over the West Branch through a covered bridge. Along with the railroad and the creamery, only traces of the bridge at Hawley remain. *WILLIAM SCHRIVER COLLECTION*.

BOTTOM: Yet another covered bridge crossed the West Branch of the Delaware River at Colchester. The O&W did not pass through the town of Colchester but did have a station, four miles north of Walton, which carried the name. The scene at right was taken in the vicinity of that station. The town of Colchester, including the village of Downsville, was served by the Delaware & Northern. *O&W SOCIETY COLLECTION*.

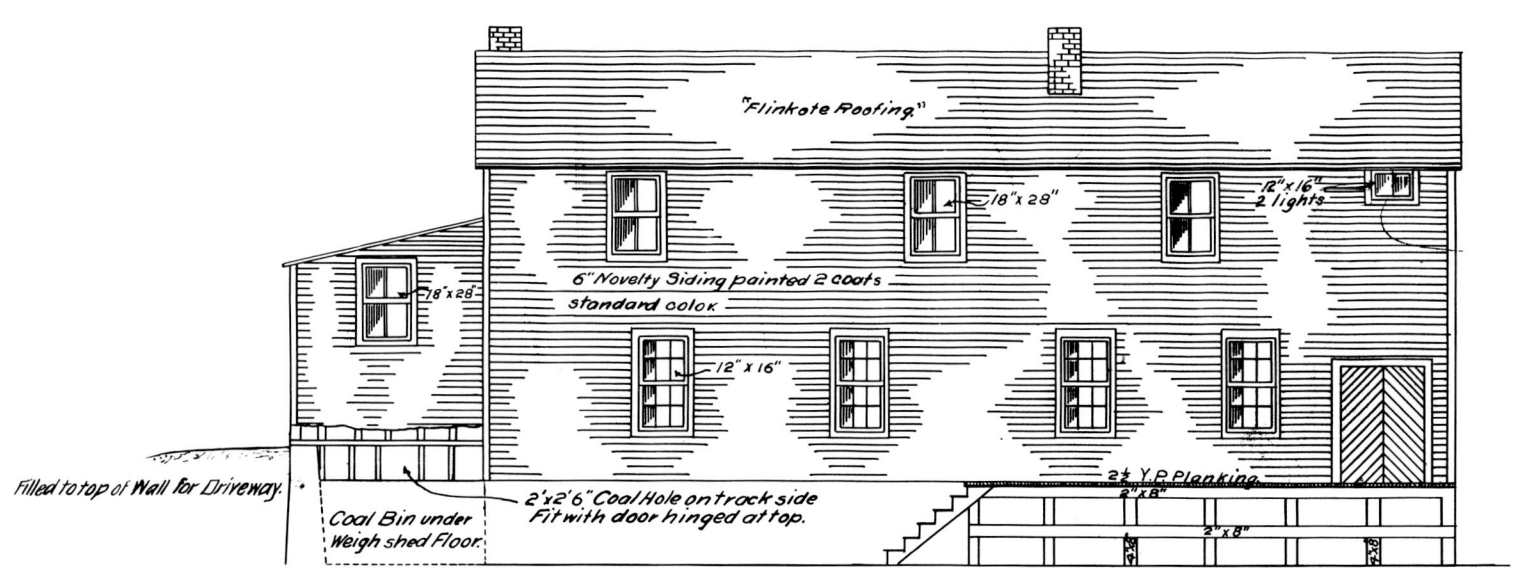

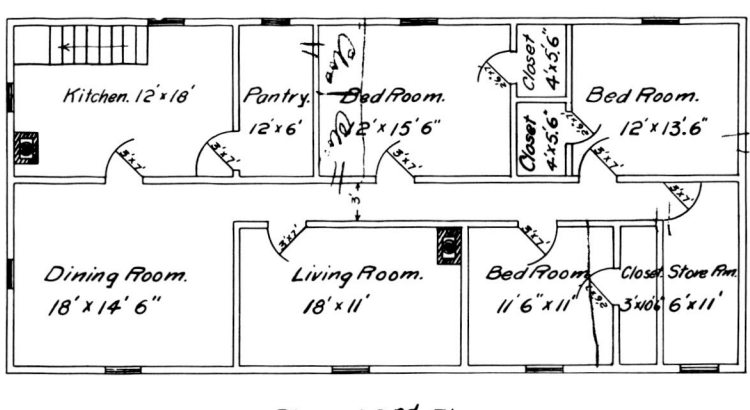

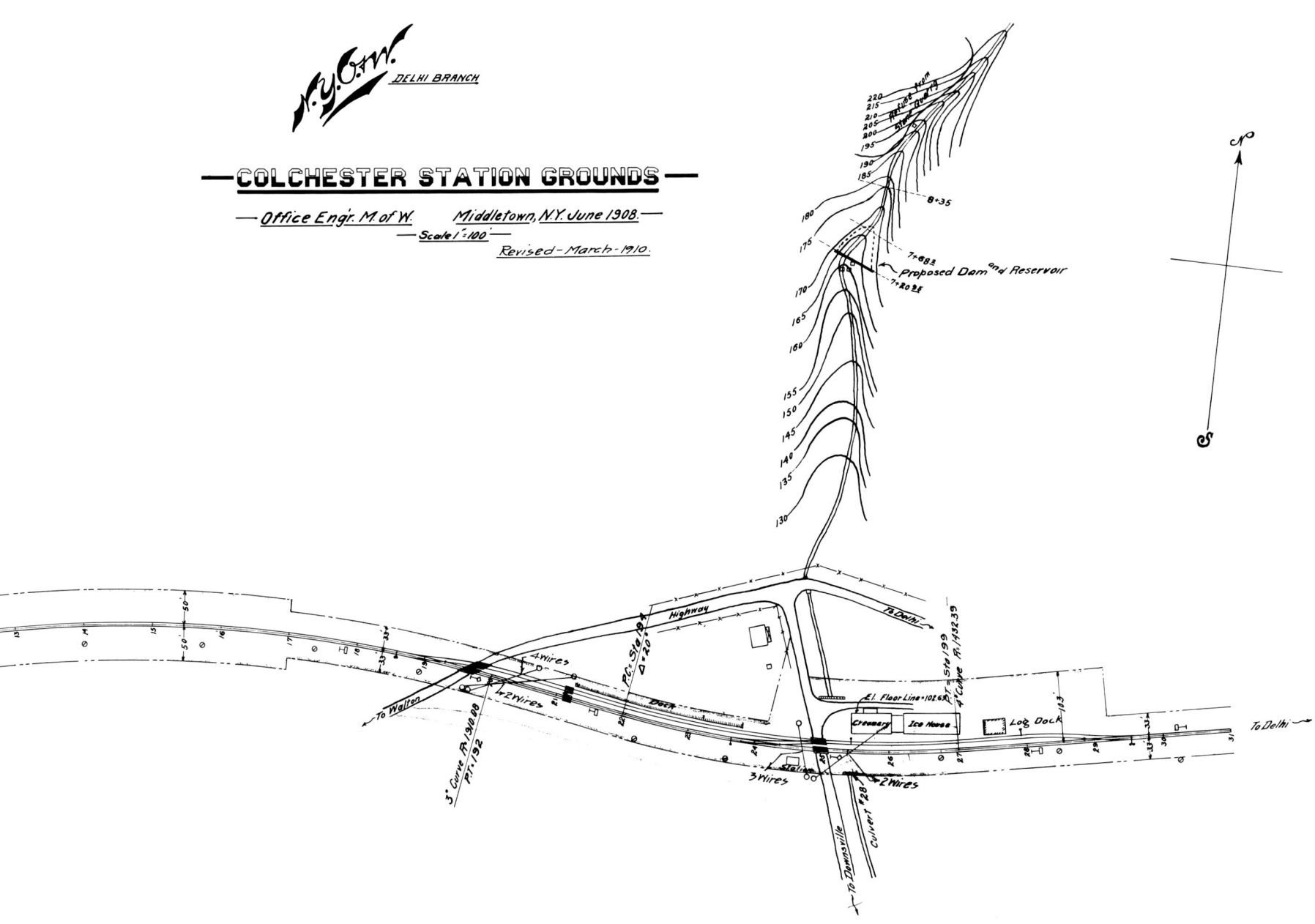

ABOVE: *A southbound train is just north of Walton in the general area of Colchester in this view taken from the Bear Spring Mountain.* JOE BUX COLLECTION. BELOW: *The Hawley Mill was along the present Route 10 not far above Walton. A dugway from the West Branch led water to the mill to provide power for its woodworking functions. This view looks south with the railroad right-of-way to the immediate right.* WALTON HISTORICAL SOCIETY COLLECTION. COURTESY OF LAWRENCE GIFFORD.

platforms, a joy to behold and I now found myself more anxious than ever to get aboard.

At last the train was made up ready to start its leisurely peregrination to Delhi. Here let me inject a word about the engine, it was a single-cab 2-8-0 of the 300 series, class W.

A railroad man in faded denims now approached me and identified himself as conductor at the same time rightly assuming me to be a passenger.

'I am going back to the coach now,' he stated. 'Don't try to jump on as I stop the train right here at the station.' I wouldn't have minded walking past the 7 or 8 freight cars to the coach but apparently he wanted to accord me complete service.

Once aboard I found the half-section devoted to passengers to consist of worn black leather seats reminding me of the mohair upholstery of the past, when as a child I encountered the slippery surface on old-timer parlor furniture. Oil lamps swung from the clerestoried ceiling and small oil lamps reposed in wall brackets in a couple of strategic locations. A pot-bellied stove stood in a corner. The crew had placed coffee cans about as ash trays and incidentally the car was clean. I found that the car was at once caboose and coach.

The conductor told me I was free to walk about but for mercy's sake don't fall out, hang on to the overhead grab rail over the side door of the baggage half. In this last, the baggage was auto tires, bundles of brooms, packages and other LCL items.

I watched the steepled station recede from the rear platform and shortly we traversed a low wooden causeway over a swampy meadow. The conductor dubbed it "the Jacob's ladder."

Next we passed the small Bridge Street station for Walton boasted two, this one very small.

Then the train chugged on along the placid Delaware in this area it being the West Branch and giving no hint of the great stream which it becomes at Philadelphia and Camden.

Presently we arrived at Colchester where we ground to a halt to dispense LCL freight. Then on to Hamden. Here as I remember the tracks ran perilously close to dooryards and front porches of the residents of the village and the train certainly furnished a spectacle to the otherwise somnolent scene. Here again freight was discharged.

Continuing to Delancy and Frasers proved very similar. Both places as well as those above had stations.

Up to this point I have failed to include the mention of many sights and sounds. The following may atone. Even small engines sound big and the whistles of ours had a mournful tone and was blown frequently for the many dirt-road crossings, the rumble of the cars ahead, the clicking of the rail joints, the hundred and one creaks and squeaks of the body of the coach, all served to create an awareness of our big-little giant ahead.

At one point, somewhere near Delhi, the conductor called my attention to huge mounds over near the river. They were in a farmer's field, almost like small hills. They were grass-grown and he told me they were thought to be Indian chiefs' graves. Whether they are or not, they give rise to thoughts of the pyramids or other ostentatious reminders of the passing of the great.

Just outside Delhi the train braked to a halt. The conductor deprecatingly asked me if I would mind riding the steps of the engine.

'You see,' he averred, 'unless we have lady passengers and you are the sole rider, we generally cut off the coach out here. It interferes with switching.' Needless to say, I agreed and he handed me some waste.

We headed for the engine and mounted the pilot footboard. When we started up, the feeling of the surge of power was exhilarating. A glance upward at the smoke box and the stack belching smoke, gave the impression that the engine reached the very sky. We approached some box cars on a siding to push them to Delhi. Riding the step and in such close contact with the car I felt that we were going to be crushed. He smiled and yelled above the thunder of the behemoth. 'Just hang on, and you can't get hurt.' As the couplers crashed together I was thankful for their presence.

In Delhi proper I stepped down wiping my hands partially free of grime with the waste he had provided and proceeded with him to the freight station. I noted with a wrench of the heart that the little brick station was gone. I had seen it in the 30's when I had been to Delhi by auto to visit relatives.

The agent assured me the freight station served just as well, as passengers were not frequent enough to merit another more pretentious building.

I wandered over to the main street to find a lunch room with the admonishment of my mentor,

ABOVE: We are looking south as a camelback 4-4-0 with a Delhi-bound train slows for a stop at the plank platform that was part of a trestle at the Bridge Street station. O&W COLLECTION. BOTTOM LEFT: The station at Bridge St., was sometimes referred to as "the city station," and the crowd on the platform may surprise those who question how much use the small station received. WILLIAM SCHRIVER COLLECTION. LOWER RIGHT: We are standing on Bridge St. and looking north at the depot as a southbound train arrives. Bear Spring Mountian rises behind the train. BRUCE TRACY COLLECTION.

ABOVE: The earlier Bridge St. Station, the West Branch of the Delaware, and an elevated section of the Delhi branch are clearly visible from the state armory tower. Walton's business district was one block west of the track in this view. The O&W's main line to the north went up the left side of the valley that fades into the distance. WILLIAM SCHRIVER COLLECTION.

the conductor, not to go too far; while they would not leave without me, he related, 'It would be best to be on hand when switching was complete.'

After lunch at a quaint restaurant, and receiving many quizzical tho friendly glances from the good residents, as I was a strange face, I strolled back to the freight station. Here the locomotive was still chuffing about making the return train. The agent showed me a 1917 timetable of which he was very proud, and recounted many bits of past O&W history and anecdotes for obviously he was long an employee.

The return to Walton varied in one respect as the engine hauled the train with the tender forward. I would have thought it could have been turned on a wye as the Delhi yard was sizable, but I maintained a studied disregard and appeared not to notice when, as at Walton, the coach was stopped in its proper end position at the platform.

Again, we stopped at each station, taking on crates of eggs, etc.

Just before we reached Walton, the conductor yawned and told me the train was out of Cadosia at 3:00 AM and serviced stations on the main line as far as Walton. It was about 2:00 PM as he spoke. He further stated that it was a passenger train only between Walton and Delhi and back.

As I climbed down at Walton I remarked that he would be glad to be back at Cadosia. He responded with, 'You can say that again.'

I waited on the platform a little while and noticed they were turning the engine on the Walton wye so as to run pilot first to Cadosia. After the train left I wended my way back to the hotel, well pleased with my experience. [The reader is directed to Addendum E for commentary on Mr. Mitchell's trip.]

In 1946 the Delhi mixed was numbered 801-802 and still originated at Cadosia, with an early afternoon arrival in Delhi. Although the combine was put on at Cadosia, it was only for the use of the crew until Walton. Passengers could then ride in the car between the latter point and Delhi as Mr. Mitchell did. A W-class 2-8-0 or an occasional U-class camelback 2-6-0 was the most frequently assigned power, with a half-dozen or so freight cars, a milk car, and the wooden combine attached. Other than the milk, there was little originating traffic on the branch. Feed, coal, lumber, ashes, fuel oil, petroleum products, groceries, farm supplies, retail goods, and an occasional car of new autos or farm machinery made up the bulk of the inbound business. Much of the coal was consigned to creameries and to the state college.

In the mid-1940's, milk cars from the Boston & Maine, New York Central, and Delaware & Hudson were used on the branch for can loading. The war had upset the usual traffic patterns and milk markets, and the O&W had very few of its own milk cars in condition for interchange service. Some milk from the Delhi area was going to New England for processing. The cans must have been heavily iced to keep the milk fresh for the long trip.

The O&W's first diesels were a group of five General Electric switchers which were purchased late in 1941 and early 1942 and assigned primarily to Northern Division locations. Later they handled some of the branch runs. The Delhi line was basically *a loads in and empties out* type of traffic with an upgrade pull against the loaded run. The business was still great enough to be beyond the 380-h.p. of a GE unit, so a steam engine remained in charge of this run. However, at least one O&W employee recalls hearing that a GE unit once made the trip.

General Motors FT road diesels came to the O&W in 1945 to work main line assignments. Their length precluded use on the Delhi branch, and much of their 2700-h.p. would not have been needed. F3 diesels,

A southbound Delhi branch train pounds over the timber trestle and West Brook before rounding the curve that will bring it onto the main line. WILLIAM SCHRIVER COLLECTION.

Cows graze on the flats west of the Delhi branch trestle and behind the Munn Piano Co. The Smith and St. John feed mill is to the extreme right. Not surprisingly, Walton's small industrial district developed along the O&W's main line and Delhi branch. WILLIAM SCHRIVER COLLECTION.

also from General Motors, came in 1948. The 501 and 502 made some of their earliest trips on the Delhi branch. Along with a third unit, the 503, they were specially equipped with footboards on both the front and the rear. This gave them some advantage for branch line and passenger service where trainmen frequently had to ride the footboards during switching and *running around* the train moves. These diesels were rated at 1500-h.p. per unit, and could be turned on the table at the end of the branch for the return trip to Walton and Cadosia.

The F3's were an interim replacement for steam in the spring of 1948 when they bumped the 321, a 2-8-0 that was the last steam locomotive on the Delhi branch. In the summer of 1948, 1000-h.p. NW2 switchers arrived from General Motors. The ninth unit out of the 21-unit switcher order was specifically marked for the Delhi run. The NW2 was a more versatile and practical unit for such work since it did not have to be turned at the end of the run and the enginemen had greater visibility to perform the switching tasks.

Since 1937 the railroad had been in bankruptcy and efforts were made on a number of fronts to hold the company together. Meetings had been held in Delhi, Walton, Sidney and other O&W communities to explain the railroad's problems, seek financial relief and develop grass-roots support. Although outright abandonment of both the Delhi and Monticello branches had been considered, the company seemed to stick to an *all or none* philosophy in maintaining service on all lines. R. E. Wright, a company official, came up from Middletown to speak to the Delhi Kiwanis Club. He reminded them of the 1865 organizational meeting held in their community and of the continued need for local support if the branch and the railroad itself were to continue. Perhaps his efforts were responsible in part for the building of a new G.L.F. feed sales business established in 1941.

The May, 1942, floods that were highly destructive to the Scranton Division also did some damage to the branch in Delaware County. Repairs were made, since the war-imposed restrictions on highway transportation had precluded any attempt to abandon service on the branch to Delhi. But there was also some promise of better times. The Delaware County Farmers' Cooperative planned a new $500,000 dairy processing facility in 1945, and a few years later the Dairymen's League remodeled and expanded the Merridale Dairies Plant which it had purchased earlier. It is not unlikely that exertions such as these extended the life of the railroad for a decade or more. Ultimately, though, all the promotion, economies, and deferments could not tip the scale or even make it balance against factors over which the company had little, if any, control. The 1948 main line passenger service cutback to Roscoe left the Delhi mixed train without a train connection, and it was dropped during the winter of 1948-1949.

During the 1950's, local and state-level politicians drove to Albany or flew to Washington in final attempts to keep operations going. In 1957 the decision came down to the wire, and the railroad lost. A small newspaper item summed up the 20 years of effort: "Ebenezer Middlemast, who saw the first train arrive in Delhi 85 years ago, Howard Currie and H. Glen Harper rode from Delhi to Walton in the caboose of the last train on March 29th."

THIS PAGE: A lengthy portion of the Delhi branch within the village of Walton rested on trestle-work to keep it out of the soft, marshy, low ground along the West Branch. Wooden piles were replaced by concrete piers which were later buried by fill material. Each change reduced the maintenance costs and insured more reliable future operation. These views of bridge 1 on the branch were made during a 1912 reconstruction. JOHN MOFFAT COLLECTION.

Walton's second main line station, of brick and concrete construction, was possibly the most elegant on the O&W.
JOHN PICKETT PHOTOGRAPH.

Chapter 7: Walton

In 1931 there were forty-five people in Walton employed by the O&W with a monthly payroll of five thousand dollars. In spite of the 'depression' the O&W was paying its way, being one of the few railroads doing so then.

Frank and Helen Lane, *Walton Yesteryears* (Walton: Reporter Co., Inc., n.d) 150

Perhaps more than any other community on the New York & Oswego Midland main line, Walton faced restrictions upon its commercial and industrial development because of geography. The village sits on a flat, where streams known as the East, West, and Third Brooks flow into the West Branch of the Delaware River. Five rugged hills surround the village: Bear Spring Mountain, Dunk Hill, Pine Hill, Pines Brook Hill, and a 2036-foot high ridge along which the NY&OM builders cut a right-of-way as they came in from the north. Only the West Branch offered a way in or out of the hills, and that was initially limited to hearty pioneers coming down a rugged river path from the north and the log rafts of early lumbermen heading south. Later, after rough roads and a community were laid out, wagons and teams leaving town immediately or eventually faced long arduous upgrade trips in any direction as well as the difficulties of the season. These factors limited the community's ability to import and export raw materials and manufactured goods in quantity, and so restricted Walton to a local economy.

Walton historians Frank and Helen Lane speak of their community as progressing through three economic periods: lumbering, sheep raising, and dairying. The streams made the first two possible by providing transportation for logs and then power for lumber and woolen mills. The railroad was the catalyst for the third. It brought western grain to New York State in quantity for dairy cattle feed and provided quick transportation to city markets for farm production. Essentially, it brought the area from a level of comfortable subsistence farming and a local economy into the national commerce.

Talk of a railroad through the Walton area went back to 1853 when a Newburgh-to-Syracuse route was proposed. Three decades later, the West Shore route would link those cities, but not via Walton. The town would get its railroad a little sooner. There were hundreds of *paper railroads* in those days with communities linking themselves together with lines on maps of questionable accuracy. Walton may have figured in a number of these schemes as well, but eventually the New York & Oswego Midland approached from the west. The NY&OM had considered two routes between Sidney and Roscoe. One was via Delhi and was discussed in the last chapter, and the other was through Walton. Both routes presented great geographic obstacles, but the Walton route was less expensive. Consequently the Sidney-to-Walton contract was let on September 10, 1869. The construction firm of Jarvis Lord from Rochester, N.Y., dug out the 21-mile right-of-way and also put up the masonry. The telegraph line was finished for the whole length of the railroad in May, 1872, and progress on individual sections could now be reported to all on-line communities. In the next month, the 147 miles of track from Oswego to Walton were put in, and the line to Delhi was completed.

The first Midland train came in from the north, and the Walton *Chronicle* of December 28, 1871, reported the following:

> Last Thursday at five P.M., the first locomotive entered this village via the Midland railroad. Engine No. 2, the Madison, was the first to enter, which was soon followed by No. 17, the Walton,

Engine 34, the NY&OM's "Hackensack," heads northward from Walton in the early days of the O&W. This engine eventually went to the D&H. COURTESY OF JOE BUX AND DEPOT ATTIC.

named in honor of our town.

The opening excursion of the Midland from Walton to Norwich was the headline appearing in the January 29th issue of the paper.

The 25th of January 1872, will long be remembered by the citizens of Walton as the commencement of a new era in its history. The time which had long been prophesied, but which many of the incredulous thought would end in prophecy, has arrived. Last Thursday morning, at half past seven o'clock, the five beautiful passenger coaches which had been furnished the citizens of Walton, were backed up to the river bridge, and in a very short time every seat was occupied; many had to stand up. At eight o'clock, the hour set to start, the gentlemanly conductor, J. K. Walker, cried, 'All aboard,' and P.M. Crane, the trusty and careful engineer, who has done his share of the pioneer work from Sidney to Walton, pulled the throttle of his engine, 'The Volney', No. 26, and the first passenger train from Walton moved slowly away while the band played *The Midland Grand March*, arranged expressly for the occasion by Professor E. Coe. Hundreds stood at the starting point to see us off, and waved us a safe trip, with their handkerchiefs, as we swept gracefully around the western side of our village, and then we go on through the Shepard and Thompson cuts where we bid a brief adieu to our quiet homes in the little valley of the Delaware.

The return train left Norwich at four that afternoon. The cost was $1.45 for the round trip.

The Walton-to-Liberty section was not completed until mid-1873, with the first through train making its run in August of that year. Unfortunately, that year also marked the beginning of a financial panic that would later cause the railroad serious problems.

When the track work was completed, Walton had three rail routes out of the village, and all of them were essentially uphill. However, the southbound run dropped down the river grade for a few miles before entering the 1.53 percent grade that led to Apex.

With the railroad came many commercial opportunities. The Crawford Brothers entered the wholesale feed business and enlarged their facilities several times. They shipped carloads of dairy and poultry feed, not only locally, but throughout the northeast. Special rail transportation rates under the heading "milling in transit" allowed this grain to be processed into animal feed and then continue on to a final destination. Many milling companies used these rates to the benefit of local tax and employment rolls. Crawfords' four-story structure housed the milling, mixing, and bagging machinery until it was destroyed by a spectacular fire in 1956.

Camp Milling, another feed company, brought thousands of cars of grain into Walton each year and generally performed the same operations and provided the same services. Lee Camp, born in New Berlin, operated a feed dealership there and expanded into Walton when he purchased the Kilpatrick Feed Mill in 1914. Camp Milling still employed as many as 40 people in Walton when the O&W ceased operations in 1957. It also had retail facilities in a number of other communities served by the O&W. The loss of rail service brought an end to its wholesale division in Walton. (Please see Addendum D for detailed information on the feed milling business.)

James Munn founded the Munn Piano Company. Using local maple lumber, his plant produced the "Old Delaware Beauty" piano. He employed the Walton Foundry to make the cast-iron frame. This business reached its height in 1905 and then dropped

RIGHT: The predecessor of Walton's beautiful masonry station of more recent memory was this building of board and batten construction. The continued growth of the railroad's operations required larger facilities from which business could be transacted and train movements overseen. The engine to the left of the station is on the north leg of the wye that led to the Delhi branch. O&W SOCIETY COLLECTION.

BELOW: This 1880 view of Walton looks north toward the passenger station and shows how small the yard was in the year that the O&W emerged out of the old Midland. Link-and-pin couplers were still in use and many of the boxcars bear New York, Lake Erie & Western reporting marks. A boardwalk crossing the Delhi branch is protected by a diamond-shaped crossing sign in the background. O&W SOCIETY COLLECTION.

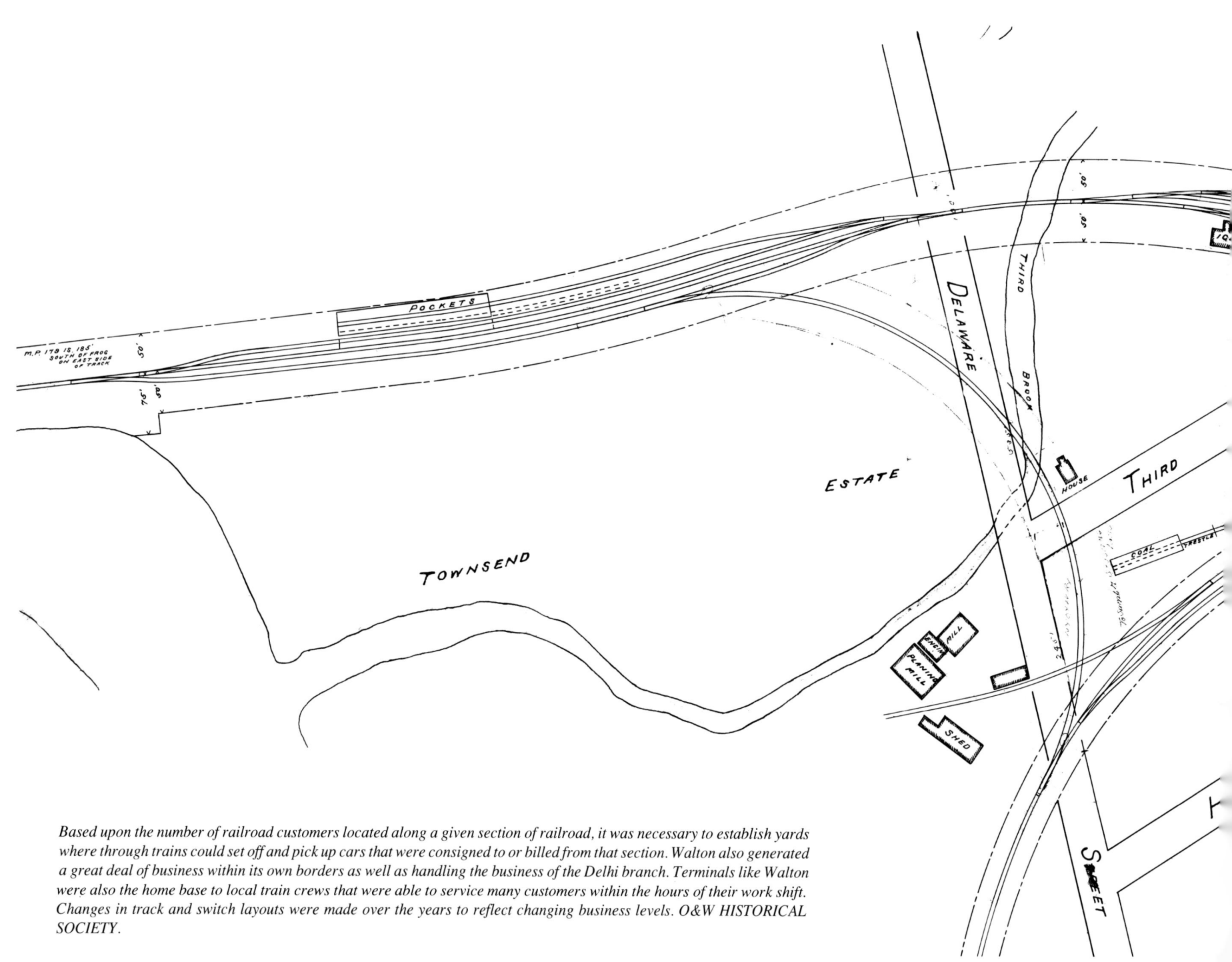

Based upon the number of railroad customers located along a given section of railroad, it was necessary to establish yards where through trains could set off and pick up cars that were consigned to or billed from that section. Walton also generated a great deal of business within its own borders as well as handling the business of the Delhi branch. Terminals like Walton were also the home base to local train crews that were able to service many customers within the hours of their work shift. Changes in track and switch layouts were made over the years to reflect changing business levels. O&W HISTORICAL SOCIETY.

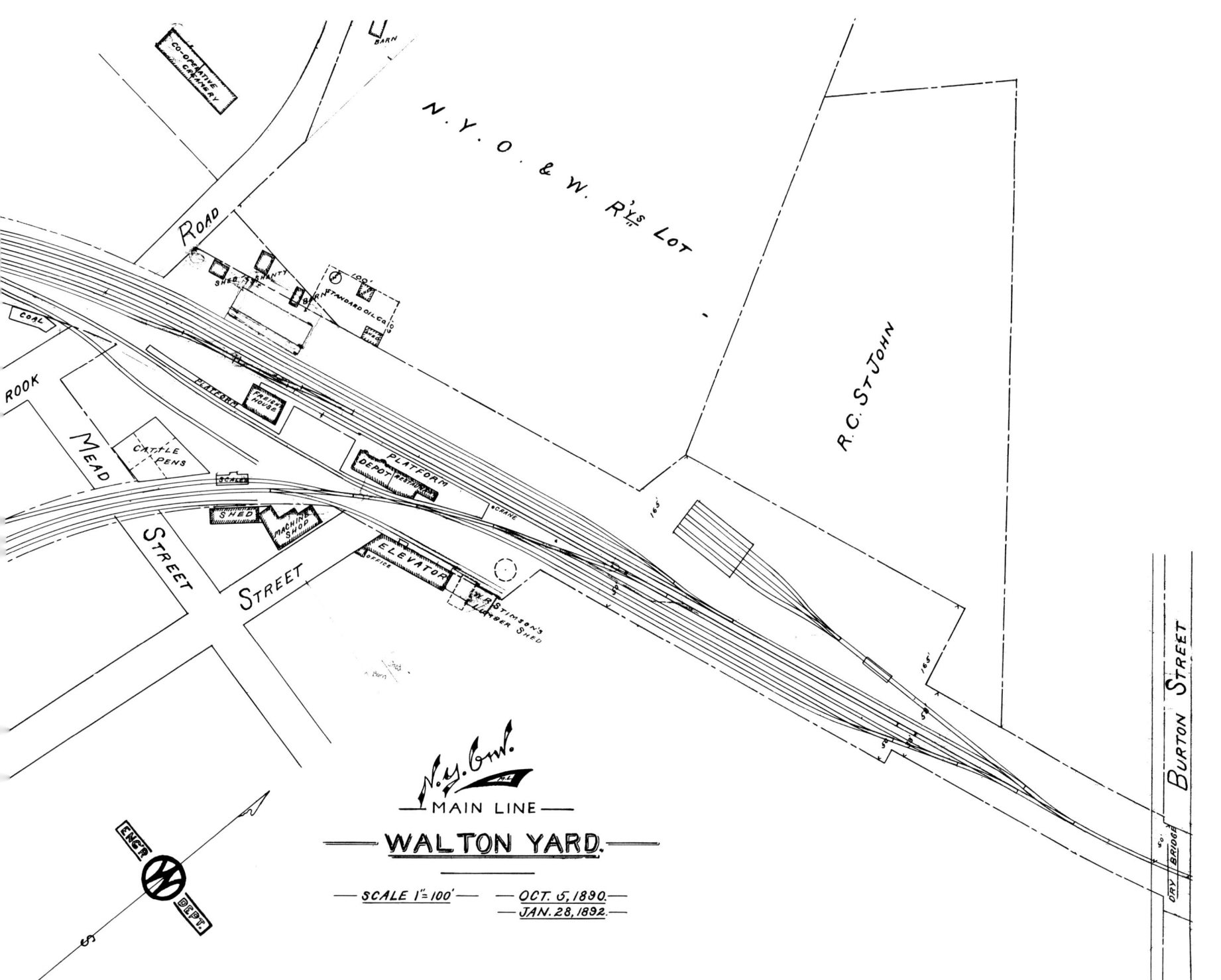

The large Walton coal trestle, located south of the depot, was used to refuel locomotives and possibly to transfer loads between hopper cars. The chutes at the trestle's far end could quickly dump several tons of coal into a tender. The hinged ramp at mid-trestle was not as simple to use. Inside the structure, coal was dumped from railroad cars into small four-wheel hoppers similar to those used in coal mines. These cars moved on a track directly below railroad cars and which led to a turntable behind the hinged ramp. The table was turned 90 degrees and the small hopper was pushed out on the ramp to dump its load into the tender or car below. Laborers worked in the dusty, dark interior using muscle power and shovels to transfer the coal. The gloomy recesses must have provided hours of fascination for local children. TWO TOP PHOTOGRAPHS: JOHN MOFFAT COLLECTION. RIGHT: O&W SOCIETY COLLECTION.

off as new competitors entered the market.

The Julius Kayser Co. came to Walton in 1919 after labor problems in Sidney and took over the former Munn Piano building. Kayser specialized in the weaving of silk and, later, rayon. In 1951, the company moved to the South. The Walton Wood and Metal Co., often known as the Walton Novelty Works, manufactured sleds, toys, and baby carriages. This firm was succeeded by the S. J. Baily and Son Woodworking Co., which produced unpainted furniture.

About 1900, Anglo-Swiss Condensed Milk Co. established a plant in Walton. Anglo-Swiss had several facilities along the O&W, and they all came under Borden's ownership at a later date. Borden's original location in Walton was within the commercial triangle formed by the wye where the Delhi branch headed north. They later built a much larger facility across the yard from the station. This was eventually sold to Sheffield Farms. The present Del-Met manufacturing company is now located in the building. After the Dairymen's League was organized, it established a Walton creamery in Borden's original building.

Breakstone dairy products was started by two brothers who took over a small, locally owned farmers' creamery. Breakstone is now part of Kraft Inc., a large food company, and the Walton plant is still active although it no longer ships fluid milk. Walton Milk and Cream was another dairy product producer in the community.

Webster's Bakery shipped locally baked goods via the O&W to other Delaware County communities. Rural communities north and south of Walton looked forward to the arrival of passenger trains that brought bread and cakes still warm from the oven. A bakery owned by Otto Hoos may also have used the railroad. Other businesses that depended upon rail service at one time or another were the Walton Foundry, Standard Oil, Vanakin Lumber, Grange League Federation (GLF), Tweedie Construction Co., and the New York State Highway Department.

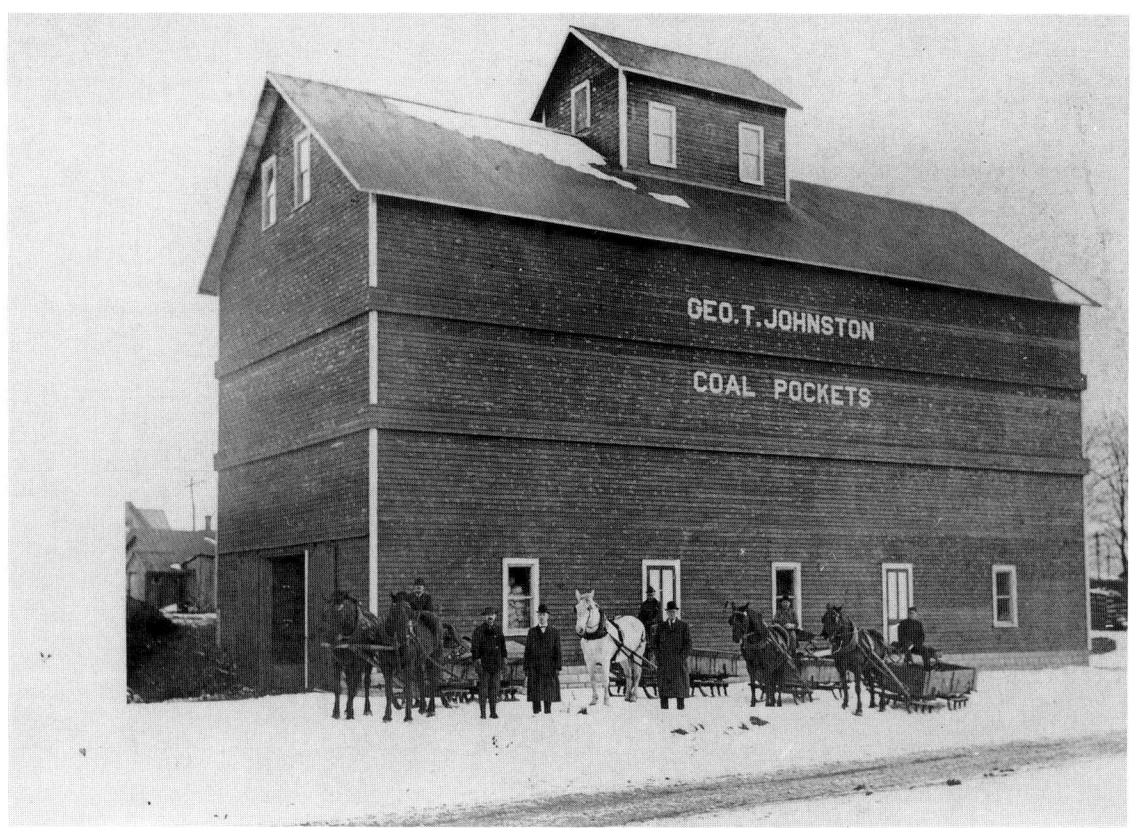

Many of these businesses operated under one or more names as they were sold and resold through the years.

The railroad's large wye not only provided flexible access to the Delhi branch, but made it easy to turn locomotives, freight cars, and entire passenger trains. This latter ability was useful for the runs that terminated at Walton. The village had at least three different passenger stations. The original board-and-batten structure on the main line was replaced by a larger structure of brick and concrete in 1904. It was a substantial, commodious building of which the community was proud. It originally included a restaurant. Few communities on the NYO&W re-

Coal, with its several advantages over wood, became the home heating fuel of choice in cities and villages and, with few exceptions, would not have been available in most communities without the railroads. Most villages had more than one retail outlet and Johnston's was one of several in Walton. WILLIAM SCHRIVER COLLECTION.

ABOVE: The sign on the first boxcar says that the string of cars is the major part of a seven-car shipment of 10,000 sleds going to one customer. The sleds were made by the Walton Toy Company. The photograph was dated November 24, 1926, which provided enough time for the sleds to reach markets for Christmas sales. The ample hardwood resources of the region made novelty and toy companies possible. WALTER RICH COLLECTION. LEFT AND BELOW: The Walton Wood & Metal Co., housed in a complex of wooden and concrete block buildings near the O&W, is either the predecessor or the same company as the Walton Toy Co. TWO PHOTOGRAPHS: WILLIAM SCHRIVER COLLECTION.

This wooden building was acquired by Borden's in 1901 and converted into a creamery. It was used until a larger plant was erected in 1911. This building was destroyed by fire in 1915 and the site was eventually acquired by the Dairymen's League, which built a new creamery in 1925. AUTHOR'S COLLECTION.

Borden's second plant at Walton took this imposing form. The facility was conveniently located next to the O&W yard. It was sold to Nestle's during World War I, closed during the Depression period, and was later purchased and operated by Sheffield Farms. It is now occupied by Del-Met, a manufacturer of automobile parts and accessories. LAWRENCE GIFFORD COLLECTION.

THIS PAGE: Steam locomotive aficionados seldom considered camelbacks to be handsome engines. Unique and utilitarian might be better descriptions of the design that found such wide acceptance on the O&W. The 165 and little friend are seen at Walton in 1902, while engines 135 and 214 visited in the mid-teens. COURTESY OF JOE BUX AND DEPOT ATTIC. Engine No. 2 was in town during the same period. CHARLES A. BROWN COLLECTION. OPPOSITE PAGE: The 275 with its relaxed engineer was photographed in 1932. J. R. QUINN.

ABOVE: Engine 251 is "popping off" with a roar of steam. The fireman has achieved maximum boiler pressure which will be helpful in climbing the southbound grade to Apex. However this release of excess pressure through the safety valve was wasteful of both coal and water and could bring a reprimand from any company official who might be about. It took skill and practice to keep the pressure just below the blow-off point. COURTESY OF JOE BUX AND DEPOT ATTIC.

LEFT: Train 9, the northbound milk, is setting off empty cars at the north end of the yard on January 15, 1933. The consist shows a mix of 1000-series cars and two taller cars that may well belong to the recently converted 1200-series. COURTESY OF JOE BUX AND DEPOT ATTIC.

At the north end of the yard, all tracks converged into the main track to enter a cut, pass under the Burton St. bridge and begin the climb to Northfield Tunnel. Engines for the Delhi branch, yard and helper service, were maintained in the shed at the right. Southbound engineers on locomotives descending into Walton had to keep their trains under careful control in the event they found other crews working on or near the main line in this vicinity. WALTER RICH COLLECTION.

STATION AT WALTON N.Y. FOR ONTARIO & WESTERN R.R.
JACKSON ROSENCRANS & CANFIELD ARCHITECTS 106 FIFTH AVE NEW YORK

ABOVE: An architect's drawing of the new Walton station showed a pleasing blend of European influences with perhaps a leaning toward the Bavarian style found in southern Germany and eastern Europe. The corners displayed handsome brick quoins, and a Gothic clock tower was capped by a finial. Some of the details were also found on several smaller stations the railroad had erected earlier. This included the hipped roof and three high windows in the end structures. COURTESY OF JOE BUX AND DEPOT ATTIC.

BELOW LEFT: The engineer of the often photographed 245 leans way out to watch the signals of the car inspectors as he couples onto a southbound train at Walton in 1938. Baggage-mail car 168 is equipped with a mail bag hook to make pick-ups on the fly. BELOW RIGHT: A well-groomed E-class 4-6-0 has a light train for the south on a spring day in 1941. The conductor has his watch in hand and will give two short pulls on the communicating whistle at the proper moment. TWO PHOTOGRAPHS: COURTESY OF JOE BUX AND DEPOT ATTIC.

BELOW: A passenger platform that serves three tracks attests to the operating flexibility required at the Walton terminal of the O&W in 1915. The train order board is out in both directions and it would have been unusual in this busy period for any train to pass through Walton without receiving an order. RUSTY RECORDON COLLECTION. LEFT: U-class engine 242 and what seems to be a W-class 2-8-0 wait at Walton before picking up their train and rolling south. The empty cab of the 242 suggests that the engines are not moving. Through freights often stopped at Walton to refill the locomotive tenders with water and coal and to have the fire-cleaner shake and trim the bed of glowing coals for better steam production. In the meantime, engine crews could pick up food and messages at the station. J. R. QUINN PHOTOGRAPH.

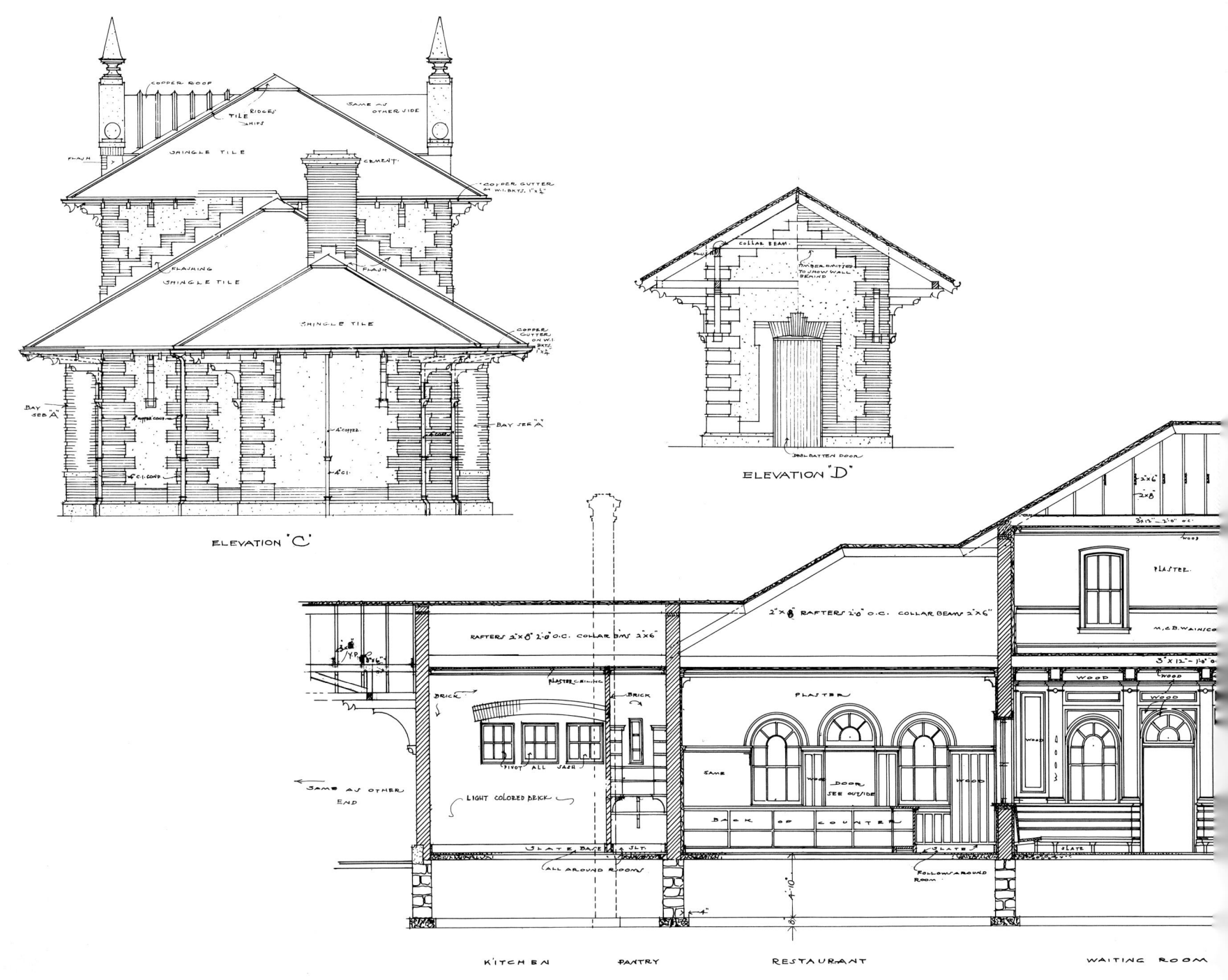

Walton station was one of the largest and finest on the railroad. It housed a number of railroad functions in an elegant style. It is unfortunate that an adaptive second use for the building could not be found. *O&W SOCIETY COLLECTION.*

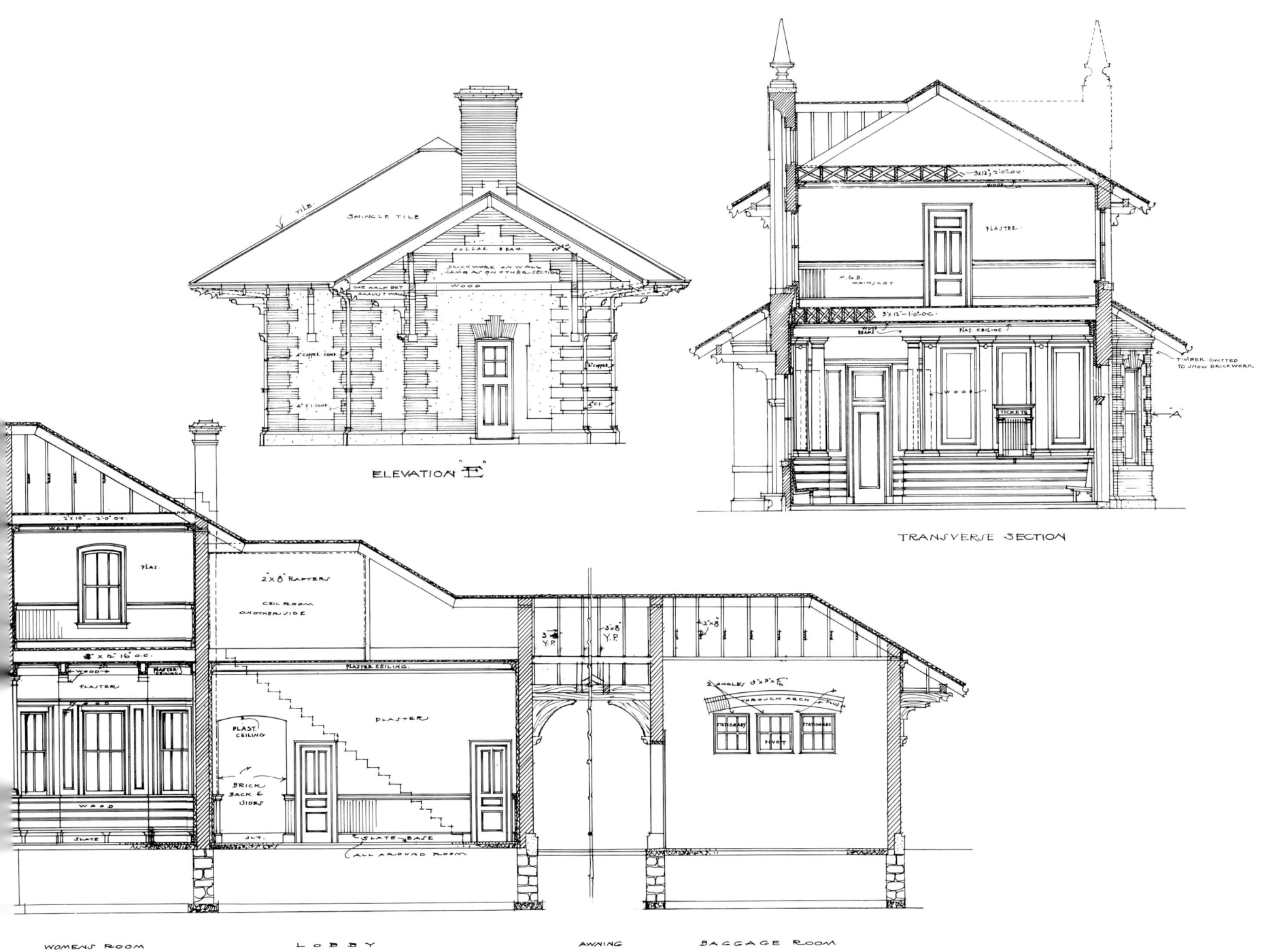

ABOVE: Those concerned with the aesthetics of O&W steam locomotives credit the class Y 4-8-2's as one of the most graceful designs on the railroad's roster. Here is the 410 with the original small tender with which they were equipped. Later, most of the class were re-equipped with larger tenders from the X class 2-10-2's and then required fewer coal and water stops. The smoke indicates that the fireman is preparing for the demands of the grade that will be encountered on the way to Cadosia. COURTESY OF CAL'S CLASSICS.

RIGHT: On February 28, 1941, a company official took this photograph from the rear of train No. 10 as it left Walton. It was used as evidence for an investigation into the death of a trainman who was killed two days earlier. JOHN FORNI COLLECTION.

Originally streamlined to head the "Mountaineer Limited," engine 405 was frequently found on other passenger trains and on an occasional freight as well. Industrial designer Otto Kuhler applied some sheet metal and colorful paint to this 4-8-2 type and so placed the O&W into the group of railroads that used smooth design and bright colors to attract passengers. AUTHOR'S COLLECTION.

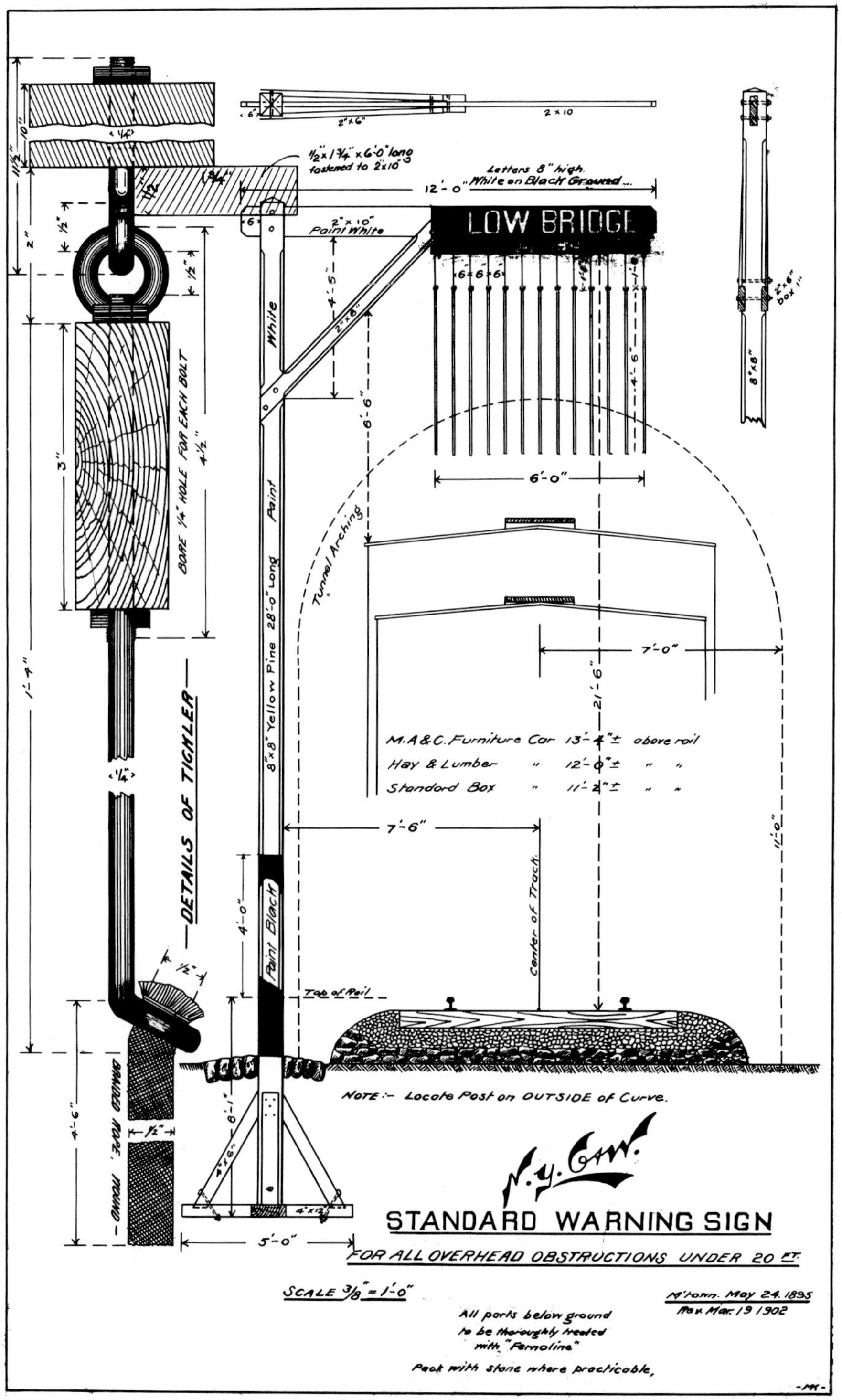

LEFT: Trainmen had to be warned of close overhead clearances so that they would not be knocked off freight cars while applying brakes or watching for signals when switching. These "tell-tale" warning devices were placed on both sides of main-line clearance obstructions, and if they brushed a brakeman's head or back, he had to crouch down or lie flat on the car's roof-walk to avoid injury. A pair was located at the Burton St. bridge. O&W SOCIETY COLLECTION.

BELOW: No. 324, a W-class 2-8-0, perhaps the most versatile and sturdy of all the O&W's steamers, works in Walton. TWO PHOTOGRAPHS: WALTER RICH COLLECTION.

ABOVE: One of Walton's large feed mills is switched by engine 284. These camelbacks were not well suited to switching chores since the fireman and the engineer had separate work stations and did not share the same cab as they did on "single-cab" engines. It was also more difficult for the engineer to operate the throttle, reverse lever and brakes in the confined cab. WALTER RICH COLLECTION. TOP RIGHT: The 311 moves around the north leg of the wye while providing some of the daily service the town's industries required. O&W SOCIETY COLLECTION.

RIGHT: Not long after its arrival on the property, an FT diesel sits in Walton with a southbound extra. The brake shoes and wheels are still hot after the descent from Northfield, but they'll cool during the next part of the trip, which will be up an ascending grade. There may have been a setout or pickup here and a crewman checks his paperwork before the trip resumes. WALTER RICH COLLECTION.

ABOVE AND BOTH BELOW: The new 118 and the hump-backed combine, No. 122, were working partners for several years and showed the great contrasts that were not unusual for the O&W. The combine's dark, weathered green finish was dull when compared to the diesel's shades of gray, yellow and orange. JOHN PICKETT.

ABOVE RIGHT: The O&W had not achieved a decade of total dieselization before its abandonment in 1957. Throughout the railroad's nine years of existence after the retirement of the last steam locomotive in 1948, many vestiges of the steam age still existed. The great water tank, visible above the boxcars in the left photograph and in close-up detail at the right, was one of the most obvious. The roof dormer, wooden finial and sawtooth skirting were features unique to the O&W. Some of these tanks, resting on heavy, creosoted timbers, remained to service steam-powered work equipment. Some were filled by steam-powered pumps. HAL CARSTENS.

Diesel 801 leads the next to last southbound train through Walton on March 29, 1957. The consist has a few off-line boxcars going back to their home roads and two switch engines from Norwich. This run would prove to be the 801's last, but the switchers had served only a quarter of their useful lives while on the O&W. WALTER RICH COLLECTION.

ceived as elegant a station building.

The Bridge Street station was a small depot on the Delhi branch at mile post 180. It was constructed in 1904. The company said it was built to serve Walton village as well as branch passengers. Its location was a convenience for passengers who came down the Bear Spring Mountain road or from the area east of the West Branch of the Delaware River. The frame building was replaced by one of masonry in 1911 or 1912. It was out of service prior to 1941 and was sold that year for $100.

As the Western Gateway to the Catskills, Walton enjoyed a brisk business for many years. Many excursions and passenger extras terminated at the main station at Howell Street. In the summer of 1898, there were five passenger trains in each direction, including the milk trains and the Delhi-Utica service. Several additional mixed trains worked the Delhi branch. In the summer of 1920, six weekday main line trains stopped at Walton. However, by the spring of 1939 the service was reduced to Nos. 1 and 2 milk trains 9 and 10. The Delhi branch was down to a pair of mixed trains. Main line passenger service to Walton ended in 1948 when Nos. 1 and 2 were cut back to Roscoe.

Because of the many shippers and consignees in the area as well as those on the Delhi branch, there was a yard in Walton for switching and storage of cars. Local freight trains and various passenger trains originated here as conditions and service requirements dictated. Through freights would set out or pick up blocks of cars, and locomotives would take coal and water to continue their runs. An enginehouse served as a shop facility to handle minor repairs on both locomotives and cars that were assigned to or were passing through Walton. The arrival of General Motors FT road freight diesels in 1945 meant that certain jobs would soon be eliminated by the new form of motive power. The 2700 h.p. two-unit diesels did not require a hostler to fill them with fuel and water. They did not need fire cleaners, pipe fitters or boilermakers to keep them in running condition. Fuel and service facilities were concentrated at only a few points and Walton was not among them when the diesels totally replaced steam. This took place in 1948 when additional main line and switching diesels arrived. They lacked the drama of steam power, but their greater efficiency saved the railroad thousands of dollars and granted the line a few more years of existence. Along with Delhi, Walton was one of the few communities of any real size that the O&W could consider captive as far as rail service was concerned. As late as 1950, the railroad employed about 40 people locally and served enough industries and businesses to keep a locomotive and switching crew busy during daylight hours. The shutdown of the railroad in March, 1957, meant some loss of jobs and certainly a slowing of economic development. Fortunately for the village, paved highways had definitely improved Walton's accessibility by motor transport, and that mode assumed the remaining railroad business.

A camelback helper shoves against the four-wheel caboose of a northbound coal train near Northfield station. The area is just as wooded and rural today as it was at the time of this photograph. JOHN AND SUE HUDSON COLLECTION.

Chapter 8: Walton to Northfield

Bluestone is found in small pockets on the hillsides, and provided an ideal supplement to the hill farmer's income. Many a farmer found and opened a bluestone quarry on his farm, working it between seasons with his sons or with the aid of itinerant quarrymen.

Douglas DeNatale, *Two Stones for Every Dirt*, (25)

With the exception of some 40 route miles between Oneida and Lake Ontario, very little of the New York, Ontario & Western's main line was level. The O&W's route and the geography of New York state did not mesh very well for several reasons. The line crossed nine summits reached by 18 grades that ranged in elevation from a modest 26.4 feet to a tough 105.6 feet per mile. The route did not select broad river valleys and follow them for long distances as, for example, the New York Central did along the Mohawk and Hudson Rivers or the Erie along the Delaware and Canisteo Rivers. The O&W seldom got as much as 20 miles of distance from a river valley before it climbed out, crested the divide, and headed down the other side of the ridge. This angular imposition on the drainage pattern of the land was highly influenced by the company's plan to serve those towns and cities that raised the funds for construction.

After Young's Gap, just north of Liberty, the next highest point on the main line was at the south portal of Northfield Tunnel. It was a 7.5 mile climb from the north end of the yard at Walton to the tunnel. After passing under the Burton Street bridge in Walton, the route followed the valley of the West Brook. The grade was approximately 75 feet per mile on the right-of-way that was cut along the west slope of the valley. This valley was not very wide and was used by farmers for side hill pastures and some cultivation. Near a location known as Churchill's, bridge 190 crossed the Walton-Sidney Center highway. Beyond this was a passing track known as Ogdens (M.P. 182.62), which was installed in 1893. Wooden signs marked both ends of this 2000-foot siding that was frequently used for meets between scheduled trains prior to 1920. The location was named for a family that lived in the vicinity. William Butler Ogden, a famous son and referred to previously, left Delaware County to become the first mayor of Chicago and founder of the Chicago & North Western Railway.

The valley continued to narrow and at the location called West Brook (M.P. 184), there was a small flag-stop station. The site, if not the actual flag stop, was later used for a section house. In addition, the railroad served a creamery, a mail crane, and a stone dock located on a short siding.

Delaware County is underlaid with deposits of fine-quality bluestone and all the railroads within its borders carried this natural resource to city markets. It is a durable yet easily worked material and is used widely for flagging, curbing, and building purposes. The stone docks were loading platforms built of heavy timber, and the name referred to their loading function rather than their construction. The height of these docks matched that of railroad flatcars so the blocks and slabs could be easily loaded. Some of the bigger docks were equipped with derricks to lift the heavier pieces. The company made note of the bluestone business in its annual report of 1885, saying that such deposits existed over a 125-mile distance between Summitville and Oxford. The report claimed that the business had undergone a 100

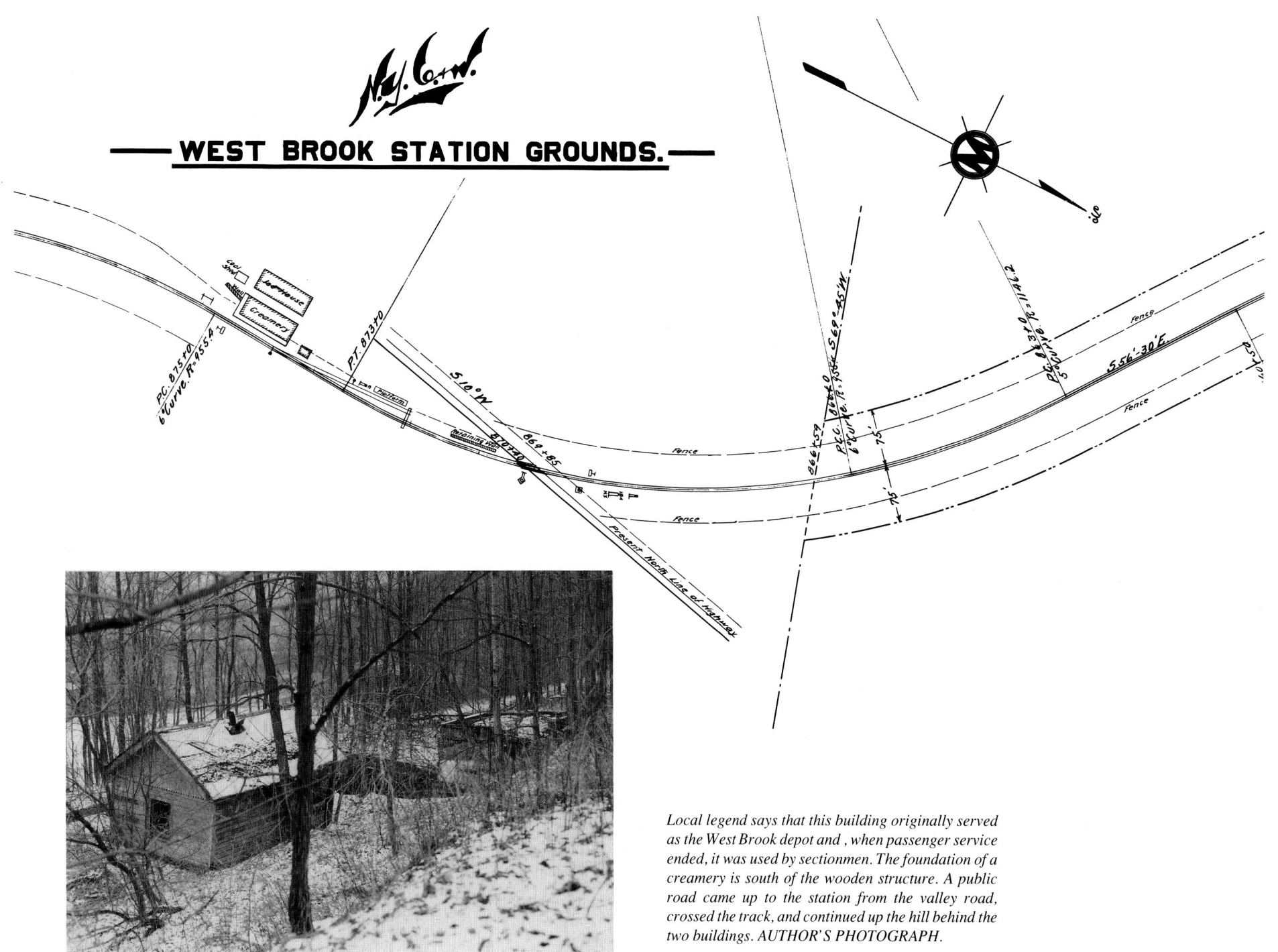

Local legend says that this building originally served as the West Brook depot and, when passenger service ended, it was used by sectionmen. The foundation of a creamery is south of the wooden structure. A public road came up to the station from the valley road, crossed the track, and continued up the hill behind the two buildings. AUTHOR'S PHOTOGRAPH.

percent increase during each of the previous three years.

A little farther west was another location named for local landowners. It was referred to as both Tweedie's and Russell's (M.P. 184.95), since property of both families adjoined the right-of-way. A short siding here had a timber dock for the loading of logs.

At this point, the valley divides and the railroad, continuing upgrade, followed the west fork along a tributary of West Brook called Webb's Brook. Older names for this region near milepost 186 were Woodford Valley and North Walton. The railroad called it Northfield (ZA, M.P. 186.65) sometime after the tunnel was built although the village of Northfield was better than a mile distant. The "ZA" telegraph call letters came from the earlier Zig Zag designation for the switchback route over the hill. In 1893, a 2400-foot passing track here replaced a short siding. In addition, there was a second, earlier siding known as the North Walton spur. It was in use at the time of the switchback operation, and it was eventually double-ended by the installation of a switch at its north end. A stone or timber loading dock was built along this siding. A small passenger station and freight house were located on the west side of the track between the two sidings and about 1700 feet south of the tunnel. Since most of the roadbed has been eroded away by the brook, with the aid of several colonies of determined beavers, it is difficult today to locate either the roadbed or the station site.

It is doubtful that the operator here had much to do in the way of car accounts, billing, or ticket sales. Train orders and operational activities, local freight, and express were the main reasons for the station's existence. During the years of the switchback operation, the station was probably active as northbound trains were divided into sections to go over the hill, and arriving southbound sections were put back together. Pusher engines, from both Sidney and Walton, required permission to return to their

Southbound freight No. 32, behind engine 316, collided with northbound engine 275 that was hauling milk and passenger train No. 11 near Northfield station in 1917. The impact sent the rear truck of the combine several feet forward and the first boxcar of the freight telescoped onto the tender of the 316. TWO PHOTOGRAPHS: COURTESY OF JOE BUX AND DEPOT ATTIC.

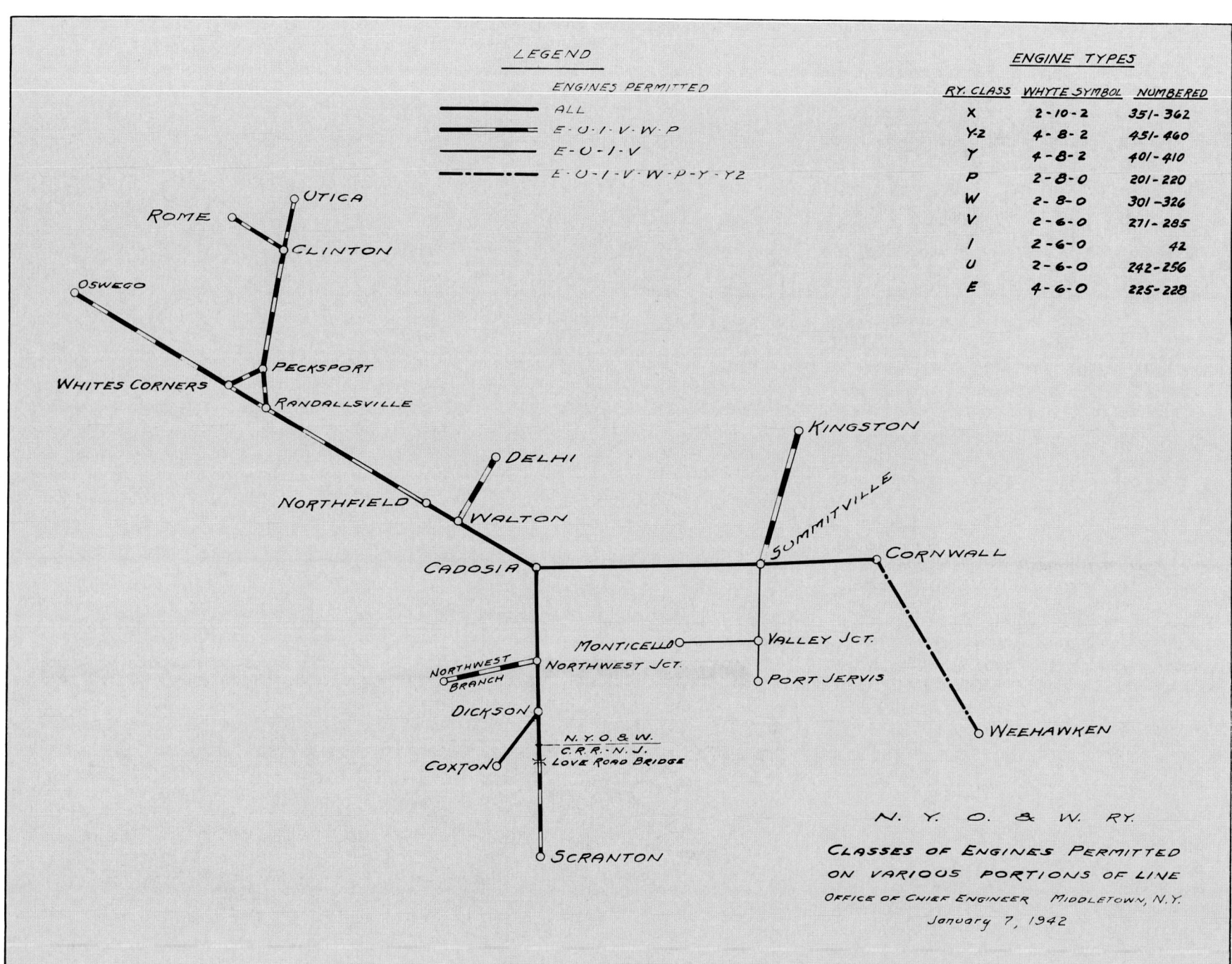

ABOVE: Bridge 186.2 crossed the West Brook and the Walton-Merrickville Road about a mile south of Northfield station. The bridge has been removed and the road paved, but some of the stone abutment structure remains. STERLING KIMBALL.

OPPOSITE PAGE: All the directives of the operating department were important to the safe and efficient operation of the O&W. One that required especially scrupulous obedience was that which limited classes of motive power to specific sections of the railroad. Note that the northern limit of the solid line—territory over which all classes of steam locomotives were permitted to operate—is at Northfield on the main line. O&W SOCIETY COLLECTION.

RIGHT: The tunnel, cuts and drainage of the Northfield area required the constant attention of section crews. Many new immigrants found work on these O&W section gangs and they, in turn, encouraged others to leave their European villages and join them in America. A scaffold arrangement on flanged wheels was used for work on the walls and roof of the tunnel and can be seen behind the platform on the left. WALTER RICH COLLECTION.

respective terminals. Under normal circumstances, all 4-8-2 and 2-10-2 type steam locomotives, the largest steamers on the O&W's roster, were restricted from operating north of Northfield. They could push a freight to this point, uncouple, and after getting a train order, return to Walton. The tunnel's width and height were greater than the same dimensions for the locomotives but they were not sufficient to allow for the lateral movement of these longer engines while under power.

The arrival of the diesel road locomotives in 1945 eliminated the need for the pushers. The new form of motive power was not restricted by tunnel clearances, and its multiple-unit flexibility permitted the placement of all needed power on the head end under the control of one crew.

The construction of the tunnel not only made operations more efficient but also much safer since it employed automatic signal protection at both ends. The original arrangement was replaced by more advanced motor signals in 1910 and supplemented by a telephone line into the station. Between the tunnel and the station was a very solid timber bridge that was built to allow a local farmer passage to his fields. Much of this particular hundred-year-old structure still stood in 1992 along with stone retaining walls south of the tunnel portal.

The area seems very quiet today, but it had moments of high drama when the railroad was in operation. On August 13, 1891, the engineer of a northbound freight was killed when his locomotive was hit by a pusher engine running in reverse. The pusher engineer had been on continuous duty for 48 hours and had fallen asleep at the throttle. A federal law was passed the following year mandating that railroad men have eight hours rest after 24 hours of continuous service.

In July of 1897, the night operator at Northfield discovered an attempt by tramps to wreck train No. 5. A common trick used by itinerants was to place small amounts of debris on the track to stop trains. An engineer could not always be sure that the debris would not derail his train. After the train had stopped to permit a crew member to clear the track,

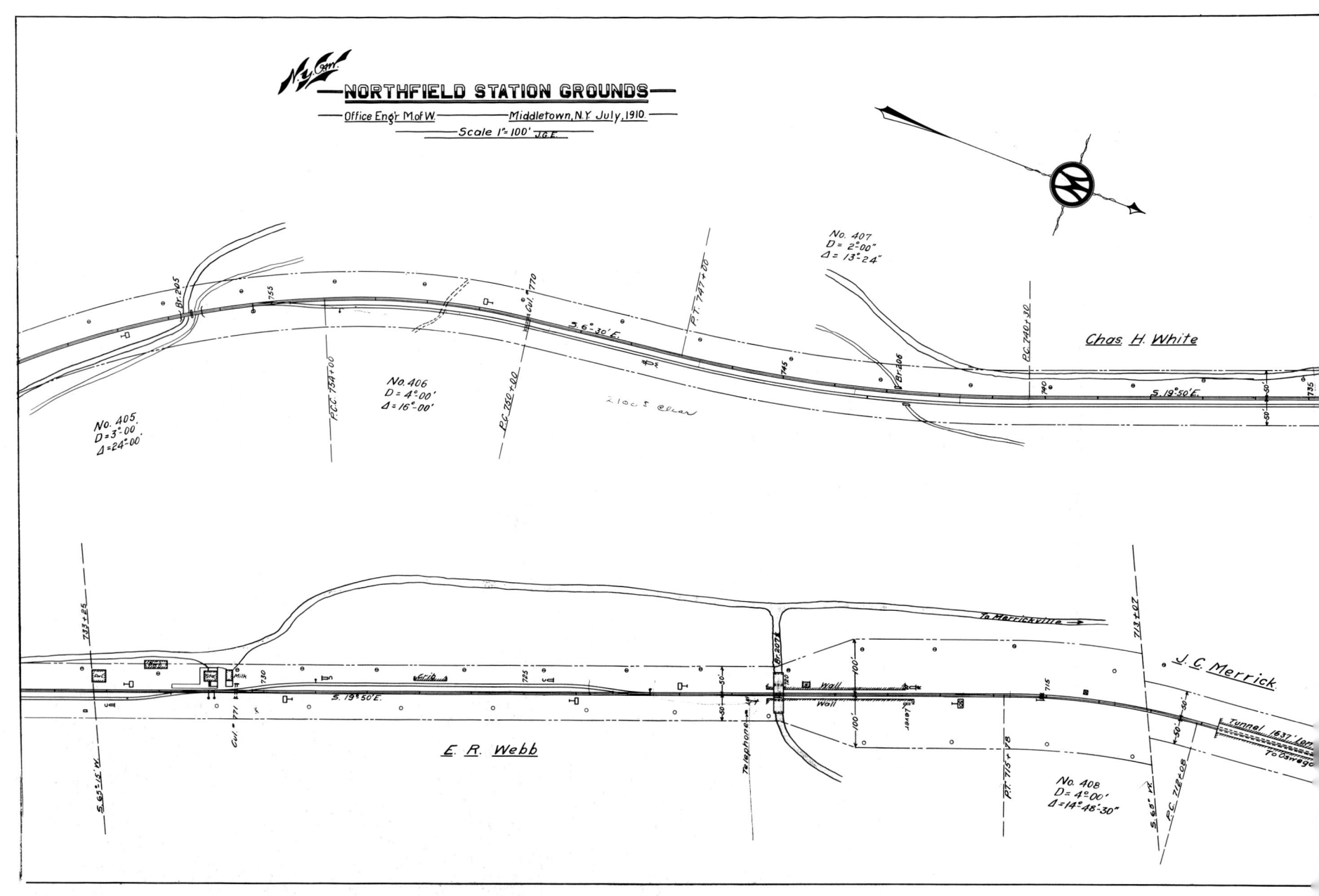

Time has erased a large part of the O&W's presence in the vicinity of Northfield. The combined efforts of beavers and running water, no longer held in check by railroad maintenance crews, have reclaimed the area from which they were displaced over a century ago. O&W HISTORICAL SOCIETY.

North and south views at Northfield show the track, structures and signal layouts. Northfield was one location at which the O&W employed a Hall signal. This type was invented by Thomas S. Hall and was later produced by the Union Switch and Signal Co. The disc rotated 90 degrees to present a clear or stop indication. The lantern on top gave an illuminated night-time indication. Signals at both ends of the tunnel served as protection against a possible human error of permitting opposing trains to use the tunnel at the same time. TOP: DIVER COLLECTION, CORNELL UNIVERSITY. BOTTOM: WILLIAM SCHRIVER COLLECTION.

The day operator at Northfield stands amid the structures and devices of his trade. He frequently handled the two switches to the right in preparation for meets and assisted in the loading and unloading of package freight, express and mail. Note the sack in the mail crane awaiting pick-up. O&W SOCIETY COLLECTION.

ABOVE: Northfield's small combination station still stood in 1963 but was well hidden by the brush and trees that grew well in the damp environment. The abandoned railroad buildings were sometimes stripped of doors, windows or lumber that might have secondhand usefulness in the neighborhood. CARL A. OHLSON COLLECTION,

TOP RIGHT: Broken rock and tunneling rubble are still visible south of the cut leading to the south portal and east of the right-of-way. Tracks of the construction railroad terminated in this area for the dumping of the excavated material. The arrow points to a farm bridge over the right-of-way just south of the tunnel cut. BOTTOM RIGHT: Steel arches that supported forms for tunnel work lay in the woods east of the station site. Cement was poured or pumped behind the forms to hold potentially loose material in place. Local farmers reportedly took serveral pieces over the years for farm use. AUTHOR'S PHOTOGRAPHS.

the perpetrator would lodge himself in some hidden location on the cars and get a free ride to his destination.

In the late 1940's a freight car derailed in the tunnel and damaged many ties as it was dragged through. Once out of the tunnel it caused a pileup near the south end.

Chapter 9: The Zig Zag and Northfield Tunnel

To avoid stopping with the pusher engine in Northfield Tunnel, south-bound trains will either pull in siding or south on main track until pusher is clear of tunnel, observing all operating rules. Operators at Northfield will open the switch when signaled by engineman.

NYO&W Railway Company, Supplemental Instructions for the Government of the Operating Department, April 15, 1927, (73).

Using wooden trestles in place of fills, grades instead of deep cuts, wood instead of iron or masonry, softwood instead of hardwood ties, and postponing of stone ballasting were some of the time and money-saving practices followed by most new railroads in the 1800's. Many of those lines never did earn enough money to return to the areas of quick construction and do the job in a more permanent manner. Others, including the New York, Ontario & Western, spent millions of dollars in later years to provide a more durable, safer and efficient physical plant.

Perhaps DeWitt C. Littlejohn and his corps of company officers and engineers down-played to the public the fact that they believed in or followed any of the above expediencies as they went about the building of the New York & Oswego Midland. Construction funds were in limited supply and moving trains on completed sections of railroad spoke louder than promises of prosperity. The quickest, and frequently the cheapest, took precedence over what was best. In defense of those early railroaders, it must be remembered that such thinking was not necessarily wrong. Passenger and freight hauling trains did much to boost a new railroad's credibility and aid in the sales of stocks and bonds for further construction.

The building of a tunnel is a very expensive and time-consuming project and one may speculate on why the Shawangunk Ridge, Fallsburgh's Tunnel Hill, and Hawk Mountain had holes cut through while Northfield Mountain initially did not. Money may have been more available when those three locations were reached. Perhaps there were fewer alternative routes at these places or it might be that the officers decided that the greater traffic density of the southern counties justified the financial outlay at an earlier date. Whatever the reasons, the New York & Oswego Midland decided to go over and not through Northfield Mountain as construction crews moved through Delaware County.

Locating engineers laying out the grade west from Walton and east from Sidney looked for the lowest point across the divide between the Delaware and Susquehanna River drainage. The pass they found was not spectacular in the scenic sense but considering what many other railroads had to contend with in the way of geographic barriers, the OM got off relatively easy.

Two examples may make this point clear. The nearby Buffalo & Susquehanna required multilevel switchbacks to lift its main line hundreds of feet over mountains in central Pennsylvania. Far to the west, the Denver & Salt Lake had to build 35 miles of line

The completion of the stone arch over the south portal of the Northfield Tunnel is good reason for a photograph. Approximately 40 laborers, muckers, drillers, masons, along with a mule driver and his mule, stand in and about the excavation they have created. A "stiff-leg" derrick lifted the blocks of cut stone into position. D. DIVER COLLECTION. CORNELL UNIVERSITY.

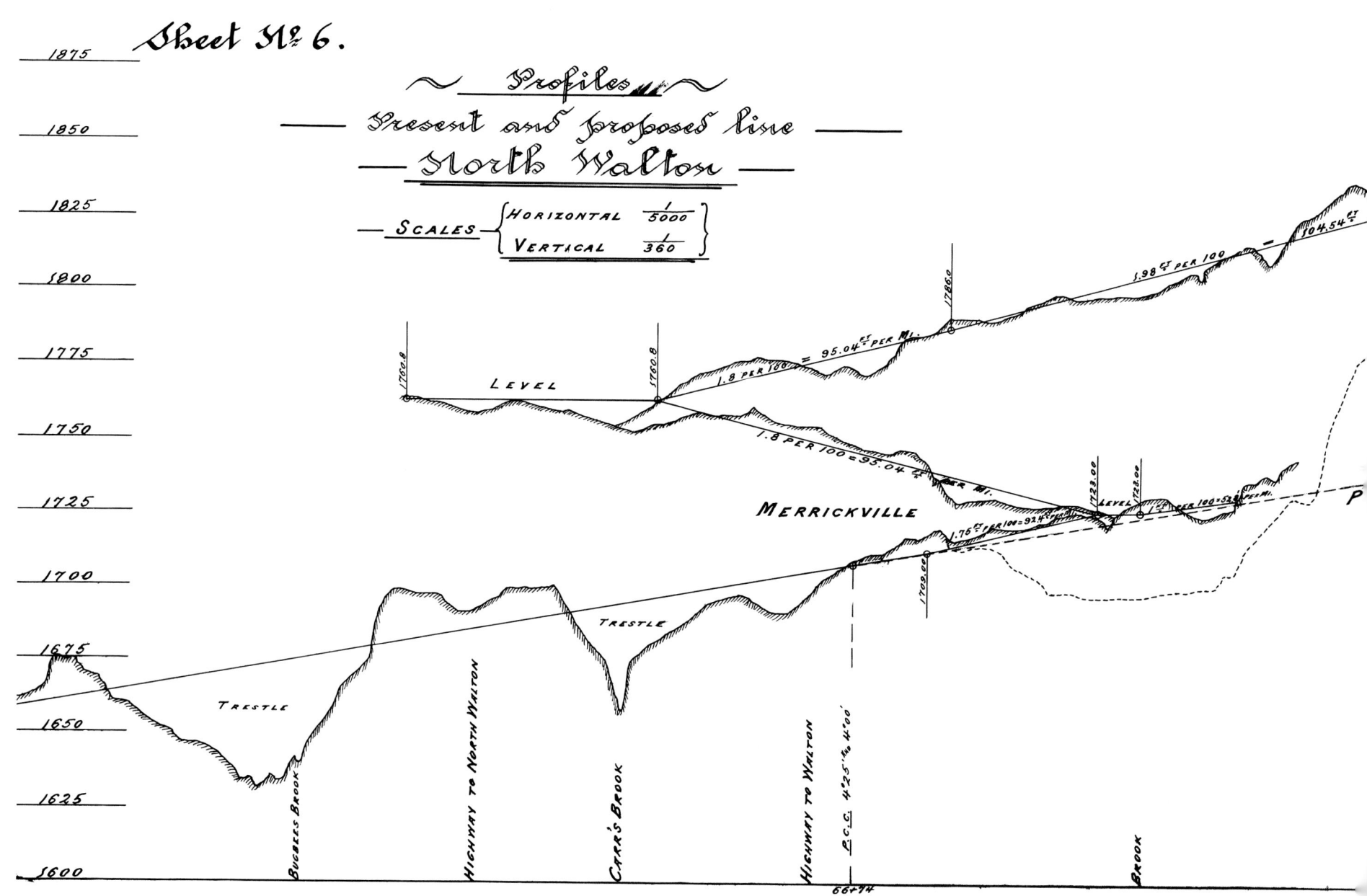

This plan allows comparisons to be made regarding grades, distance and elevation between the switchback and the tunnel routes. *O&W SOCIETY COLLECTION.*

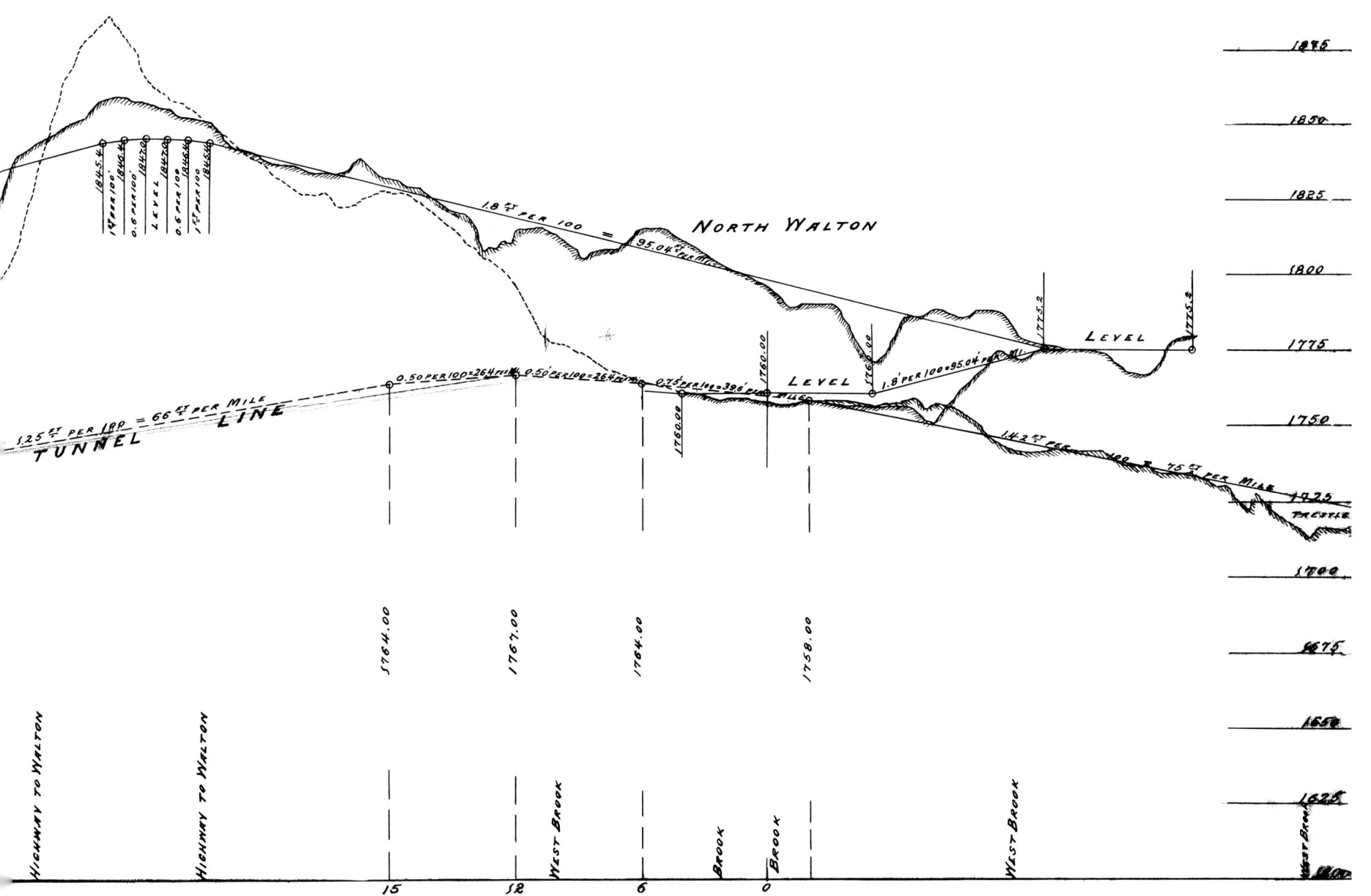

TOP AND BOTTOM, LEFT: Most of the excavation in the north cut was completed by September, 1890, and the slower tunneling work appears to have begun. Fortunately for the railroad, the rock was not a very hard variety; so drilling and blasting efforts were not as difficult as those confronted at similar projects. Water and fuel had to be supplied to the steam shovel and the foreground pipe in the second photograph may have been a water line. TWO PHOTOGRAPHS: COURTESY OF JOE BUX AND DEPOT ATTIC.

BELOW: Both standard and narrow-gauge equipment was used in the south cut. There is a large mound that appears to be man-made in the vicinity of Northfield station, west of the right-of-way. The fact that the work cars are open on the west side adds support to the theory that the mound is made of material removed from the tunnel. COURTESY OF JOE BUX AND DEPOT ATTIC.

in Colorado to cover a distance that the Moffat Tunnel would later reduce to eight miles. The statistics for Northfield were not nearly so impressive. From an elevation of 1236 feet at Walton, the line had to climb 524 feet to North Walton, later to be known as Northfield. The distance was 7.2 miles. All grades were under 2 percent and only two additional miles were required to cross the hill. Trains traversing the switchbacks had to change direction only three times when making the crossing.

The switchback on the North Walton (south) side of the hill had a tail track that was about 600 feet long. The route then proceeded upward through a series of gentle curves and went through the gap at an elevation of 1847 feet. The track was directly on top of the future tunnel alignment and next to the public highway. The descent of the Merrickville (north) slope was somewhat steeper. A section of 1.98 percent grade was necessary as compared with 1.8 percent on other parts of the switchback grades. It was also a little longer than the line on the south grade and made a sharp curve toward the east as it approached the tail track switch. The tail track itself was close to 1000 feet in length. The steeper grade of the north slope may account for the additional length.

The North Walton spur, referred to in the previous chapter, provided a southbound train with a storage track for cars when trains had to double or triple the hill. On the switchback, the south side tail tracks and spur were level as was the northside tail track. (The tail tracks were sections of track on which the train stopped before reversing direction.) Due to the back and forth movement in traversing the switchbacks, the section of line was referred to as the Zig Zag, (without a hypen). The name was officially recognized and used by the company.

The operators at North Walton and Franklin controlled operations over the hill. Merrickville did not have a station or operator at this time. The two operators had very important functions. They had to work together closely to avoid putting opposing

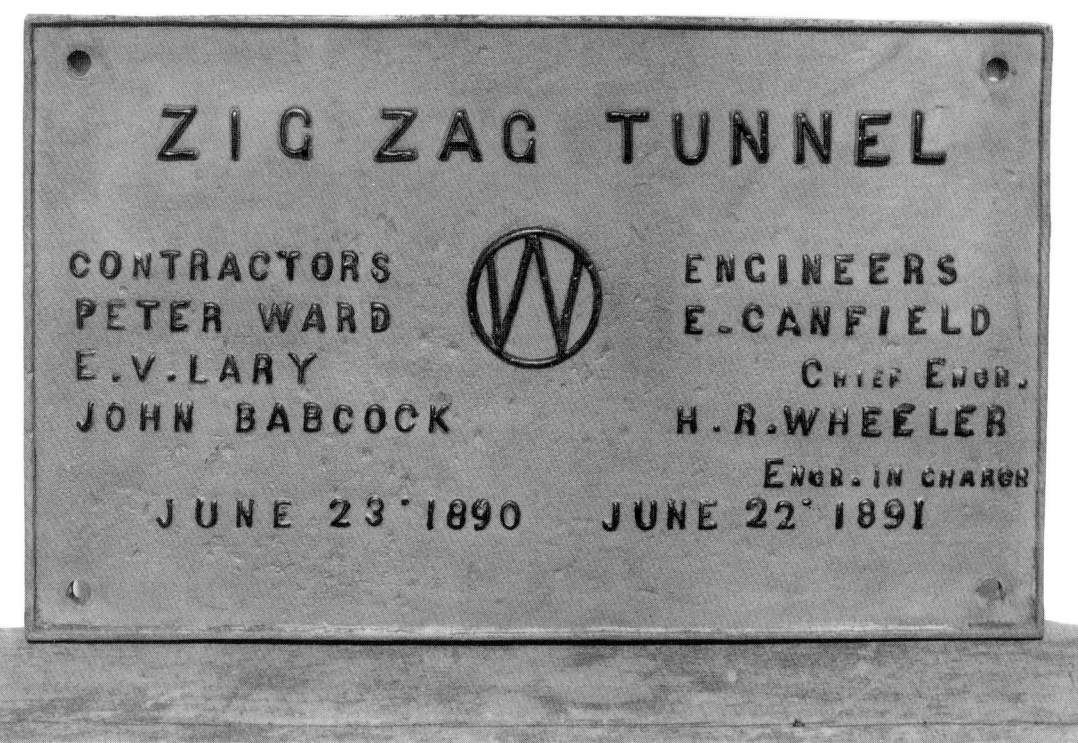

One of the cast plaques which appeared above the keystones at both ends of the tunnel rests in a Delaware County collection. AUTHOR'S PHOTOGRAPH.

trains on the hill at the same time. Movement over the hill called for alert railroading on the part of engine and train crews. Runaways on the grades were a deadly hazard. The dispatcher had to plan carefully before allowing trains to leave Walton or Sidney. Operational decisions were shaped by siding and switchback limitations, locomotive tonnage ratings, the proximity of first class trains, and a myriad of other considerations such as water and fuel requirements, hot bearings, breakdowns, vagaries of train crews, human error, and weather conditions.

The switchbacks were never considered a permanent feature of the Oswego Midland. As soon as revenues justified the undertaking, a tunnel was to replace the three miles of railroad on the hill. But, such financial justification would not occur during the OM's short, 13-year life span. When the New York, Ontario & Western was formed in 1880, the officials regarded the switchbacks as one of the weakest operational links on the line and a priority improvement to be undertaken as soon as possible. It was estimated that the switchbacks were costing the company $18,000 per year in operations and maintenance. Only a few years after the O&W's formation, an annual report said of the switchbacks:

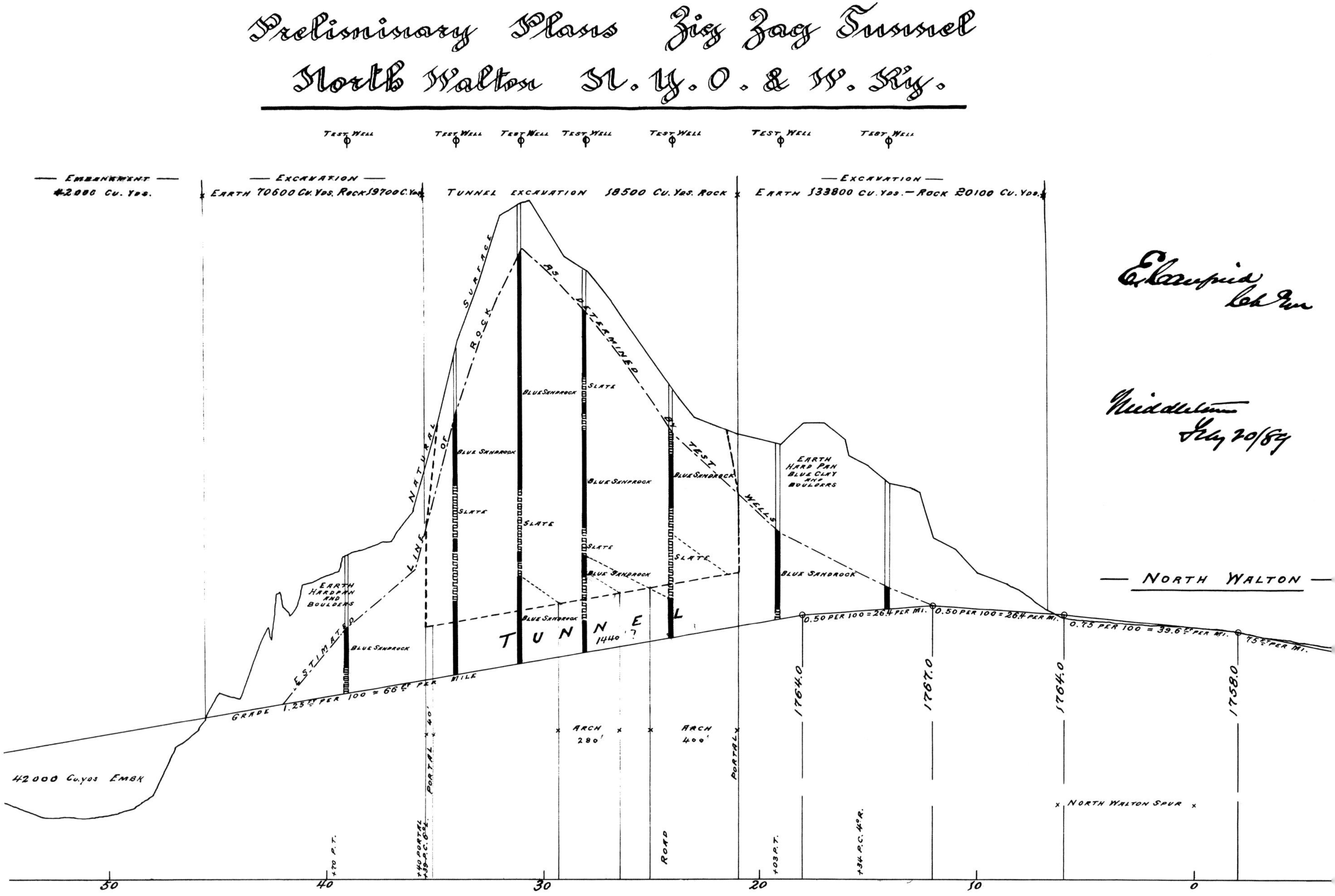

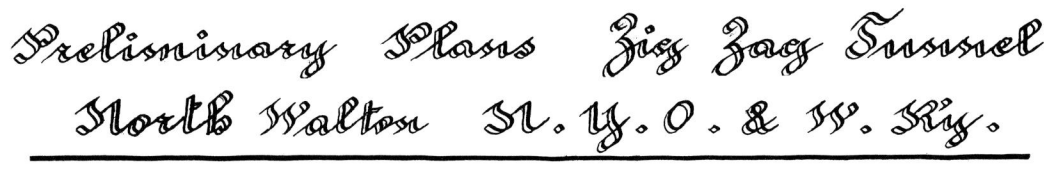

The profile for the tunnel shows that seven test bores or wells were driven to determine the subsurface conditions. The necessity of a long fill on the Merrickville side can be seen as a depression north of the cut. According to one plan, it would require 42,000 cubic yards of fill. Apparently the exact location of where the cuts would end and the tunneling begin had not yet been decided. O&W SOCIETY COLLECTION.

"Nearly all trains are necessarily divided into sections, causing delay, inconvenience, and consequent expense."

In 1887 and 1888, preliminary test borings were made to determine the nature of the material through which a tunnel would pass. The borings were made at intervals of 150 to 200 feet and ranged in depth from 42 to 155 feet. Red shale and blue sandstone were found 25 feet below the surface. Fortunately for the company, this type of rock can be cut through without great difficulty. Some 240,000 cubic yards of earth, and loose and solid rock had to be excavated from the tunnel and both approaches.

Details, plans and estimates were prepared by the railroad's chief engineer, Edward Canfield, after analysis of test borings and surface studies. The proposed tunnel and its approaches were estimated to cost $280,000 for a length of 2500 feet. Excavated material would be used in fills on both approaches to the tunnel.

Additional support for boring the tunnel came from a study which found that the operating savings would be greater than the interest on the cost of the construction. During the period just prior to construction, the railroad's tonnage had increased 48.6 percent and was still climbing. At the same time the O&W's largest expansion project, the 54.5 mile Scranton Division, was undertaken and meant additional traffic. To finance the tunnel, build the new line, redeem earlier bonds, and purchase new equipment and rolling stock, a new bond issue of $10,000,000 was sold in 1889 and secured by a mortgage that essentially covered the entire railroad.

In June of 1889, the tunnel contract was let to the construction firm of Peter Ward, E.V. Lary, and John Babcock of Newburgh, N.Y. Work on the approaches began the same month with tunneling beginning a year later. The tunnel was opened for traffic on June 25, 1891, almost two years to the day after work had begun. Locally it was referred to as the Zig Zag Tunnel in memory of the switchbacks it replaced. Even before the official opening, the Walton *Reporter* said in January, 1891:

The Zag Zag Tunnel is a reality. The breezes of the Susquehanna Valley blow through and mingle with those of the Delaware. One of the greatest obstructions to travel and traffic over the Ontario and Western Railroad will soon be a thing of the past.

The 1636-foot tunnel cost $282,560.18. It had the same clearances as the other three tunnels on the line: 14 feet between bench walls and 16.5 feet from the top of the rail to the soffit in the arch. Lining was required for 874 feet, or about half the length. Some 640,000 bricks were needed in the arch lining. Tunnel and approaches were laid with treated oak ties and 67-pound steel rail on stone ballast. This firm roadbed was essential because of wet conditions in and about the tunnel area. Quicksand was in fact reported during construction. (The problems which the railroad had with drainage are still evidenced today by the drainage ditches along the tops of the approach cuts.) Signal protection was installed at both ends.

Comparisons of proposed and final statistics show that the engineers had calculated quite carefully. The final cost exceeded the estimates by only $2569—a cost overrun of less than one percent. Two miles of train travel were saved as well as a great deal of time formerly spent in breaking the train into sections to cross the hill. The grade on the north side was reduced by 37 percent and on the south side by 25 percent. The actual summit of 1767 feet was not in the tunnel but near the beginning of

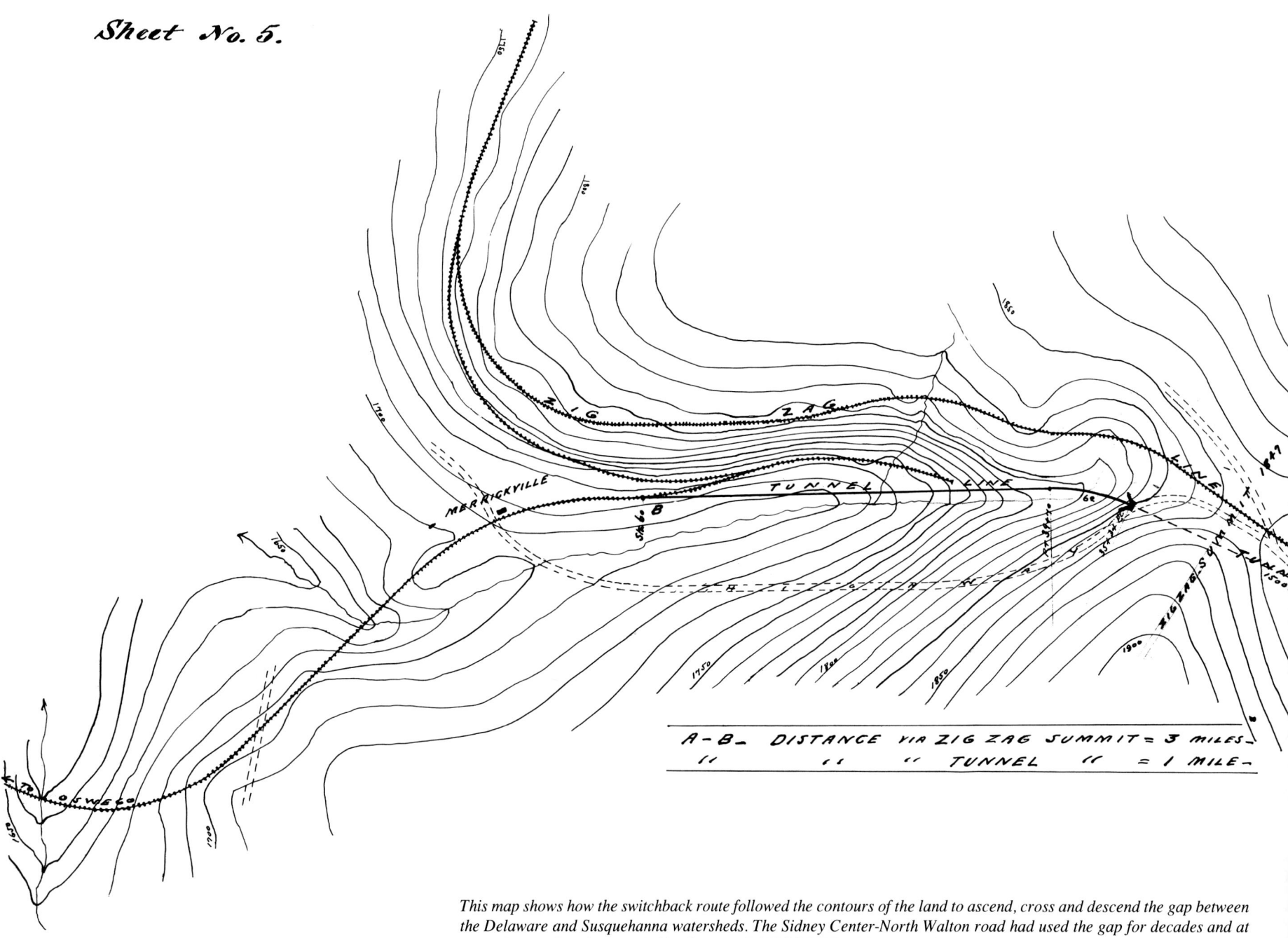

This map shows how the switchback route followed the contours of the land to ascend, cross and descend the gap between the Delaware and Susquehanna watersheds. The Sidney Center-North Walton road had used the gap for decades and at one point, ran beside the switchback route. O&W SOCIETY COLLECTION.

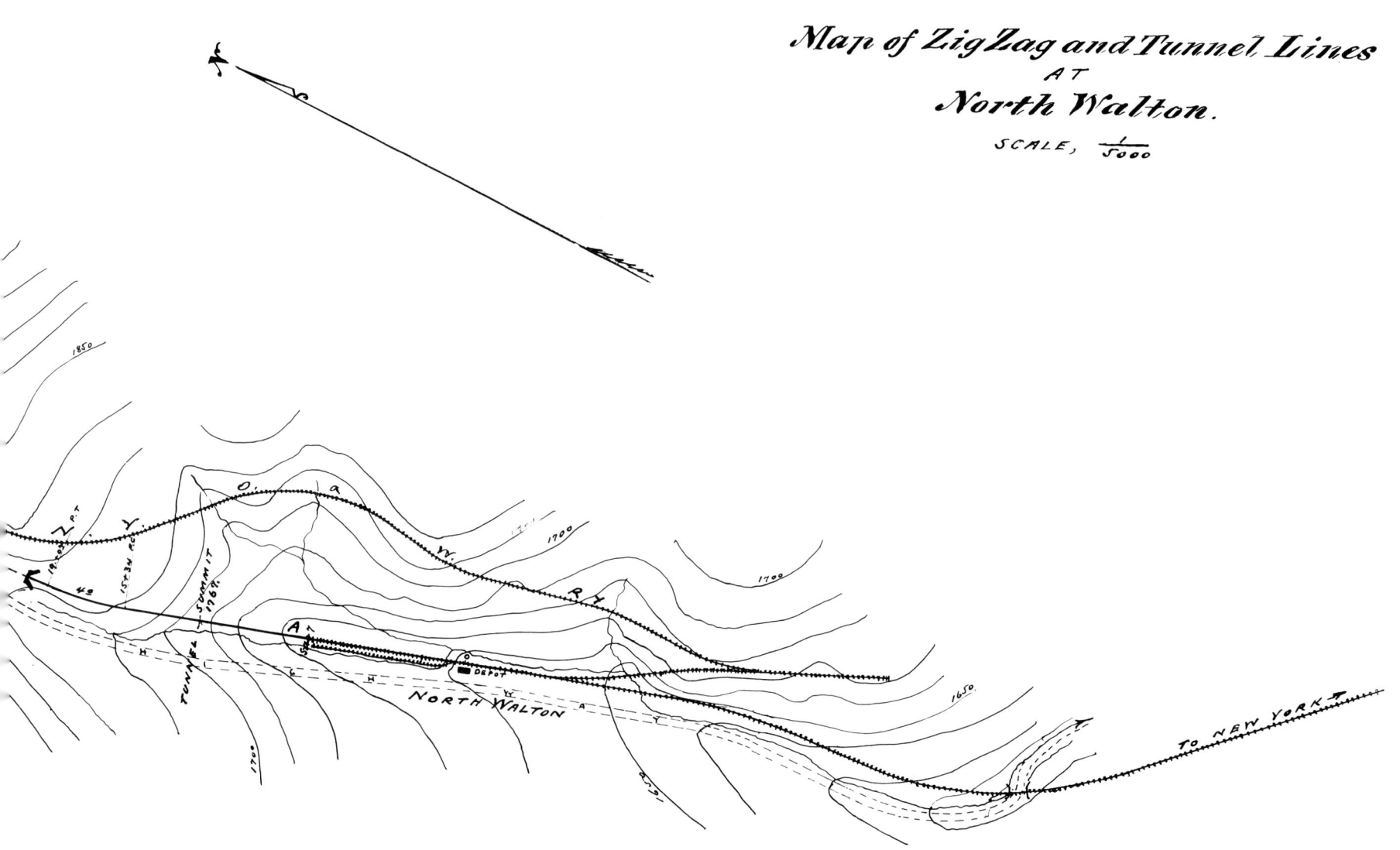

A railroad employee, lantern in hand, stands before the north portal of the tunnel. The year of the tunnel's completion, 1891, has been cut into the keystone. Since abandonment, the seasonal action of water and ice and the lack of maintenance made the tunnel dangerous to enter. CARL OHLSON COLLECTION.

Tunnel watchmen were charged with the task of reporting any hazardous condition in both the tunnel and the approach cuts. They were expected to walk through the tunnel several times daily and use their flagging equipment to stop a train should a dangerous situation be found. A standard design watchman's shanty was provided for these men at the north portal. BRUCE TRACY COLLECTION.

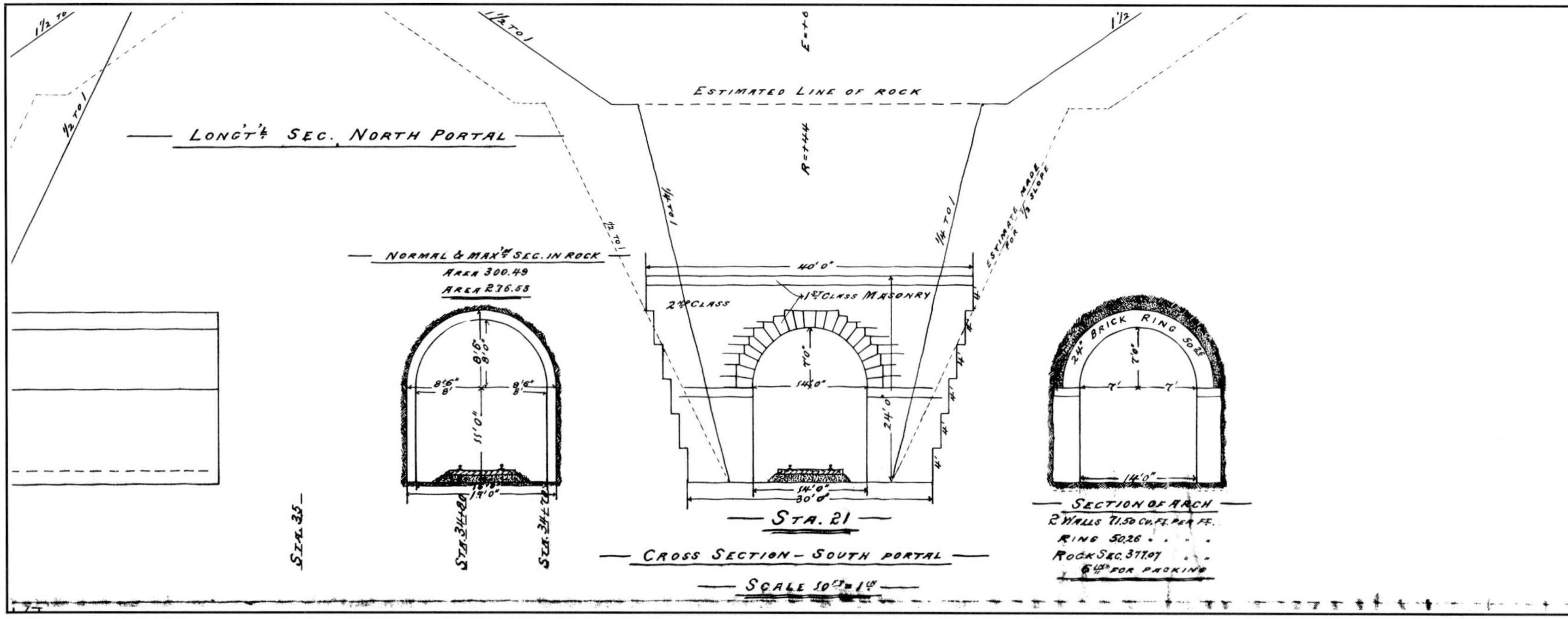

the cut at the south side causing water to drain northward through the tunnel. The railroad had a marker here to indicate the elevation above sea level.

With an almost mystical belief in the future of Oswego, located on Lake Ontario, the O&W completed a number of physical improvements in 1922 including dock work for handling rail-to-lake business. Arrangements were made with a steamship company to handle traffic between Oswego and all Great Lakes ports. The railroad was also anticipating the enlargement of harbor facilities by the federal government and a deepening of the Welland Canal by the Canadians. Clearance restrictions and tolls on canal use had put Lake Ontario ports at a disadvantage. Meanwhile, with these improvements to the north, the railroad was concerned with the clearances in the Northfield Tunnel. An incident on February 2, 1923, pointed out the need for engineering attention. A mass of stone and earth collapsed and closed the tunnel. Trackmen, inspecting the tunnel after the passage of train No. 12 and shortly before the arrival of train No. 2, discovered the cave-in. It had been some thirty years since the tunnel had been completed and heavy maintenance work was necessary.

In 1926, the company undertook the task of enlarging the bore to permit the passage of the larger freight cars that had come into use. Prior to this it had been necessary to employ the expensive practice of unloading and transferring freight from larger to smaller cars for the passage through the tunnel. To achieve greater clearance for the higher cars, material was excavated from the floor of the tunnel. This also required rebuilding the approaches for a smooth transition. Even the improved tunnel clearances were not adequate for X-class 2-10-2 and Y and Y-2 class 4-8-2 engines for reasons mentioned earlier. After clearance work had been completed, a new lining was installed. Steel arches of channel and I-beam configuration that were used in this and later tunnel maintenance projects may yet be seen near the site of the Northfield station. In 1955, a Gunite

In a time of simpler pleasures, a walk to the north tunnel portal on a Sunday afternoon occupied a couple and their friend in 1907. Even at a slow pace, an hour would be adequate time for a round trip from Merrickville. WALTER RICH COLLECTION.

lining (the patented process of spraying cement over a surface) was applied in the tunnel and the portal was faced with concrete stucco.

During periods of freezing weather, ice became a problem. Most tunnels pierce the ground water table, but generally the situation stabilizes after a few years and water flow diminishes. However, Northfield required a boiler that produced hot water or steam to control ice formation. This boiler was in a shed near the south portal. It required the services of a watchman and probably additional sectionmen during the winter season. Unlike other railroads, the O&W did not use doors to close the tunnel to winter winds nor did it run ice breaker cars to clear icicles from the ceiling.

Smoke and gas in the bore provided several minutes of very unpleasant conditions for engine crews. Since trains were pulling upgrade they had to work steam through the tunnel. NYO&W General Road Foreman Fred Lewis said that it was standard procedure to put in a good fire approaching the tunnel and then get down on the deck and bury your face in a damp bandanna or a wad of cotton waste. The diesels put a happy end to such practices for those who had to endure them.

The tunnel and its approaches still exist for the cautious historian to find. Each year, however, more pieces of the retaining walls and concrete facings are falling onto the right-of-way. Summer foliage makes the tunnel difficult to locate and gain access. The legendary old switchback can also be traced out by the persevering. Most of the south entry is gone, but the second switch, tail track, and route over the hill are visible. Parts of this run through private property, and permission should be obtained before entering.

ABOVE AND LEFT: Engine 255 is on a work train that had business on both sides of the tunnel. The top left view appears to be at Northfield with the photographer standing on the farm overpass. In the bottom left photograph, the crane is lifting pieces of steel tunnel lining and placing them in a gondola car. Above is engineman Ted Lewis who was assigned to the job. TED LEWIS COLLECTION.

RIGHT: A view from inside the tunnel shows pipes that were used for the steam-heated ice control system. Seeping water and constant heating and cooling of rock masses created instabilities that were often difficult to detect and made daily inspections mandatory. JOHN PICKETT.

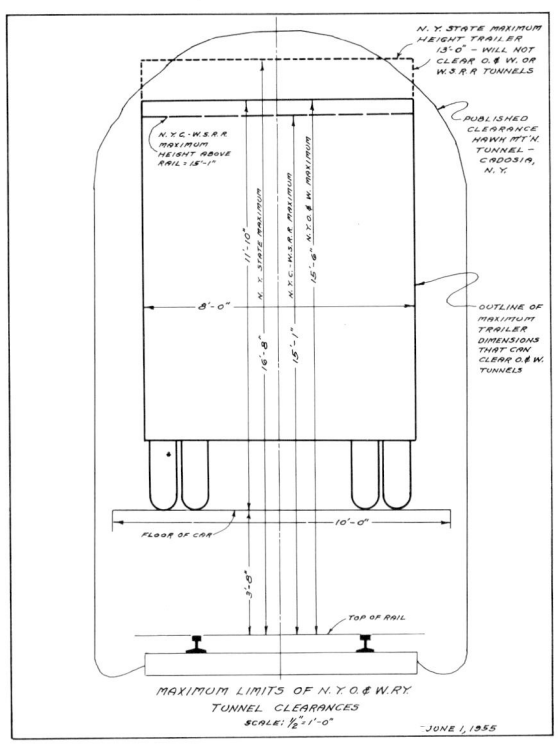

LEFT: Daisies, weeds and rust claim the main line at the south portal in this post-March, 1957, scene. The steam plant stood for a few years after the railroad closed and scattered remains may yet be found. Rock and earth are sliding into the cut as water and ice continue their constant effort to reduce the building of man and nature. The photographer was standing at the high point of the grade between Walton and Sidney. STERLING KIMBALL.

BELOW: An aerial view shows many of the features around the south portal of the tunnel. This appears to be a post-abandonment photograph shortly after the track had been removed. The arrow shows the switchback right-of-way. CARL OHLSON COLLECTION.

ABOVE: A few color photographs show piggyback (trailer on flatcar) service did exist on the O&W. There were restrictions on such service due to clearances, and such restrictions would have continued to plague the O&W had it survived beyond 1957. The high cost of increasing cut, tunnel and other right-of-way clearances could only be justified by a large volume of traffic, which the O&W did not have. This diagram, dated June 1, 1955, shows that New York State's maximum height trailers already exceeded dimensions that the O&W could accept. O&W SOCIETY COLLECTION.

The great trestles at Sidney Center, identified as Maywood by the railroad in order to avoid confusion with the larger community of Sidney, were the dominant features of the 13 miles of line covered in this chapter. Trestles 216 and 217 did not display the classical grandeur of Erie's Starrucca, Lackawanna's Tunkhannock or B&O's Relay Viaducts, but they none the less imparted a distinction and identity to a community. O&W SOCIETY COLLECTION.

Chapter 10: Merrickville to Sidney

The importance of the railroad station in a small town of the 1890s cannot be comprehended by a generation brought up on the automobile. In those days the rails were just about our only means of long-distance land transportation.

B. A. Botkin and Alvin Harlow, eds., *A Treasury of Railroad Folklore* , (184).

Leaving the Northfield tunnel, the railroad passed over a fill constructed with broken rock and excavated tunneling rubble. Below the fill was a beaver pond that was a local source of ice. Before passing through the cluster of buildings in the center of Merrickville (MK, 187.94), the railroad served a creamery that was built upon the abandoned Zig Zag right-of-way. Near the depot site was another creamery which was destroyed by fire in 1906. A depot built in 1911 also housed the post office. No telegraph call letters for Merrickville appear in the company records until the 1930s, at which time Northfield was closed. It is possible that there was a consolidation of agencies with the operator's responsibilities moved to Merrickville until it, too, was closed in 1951. A water tank was erected here in 1904 and delivered water via a standpipe at trackside. This tank proved to be one of the last surviving examples of such a structure on the NYO&W, and stood until 1986. An 1800-foot passing siding curved through the village and at least one commercial siding served local customers.

Several stores and a feed mill owned by the Hyzer Brothers did business in the village which took its name from John Merrick, who settled in the area in the 1800s.

Curving to the left leaving Merrickville, the railroad wound along a hillside just above the present Franklin Depot Road and passed through second growth woodland and rocky pastures. Before entering Franklin Depot (FE, 189.71) there was a switch for a 2000-foot passing track. Franklin Depot was not quite two miles north of Merrickville and about four miles south of the village of Franklin. It came into existence because of the railroad. The depot, creamery, stone dock, cattle pens, and coal trestle were located along the tracks, with a store, hotel, and feed mill close by. A 900-foot siding on the west side of the main line served some of these establishments. The creamery was closed by 1935 and the feed mill burned in the late 1940s. Both long sidings were gone by 1949, with only a 400-foot spur remaining. Such sidings were frequently employed for storing maintenance equipment and the boarding cars used by track, signal, and other maintenance gangs. Also, trainmen sometimes discovered mechanical problems on cars in their trains. A convenient siding allowed them to set the car out for repairs while the train proceeded on its run.

The demise of the local businesses meant that trains had little reason to stop at Franklin Depot. Just north of the station the line made a curve to the right and crossed trestle 210, whose abutments are yet visible. Trestle 210, called Franklin Trestle, crossed Goodrich Brook and was originally constructed on 49 timber bents. It was almost 300 feet long and 50 feet high and was rebuilt in steel in 1905.

The railroad's right-of-way northward from Franklin Depot often served as a line of demarcation for land use. The uphill side was frequently covered by second-growth timber or brush. The downhill side, from the cinder ballast edge to the stream below, was used for pasturage or tillage. Many of the cattle passes that permitted farm animals to pass under the railroad are still intact. Most of them were constructed with stone abutments and iron beams in

ABOVE: The building at the right may have been part of a feed business that was operated by the Hyzer Brothers. The foundations of their other buildings exist today just north of this location. WALTER RICH COLLECTION.

BELOW: It was O&W practice to have station signs indicate the mileage to the railroad's end terminals. For through passengers it might have indicated the tedium yet to be endured. This station was built in 1911. JOHN AND SUE HUDSON COLLECTION.

ABOVE: Looking south from Merrickville, the track curves to the right and disappears in the cut leading to Northfield Tunnel. The signal is a lower quadrant semaphore type and the blade is in the clear position. A horizontal blade meant stop. JOHN PICKETT.

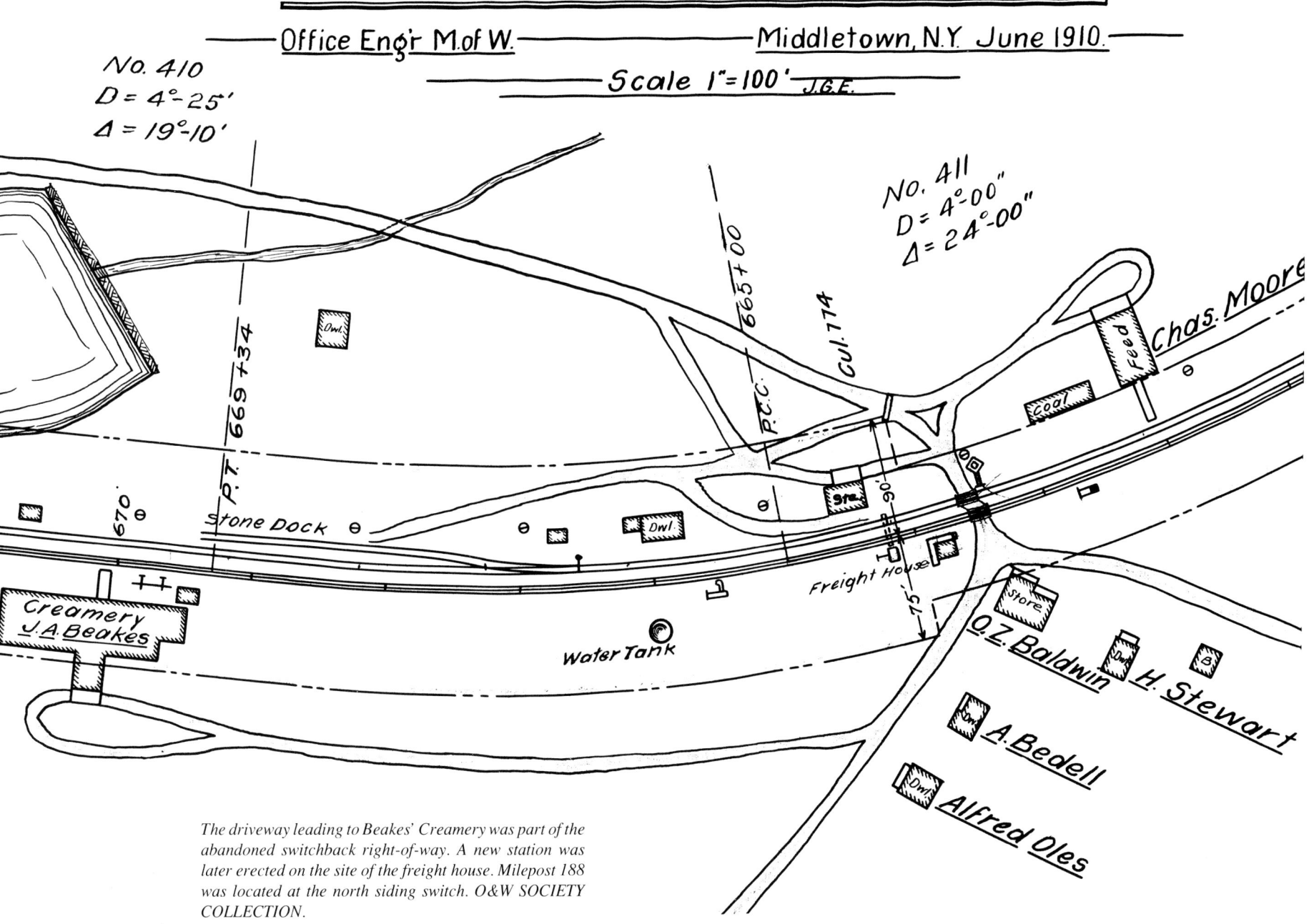

The driveway leading to Beakes' Creamery was part of the abandoned switchback right-of-way. A new station was later erected on the site of the freight house. Milepost 188 was located at the north siding switch. O&W SOCIETY COLLECTION.

LEFT: Baldwin's general store and post office was located on the main road through town and close to the depot. This was convenient for picking up merchandise shipped in by wholesalers. Small outgoing orders would leave via the mail crane next to the children. WILLIAM SCHRIVER COLLECTION.

BELOW: An August 1910 scene shows most of Merrickville and the track curving north toward Franklin. A small part of an ice pond and the main line is visible at the extreme left edge. The road serving the white-roofed creamery was part of the old switchback right-of-way. The creamery was known as Beaker's and produced several kinds of Italian cheeses. COURTESY OF JOE BUX AND DEPOT ATTIC.

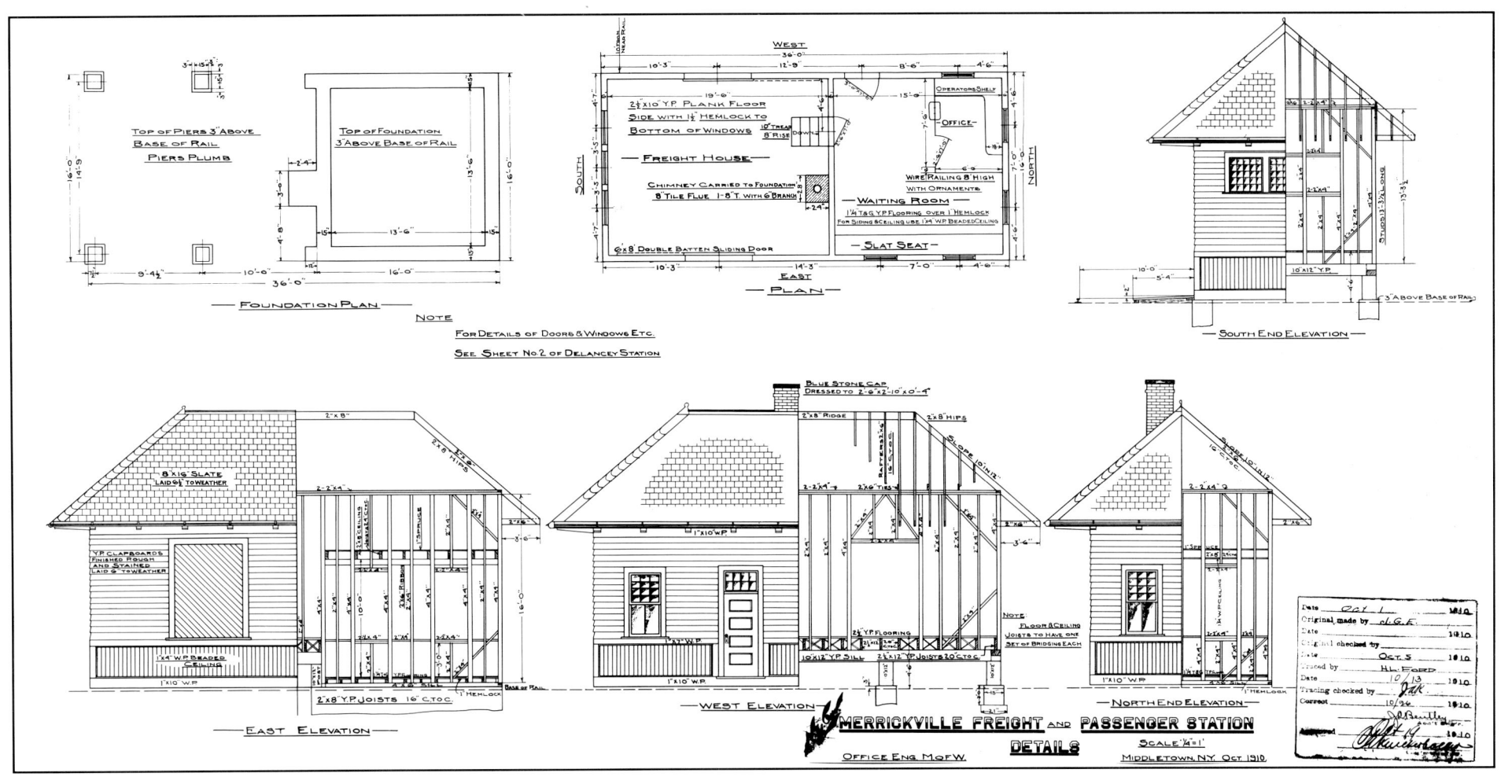

Using some details from the Delancey station, Merrickville's new depot was built late in 1910 or in 1911. The agent worked in a small office that was separated from the waiting room by wire screens. O&W SOCIETY COLLECTION.

Cattle fences, as seen in this early view at Merrickville, were found along miles of the O&W's right-of-way. This view is looking toward Walton. The station was later erected on or near the site of the small building at the crossing. JOHN MOFFAT COLLECTION.

Twisted metal roof sheets and the smoking rubble of a creamery fire greet the southbound milk train on its arrival in Merrickville. The limited processing ability of the early plant is evident by the lack of pipes, tanks and other hardware amid the ruins. A boiler and some steam or hot water lines were the extent of the plumbing. WILLIAM SCHRIVER COLLECTION.

LEFT: In 1948, Merrickville station still functioned as a train order office. The large white box above the steps contains a dispatcher's phone that can be used to reach the Middletown dispatcher's office when the station is closed. JOHN PICKETT.

BELOW: When the railroad no longer needed the Merrickville water tank, a local resident adopted the structure for water storage. It was the last 'in place' example of a steam-era facility along the O&W right-of-way. CARL OHLSON.

There is no commercial activity at Franklin Depot in the present day, but there were several businesses there in the early decades of this century, as the photograph at left shows. The station had a train order signal which is not present in the picture below. The latter photograph may have been taken after Merrickville opened as a train order office, taking the function away from Franklin Depot. BOTH PHOTOGRAPHS: SALLY DAVIS COLLECTION. COURTESY OF BRUCE TRACY.

Where we telephone to find out what time it "was"

LEFT: Those familiar with Franklin Depot today will marvel at this crowd on the station platform in 1907. A church group or fraternal organization might be going on an outing or to a convention in a neighboring town. Many of the passengers are facing south as if awaiting a northbound train. WALTER RICH COLLECTION.

BELOW: Franklin Station ground as 'revised March 24, 1914.' O&W SOCIETY COLLECTION.

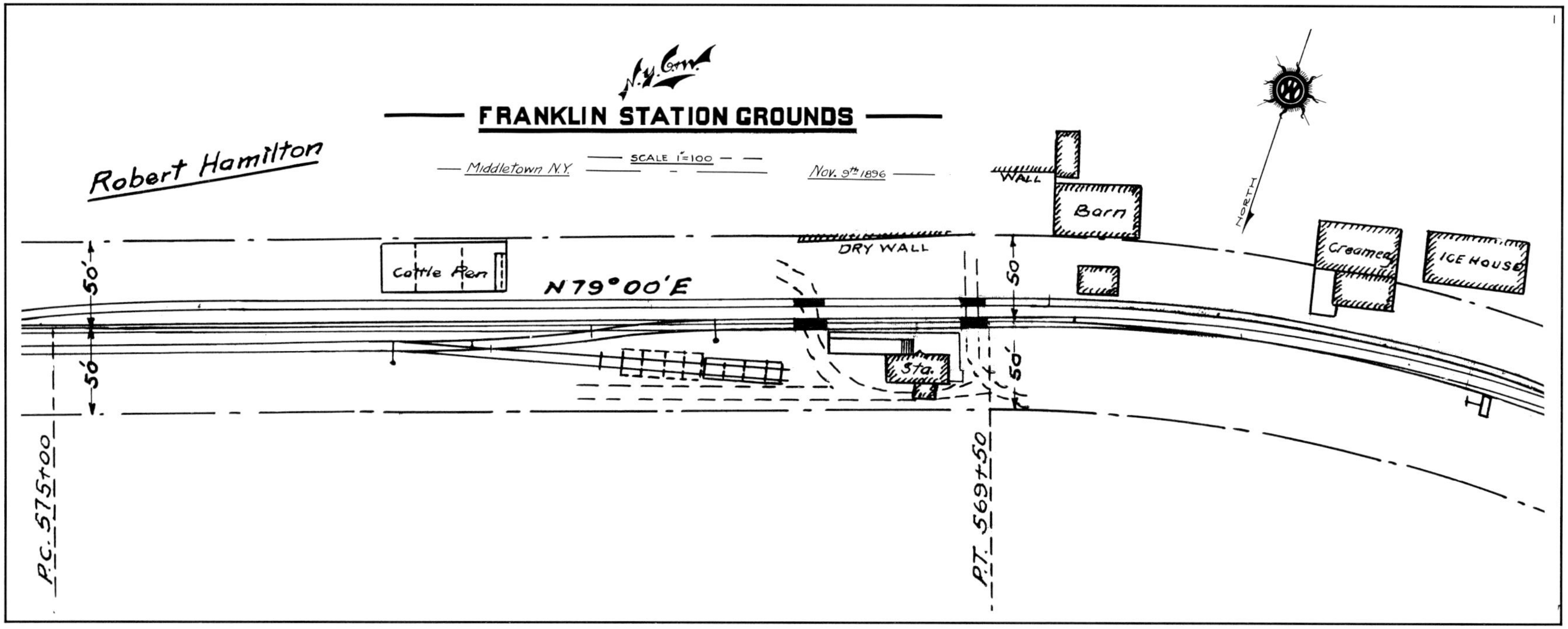

ABOVE AND LEFT: Three photographs show construction details on the new Franklin Depot trestle. Bridge 210 will be shorter (288 feet) since both approaches are losing some length to fills. Poured concrete and steel are replacing timber and the structure is wide enough for two tracks. O&W SOCIETY COLLECTION.

RIGHT: A new underpass, at the south end of 210, was part of the reconstruction. Poured concrete was relatively new for heavy construction and the O&W joined a growing list of railroads that adopted its use. Old rails were used as reinforcement. Beneath the fill is the earlier wooden trestle that passed over this road. O&W SOCIETY COLLECTION.

Left: Circa 1905, we are looking south with the Franklin Depot station located in the middle of several businesses that depend upon rail service. COURTESY OF JOE BUX AND DEPOT ATTIC.

LEFT: The engineer of this southbound is breaking for a stop at Franklin Depot as he crosses Goodrich Brook and the farm road that passes under the new trestle. While it looks suspiciously like a milk car, the lead car probably carries baggage. O&W SOCIETY COLLECTION.

BELOW: This August, 1958, view shows that some of the fill around the pillars of the north abutment has eroded away. The extra width for the second track proved unnecessary. STERLING KIMBALL.

N. Y. AND O. MIDLAND R. R. VIEWS.

Sidney Center Trestle. ---- Iron and Wood.

Length of Iron, ---- 1410 feet | Length of Wood, ---- 972 feet.
Highest Point, ---- 100 " | Highest Point, ---- 52 "
Total Length from East end of Iron to West end of Wood, ---- 2790 feet.

PHOTOGRAPHED BY
BURTON HINE, Walton, N. Y.

TOP LEFT: We are looking south over the original Oswego Midland-built trestle 216. Note the hand-hewn ties, light rail and lack of rock ballast. The original combined length of both trestles was 2400 feet, which was later reduced. TOP RIGHT: Trestle 217, and possibly 216 as well, had not yet had safety railings applied in this early OM view. The stretch of track between the two trestles was approximately 300 feet long. This was later lengthened as fill was added to reduce trestle lengths. These two photographs were published as stereo views, with the information shown at left on the obverse. TWO PHOTOGRAPHS: O&W SOCIETY COLLECTION.

the 1890s and early 1900s. Some of these are maintained by the present property owners who, in some instances, allow the right-of-way to be used by recreational vehicles.

The route continued north, winding along the edge of Hodge's Hill with Carr's Creek about 100 feet below. Soon after passing milepost 192, the railroad rounded the shoulder of the ridge and made a great horseshoe curve over two trestles and around the village of Sidney Center—later to be known as Maywood (SC, 193.08). Construction from the north reached this point on July 1, 1870. However, the two great trestles were not yet in place and were not completed until October 4, 1871.

Sidney Center sits in the junction of three valleys and gave the New York & Oswego Midland the problem of crossing two valleys and the hill that separated them before it continued north. The first trestle, bridge 216, was almost 1400 feet in length and 100 feet high. The line then gained a small hill over which the right-of-way curved to the right for a few hundred feet. A second trestle, shorter and not as tall as the first—470 feet and 40 feet respectively— was bridge 217. It took the line over a smaller valley and the road that led to the depot and creamery. These measurements are approximate, and the true distances varied over the years because of improvements. The height, length, and curvature of the trestles, as well as the geographic setting, provided one of the railroad's most spectacular scenes. Machinery and rolling stock weighing hundreds of tons passing overhead with passengers peering down into back yards left impressions that are still bright for many residents more than 30 years after the railroad's abandonment. Mrs. Wannita Kilmer remembers childhood and adolescent years in Sidney Center within the sights and sounds of a busy O&W:

> I had a box seat on the 50-yard line and was a one-person cheering section for the O&W. My youthful days were pretty much involved with the railroad. When the trains from Walton came around the bend and onto the large trestle, they always blew their whistle. That was my signal to rush outside and wave as the train went by. Often I was at the feed store near the depot and watched the trainmen throw switches so cars could be put in the siding and empties taken out. Three to five cars of feed were unloaded daily. We children were often warned to never cross the tracks when a train was due or was switching. What adventuresome child heeds such advice? When salesmen ran up beneath the small trestle to catch a train, we knew they would lose the change in their pockets, so we ran over to pick it up.
>
> I went to Walton High School via the O&W. When we passed through the Northfield Tunnel, we always bent our heads because the big boys threw spitballs at us. A rough estimate would be that one third of the students attending Walton and Sidney high schools were from surrounding communities and rode the O&W to school.
>
> During World War I, a detachment of soldiers was placed just above the small trestle. They patrolled both trestles 24 hours each day. Guarding the Northfield Tunnel was also their responsibility. They called out each hour saying 'All is well.'
>
> The Borden's creamery had an icehouse and I believe the ice came from East Masonville Pond. Many times I watched the men load the cans into the cars and then cover them with chopped ice. In the winter, we skated on the mill pond under the

This group's apparent lack of concern for an approaching train is due to the posted speed restriction on trestle 216. WALTER RICH COLLECTION.

The dominant feature of the O&W's right-of-way between the Northfield Tunnel and Sidney was the sweeping curve and trestles at Sidney Center. The railroad's alignment around the village was the O&W's version of the famous Horseshoe Curve of the Pennsylvania Railroad. The O&W's Sidney Center curve lacked the traffic density and heavy grades of the PRR, but it had a great deal of rural charm and small town atmosphere. A storage shed, the station and creamery, and the right-of-way heading north through a cut are visible in the left of the picture below. New abutments have been poured for both ends of trestle 217 and a substantial section of the south end is being buried by fill. The wooden bents and stringers are soon to be replaced by steel. *TWO PHOTOGRAPHS: COURTESY OF JOE BUX AND DEPOT ATTIC.*

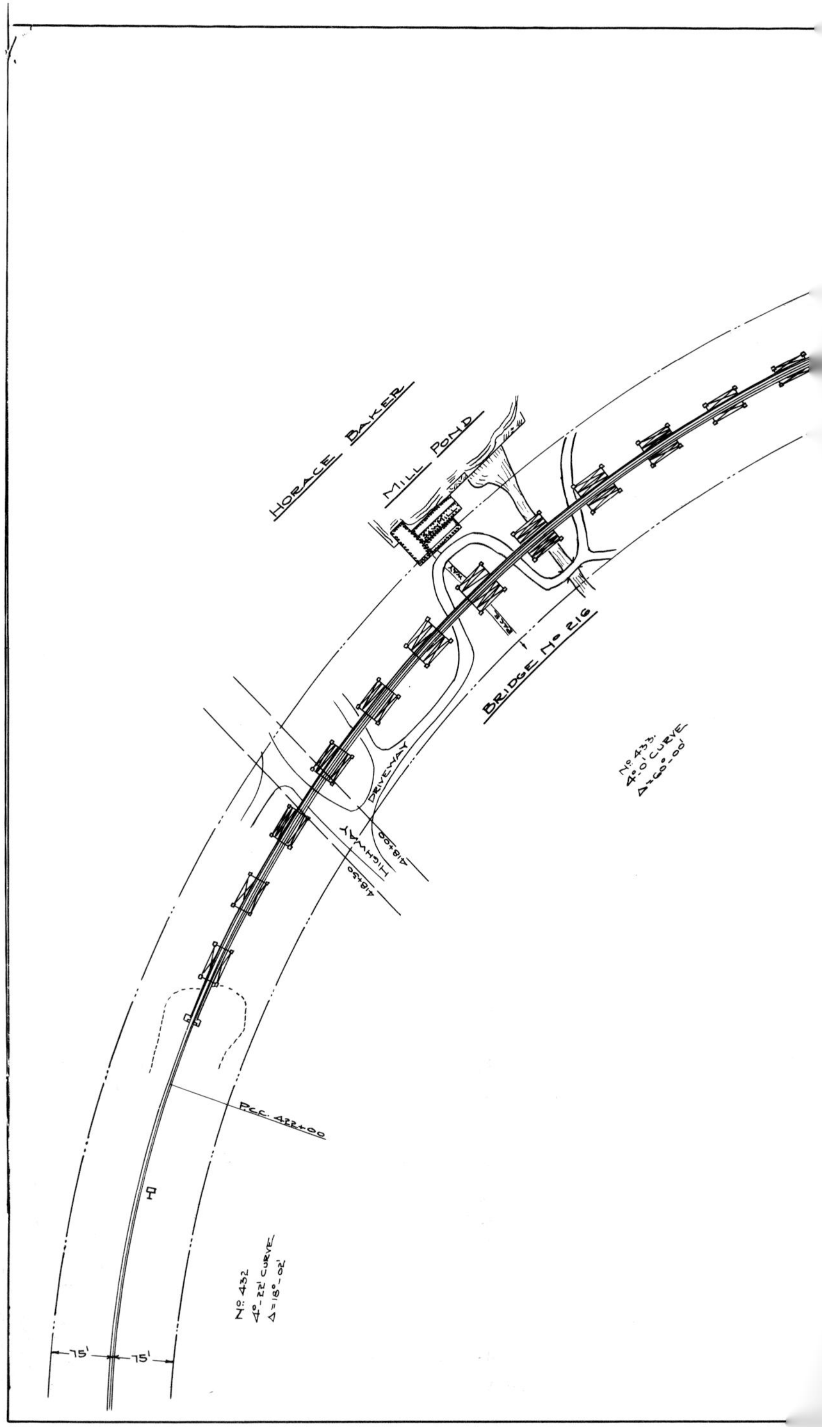

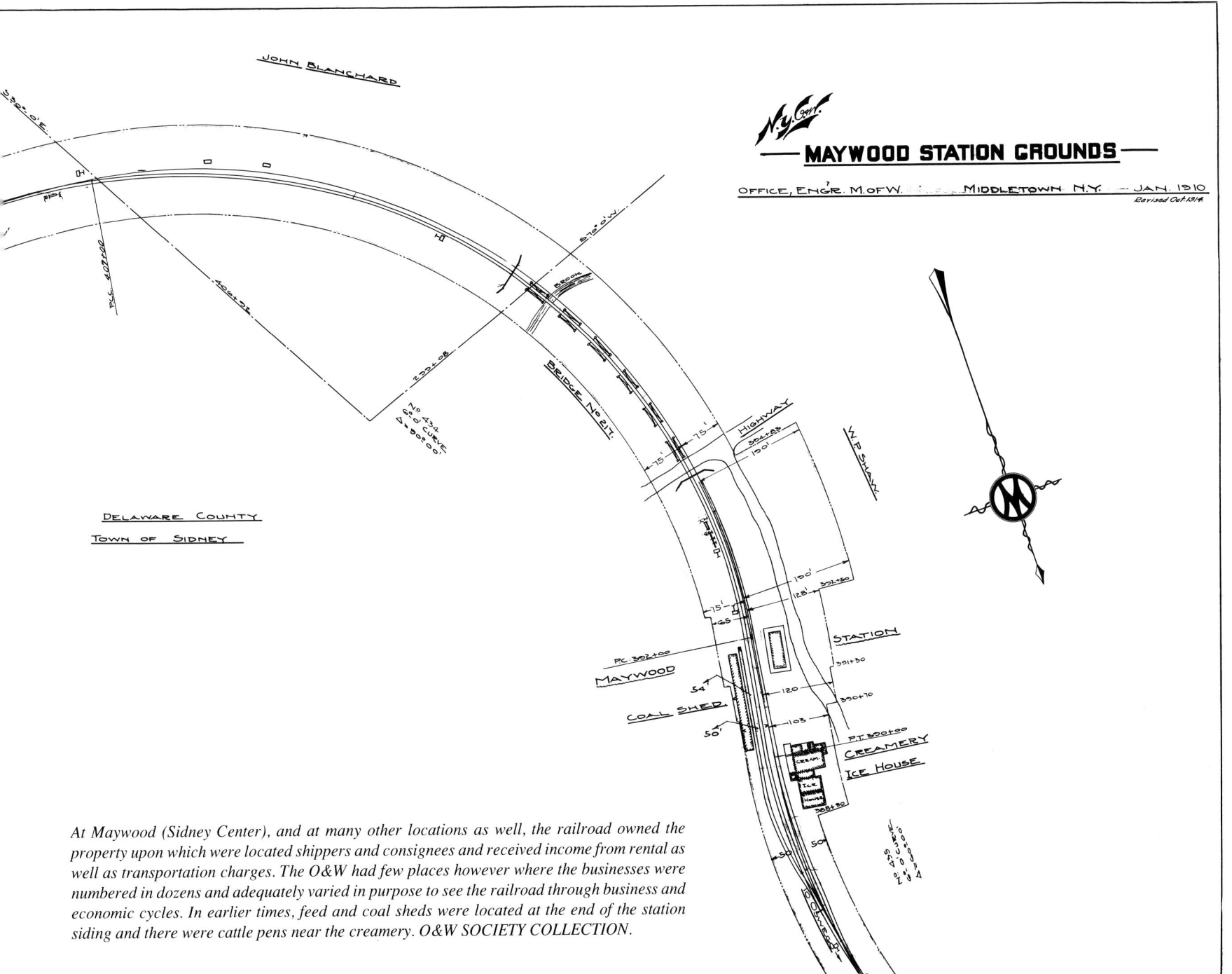

At Maywood (Sidney Center), and at many other locations as well, the railroad owned the property upon which were located shippers and consignees and received income from rental as well as transportation charges. The O&W had few places however where the businesses were numbered in dozens and adequately varied in purpose to see the railroad through business and economic cycles. In earlier times, feed and coal sheds were located at the end of the station siding and there were cattle pens near the creamery. O&W SOCIETY COLLECTION.

The greater part of Sidney Center is visible from the hill behind trestle 217. Depot Street comes up from the village and passes under the north end of the bridge. The double-track width of the trestle support structure can be seen from this aerial perspective. JOHN MOFFAT COLLECTION.

Depot St. went under the north end of trestle 217, where a side road led up to the depot and creamery. Although the railroad half-circled the town it was probably the most convenient location for the station. When passenger service ended, the public had little reason to refer to the town as Maywood and it is now Sidney Center again, and probably had been all along, as far as residents were concerned. WALTER RICH COLLECTION.

big trestle. There was never any fear of the trains going by on the trestle over our heads. I will always think that the engineers who designed those two trestles were geniuses. As you rode over them, if you didn't look out the window, you would have thought you were on straight track. Fast freight trains never rocked as they came across.

The higher and longer of the two, bridge 216, was originally built of iron while No. 217 was built of wood. These trestles were redecked at least once before they were replaced by steel viaducts. No. 216 was upgraded in 1890 when the older deck was replaced with Georgia pine. Pictures clearly show two versions of both bridges. In the mid-1890s a steel structure superseded the original iron of No. 216. This steel viaduct was reported by the company as being 90 feet in height, with a length of 1220 feet consisting of 40- and 50-foot spans. The length was reduced by filling in 190 feet of the older trestle work. This required new piers and abutments which made great use of poured concrete. From 1890 on into the twentieth century, the O&W put a great deal of money into plant improvement, with the Maywood trestles being a representative sample of the effort. Bridge 217 was partly rebuilt in 1880 and rebuilt again with Georgia pine in 1889. Since this structure was not as high or long or built to as great a curve as No. 216, it was not replaced with steel until 1906. It was also shortened by filling part of the southern end. The second viaduct contained 13 spans and was 468 feet long. At that time, the O&W's traffic and financial outlook was very promising and it seemed reasonable to plan for future double tracking. The concrete abutments were made wide enough for two tracks, but the operational necessity for such expansion never came.

Mrs. Kilmer relates a hair-raising experience on bridge 217.

One summer day, against all parental admonitions to never go on the trestles, my sister, two nieces, the boy next door, the section foreman's son and I ventured out on the smaller trestle. We were sure no trains were due, but not all of the freight trains ran on schedule. We were nearly halfway across when we heard the whistle of a train coming around the bend from Walton. We all started to run to the end of the trestle but my younger niece couldn't keep up. My older sister, older niece, and the boy next door made it. The section boss's son and myself stopped to help my younger niece. He said, 'We can't get off in time,' so we stepped out onto a place the section hands used. He said to the niece, 'Grip the outside rail for dear life. Nina, you lock hands with me behind her and grab the rail with the other hand.' The suction as the train went by was great, but we held on. We caught it from our parents and the men on the train, but they also said, 'We compliment you for knowing what to do.' We had learned our lesson and never tried that again.

Northbound train 11 of July 4, 1932, is behind engine 273. Unfortunately fuzzy, the photograph still shows the trestle's graceful curve and farm pastures above and below the right-of-way. The Walton-Sidney road passes under the far end of the bridge. CARL P. MUNCK COLLECTION.

In order to avoid having two communities on line with the same or similar names—Sidney Center and Sidney—the railroad designated Sidney Center as Maywood or Maywood Station. The name change took place on June 27, 1897. The purpose was to avoid possible confusion in train orders, waybills, and passenger destinations. A station, coal shed, and Borden's creamery were located on the west side of the track, near the north end of trestle 217. There were also two single-ended sidings leading into the main line at the north end of the station complex. George A. Boice was the last agent at Sidney Center. He locked the door on December 28, 1939, when the railroad closed six stations to reduce expenses.

A final comment from Mrs. Kilmer:

Even the children at School Nine could look out the window at the trains as they came around the bend after passing the creamery. Many times I was told to take my seat; the train could get along without my watching it!

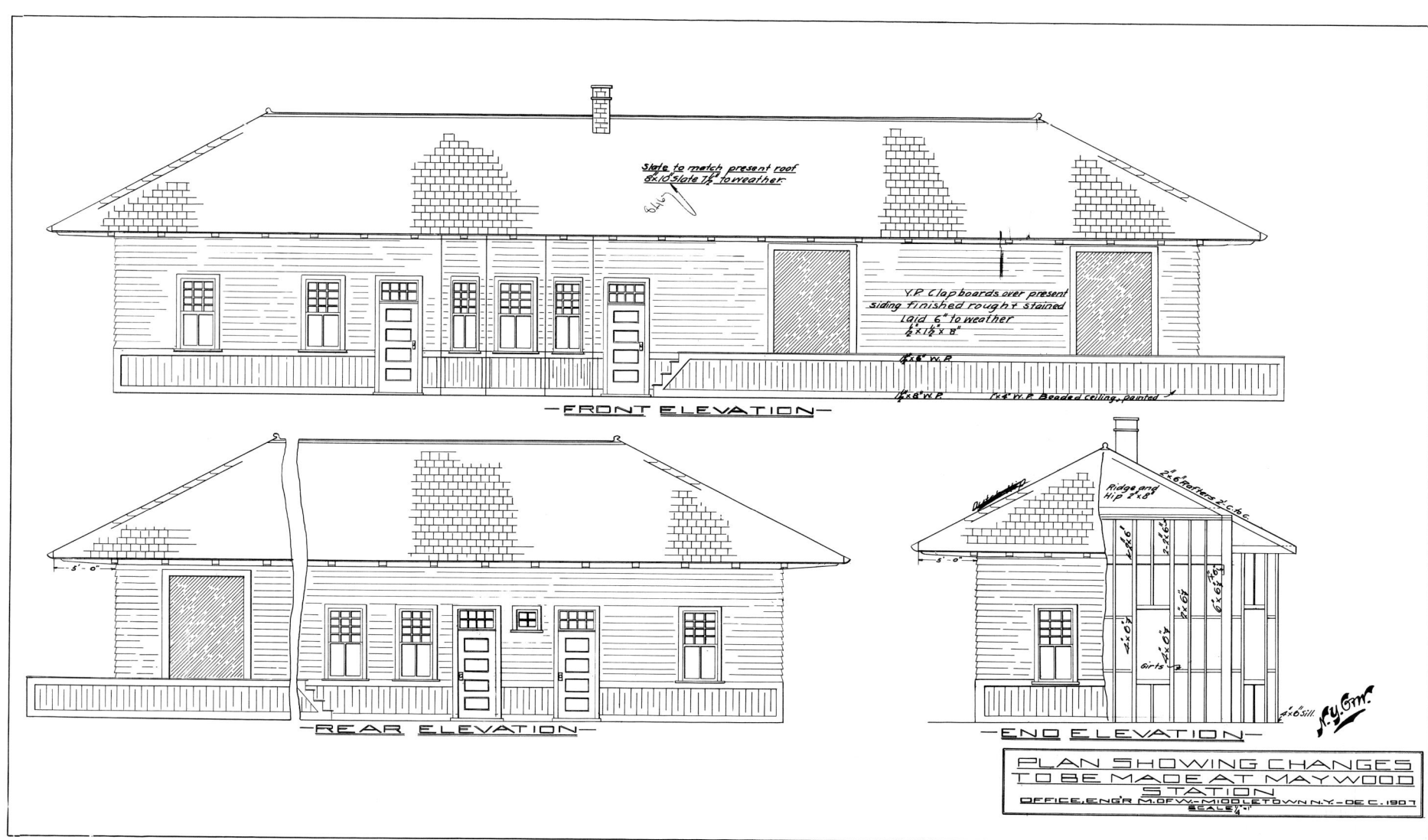

LEFT: The northbound milk train is stopped at Maywood while a brakeman walks forward, seemingly intent on some task. He may throw the switch that will allow a car to be picked up or placed. If that is his intention, he will also have to throw the derail on the right to allow access to the siding. BOB LORENZ COLLECTION.

BELOW: Two scenes show contrasting appearances of Maywood station in 1936, at left, and August, 1958, at right. The dark brown paint or stain used on many O&W depots tended to make them look poorly maintained, especially in black and white photographs, even before deferred maintenance became a money-saving policy. In fresh paint, however, the brown siding, green wainscoting and red sashes must have presented a dignified and handsome appearance. LEFT: WALTER RICH COLLECTION. RIGHT: STERLING KIMBALL.

It is not indicated by a sign, but the Maywood creamery was once part of the Borden's holdings. Standing by the coal yard, the white-clad, rubber-booted workers take a few minutes from their steamy labors. The cases on the platform indicate a bottling or condensing operation large enough to ship carload lots. O&W SOCIETY COLLECTION.

LEFT: *Within the shadow of trestle 216 was a pond that supplied waterpower for a sawmill and ice in the winter.* COURTESY OF JOE BUX AND DEPOT ATTIC.

BELOW: *The 1895 rebuilding of bridge 216, when steel replaced iron, was marked by this cornerstone and the contractor's name. The stone was in a pier next to one of two roads that passed under the bridge. It is believed to be in the collection of a local historical society.* STERLING KIMBALL COLLECTION.

John Bauman of Carbondale, PA brought the trestles down after the trains stopped running in 1957. Because of the depressed prices for scrap steel in this country at the time, the metal was sold to France and Belgium.

The railroad exited Sidney Center through a cut and proceeded a half mile west to a location known as Niles (193.57). It was also known as Niles Switch. A 2400-foot passing siding was constructed and at one period was used for at least three daily scheduled meets involving six trains, as indicated in an employees' timetable. Some type of provision must have been made for travelers to board and detrain, since it is listed as a stopping point for passenger trains. This seems strange since there was a depot and ticket agent less than a mile away. The name came from a local family and the siding was marked with wooden name signs at each end. Although there is no firm evidence in this case, it was not uncommon for a land owner to deed property to a railroad in exchange for having a train stop on demand for his convenience. As with sidings at Northfield and Merrickville, Niles remained in place if not in service into the 1950s and possibly until 1957.

Slightly more than two miles west was a hamlet known as Youngs (YO, 196.23). The 1873 Midland Travelers' Guide described Youngs as having "a small station and post office and it is about a mile and a half from the village of Unadilla on the Albany & Susquehanna Railroad." Youngs got a new station in 1915. A Borden's plant, stock pen, feed and farm supply dealer, and freight house shipped or received freight via a pair of sidings. There was an earlier creamery here run by J. C. Righter. It was located on the lower side of the track, whereas the later Borden's was on the uphill side. The Borden's creamery closed in the later 1930s, and its farmers then had to deliver to the Sidney Center plant or change their dealer affiliation. The small commercial center at Youngs was reached by a dirt road that ran a short distance south from the village. About a quarter-mile north of the station stands a fill that bridged a small stream called Ford's Brook. The

LEFT: Between Sidney Center and Niles, the right-of-way went through a rock cut. This view was taken during the Midland days and may well date back to the opening of the route. The view looks north. O&W SOCIETY COLLECTION.

ABOVE: The road through the village of Youngs went over the track on a timber bridge west of the station. Close-clearance warning devices (tell-tales) still stood on both sides of the bridge in this August 13, 1958, photograph. STERLING KIMBALL COLLECTION.

LEFT: Between Niles and Youngs was bridge 223 at M.P. 194.82. Known as Southwick's Trestle, it was 180 feet long and 39 feet high. STERLING KIMBALL.

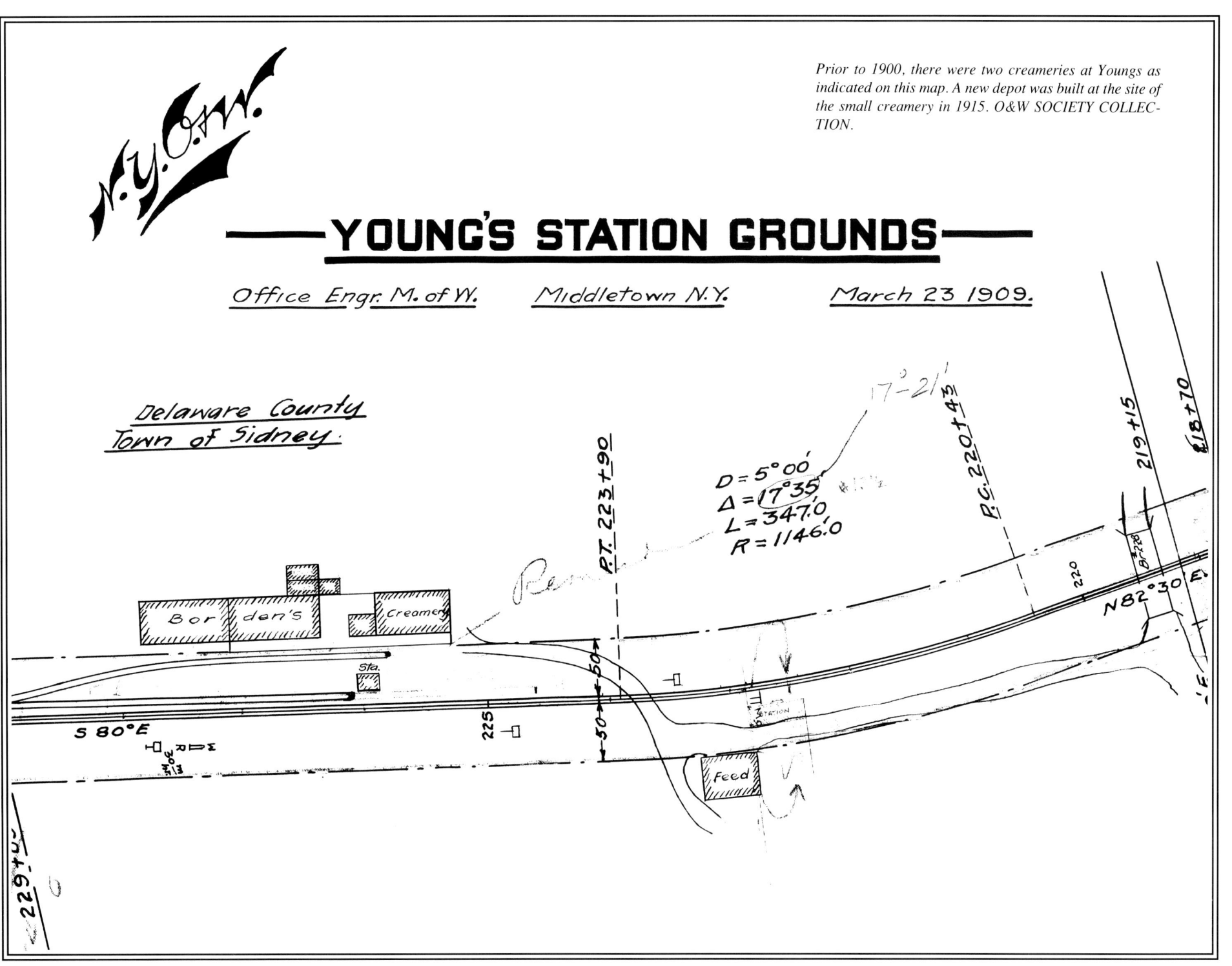

Prior to 1900, there were two creameries at Youngs as indicated on this map. A new depot was built at the site of the small creamery in 1915. O&W SOCIETY COLLECTION.

![Youngs, N.Y.]

The first station at Youngs lacked a platform for the convenience of passengers and looked neglected. Its condition was noted in a critical letter from the state Public Utilities Commission. A boxcar occupies the siding at the creamery. WALTER RICH COLLECTION.

Recalling the days when he delivered milk to the Borden's plant, Harold Dumond of Youngs points to the remnant of the concrete delivery platform of that creamery. AUTHOR'S PHOTOGRAPH.

RIGHT: After noting the condition of the older structure, the Public Utilities Commission ordered the O&W to build a new station at Youngs. This was done in 1915. The new building was closer to the center of the little village and was reached by a dirt road that is all but gone today. The white post, noted in earlier photographs, was also employed here as part of the train signaling system. JOHN AND SUE HUDSON COLLECTION.

BELOW: With its very small population, Youngs was only a flag stop for many trains. Passengers wishing to board through trains had to go to a station farther south, or north to Sidney. Sometime in the 1930's, Youngs ceased to be listed as a passenger stop. The railroad was inconsistent in the spelling of the village name, using both Youngs and Young's. WALTER RICH COLLECTION.

ABOVE: Two hopper cars sit on a coal trestle at Youngs. Although its markings are not visible, the details on the steel car appear to be of O&W design. Placing cars on such a trestle was tricky and occasionally one was pushed off the end. O&W SOCIETY COLLECTION.

Built in 1892, the South Unadilla station served the freight transportation needs of the immediate vicinity. There was at least one bluestone shipper here as well as pens for the shipping and receiving of animals. In all, the railroad listed over 30 shippers and consignees at this location in 1910. The flag displaying green over white demonstrates the origin of the term 'flag stop.' It means that passengers wish to board the next train approaching the depot and the engineer must respond to the signal with two short blasts of the engine whistle to indicate acknowledgment. COURTESY OF JOE BUX AND DEPOT ATTIC.

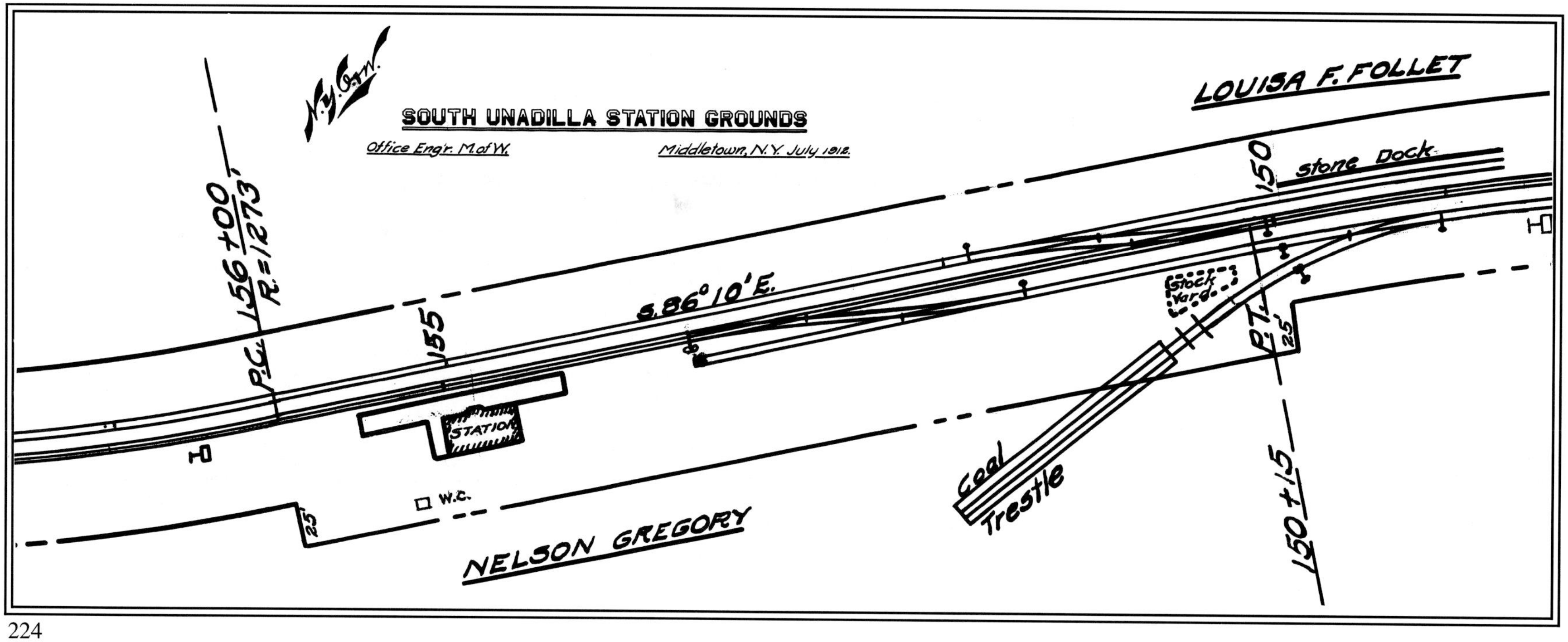

brook was originally crossed by a trestle which was later filled in, and a public road now uses the fill. Sometime prior to 1939, Youngs was eliminated as a passenger stop.

Proceeding northward, the railroad continued to hold to the hillside above the main highway, and 1.5 miles later entered the wider valley of the Susquehanna river at South Unadilla (UD, 197.56). A new station was built here in 1892 or 1893. As with Northfield and Franklin Depot, this station served an area rather than a single community. The station area supported some commercial activity although it was a good half mile from the cluster of houses and highway intersection that was South Unadilla. A retail coal trestle, team track, and cattle pen were constructed north of the station. There was also a passing siding that was installed in 1893 but removed sometime before operations ceased in 1957. Farther north was another siding that might have served a stone quarry. Presently the station site is occupied by a bluestone company. Between this point and Sidney, there was a location known as Gillette. The building of Interstate Route 88 has destroyed some of the right-of-way north of milepost 198. It was in this section that the right-of-way left the hillside and cut diagonally across the valley. Passengers and trainmen were able to look up and down the valley of the Susquehanna River as their train descended from the hills. About a half mile north of milepost 199 was the yard-limit board marking the Sidney switching limits.

LEFT: It was the station agent's responsibility to keep the platform clear of snow and to maintain the building, grounds, and all appliances related to them in good order. The curtained gable windows indicated that the agent was in residence and thus charged with the upkeep of his own quarters as well. O&W SOCIETY COLLECTION.

Perhaps while waiting for someone to come in on the next train, a family used the station as a picture backdrop. The depot might also have been a destination for a Sunday afternoon drive in the touring car. COURTESY OF JOE BUX AND DEPOT ATTIC.

TOP LEFT: Steam derrick SD-1 works the west end of a major derailment at South Unadilla on June 28, 1908. The rear end of the derailed train sits in the passing siding across from the station. A large audience on the hillside at right tries to second-guess the wreckmaster on which car will next be pulled from the heap of shattered wood and metal. WALTER RICH COLLECTION. TOP RIGHT: Sacked freight salvaged from the wrecked boxcars is piled above the cut. Two or more gondola-loads of coal will also have to be picked up. Frugal area residents will visit the scene and get away with several buckets and sacks of coal to reduce next winter's fuel bill. O&W SOCIETY COLLECTION.

LEFT: The main concern at a derailment site is to get the line open as quickly as possible to avoid further traffic delay and loss. An engine down an embankment required a planned recovery effort, and might lie where it came to rest for several weeks before salvage efforts began. This may be the engine involved in the wreck shown. JOE BUX COLLECTION.

A pair of camelbacks bring a long train that includes 14 milk cars over bridge 230 at South Unadilla. This trestle was filled in sometime after 1903. In this very unusual view, we are looking back from the cab of the first locomotive, through and past the cab that sheltered the fireman. COURTESY OF JOE BUX AND DEPOT ATTIC.

Sidney's Union Station was viewed with pride by the community according to editorial commentary in the local paper. Interline passengers to and from the D&H were mere steps away from connections. The signal at the left kept O&W enginemen from blocking the Main Street crossing while waiting to cross the D&H. If it was set at stop, they did not have permission to cross the D&H and would wait, clear of the busy crossing, until permission was granted by the towerman. O&W SOCIETY COLLETION.

Chapter 11: Sidney

The efforts of the O&W Company in improving its property in Sidney during the present season have been viewed with lively satisfaction by the many friends of that popular and very progressive railroad company. Although the O&W Company owns in Sidney only a comparatively small strip of land, none daunted it has set bravely to the task of improvement. In this it has succeeded admirably, much to its credit and the public good.

Sidney Record, September 27, 1902

High spirits reigned in the western corner of Delaware County on October 22, 1866. The Albany & Susquehanna Railroad Company, chartered several years earlier to build a line between Albany and Binghamton, reached Sidney Plains on that date. Transportation over dirt roads and along unimproved rivers had limited business and agricultural development in the vicinity as it had in all rural areas. Albany and Binghamton were now only a few hours away via the A&S, and much of the region's rural isolation was over. The road was completed to Binghamton in January of 1869, largely with the assistance of state aid and town bonding funds. The line soon became a major link in a coal route from Pennsylvania to Albany after it was leased by the Delaware & Hudson Canal Company. This route came to include the Jefferson Railroad that ran from the coal fields to an Erie—formerly New York & Erie—connection at Lanesboro, Pa. The NY&E provided a link from that point to Binghamton and the A&S ran north from there.

In June, 1868, two years after the arrival of the A&S, contracts were awarded for the construction of the New York & Oswego Midland. Sidney Plains was the halfway point between Oswego and Middletown and was a convenient supply and storage depot. The A&S provided a route for incoming rail, track fittings, lumber, labor and other necessities for building the NY&OM. Once the track was down, locomotives and rolling stock made their OM entry via the A&S into Sidney Plains.

Thanks to the forces of nature the community did not have to seek out the OM and entice it to enter. Sidney Plains was one of four geographic points within the state that A.C. Powell, the Midland locating engineer, said the road had to pass through. Powell, in a pamphlet prepared for the company, claimed that "nature determined these four points and the board of directors had the responsibility to locate the line between them."

On June 15, 1870, the OM was opened for service between Norwich and Sidney Plains, giving the region its second rail outlet. A Midland timetable for that month showed two passenger trains and one freight running between Oswego and Sidney Plains. This newly completed section included the great Lyon Brook bridge and heavy grades to Guilford Summit that were north of Sidney Plains. The contract to continue the railroad south from Sidney Plains to Walton was awarded in September of 1869 and again the work took two years to complete. The road would not be a through route for two more years, but local travel and freight business was encouraged and established as each section opened. A grade-level crossing between the OM and the D&H was constructed at Sidney Plains without the difficulty that often occurred when such a junction was

229

RIGHT: *Laborers, or possibly immigrants, await an O&W train at the old Sidney station. The board and batten construction and simple brackets under the eaves typify the lack of elegance found in many railroads' original structures. After the great investment began to earn income, communal requests for more attractive facilities were sometimes granted.* RICHARD ARRANDALE COLLECTION.

BELOW: *This view shows the north end and D&H side of Sidney's first station.* WILLIAM SCHRIVER COLLECTION.

attempted. At least no mention is made of the A&S stationing club-wielding workmen at the site to prevent the OM from coming through.

In 1870, the A&S was leased by the D&H Canal Company. This lease would prove beneficial to the New York, Ontario & Western in a few years. Interchange with the D&H provided both through and local traffic in great quantity. In 1937, the year the O&W entered bankruptcy, the interchange at Sidney amounted to 3560 cars.

A third railroad was planned for Sidney in the form of an electric interurban line that would run to the village of Franklin. A contract was reported late in June, 1903. Some grading was done and a powerhouse was built, but financial and legal obstacles kept the line from completion. The power plant did provide part of Sidney's electricity for a short while. It is very likely that the route of this electric line followed one of the old OM proposed routes up the Susquehanna to the Ouleout Creek and then on to Franklin. If the line were completed, it would probably have pulled some local passenger traffic from both the O&W and the D&H. Another proposed trolley route was planned to run north to connect Sidney Plains with Utica via Morris.

With two railroads in the village, commercial development began in earnest. The railroads provided direct employment for many and encouraged the expansion and establishment of other businesses which required additional workers. All of these people, in turn, required goods and services. Initially a foundry, wagon shop, several blacksmiths,

It is difficult for the present generation to realize how much activity took place at a local railroad station. These two views, on different occasions and opposite ends of Sidney's original wooden station, illustrate the point. In both photographs, the D&H seems to be getting most of the business. TWO PHOTOGRAPHS: RICHARD ARRANDALE COLLECTION.

Main Street Crossing, Sidney, New York.

LEFT: The O&W's planked crossing occupies the foreground in this view which looks north on Sidney's Main St. It is protected by the flagman, perhaps the vigilant Mott Videtto himself, seated on the streetside bench where he could greet passing townspeople by name. The D&H employed its own crossing watchman whose shelter is visible just above the station baggage carts at the left. WILLIAM SCHRIVER COLLECTION. *LOWER LEFT: The Hotel Sidney was conveniently located on Main Street near the station. It served both travelers and railroad men until it was destroyed by fire.* O&W SOCIETY COLLECTION.

BELOW: The O&W's beautification projects in Sidney showed a fine degree of civic interest on the part of the railroad and was applauded by the citizenry. Many railroads employed gardeners to tend such projects, and they traveled between towns on their railroad passes. RICHARD ARRANDALE COLLECTION.

169—Hotel Sidney. Sidney, N.Y.

This view of an eastbound milk train in Sidney was apparently taken by an engineman of a waiting westbound train. The milk trains usually had a combine on the rear for the use of the crew and those travelers who, for whatever reasons, had to travel the milk trains. In later years, a caboose was sometimes added. ROBERT HARDING COLLECTION: COURTESY OF JOE BUX AND DEPOT ATTIC.

a single creamery, hotels, a paper mill, and a newspaper called the *Midland Times* were the businesses in the community. Sidney was incorporated as a village in 1888, and it was probably at this time that the name was shortened from Sidney Plains to Sidney.

The closing years of the 19th century saw many additional new industries come into the village. A silk mill, glass works, cart and carriage company, novelty works, woodenware, and cigar factories were established. Later a knitting mill arrived and the Sidney Mill and Lumber Company became a manufacturer of lawn swings. The dairy business picked up with the coming of a French cheese manufacturing firm that required local milk in quantity. The railroad built a creamery in 1896 and a new icehouse in 1909. For a short time, Hatfield automobiles were also made in Sidney. A Methodist Church organization, the Sidney Grove Camp Meeting Association, provided both the O&W and the D&H with passengers and passenger extras during the warmer months.

Probably the best known of all the industries in Sidney was the Scintilla Magneto Company, which later became a division of Bendix Aviation Corporation. This firm established itself in the former Hatfield buildings. From a simple 15-employee beginning, it grew to become Sidney's major employer. Its peak period came during World War II. Some 8600 people were employed in 1943 producing electrical components for aircraft. In January of that year, the O&W instituted Commuting War Workers' Specials from both Walton and Norwich to transport the workers, since gasoline and tires were rationed. The railroad reported that it carried 487,156 passengers on these trains during a 13-month period. Wooden coaches 262-268 inclusive were reportedly assigned to this service. Special buses brought workers from points as distant as Susquehanna and Forest City, Pa. The D&H also provided some special transportation to Scintilla.

The population of Sidney Plains was about 500 at the time the Midland came through. Like many other communities of its size on the line, it pressured the OM to locate its shops in the village, and this was a lively newspaper topic at one time. However, it was Norwich, 25 miles to the north, that became the operating center of the Northern Division. Sidney would eventually have a small roundhouse, car shop, icehouses, water tank, coal dump, and other modest facilities for repairs and operations. A yardmaster oversaw local operations and had the services of an engine and yard crew. These jobs remained until the road closed but were limited to only the day shift as the end approached. Pusher engines were often required in steam days, since Sidney was in a river valley. From the 1930's until the end of steam operations, this was usually a W-class engine. On some occasions a pusher that had coupled onto a south-bound freight at Norwich went on through Sidney and on to Northfield with a train.

The many train movements kept Main Street crossing watchmen very busy. At the turn of the century Mott Videtto was an O&W employee assigned to that job. He worked out of a wooden shanty for 48 years and had a counterpart at the neighboring D&H crossing who put in the same amount of time. In 1916, the O&W had six tracks

233

A series of Sidney pictures from the Robert Harding collection show some of the men and machines that called at the busy O&W location daily. Clockwise from top left: Engine No. 4, on the New Berlin train, has been decorated for July 4, 1904. Engineer Archer Weedon stands on the steam chest, fireman Bill McDonald stands in the gangway, and Bryon Ducollon, conductor, is second from the right. Engine 146 is ready to make its first run north to Norwich with milk train 9. Another engine used on the New Berlin run was the 115 seen at Sidney circa 1904. Train No. 6 with engine 68 is stopped near the car repair track just south of the station. The stock car in the background is lettered N.Y.O.&W. FOUR PHOTOGRAPHS: COURTESY DEPOT ATTIC AND JOE BUX.

TOP: The locomotive coaling ramp at Sidney was similar in appearance and operation to the one at Walton. Several drop-bottom coal gondolas were being placed for unloading. Assigned laborers had to spend several hours each day in dumping and shoveling coal and filling tenders. O&W SOCIETY COLLECTION. BOTTOM: This scene at the Sidney coaling dock offers the opportunity to better understand the facility's operation as explained in the Walton chapter. The four-wheel cart on the ramp is about to drop its coal load into the tender with an accompanying cloud of dust. RICHARD ARRANDALE COLLECTION.

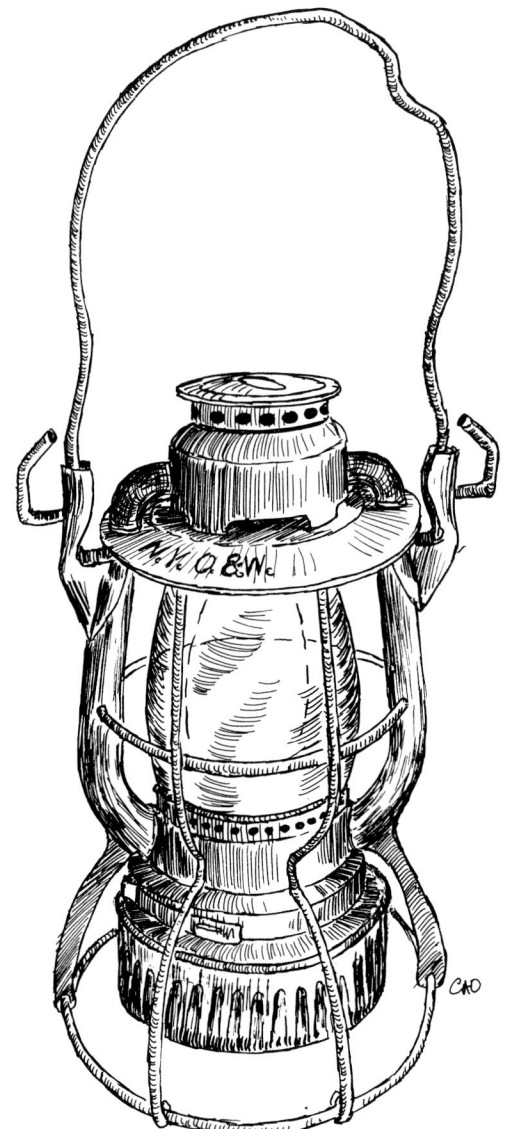

Coaling, watering, a wipe-down, and other services having been completed, the 241 is ready for another assignment. Sidney's four-stalled roundhouse and shopmen serviced assigned locomotives and through power that needed minor mechanical attention or routine servicing during a brief visit. O&W SOCIETY COLLECTION.

LEFT: Engine 42 was frequently found in Sidney. On the pilot is Charles W. Shofkom, a hostler whose O&W career began in 1912 as an engine wiper. Coincidentally, his career with the railroad spanned 42 years. RALPH SHOFKOM COLLECTION.

BELOW: The southbound milk train has two boxcars between the milk cars and the combine; so the conductor's signal must be relayed to the head end by hand signals when it is time to leave. To the right is the 301 with a tender that was originally attached to a Y-class 4-8-2. The W-class 300's were most frequently found on the northern end of the O&W where they turned in satisfactory performances in all types of service. COURTESY OF CAL'S CLASSICS.

A New York Division Railroad Enthusiasts' Special pauses at Sidney on an unspecified date. Such trips frequently utilized several railroads to make a circle trip. For example, Sidney offered the opportunity to switch from the O&W to the D&H for a run to Binghamton where the Lackawanna or Erie might be used to get back to the metropolitan area. COURTESY OF CAL'S CLASSICS.

across Main Street while the D&H had four. Near the crossing was the passenger station which was replaced by joint O&W-D&H passenger- and freight-handling facilities in 1913. The passenger station was north of Main Street and the freight house was south of it.

Through the years of the OM's and the O&W's existence, the dividing line between the Northern and Southern Divisions seemed to be the Susquehanna River at Sidney. However, Sidney's function as a crew-change point seemed to fluctuate. Many passenger runs originated or terminated there and for many years the New Berlin branch local freight began its daily run from the Sidney yard. The through freight and passenger runs, however, changed crews and usually motive power at Norwich. D&H interchange, local service, and general yard work required 24-hour switching, and several crews were employed for that service. The crashing and stretching of couplers and draft gear and the coal smoke from two busy railroads gave Sidney the unmistakable atmosphere of a railroad community.

Both the OM and the O&W had a close relationship with the D&H Canal Company and its subsidiary A&S. The connection at Sidney was the key piece to a mutually profitable operation for the two roads. Some background is necessary to see how this came about. The D&H Canal Company, looking to possible expansion and further outlets for their coal, gained possession of the 31-mile Utica, Clinton & Binghamton Railroad that ran from Utica to Randallsville, N.Y. It also leased the 13-mile Rome & Clinton that ran between its namesake locations and connected with the UC&B at Clinton. Both properties were then sublet in 1872 to the NY&OM, which operated them until it entered receivership. When the OM could no longer handle its own business affairs, the D&H assumed operation of its two properties as well as the OM between Sidney and Randallsville in 1875. The UC&B and R&C were operated under a variety of arrangements until the O&W leased them in 1886 for some $70,000 per year. Rather than arranging a trackage-rights agreement to bridge the 45 miles between Sidney and Randallsville, the D&H chose to have the O&W handle the coal traffic as well as all other rail business to Rome and Utica. Further D&H Canal Company expansion came in 1881, when the company built a coal dock at Oswego on the east side of the Oswego River. This was at the point where the river flows into Lake Ontario so the dock was accessible to American and Canadian colliers. The D&H owned the trestle, but it was maintained and operated by the O&W. The O&W apparently had some use of the trestle also. Lake vessels loaded directly from the dock and, by way of the Welland Canal, could reach the upper lakes. Initially the D&H and the O&W were in a partnership that required the O&W to provide some of the hopper cars for coal loading.

In July of 1890, the O&W opened its new Scranton Division with the primary intention of becoming a major coal hauler. Late in 1893 it reported that it was hauling the output from 16 on-line breakers, and in 1895 it claimed the loading of 600 hoppers in a single day. Although it became a competitor of the D&H, the O&W continued to haul an important part of the D&H's tonnage from Sidney to western New York and the Great Lakes. Within a year of entering the coal business, the O&W constructed its own coal trestle at Oswego. In 1891 an arrangement with the R&C at Rome provided the O&W with a facility to transfer coal to Erie Canal boats. The demand for the anthracite at this time was more than sufficient to support the two carriers and their affiliated coal producers.

The O&W expressed an early and repeated concern about the size limitations on ships and the tolls collected by Canadians for use of the Welland Canal. (The natural connection between Lakes Ontario and Erie, the Niagara River, is not navigable due to the falls. The canal, built by the Canadian government and opened in 1829, provided a navigational link between the two lakes and thus an entrance to the upper lake ports for Lake Ontario interests. The canal was enlarged and modernized several times and still functions.) Both the O&W and the D&H believed that a reduction or elimination of the tolls would bolster coal movement. In 1893 the tolls were cut 50 percent. However, the O&W still hoped for their total elimination or the construction of a new canal by the American government.

In 1894, the D&H shipped 362,742 tons of coal through Sidney, making it the best year for the traffic. During the next year the D&H trestle was

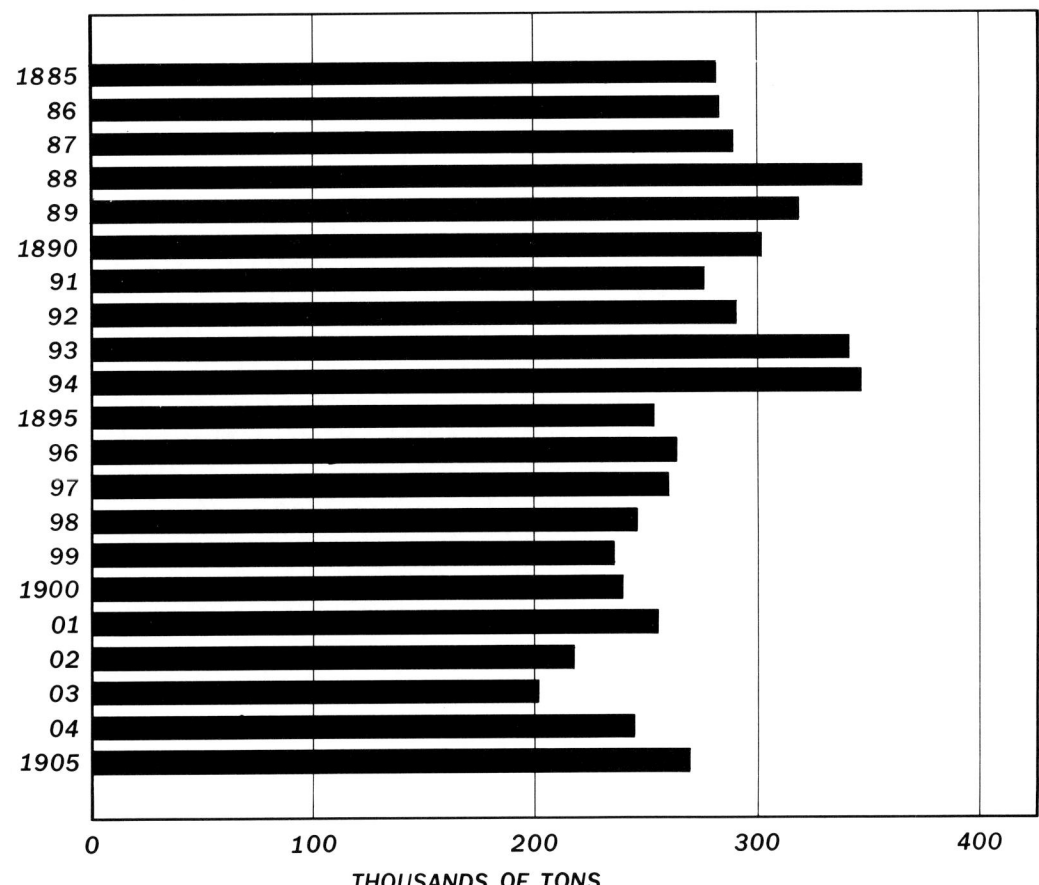

239

240

FACING PAGE: I and I-1 class engines, built in the first decade of the 20th century, worked a number of assignments out of Sidney including the New Berlin branch jobs. The 42 is at the south end of the yard near the company icehouse. This engine was destined to be the last remaining O&W steam locomotive. The 44 takes a turn at yard work while assigned to an extra train. The white flags will indicate it as such to all operating personnel. TWO PHOTOGRAPHS: J. R. QUINN COLLECTION.

RIGHT: Engine 35 was rebuilt into a 4-6-0 in 1919 and remained on the property until 1948. Here it is at the north end of the yard and appears to be coming off, or going out to, a northbound train. COURTESY OF CAL'S CLASSICS.

rebuilt with its length extended to 1000 feet. The added length also gave it a coal storage capacity of 4500 tons.

While years of profit still remained in the business, it was already beginning to drop off. By 1906 the O&W no longer reported the D&H coal tonnage through Sidney in the annual reports, but small amounts of such traffic continued even into 1957. Use of the D&H trestle continued to decline, and it was out of service by World War I. By comparison, the O&W's trestle was in use until the mid-1930s.

Controlling the important junction between the two lines at Sidney was the D&H's "GX" interlocking tower. The two-story building and its interlocking machinery were erected in August, 1902, and replaced a simple signal pole that had served up to that time. Improvements to the interlocking apparatus were made in 1911. The usual arrangements for such crossings was for the second railroad to assume the costs and responsibilities for crossing the line which arrived earlier. Instead the D&H, with its greater traffic density, accepted the responsibility—perhaps figuring upon greater control over train movement. The O&W probably paid a prorated share of operational and maintenance expenses. Some D&H employees must have felt that their trains were always superior to the O&W's regardless of rules or agreements. The following is from the July 6, 1907 *Sidney Record*.

At about noon last Monday a D&H engineer attracted general attention in town by vigorous and continued blowing of his locomotive whistle. He wanted the towerman to give him the crossing while the same was in use by an O&W train. It is a way with some interesting people to make a big noise when they want something they are not entitled to.

The tower was manned 24 hours per day and controlled interchange as well as through movements by the use of 24 mechanical levers. Being a mechanical plant, GX required a skilled operator to move the many feet of pipe, bell cranks, and levers that controlled switches, signals and derails. The towerman also controlled the Union Street gates by a pneumatic system. At the time of the O&W closing in 1957, GX was believed to have been one of the two last functioning interlocking plants on the railroad, the other being CN tower at Cornwall.

Approaching the D&H crossing from the north, O&W trains had to slow down for the sharp curve as well as Union St. crossing. The pipe connection to a switch, signal or derail is at right. CLYDE CONROW COLLECTION.

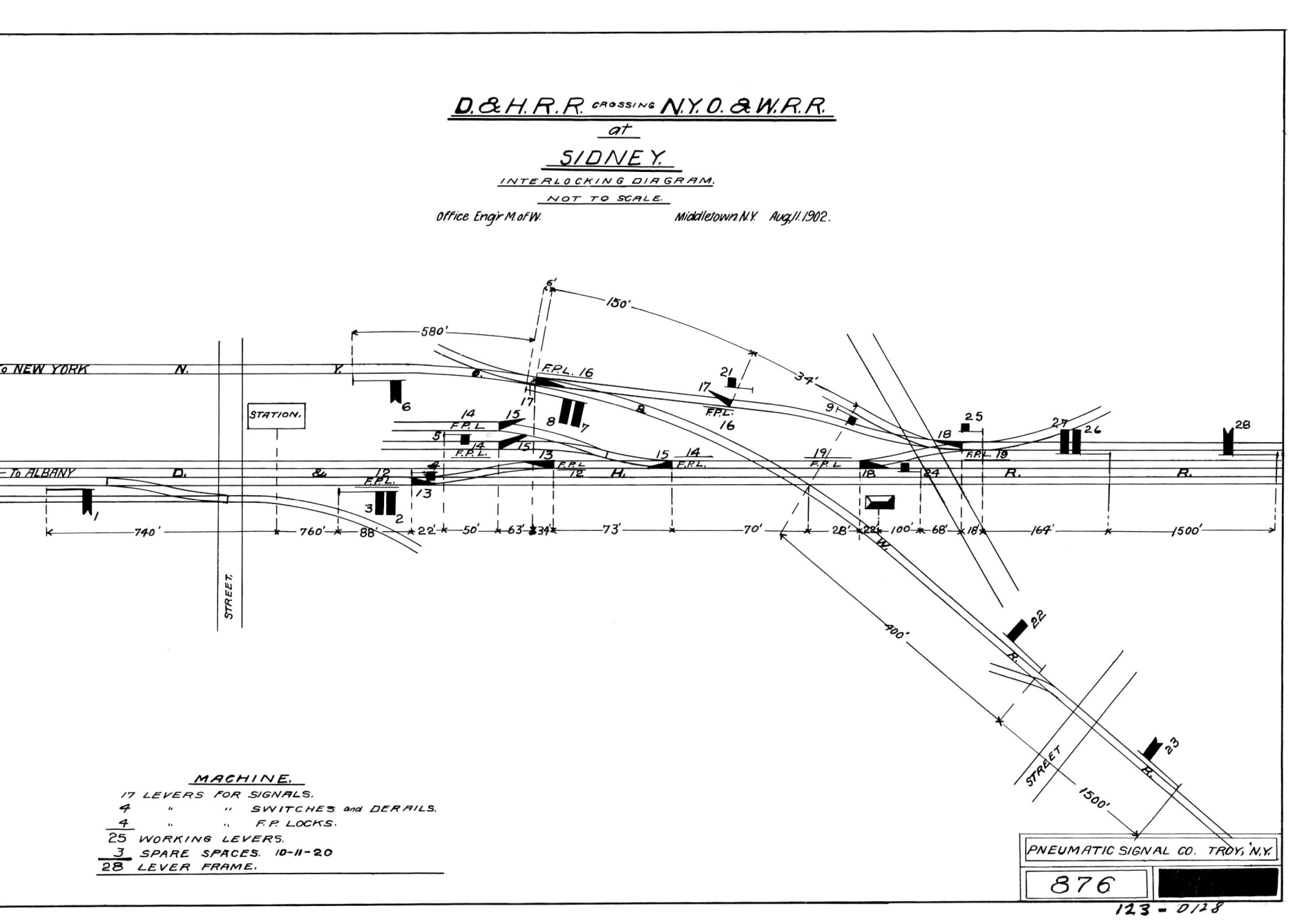

RIGHT: A young towerman (signalman) takes his ease in the second story quarters of GX tower. We can be sure that he will find it easier to throw the levers at this season without snow and ice to block the movement of rods, cranks and switch points. It is also his responsibility to notify each road's dispatcher every time one of its trains enters or leaves his control. WILLIAM SCHRIVER COLLECTION.

BELOW: A northbound O&W train has been given the highball indication at the crossing and proceeds across the D&H tracks. Hidden behind the tower is the other ball, suspended at a lower elevation, to hold D&H trains. More modern signaling has replaced the pole, ball, ropes and pulley system but the term 'highball' remains in the railroad jargon to this day. ROBERT HARDING COLLECTION. COURTESY OF JOE BUX AND DEPOT ATTIC.

ABOVE: Looking from the tower, south on the O&W and north on the D&H, the viewer can see that the photograph was taken in a time when railroads were the dominant force in transportation. The interchange tracks at the left are almost full and the O&W yardmaster is trying to figure just where he can squeeze in another car. The twin-blade O&W home signal is at stop for the northbound; so perhaps a D&H move was imminent. The pipes to the left of the D&H track connect the levers in the tower to signals, switches and derails that make up the interlocking system. E.V. CAMPBELL COLLECTION.

ABOVE: The D&H's double-track main comes from Wilkes-Barre and Binghamton on the left and heads toward Albany to the right. The O&W leaves Sidney in the lower right, crosses the D&H, and curves to the right toward New Berlin Jct. Union St. crosses both railroads and runs between the tower and the D&H's water tank. The lowest track paralleling the D&H main is the O&W's siding into the Scintilla Works. RICHARD ARRANDALE COLLECTION.

RIGHT: Looking north on the O&W from the vicinity of the tower, circa 1918, we again see the tracks used for interchange with the D&H filled with freight cars. The interchange volume might have been so great as to require several 'clean-out' moves per day. BRUCE TRACY COLLECTION.

RIGHT: A W-class locomotive has derailed its tender, and the crane has come down from Norwich to set things right. Judging from the depth the tender has plowed into the ground, it must have been loaded with coal and water and operating in reverse when it derailed. O&W SOCIETY COLLECTION.

BELOW: In June, 1941, the versatile No. 42, with a tender that appears fresh out of the Middletown backshop, moves about the Sidney station area. The fireman leans out to check for smoke, or see if the crossing flagman has traffic stopped, or to take a signal from a brakeman. Because it was bisected by a busy street and had very active freight and passenger stations, switching operations at Sidney had to be conducted with greater than usual attention. DEPOT ATTIC COLLECTION, COURTESY OF JOE BUX.

LEFT: About 1950, one of the O&W's first diesels shuffles a milk car at a location believed to be Sidney. The car may be in service to a Northern Division milk plant or may be assigned to a point on the Unadilla Valley Railway. Regardless of origin, it will no doubt make a number of round trips on trains 9 and 10. JOHN PICKETT.

BELOW: It is about 2:00 PM on March 29, 1957, and one of the last through trains is seen passing the freight house at Sidney. Empty and rusted yard tracks, closed offices, furloughed employees and a silence over the right-of-way signaled a mark on the time line that was difficult for many to comprehend. WALTER RICH COLLECTION.

RIGHT AND BELOW: The D&H's original proposal for the new joint station called for a more ornate building as may be seen in the plan below. The postcard view shows the D&H side as built. Since the D&H ran more trains through town, it is assumed that it paid a greater share of the prorated costs of operation and maintenance. O&W SOCIETY COLLECTION.

RIGHT AND BELOW: The D&H was a very important interchange partner for the O&W, and it had a passenger and freight business that was greater than the O&W's. In the bottom photograph a northbound passenger train, with an Anglicized 4-6-2, makes a Sidney stop on a run from Binghamton to Albany. The O&W went to General Motors diesels and the D&H chose American Locomotive Company engines like the RS2 on a southbound train at right. Both photographs were taken in June, 1948. JOHN KRAUSE.

RIGHT: The O&W used both its smallest steam switchers and its smallest diesels at Sidney. The 53, a class L 0-6-0, simmers just south of the Main Street crossing. JOHN KRAUSE. BELOW LEFT AND BELOW RIGHT: The 103 and 104 were two of the five General Electric engines purchased in 1941. The 103, photographed in 1942, shows the original color scheme of maroon, black and silver. After the General Motors diesels arrived in 1945, the little GE's were repainted in the gray, yellow and orange to match them. The 104 was photographed in 1951. ENGINE 103: O&W SOCIETY COLLECTION. ENGINE 104: COURTESY OF JOE BUX AND DEPOT ATTIC.

ABOVE AND RIGHT: A modern, joint freight house was also part of the improved facilities at Sidney in 1913. At that time, less-than-carload traffic made up a large percentage of railroad business, and many employees and several facilities were assigned to sorting and forwarding package freight. Either the photographer took the rear view when the switcher was making a new car arrangement or the cars were deliberately pulled out for the picture. It is extremely doubtful that the transfer platform was ever empty of cars. O&W SOCIETY COLLECTION.

FACING PAGE: Sidney's urban bustle is apparent in this turn-of-the-century scene when the O&W and D&H were all-pervading influences in the community. The earlier, wooden freight and passenger stations bracket Main St. with the Hotel Sidney and another hostelry behind them. The O&W's tracks are on the near side of the freight house with Wood's Mill in the immediate foreground. In the background, the valley of the Unadilla River opens to the north. RICHARD ARRANDALE COLLECTION. BELOW: An 1882 map of O&W and D&H properties in Sidney presents a puzzle. The passenger station is farther north than any that appear in this chapter's photographs. Were there two different wooden stations or was the station moved? Turntable, enginehouse, and track scale were moved in later years and the yard was enlarged. O&W SOCIETY COLLECTION.

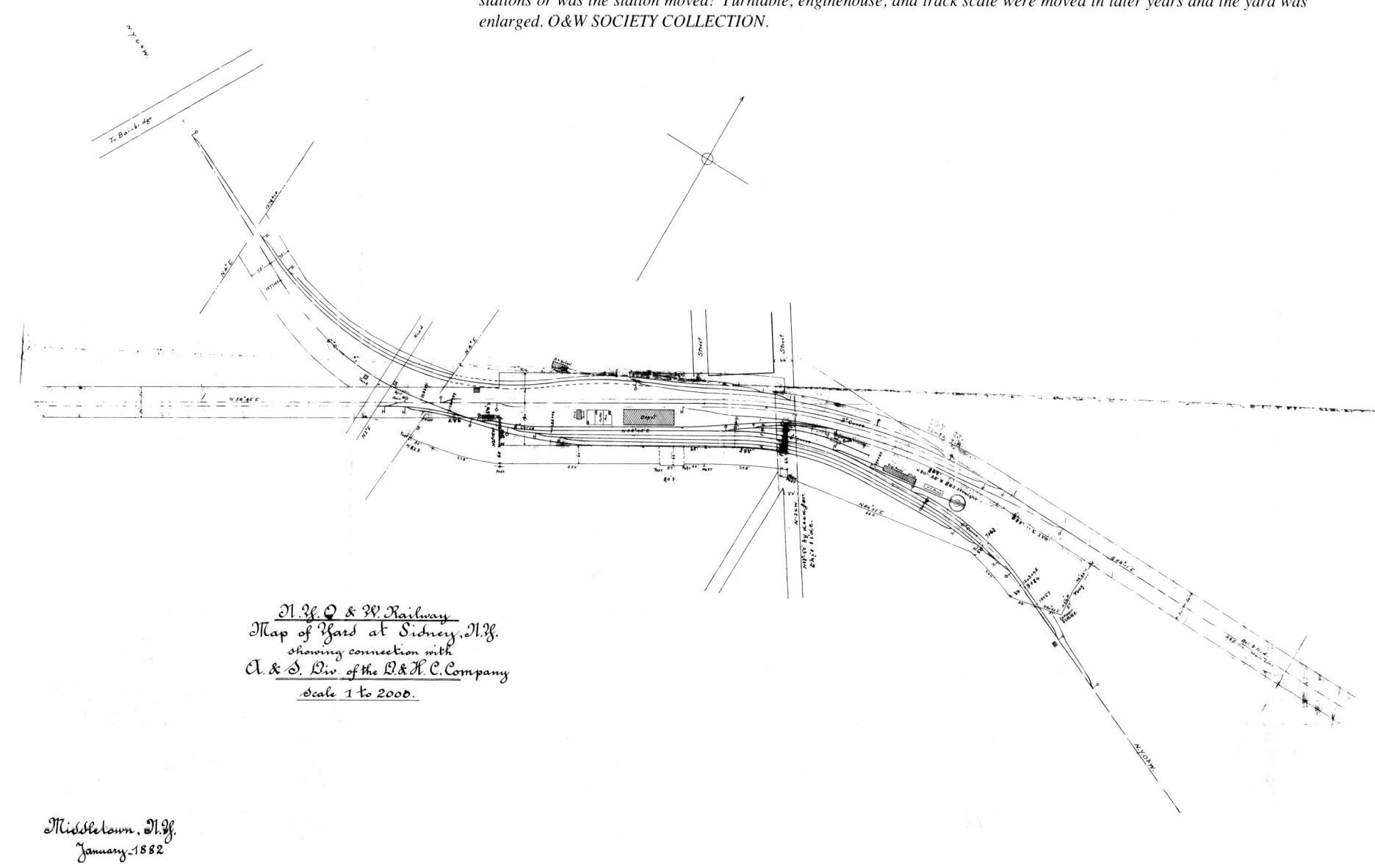

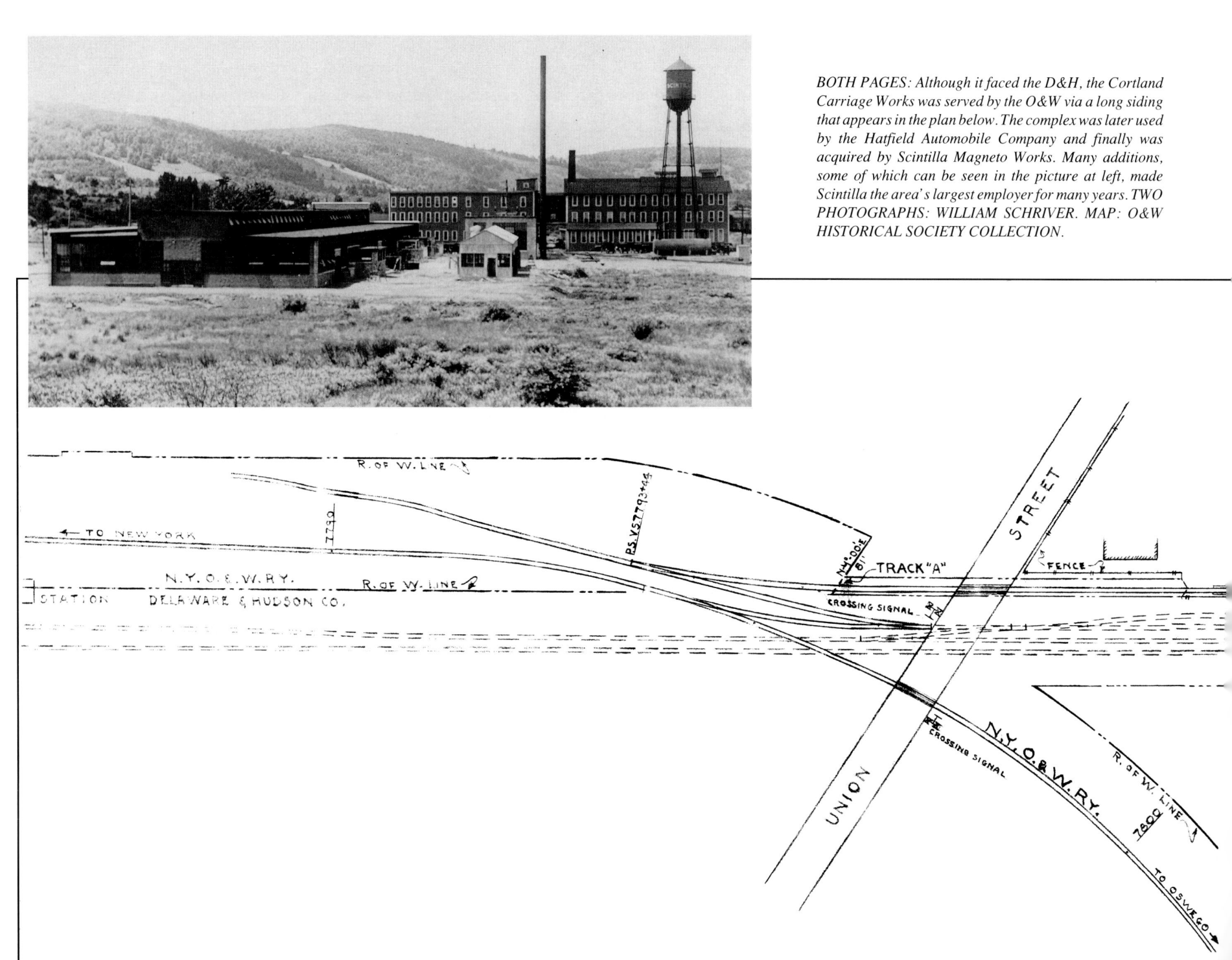

BOTH PAGES: *Although it faced the D&H, the Cortland Carriage Works was served by the O&W via a long siding that appears in the plan below. The complex was later used by the Hatfield Automobile Company and finally was acquired by Scintilla Magneto Works. Many additions, some of which can be seen in the picture at left, made Scintilla the area's largest employer for many years.* TWO PHOTOGRAPHS: WILLIAM SCHRIVER. MAP: O&W HISTORICAL SOCIETY COLLECTION.

BENDIX AVIATION CORP.
SCINTILLA MAGNETO DIV.

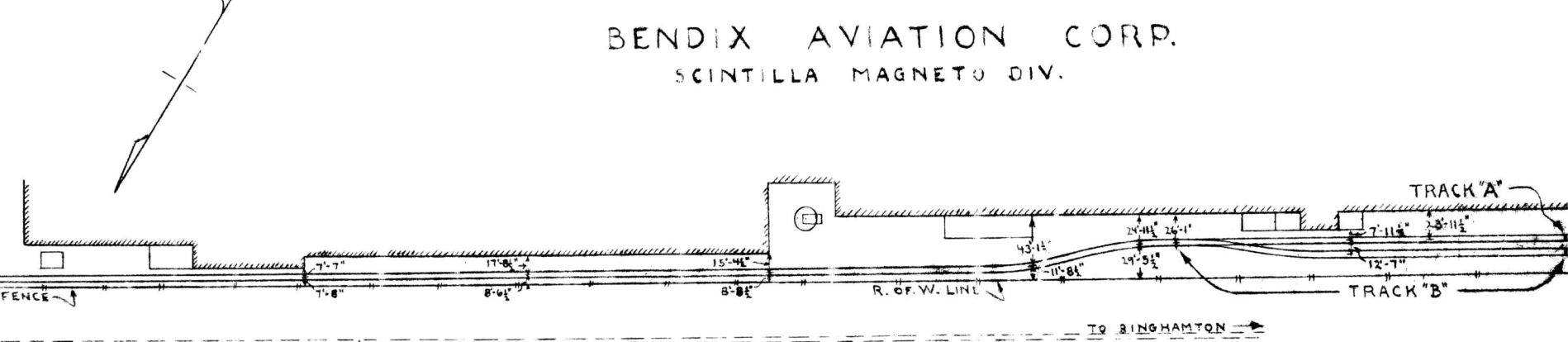

TRACK "A" LENGTH OFF RAILWAY PROPERTY = 2,000'±
TRACK "B" LENGTH OFF RAILWAY PROPERTY = 360'±

N.Y.O. & W. RY.
LOCATION OF TRACKS SERVING
BENDIX AVIATION CORP.
SCINTILLA MAGNETO DIV.
SIDNEY, N.Y.
SCALE: 1" = 100'   MARCH 29, 1948

ABOVE: Clark's Sash and Blind factory had direct O&W service via its own siding. The factory also produced turned, ornamental woodwork by the use of belt-driven lathes which were powered by steam engines. BELOW: The French Cheese Factory does not appear to be near the O&W or the D&H but its size suggests a quantity of production that would use rail service to reach wider markets. An O&W business directory listed a manufacturer of Camembert cheese in Sidney and this might have been the same. TWO PHOTOGRAPHS: JOE BUX COLLECTION.

ABOVE: Any business that meant loads in and loads out was most welcome on a railroad. The Sidney Novelty Co. required inbound coal and possibly lumber. Outbound manufactured items moved in boxcars. JOHN AND SUE HUDSON COLLECTION. BELOW: Kayser Silk Mill did not have direct O&W service but the railroad's business directory listed the mill for many years. The O&W's water tower can be seen to the right of the middle distance with the main line to the south hidden by the low ridge above the black line of D&H cars. WILLIAM SCHRIVER COLLECTION.

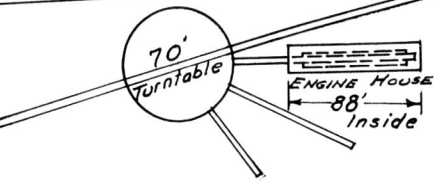

N.Y.O. & W. RY.
ENGINE HOUSE
SIDNEY, N.Y.
Scale: 1"=100'   Dec. 31, 1938

When the O&W's four-stall roundhouse burned, this building was either moved or erected over one of the pits and became the enginehouse. The building appears to be abandoned although the turntable was occasionally used by diesels. Both structures were essentially anachronisms from the age of steam. THREE PHOTOGRAPHS: RICHARD ARRANDALE COLLECTION.

RIGHT: The low ground near the confluence of the Susquehanna and Unadilla Rivers is coverd by several feet of water in the early spring of 1913. Anticipating just such a condition, the Oswego Midland placed its track on a fill through the fields bordering the river crossing. Special slow orders were probably in effect for this section of line during periods of high water. RICHARD ARRANDALE COLLECTION. BELOW: This view looks north, through the O&W's bridge over the Susquehanna. The railroad climbed over the distant hills which formed the divide between the Unadilla and Chenango Valleys. WILLIAM SCHRIVER COLLECTION.

ABOVE: Train 30 is crossing the Susquehanna River and the engine crew is watching for the signal that will give permission to cross the D&H. An earlier 'distant' signal would have indicated conditions at the crossing but the 'home' signal at the tower will be the final authority governing train movement over the crossing. ROBERT HARDING COLLECTION. COURTESY OF JOE BUX AND DEPOT ATTIC.

RIGHT: The south span of the O&W's bridge over the Susquehanna River is already gone and demolition of the north span is well underway. After the railroad's abandonment, the state realigned the highways and eliminated two bridges in this area. ONEONTA STAR PHOTOGRAPH, WALTER RICH COLLECTION.

The switch at New Berlin Junction is lined and locked for the main line, but for the purposes of continuing our story, we shall imagine it aligned for the branch. The two signals in the distance are electrically connected to the switch and provide southbound enginemen with an idea of conditions ahead. The operator at the junction may have expedited train movement by aligning the switch in advance of approaching trains according to their destination. There is no evidence that the switch itself could be operated by mechanical or electro-mechanical means from the station at any time. COURTESY OF L & L PHOTOS AND LEN KILIAN.

Chapter 12: Sidney to New Berlin Junction.

It (New Berlin Junction) was settled in 1789 by John Merceraus and called Indian Orchard. Later called Schaners Corners, then New Berlin Junction when the railroad came through.

Unadilla Valley Historical Society, *Unadilla Valley* (124).

Leaving Sidney, the railroad ran on a fill across bottom lands that were subject to flooding by the Susquehanna River. An early map indicates that the New York & Oswego Midland passed through an Indian burial ground on this flat before crossing the river. The railroad may have had as many as three different bridges across the Susquehanna. In 1892 two 153.5-foot steel spans replaced a timber structure, reflecting the need for a stronger physical plant to handle coal traffic. North of the Susquehanna, the roadbed gained higher ground and passed under New York Route 7. Road and steam alignments and recent gravel quarrying have confused the topography here, and the railroad grade is difficult but not impossible to trace. There was a gentle curve to the left, and in less than a mile the railroad crossed the Unadilla River on another twin-span bridge, 242, which consisted of two 130-foot steel spans that had replaced the original timber. The line then crossed New York Route 8 on a though-girder span and followed hillside contours to the village of East Guilford. The railroad later called this location New Berlin Junction (NB, later NJ, M.P.203.21), since the branch to that village began here.

Leaving the junction, the main line grade continued north as it climbed toward Guilford Summit. The New Berlin branch began an immediate descent to cross a small chasm and Guilford Creek on the highest and probably longest bridge on the entire branch. This 23-mile line was part of the original Oswego Midland plan, and with its Wharton Valley extension was the only major portion of the NYO&W to be sold or abandoned after 1900 and prior to the total abandonment in 1957. Branch trains generally interchanged their cars in Sidney yard, but there were times when cars going to or from the branch were switched and stored in sidings near the junction. These siding arrangements varied through the years. At the time the branch was sold to the Unadilla Valley Railway in 1941, there were two sidings at the junction.

Automatic electric signals had been installed in 1896 to protect trains at this location, but this system may have superseded earlier electric signal installations. The station at the junction sat in the angle between the main line and the branch. An earlier station here burned in June, 1904, and its replacement presented a curious puzzle in later years. One corner of its roof was missing and no conclusive explanation has been offered. One local resident thought it was due to a derailment, but it seems more likely that additional clearance was required when track arrangements were changed. Several years after the railroad's abandonment, the building was disassembled and moved six miles north to Mt. Upton. It was reassembled by the local historical society and it now houses a modest collection of historical items, including several from the O&W and UV Railroads..

FACING PAGE: The New Berlin branch drops quickly after parting from the main line. Loaded southbound milk trains from the branch must have made noise and smoke as they pulled upgrade to enter the main line. A slow speed was necessary to allow the head brakeman to climb back aboard and the flagman to drop off, close and lock the switch, and get back on the train. All movements onto or off the branch had to be reported to the dispatcher, so the station was a train register office for many years. BOB HARDING COLLECTION: COURTESY OF JOE BUX. INSET: Two views of the same train show a set of FT's, with train 10, stopped at the junction. In the view from the caboose roof, the New Berlin branch tracks are visible at the left and include the several hundred feet of line that remained under O&W ownership after the sale of the branch to the Unadilla Valley. A dispatchers' diary entry for February 5, 1946, stated, 'No. 10 detained at New Berlin Junction until 6:30 PM waiting for UVRR milk acct UVRR had a wreck and delayed their train.' This train may be waiting for a similar reason. LEFT: O&W SOCIETY COLLECTION. RIGHT, WALTER RICH COLLECTION.

ABOVE: A southbound motorist on Route 8 has just crossed the O&W and will soon be at the junction with Route 7 near Sidney. Both the Unadilla River, visible at left, and Route 8 have been rerouted and little remains today of the railroads's right-of-way in this area. RICHARD ARRANDALE COLLECTION.

RIGHT: A lengthy local freight, bound for the New Berlin branch, crosses the Unadilla River between Sidney and New Berlin Junction. The train is at least nine cars long and gives some idea of the volume of business on one branch of the O&W at the turn of the century. Six or seven cars back, a brakeman rides the tops displaying a risky but fully accepted practice that was part of his everyday job. Imagine the same task on an icy winter night. ROBERT HARDING COLLECTION, COURTESY OF JOE BUX AND DEPOT ATTIC.

LEFT: Unadilla Valley No. 4, ex-O&W No. 42, has been turned on the table that the UV installed at the junction about a year after it bought the branch. According to the condensation line on the tender, No. 7 has about a half-tank of water for the return to New Berlin. UV No. 7 was scrapped in 1956 and is believed to have been the last surviving O&W steam locomotive. WALTER RICH COLLECTION.

RIGHT: Original bridge No. 1 on the New Berlin branch displayed design features similar to trestle 216 at Sidney Center. This trestle was replaced sometime after 1907 with a heavier structure. O&W SOCIETY COLLECTION.

Three views show the second version of New Berlin branch bridge 1. Guilford Creek was dammed to provide waterpower for a mill, and the creek is shown at a low-water stage, possibly after the mill had been abandoned. The view at right looks north over the bridge. THREE PHOTOGRAPHS: O&W SOCIETY COLLECTION.

Form D. S. 26.

New York, Ontario and Western Railway Co.
TRANSPORTATION DEPARTMENT.

C. W. LANPHER,
Sup't Transportation.

Norwich, N. Y., June 12 1890

Circular No. 317.

TO ALL CONCERNED :

On and after June 22nd, 1890, No. 5 will not register at New Berlin Junction, but the Agent or Operator will be held responsible for the registering of all regular trains. Conductors of the New Berlin Branch trains 'southbound' and of the second-class or extras on the main line south bound, will examine the register book and ascertain from the Agent or Operator at New Berlin Junction whether all trains due 'north bound' have arrived.

C. W. LANPHER,
Supt. Trans.

LEFT: *Five months' growth of weeds cover the main line rails leading south to Sidney in this August, 1957, scene. A small part of the Unadilla Valley's turntable is visible at the left as well as the O&W-style crossing sign. The UV had no customers this far south but might have come into New Berlin Junction to use the turntable on an occasional basis. H. G. BRINKERHOFF PHOTOGRAPH.*

RIGHT: *The New Berlin Junction station has been relocated and restored in Mt. Upton where it is maintained by the Unadilla Valley Historical Society. The two rooms house a modest collection of natural, agricultural and transportation history items. The track car to the right came from the Unadilla Valley Railway. AUTHOR'S PHOTOGRAPH.*

Rockdale's station was behind a row of buildings facing the state road which ran through town. The agent-operator has left his telegraph key for a moment but his discriminating ear will be able to pick out the Rockdale call from the other clattering on the wire. O&W SOCIETY COLLECTION.

Chapter 13: The New Berlin Branch

The old branch line with its rusted rails
Wends on through the ancient hills
The shadows creep as the sunlight fails,
And the calls of the whip-poor-wills
Sound in the thicket where verdure lies,
Shading the green of the grass-grown ties.

"Abandoned" by Odin Lyman and taken from, *Railroad Avenue*

In technological smugness, modern motorists zip along New York Route 8, heading for New Berlin while sitting behind digital gauges, breathing thermostatically conditioned air, and only occasionally glancing through the tinted glass to peer at the cinder path along the road. After more than a century of progress, who among the present generation can realistically imagine the all-day haul by animal team from Sidney up to New Berlin? How often did the teamsters stop to remove the accumulated winter ice or caked spring mud from the wheels on the twenty-five-mile route? A one-hour trip over the same distance in the shelter and comfort of the Midland's steam cars must have seemed a delightful luxury when the New Berlin branch service was inaugurated in 1870.

Like the Delhi branch to the east, the extension to New Berlin was one of the Oswego Midland's original planned routes. In order to aid the great Midland project and assure itself of on-line status, the town of New Berlin had bonded itself for $150,000, part of $270,000 raised from town bonds along the line. These funds were supplemented by an additional $12,300 which was subscribed privately. A grand total of $1,583,400 came to the NY&OM from town bonding in Chenango County, which was reported in 1875 to have the largest debt of this kind of any county in the state.

In one of the easier NY&OM routings, the surveyors simply followed the steam and were able to keep the right-of-way on the west, or Chenango County side, of the Unadilla River. Company engineer Gilbert estimated that 290,035 cubic yards of earth and rock had to be excavated to construct the branch and that it would cost $120,677.45 for this work plus bridge masonry, culverts, and back walls for 270 feet of bridging. On July 3, 1868, construction bids were received in Middletown for portions of the main line and the Ellenville and New Berlin branches.

Construction was begun in the spring of 1869 when the contracting company of Gage, Williams, and Jerome established a base camp about six miles up the branch near Mt. Upton. Its Irish laborers picked and shoveled their way up the valley of the Unadilla, with many additional local men performing a number of jobs. Oak and other hardwoods had to be cut to seven-foot lengths and hewed flat on two sides for ties. Drivers and teams from local farms went to work with horse-drawn dump wagons, and the local hired help earned 75 cents per day. A number of houses, barns, and schoolhouses had to be moved or torn down to clear the right-of-way. Several bridges of the Howe truss design were used to cross streams that flowed into the nearby Unadilla River.

After leaving New Berlin Junction, the branch went downgrade to bridge 1 over Guilford Creek, made a six-degree curve to the north and paralleled the present New York Route 8. Bridge 1 was constructed with wooden stringers and was later rebuilt

The northbound milk train rolls into Rockdale on an October day in 1908. Beginning at this point, empty milk cars were set out along the run which began at Sidney. BRUCE TRACY COLLECTION: COURTESY OF JOE BUX.

as a steel plate-girder viaduct. The first station on the branch was Rockdale (RD, M.P. 206.04). There was a short double-ended siding on the east side of the track, and a creamery and icehouse were built on a spur that came off the north end of the siding. There would be an active creamery here well into the present century, and at the time of the sale of the branch to the Unadilla Valley Railway in 1941, it was known as Eisenstein's. The creamery and icehouse sat back against the river in the neighborhood of several stores that fronted the same siding. Mt. Upton (MU, M.P.209.69) proved to be one of the best traffic-generating communities on the line. Borden's had established a large facility here in 1899 on the east side of Route 8. This was located on a 1000-foot spur that left the main south of the station, curved eastward, and crossed the highway. The facility was sold or leased to the Dairymen's League in the 1920's. Sheffield Farms operated a smaller plant along the main track near the station. A 1200-foot passing track, section houses, coal shed, lumber mill, and several stores lined the main track through the village. A major job in building the line was the filling of a great swamp south of the village. It took two construction seasons to create a firm roadbed.

In the early days of the branch, a fuel station was established at Rockwell's Mills (M.P. 211.33). Locomotive fuel wood was cut into three-foot lengths and stacked alongside the track. Although there was a depot here, it was not a train-order office. A short passing track, freight house, and timber dock occupied sites near the depot. A cloth mill, established along the river by Chester Rockwell in 1849, required rail service. Hardly a mile north and halfway to New Berlin was Latham's Corners (212.21), where the railroad purchased water rights and established a facility for filling locomotive tenders. The railroad had a small structure here that served as a flag-stop shelter.

The little village with the intriguing name of White Store (214.08) was also a flag stop. The name came from a store building erected in 1803 and finished with a coat of white paint. This was unusual for the period and made the building a distinctive landmark. The railroad usually added an *s* to the name and called it Whites Store. White Store Brook, some 1000 feet north of the station, was the site of a serious wreck in 1910.

A grist mill, cheese factory, and woodworking mill were three of the early industries in Holmesville (216.12). An assigned agent handled local business including that for a coal dealer. A passing siding here was 1500 feet long. There was an old creamery on the east side of Route 8 at the point where it crosses the right-of-way and enters Holmesville. It was closed by 1916.

South New Berlin (SW, M.P. 217.59) was an agency station as well as a daytime order office. A new station was erected in 1893 that had living quarters on the second floor for the agent. Three icehouses, store houses, feed store, coal shed, and creamery made it a daily stop for the way freight. The creamery was built by the National Sugar Milk Company in 1899. It later became part of Chenango Farm Products and produced dry milk. The building was still standing in 1992. Camp Lumber, I.L. Richer, and Unadilla Oil Company later moved into the village and were railroad customers. Well before an improved Route 8 existed, many of the local stores had their own freight platforms and storage rooms. The short 30-foot boxcars of the day brought goods and supplies from wholesalers by the weekly carload. This was in addition to the express and LCL business that arrived at the depot.

Davis Crossing (220.23) was another flag stop with a siding for local customers. New Berlin Center (M.P. 221.24) had very limited railroad facilities, possibly just a wooden platform. Sages Corners (222.42) was a non-agency flag stop.

ABOVE: Rockdale's main street, passing between the inn and the houses, is the present N.Y. Route 8. The dirt road at the right of the picture leads to the creamery and station and continued over the Unadilla River. BRUCE TRACY COLLECTION, COURTESY OF JOE BUX. BELOW: Small grocery shops like this store in Rockdale depended upon the railroad's local freight to keep their shelves stocked until the grocery chains established their own trucking services. Such stores often provided local postal service as well and so the proprietor had another reason to visit the depot daily. WILLIAM SCHRIVER COLLECTION.

ABOVE: The Rockdale Creamery operated under more than one name during its lifetime. A siding below the main track served the bulding. The Rockdale Company had at least one other creamery and manufactured French cheeses as well as fluid milk. The bridge in the background crossed the Unadilla River. O&W SOCIETY COLLECTION.

RIGHT: New Berlin branch bridge 8 crossed Dodges Creek north of Rockdale village. The right-of-way embankments on both sides of the stream have been removed leaving the stone abutments standing in isolation. This view looks north. AUTHOR'S PHOTOGRAPH.

The O&W facilities in New Berlin (NI, M.P. 225.36) consisted of an icehouse, engine shed, turntable, section houses, freight and passenger stations, water tank, and a three-track yard. The more extensive facilities were typical of a branch-line terminus. A locomotive required some attention after the trip up from Sidney, and cars had to be placed in some order for switching moves on the return trip. There was also a 157-foot coal shed that was built in 1888 and a stock pen used for shipping dairy cattle.

The valley residents and businesses had a functioning branch line railroad on August 1, 1870, two years before the main line of the OM was completed. Travel and freight connections could be made with the OM's main line trains that were running between Sidney and Norwich and with the A&S at Sidney. The inauguration of rail service in the valley was marked by a trip to Sidney for all who chose to ride. An engineer named Scrutton sat in the locomotive cab and was rumored to be *under the influence*, possibly as a result of earlier celebrating. Apparently his intention was to give his passengers a memorable, fast first ride to Sidney and return. Among the hundreds of riders was Jesse S. Bradley, a handicapped but game hardware dealer from New Berlin. The story was that his friends had a difficult time keeping themselves and Bradley's wheelchair on the flatcar. No doubt the new roadbed had yet to settle and required further tamping and alignment and so contributed to the excitement of the ride. (Engineer Scrutton would later be involved in a collision on the branch when he ignored a signal.)

After the branch was opened, service consisted of two trains each way between Walton and New Berlin. One was a passenger consist while the other was mixed. On May 1, 1875, the branch supposedly began operating under an unusual lease to individual conductors. This was during the OM's period of receivership during which a man named T.L. Mumford was in charge of the branch. In 1877 the OM resumed control. At a later date, trains operated between Sidney and Edmeston when the Wharton

Looking northward at Mt. Upton, one can clearly see the spur leading from the main track to the Borden's plant out of sight at right. An array of warehouses and sheds connected with businesses that relied on rail service sat near the depot. WALTER RICH COLLECTION.

LEFT: Train time at Mt. Upton in June, 1907, the year that President Teddy Roosevelt put the Army Engineers, under Lt. Col. Goethals, in charge of building the Panama Canal. Stories about the project will make the city newspapers which will be brought north on the passenger trains. O&W SOCIETY COLLECTION.

FAR LEFT: Having passed the century mark and having served the transportation needs of the community for the greater part of that time, the Mt. Upton depot now serves the community with farm and gardening supplies as part of the Agway organizaiton. LEFT: Turning about and looking north through Mt. Upton today, one can still see remnants of rail-served businesses. To the immediate right is the former Curtis mill which was part of a farm and fuel supply dealership. The farthest buildings were owned by Sheffield Farms, which operated a creamery until 1970. Between the two old rail customers is the yard of a milk trucking compnay. AUTHOR'S PHOTOGRAPHS.

Valley extension opened. Horse-drawn vehicles from New Berlin's two hotels met the O&W's trains as well as Unadilla Valley Railway's arrivals at their depot, just a few hundred yards north, after that road arrived in the village.

As it did in every region it entered, the railroad brought changes. The new ability to transport fluid milk to population centers encouraged a big change-over from cheese manufacturing to milk production. Six creameries, receiving the milk of 1,850 cows, were established around New Berlin by 1879. The completion of the OM's main line to Oswego in 1872 provided additional connections with railroads and Great Lakes vessels. The O&W established a freighter service on the lakes between Duluth and Oswego which carried coal west and brought grain east. The railroad established its own grain elevator at Oswego for storage. Some of this western grain provided feed for both dairy and beef cattle. Grain-fed animals were superior to those living only on pasturage (see addendum D). This further aided the dairy interests while offering business opportunities for distribution of feed and farm supplies. A major Unadilla Valley firm engaged in this business was the I.L. Richer Company, referred to in Chapter 6. Several similar retail establishments were located on the New Berlin branch and they were among the railroad's best customers for inbound traffic. In 1883 bricks were being made in the area and shipped out in carload lots. Furniture makers and other small manufacturers could obtain raw materials more easily than before the building of the OM and did not have to rely on the river and dams to supply energy. Coal was now brought in by rail to run the machinery with steam power.

There was a story circulated in 1875, shortly after the line had opened, that the D&H planned to buy the branch to connect with its Utica, Clinton & Binghamton line farther north. There may have been some truth in this, since the D&H tried a variety of plans to operate the disconnected UC&B. Another connection between the D&H and the New Berlin

BOTH ABOVE: An impressive line of milk wagons waits to reach the unloading door at Borden's Mt. Upton plant. Each wagonload of cans is covered by a tarp to protect the milk from dust and heat. The intersection of what is the present Route 8 and the siding leading to the creamery is marked by a diamond-shaped crossing sign. The view below was taken from the highway. Note that only one wagon at a time ascends the ramp to unload. BOTH PHOTOGRAPHS: SALLY DAVIS COLLECTION, COURTESY OF BRUCE TRACY.

ABOVE: We are looking toward the Borden's plant from the east side of the Unadilla River. The railroad runs from left to right between the line of dark trees and the slope of the hill. WILLIAM SCHRIVER COLLECTION.

BELOW: This view also shows the unloading activity but gives a better perspective on the magnitude of operations. Borden's provided housing for plant managers and workers at the site. JOHN KILLIAN COLLECTION.

branch surfaced in 1895 based upon the comment of a Sidney editor. According to the plan, the O&W would exchange the New Berlin branch for the "Utica-Randallsville" section. This seems to again refer to the UC&B, the D&H property that was leased to the O&W in 1889. The UC&B's 32-mile length matched the New Berlin line's 31 miles very nicely. If, in fact, these were the properties involved, the D&H would have also required trackage rights from Sidney to New Berlin Junction, a distance of 2.5 miles, to reach the branch. In the 1940's, the O&W did purchase the UC&B as well as the Rome & Clinton with which it connected.

A variety of service disruptions occurred through the years and not all were unpleasant. A northbound branch passenger train was stalled at the station in Rockwell's Mills during an early spring snowstorm in 1874. Chester Rockwell, owner of the mills, had planned a large dinner party that same evening, but the storm prevented the invited guests from getting through. Looking out his windows, Rockwell noted the frosted windows of the stalled train. Pulling on his boots and a heavy coat, he fought through to the station, boarded the train, and invited the shivering, anxious passengers and crew to his home. Here steaming dishes, roasts, and pies were served in abundance. Hymns were sung, stories were told, and good cheer was the order of the evening. It was after midnight when the station agent came to the door and announced that the track had been cleared. With final songs and thanks, the travelers left Rockwell's home and resumed their journey.

Lightning was blamed for a fire that destroyed the Mt. Upton depot in 1882. Over $3000 worth of freight in the building was lost. The station at South New Berlin suffered a similar fate in August, 1892. In 1905 a cloudburst and flood caused a three-day shutdown of the line. Other disruptions caused by floods occurred in 1901, 1902, 1918, and 1935. In August of 1907, another weather extreme was the cause of the wreck of the northbound milk train at White Store. The South New Berlin telegrapher was

BOTH ABOVE: Two views from the same location show a number of changes brought about when Borden's eventually sold the Mt. Upton facility to the Dairymen's League. The O&W continued to enjoy a brisk and probably larger business from the new owners. Note the coal pile and conveyor leading into the boilerhouse. BORDEN'S PHOTOGRAPH, O&W SOCIETY COLLECTION. DAIRYMEN'S LEAGUE PHOTOGRAPH, SALLY DAVIS COLLECTION, COURTESY OF BRUCE TRACY.

sent to the scene to provide on-site communication with the dispatcher in Norwich. After climbing a pole to connect the necessary wires, he reported that the great heat of the day had caused the rails to bend out of alignment and derail the train. One of the saddest occurrences was that which marked the death of a brakeman who had forgotten the close clearance between the cars and the freight house in the New Berlin yard. Such tragedies were far too common in those days when occupational safety was solely the responsibility of the employee.

In 1888 the original iron rail on the branch was replaced with steel. Due to the lighter traffic on this line, this was the last section to be relaid in steel. Another upgrading took place in 1906, when 75-pound steel replaced the 50-pound rail. Beginning in the late 1890's, cinder, gravel, and culm ballast was added to the roadbed of the branch.

The Midland had hardly been completed to New Berlin when rumors and agitation began to push the line northward toward Utica or to organize a new company to do so. The DL&W had completed its branch into Richfield Springs and offered a convenient connection at the north end of the valley. Utica was the nearest big city and provided a ready market for the valley's agricultural and manufactured products. It would also be comparatively easy, and less expensive, to make a one-day trip to Utica as opposed to going to New York City. However, it was 1889 before such a line was begun, and it was left to local interests to organize and build the Unadilla Valley Railway.

This shortline linked the DL&W with the O&W when it came into New Berlin in July of 1895. The festivities rivaled those that had greeted the Midland some 25 years earlier. The O&W profited from the day by bringing in several hundred spectators and celebrants from the south. A few homes in New Berlin had to be demolished for the connecting tracks to be installed between the O&W and the UV. They were not used as heavily as the O&W might have wished. There were several factors that affected the number of cars and types of traffic interchanged between the two railroads at New Berlin. The O&W was not the UV's favored connection, and the fact that the two never had a joint station seems to indicate a lack of cooperation as well as limited interchange.

One story that appeared in a September, 1895, newspaper claimed that an O&W agent in Utica convinced a troupe of traveling performers that they could reach New Berlin via the O&W. He neglected to say how circuitous the route would be. Rather than go via New Berlin Junction and come up the branch, the party detrained at Norwich and made a bumpy stage coach ride over the mountain. That made them late for their scheduled performance. The troupe was especially angry when they found that the Lackawanna would have taken them from Utica to a convenient connection with the UV at Bridgewater. A short trip on the UV would have completed the journey. This could only have fueled the antagonism between the two lines. Evidence seems to point to the fact that the UV had closer ties to the Lackawanna at the upper end of the valley than with the O&W during the time that the UV was under local control. After the Salzberg interests bought the line, this changed significantly with the highway traffic on Genesee Street in New Berlin

ABOVE: The bridge at White Store was of the Howe truss design. It represented a transition in bridge construction since iron tie-rods were used to replace wooden vertical members. Later designs would call for all iron or steel construction as seen in an adjoining photograph. This was probably the second bridge over White Store Brook. O&W SOCIETY COLLECTION.

RIGHT, TOP AND BOTTOM: A derailment south of the White Store Brook destroyed at least two milk cars but left the remaining milk cars, the postal-baggage and the combine car upright. The engineer bled off the air on the engine brakes to get away from the derailing cars behind. This was correct practice for the protection of the engine crew and locomotive as well as keeping the hind end from possibly ramming into the stopped locomotive, causing further damage and injury. Note that the earlier bridge has been replaced. TWO PHOTOGRAPHS: O&W SOCIETY COLLECTION.

more frequently interrupted by interchange switching between the two roads.

Another proposed route out of New Berlin held some promise for awhile. Two surveys were made and right-of-way sections were possibly purchased for a line to reach Oneonta. The 32-mile route was to begin near the Unadilla Valley Railway station in New Berlin and terminate in the Neahwa Park section of Oneonta. It would seem that the Wharton Valley extension of the O&W would have served nicely to get the line across the Unadilla River and on its way toward Oneonta. However, Unadilla Valley Railway people were behind the proposal and their attitude toward the O&W was less than cordial at the time.

Familiar passengers on the New Berlin branch as well as the main line were the drummers who made weekly trips up the line as representatives of hardware, dry goods, drug, tobacco, and liquor wholesalers. Their worldly attitude and jovial nature made them popular travelers. At stations like Mt. Upton and New Berlin, they would detrain and head into the hills with a rented livery rig to make their sales calls. The next week, an LCL car, combine, or perhaps a whole freight car would arrive with the customer's order. The agent would notify the consignee that his shipment was in, and so the national commerce came to the Unadilla Valley.

The $3000 worth of destroyed merchandise referred to earlier in the depot fire at Mt. Upton clearly shows the volume of business passing through one local station. The reader is reminded that those were 1882 dollars representing significantly larger purchasing power than today's currency. The same agency reported the following items coming in or going out by train from his location in the 1880's: chestnuts, hickory and butternuts, maple sugar and syrup, apples, peas, cheese, butter, tanbark, chestnut fence posts and coal-mine timbers, salted beef, horse and sheep hides, butter firkins and apple barrels, live cattle, sheep, turkeys, coal, wagons, cutters and bobs, plows, cultivators, drags and steam engines.

ABOVE: Cinder platforms and plank crossings were part of the simple accommodations provided for the dozen or so passengers per day that used the Holmesville depot. Several stations on the branch had structures similar to the outside-framed one in the background, where coal or some other bulk commodity might have been stored. BRUCE TRACY COLLECTION.

BELOW: This wooden bridge over Great Brook was located about a half-mile north of the Holmesville station. In 1907 it was replaced by a single-span through lattice truss. Larger and heavier locomotives and cars were not only costly in themselves, but also required related changes in the road's physical plant. O&W SOCIETY COLLECTION.

TOP LEFT: In July, 1892, the South New Berlin station was struck by lightning and burned. The new or rebuilt station is shown here. The season represented is not conducive to the activity, but in the warmer months the express and baggage wagon at this end of the depot will provide an excellent train-watching perch for local children. Signs advertise the services of both Western Union Telegraph Company and the Adams Express Company. Station agents were frequently paid commissions for handling the business of both firms. TOP RIGHT: An unusually large group appears to have detrained for a community with a population of 850 at the time of the photograph. BELOW: In the beauty of an Unadilla Valley morning, all eyes are on the approaching southbound passenger train arriving at South New Berlin, with the exception of the man wheeling a baby carriage. The agent awaits the conductor, who has news and messages from the north. THREE PHOTOGRAPHS: O&W SOCIETY COLLECTION.

This was not a complete accounting, but it serves the purpose of showing how much a part the railroad played in developing the region.

Shortly before the sale of the branch to the UV, a 1938 traffic inspection trip named the following as receiving rail service in New Berlin: I.L. Richer had three sidings, George Ellsworth had a rail siding for an unspecified purpose, and there was a cattle pen that dated back to the early days of the dairy business and also encouraged livestock shipment. The firm of Zuber and Millspaugh received petroleum products on its own siding. Petroleum product depots were found in many railroad communities after 1900. The paved all-weather highway was still in the future; so kerosene, gasoline and lubricating oils were transported from the refineries in tank cars. Sinclair, Standard and Richfield were common brand names during this period. The O&W leased parcels of land to these distributors in many villages and received both ground rent and transportation charges for carrying their products. Some of these early distribution centers are still in operation today under third and fourth-generation ownership.

One of the largest O&W customers was the Borden's condensery in Hoboken, a hamlet just across the Unadilla River from New Berlin. It was in operation from 1895 to 1920 and was said to have been Borden's largest condensery. Eagle Brand condensed milk was prepared here. A 1600-foot siding extended into this plant for delivery of inbound coal and carloads of outbound canned milk. Sheffield Farms also had a creamery in New Berlin that was switched by the UV and the cars were interchanged with the O&W for shipment south. The branch served the railroad well for many years and in turn the railroad served the valley population with freight and passenger service. In 1923 there were still two passenger or mixed trains on the line, but these were gone in 1931. For a while, the O&W did advertise bus service along the branch as far as New Berlin. There has been no evidence to indicate that self-propelled rail cars were used on the branch at any time, but it must have entered some official's mind to give one of them a try on the run up to New Berlin. Apparently to the end of O&W Service, train 510 was carried as a scheduled train in the employees' timetable. It brought the loaded milk cars to Sidney to make connections for the south.

The 1941 annual report summed up the future of the New Berlin branch:

The operation of the branch line of the railroad known as the New Berlin branch, extending from New Berlin Junction to New Berlin, a distance of 22.29 miles, and the railroad of the Wharton Valley Railway Company, a subsidiary, extending

Inspection engine 25 pauses at South New Berlin during a run in 1895. The lack of an officials' car and the officious demeanor and appearance of a single individual gives this the look of a division engineer's or roadmaster's inspection. Periodically, these middle-management officials went over their assigned territory to inspect conditions and schedule maintenance projects. DEPOT ATTIC COLLECTION, COURTESY OF JOE BUX.

from New Berlin to Edmeston, a distance of 6.83 miles in the State of New York, has become unprofitable and sale thereof was negotiated and is now in the process of consummation with Unadilla Valley Railway Company as duly authorized by the District Court of the United States and the Interstate Commerce Commission.

Seventy years of OM and O&W service to the valley came to an end, and for $25,000 and a sum equal to one-half the tax saving, if any, based upon the difference between the 1939 and 1941 assessed valuations, the property was turned over to the once unfriendly Unadilla Valley Railway. In addition, the sale stated that the UV would be allowed revenue divisions of not less nor appreciably more than $40,000 yearly, based upon the 1940 volume of traffic.

Contrasts over a span of time are presented in these views near the South New Berlin depot. TOP LEFT: The creamery was a Borden's plant at one time and is believed to have been a condensing operation. GERALD W. D'AURORA COLLECTION. BOTTOM LEFT: We look north with a water standpipe and section house barely visible in the distance and again a milk car appears behind the building on the right. CHUCK YUNGKURTH COLLECTION. BOTTOM RIGHT: a contemporary photograph shows that two of the structures have, thus far, stood the test of time. AUTHOR'S PHOTOGRAPH.

LEFT: Bridge 49 was an open-deck type that crossed a millrace just south of the New Berlin yard. It was rebuilt with steel stringers about 1912. The train to the left of the tree is southbound. O&W SOCIETY COLLECTION.

BELOW: Z&M Oil Co. leased property from the O&W to build a petroleum products storage facility about a tenth of a mile south of the station. It would take decades for petroleum to replace coal as a heating fuel but the transition had already begun by 1918. O&W SOCIETY COLLECTION.

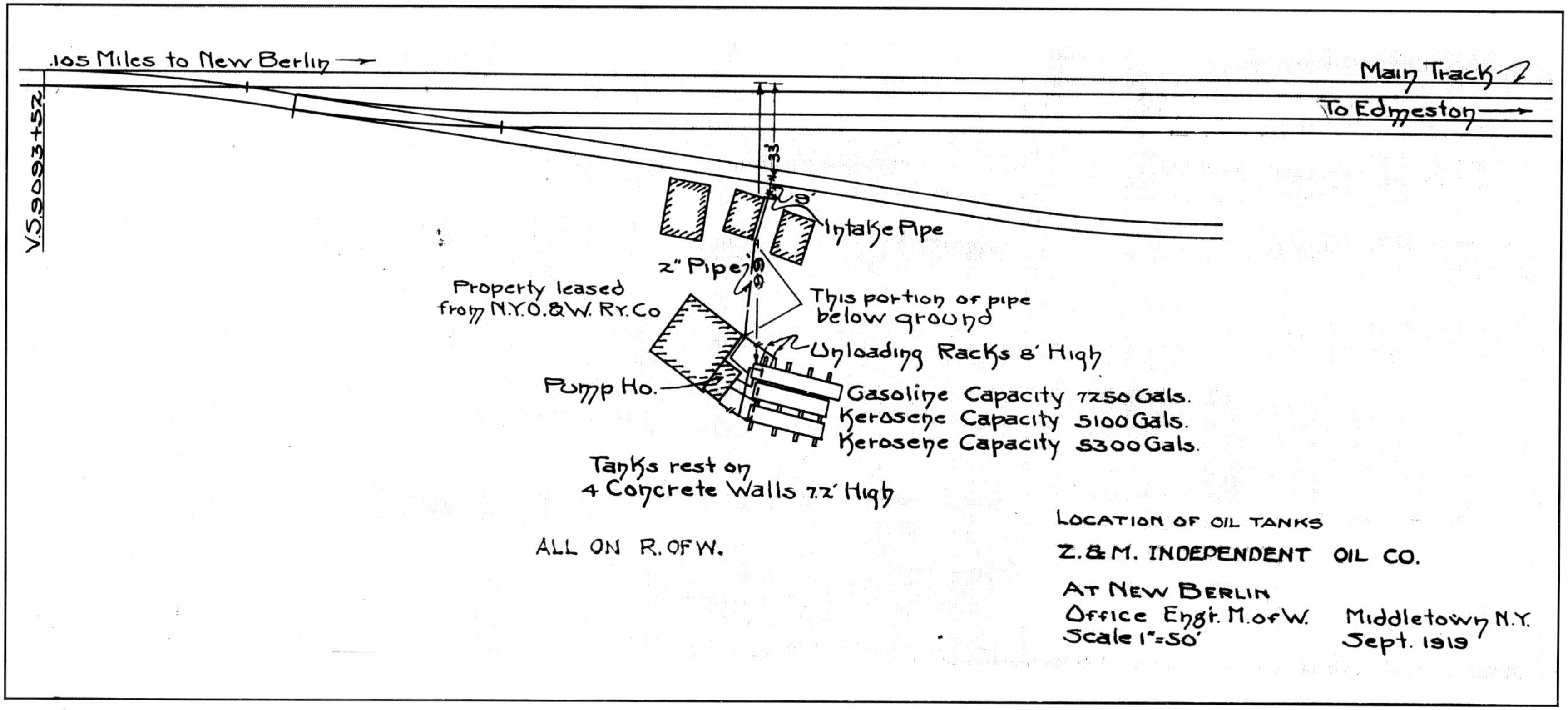

LEFT: The O&W's depot at New Berlin was the largest on the branch. Some of the business conducted here concerned package and express freight that was transferred to and from the UV. Across the three tracks in front of the station was a large retail coal trestle that marked New Berlin's reduced need for water-powered mills. O&W SOCIETY COLLECTION.

BELOW: Just a few months prior to its run with the last O&W train on the New Berlin branch, engine 33 is about to head back to Sidney with a mixed consist on July 9, 1941. Five freight cars, probably empties, and a baggage car for express service, make up the train. STEVE MAGUIRE PHOTOGRAPH, COURTESY OF JOE BUX AND DEPOT ATTIC.

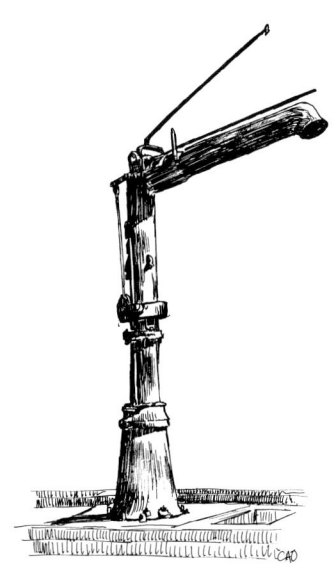

ABOVE: Looking northeasterly from New Berlin toward Edmeston, the O&W's Wharton Valley extension is seen crossing the bridge at right. The foreground track connects the UV yard (off to the left) and the O&W yard (off to the right). The small bridge crosses a millrace. Behind the bridge are houses located in the section of New Berlin called Hoboken, which was actually in Otsego County. JOE BUX COLLECTION. RIGHT: The map shows the simple terminal the Oswego Midland constructed in New Berlin. Both the UV and the Wharton Valley extension are in the future. MAP COURTESY OF FRED PUGH.

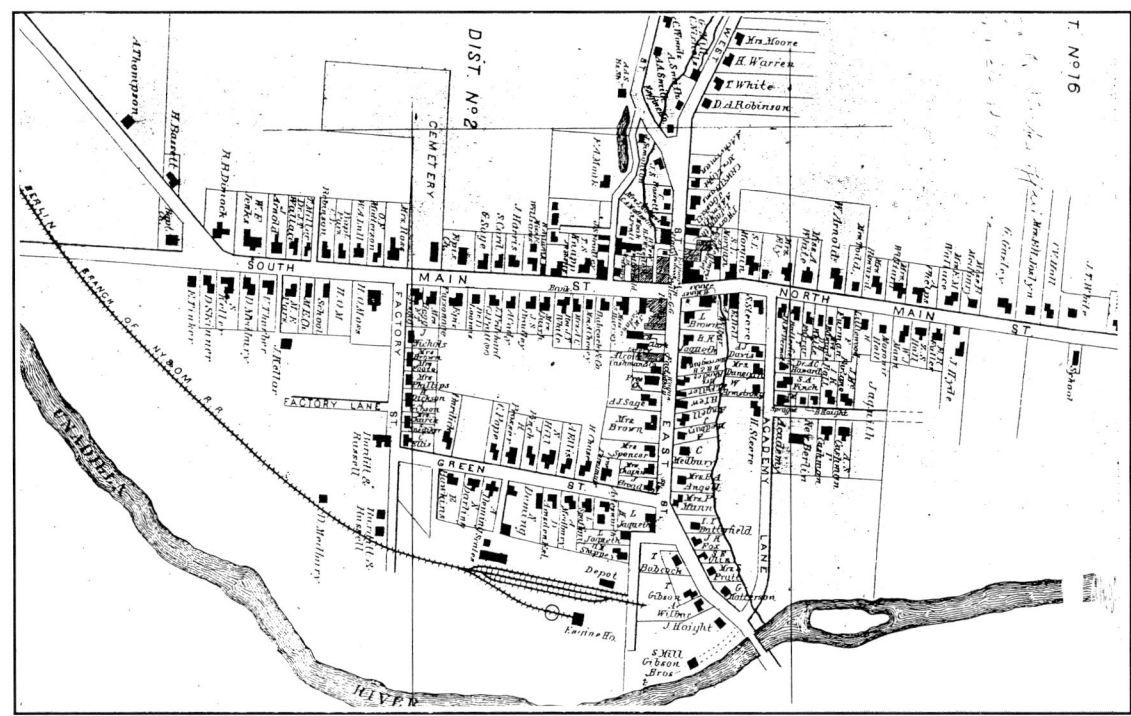

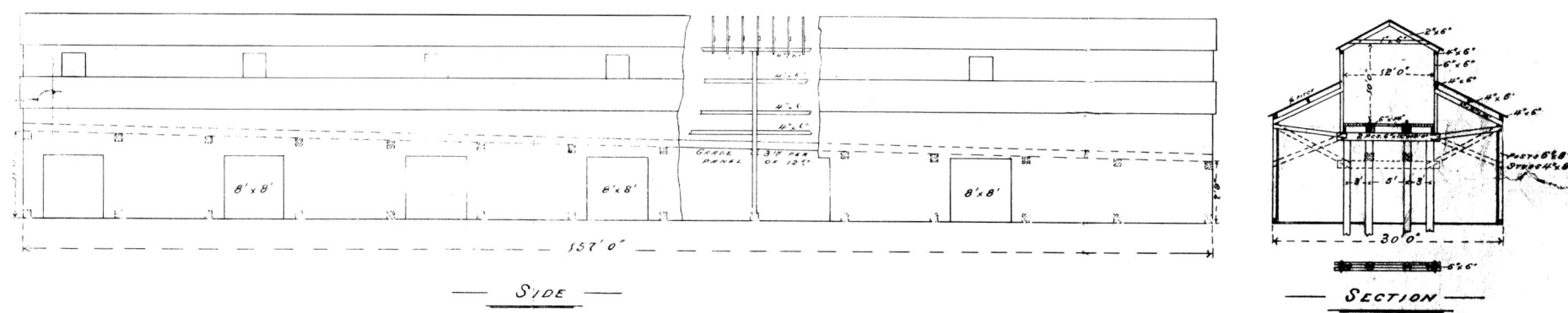

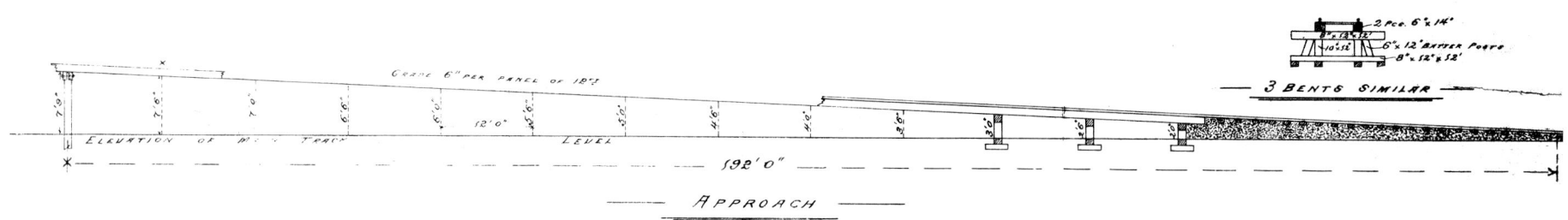

The New Berlin coal shed had a grade ranging from two to four percent and required a careful hand on the throttle to spot a heavy string of loaded hopper cars. The shed could hold approximately four cars. O&W SOCIETY COLLECTION.

Either someone forgot to block the wheels or the engineer misjudged distances when pushing loaded coal cars onto the New Berlin coal trestle. This large structure was used for the purpose of unloading and storing coal that was retailed locally. IRVING RICHER COLLECTION. COURTESY OF FRED PUGH.

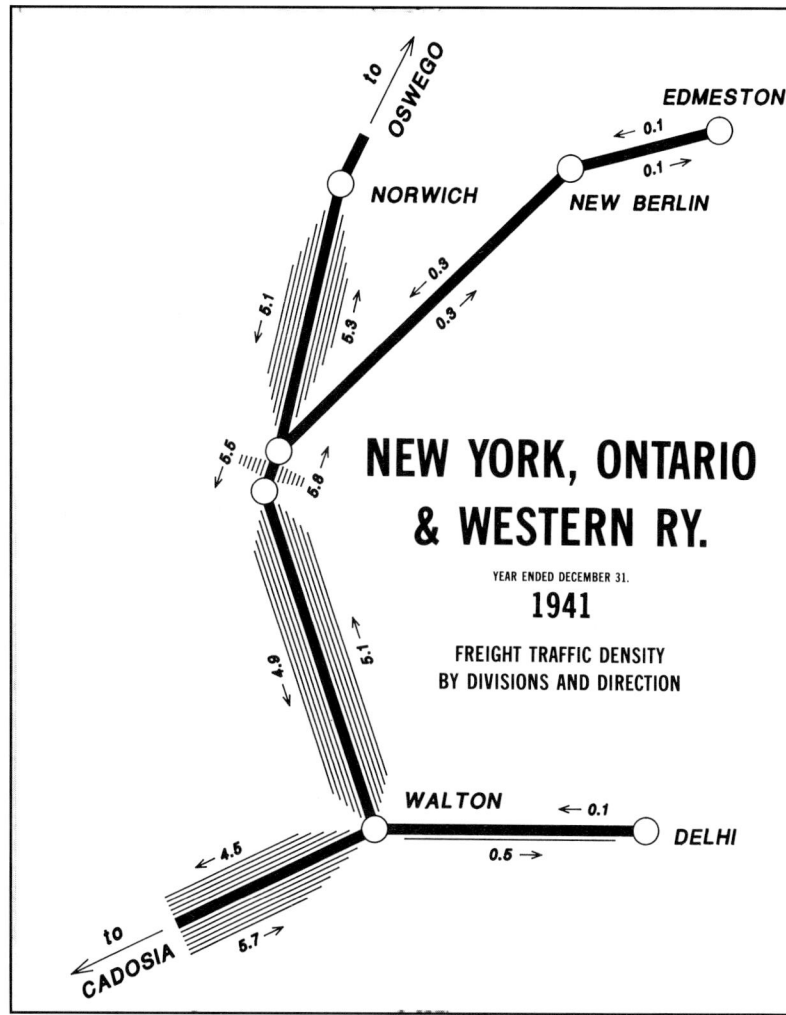

ABOVE: Traffic density over the lines covered in this book for the year 1941 is shown above. Multiply each number by 100,000 to determine the freight tonnage. CHUCK YUNGKURTH.

TOP LEFT: The Eagle Hotel was a hostelry and meeting location during the O&W's and UV's busy years. It was located at New Berlin's main intersection just a few blocks from the railroad stations and probably sent an omnibus to meet the trains. It was destroyed by fire many years after this 1913 view.
BOTTOM LEFT: The opposite side of the street presents a cosmopolitan air with a number of two- and three-story buildings offering goods and merchandise locally that would otherwise have required a trip to Sidney, Norwich or Utica. O&W SOCIETY COLLECTION.

The last O&W train in New Berlin left town on October 20, 1941. Standing in front of the engine are Frank A. Bradley, retired New Berlin station agent, and E. E. Gray, express driver at New Berlin. Standing on the foot board are L. Ward Van Buren, agent at New Berlin and conductor E. L. Stratton of Norwich. At the rear are Ira Avery, express messenger of Edmeston; engineer H. J. Howe; flagman Tom Natoll; and brakeman James McGarity. EDMESTON MUSEUM COLLECTION.

American-type engine No. 41 has been turned at Edmeston. The cars have been switched, and a milk car has been picked up from the creamery. The train is now ready to return to New Berlin and Sidney on the southbound side of a round trip. In the foreground are a slash bar, fire hoe and cinders showing where locomotive fire cleaning took place. EDMESTON HISTORICAL SOCIETY.

Chapter 14: The Wharton Valley Railway

With the acquisition of this trackage [the Unadilla Valley's purchase of the New Berlin branch and connecting Wharton Valley], the company now gained many new businesses on the line. In Edmeston there was a Dairymen's League milk plant, a Sheffield milk plant, Hardic Coal Co., Hardic Machinery and Hardware Sales, Purina Chows Feed Store and also another feed store run by the Talbot family.

Fred Pugh, *Days Along the Buckwheat & Dandelion* (66).

After four years of writing letters to officials of the New York, Ontario & Western in attempts to get that company to extend the New Berlin branch an additional 6.8 miles north to Edmeston, a committee of Otsego County men arranged to meet with the O&W officials in person. Mr. D. F. Talbot, prominent in local affairs in the western part of Otsego County, was the leading light in the matter. On June 12, 1888, Talbot and other interested men incorporated the Wharton Valley Railway. A few days later, the directors, who included six O&W men on the 13-man board, elected their officers and capitalized the company at $70,000—all stock soon to be owned by the O&W. A $75,000 bond issue was passed and had both principal and interest guaranteed by the O&W, which would purchase the entire issue at maturity.

In addition to donating part of the right-of-way, Wharton Valley residents supposedly donated $20,000 in cash for construction of the railroad. The O&W agreed to rent the Wharton Valley for a sum equal to the interest on the bonds and cost of organization expenses as well as payment of taxes on the property.

The Wharton Valley got little, if any, return on its stock which the O&W managed to buy up within a few years. When the bonds came due in November 1917, the O&W bought them up at a discount and took them out of circulation rather than pay them off. In addition to the favorable financial details, the O&W realized that the extension passed through very productive dairy country and confidently expected that the new business would more than cover the costs on the 6.8-mile extension.

The O&W's engineering and surveying staff provided the expertise for locating the route. The first shovel broke ground on Wednesday, August 28, 1888, in the vicinity of Pecktown, which later became Pittsfield. In September, 1888, William R. Haver was contracted to do the grading, masonry, and pile work. It was reported that a construction gang of 100 Italian laborers was employed. Construction materials were shipped to New Berlin, and an estimated 150 to 175 carloads of ties, spikes, and rails were needed to build the line. Necessary railroad structures were erected by the Underwood brothers, who worked overtime to complete the enginehouse and turntable at Edmeston. Homer Underwood was an original director of the Wharton Valley Railway. He is supposed to have constructed more than 50 buildings for the O&W, including the depot at Liberty in 1893. The turntable was originally located in the vicinity of the Borden's creamery but was moved south and to the other side of the main track sometime prior to 1916. A newspaper in nearby Morris reported that grading was complete and that track had been laid more than halfway to

Largest Condensery in the World, New Berlin, N.Y.

Three photographs display the immensity of the Borden's condensery at New Berlin. The facility had earlier been a cotton mill. The buildings were actually across the Unadilla River in a section of New Berlin called Hoboken and were served from Wharton Valley trackage. A coal shed can be seen in the top right view. Most plants did not rate a covered structure for delivery or storage of coal. THREE PHOTOGRAPHS: COURTESY OF JOE BUX.

RIGHT: *A milk car and gondola rest at precarious angles before O&W steam derrick SD-1 goes to work. Additional shoring and bracing may be needed for the trestle timbers before the heavy crane can begin lifting.* JOHN AND SUE HUDSON.

BELOW: *Four milk cars occupy the Borden's track and additional milk and freight cars fill the siding at the right. In addition, the mixed train is in town and must be switched for a return trip south. The farm implements and fence posts are part of the stock of a local farm supply store.* JOHN AND SUE HUDSON.

Many railroads had established dress codes for various occupations, including station agents, and strictly enforced the code's provisions. Arrangements were made to have a tailor visit various locations on the line to display his wares and take measurements. Clothing costs were deducted from wages. A collection of individuals, some probably without official business, pose at Edmeston's first station at the very northern end of the Wharton Valley Railway. EDMESTON HISTORICAL SOCIETY COLLECTION.

Edmeston by December 12, 1888. Charles I. Matteson of New Berlin wrote in his dairy under the date of November 26, 1888, that he had been given a ride on the first locomotive to run in Pittsfield. The most time-consuming part of the construction was the Unadilla River bridge at New Berlin. However, with the exception of Ferguson's Cut, just above Pittsfield, the seven-mile right-of-way was generally devoid of the heavy cutting and filling that was typical of most of the O&W main line.

On January 12, 1889, the rails of the Wharton Valley Railway were linked to the O&W at New Berlin. A final spike was driven with the requisite ceremony and was witnessed by some 500 people. The first train to traverse the line came up from Sidney with engineer Mark Brady at the throttle. The story was told that, when he returned to Sidney, he was asked what Edmeston looked like. He replied, "Well, all I could see was one house, two barns, and a hay stack."

Tradition says that the conductor on those early runs used to call out, "Edmeston—one house, two barns, and a hay stack," when the train pulled in.

Since the depot was about a mile from the center of the community and much of the commercial activity had yet to develop, the engineer's perception was probably accurate. The initial fare from New Berlin to Pittsfield was nine cents and to Edmeston was 21 cents.

Leaving New Berlin, the rails crossed the Unadilla River and entered Hoboken. Although it was in Otsego County, it was essentially a part of New Berlin and had no separate designation on the O&W. Here was the siding that entered the Borden's con-

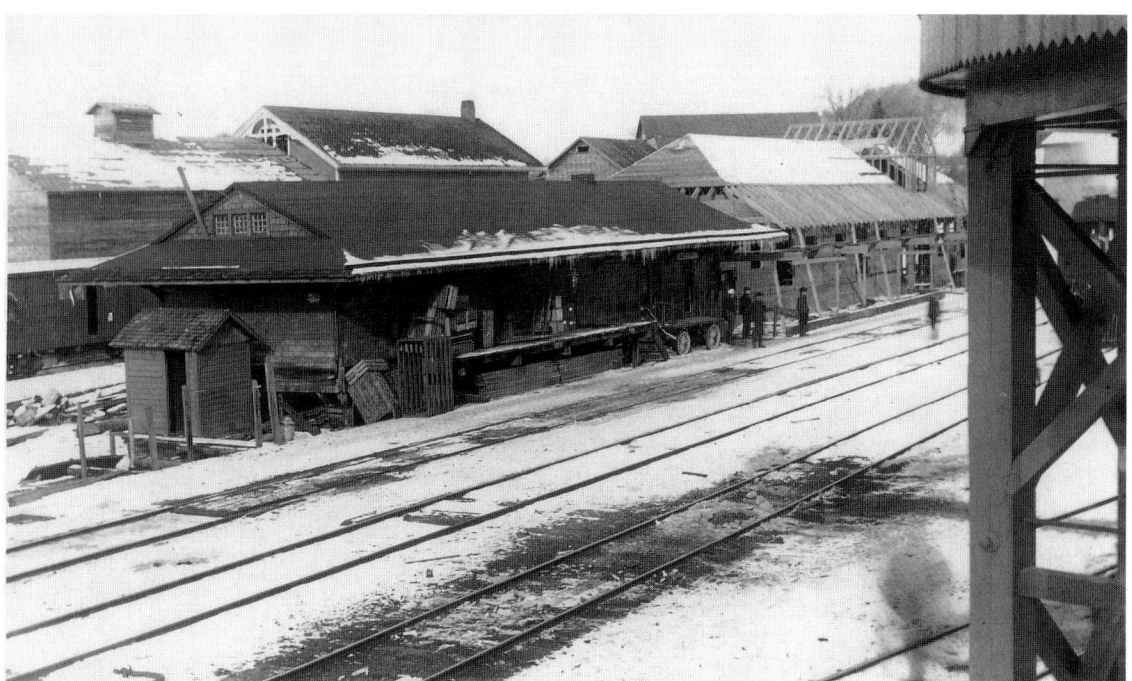

BOTH RIGHT: The O&W's second and larger station was built just north of the first one. A compact cluster of businesses, dependent upon rail service, virtually surrounded the station. The essential water tank was also nearby. The hill upon which the photographer stood may have been a glacial formation which has since been removed. TOP, JOE BUX COLLECTION. BOTTOM, O&W SOCIETY COLLECTION.

RIGHT: Edmeston's larger businesses were located around the O&W facilities south of the main section of town. The railroad's new station was truly the area's most elegant building as well as the nerve center of commercial activity and transportation. The quality of the station as well as its size and that of the nearby icehouse give evidence of the dollar-income Edmeston provided the railroad. PHOTOGRAPH, JOE BUX COLLECTION. PLAN, O&W SOCIETY COLLECTION.

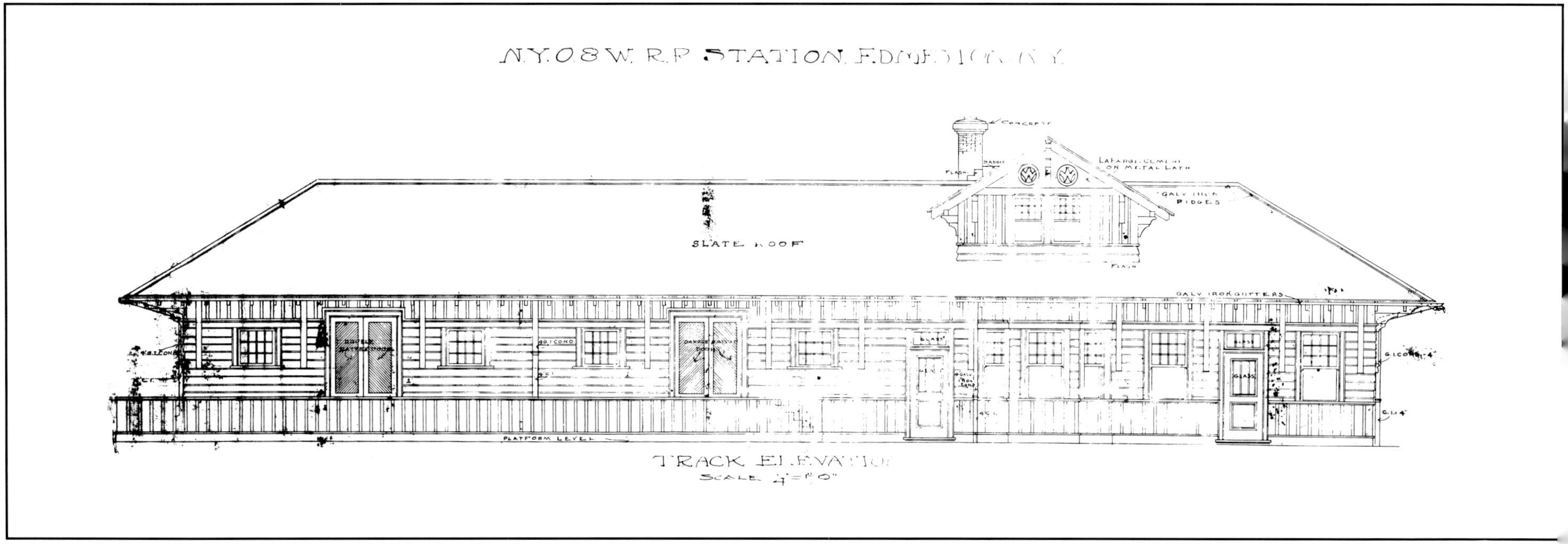

RIGHT: Bridge 73, of Howe truss design, crossed Wharton Creek at Ambler, just south of Edmeston. The map shows 1903 track arrangements at Edmeston. PHOTOGRAPH: O&W SOCIETY COLLECTION. MAP: EDMESTON HISTORICAL SOCIETY DATA.

densery. A petroleum fuel dealer would locate here around 1917. Pittsfield (M.P. 227.96) was a flag stop with a siding and a lumber dock. Just south of this point, the WV made the first of four crossings of meandering Wharton Creek. All of the longer bridges on the WV were replaced with steel by 1907. Near M.P. 229 were a switch and a platform for loading milk. It was either here or near this location that Borden's had a creamery which produced certified milk. The next station was at Ambler (M.P. 230.56), which was merely a flag stop. Edmeston (ED, M.P. 232.16) grew over the years to become substantially more than engineer Brady's first impression implied.

True to the company's prediction, the milk business did develop when Borden's built a large plant across from the depot. Later it rented this building to the Dairymen's League. The facility was an active rail shipper under both owners. Sheffield Farms was also a volume milk shipper. Cattle, farm supplies, hay, coal, LCL freight, and all the usual inbound traffic required by a rural, agricultural community kept the Wharton Valley line busy. A turntable, a commodious freight and passenger station that was built in 1907, and a number of smaller maintenance structures affirmed the O&W's presence on the southern outskirts of Edmeston. Several sidings adjoined two-story structures that served storage, shipping and distributive functions for the local commercial center. Milk trains and mixed consists, generally originating at Sidney, provided service for the 52 years that the line was under O&W operation. In 1938, the railroad still listed two lumber yards, two milk shippers, one coal and farm supply house, and two feed agencies in Edmeston.

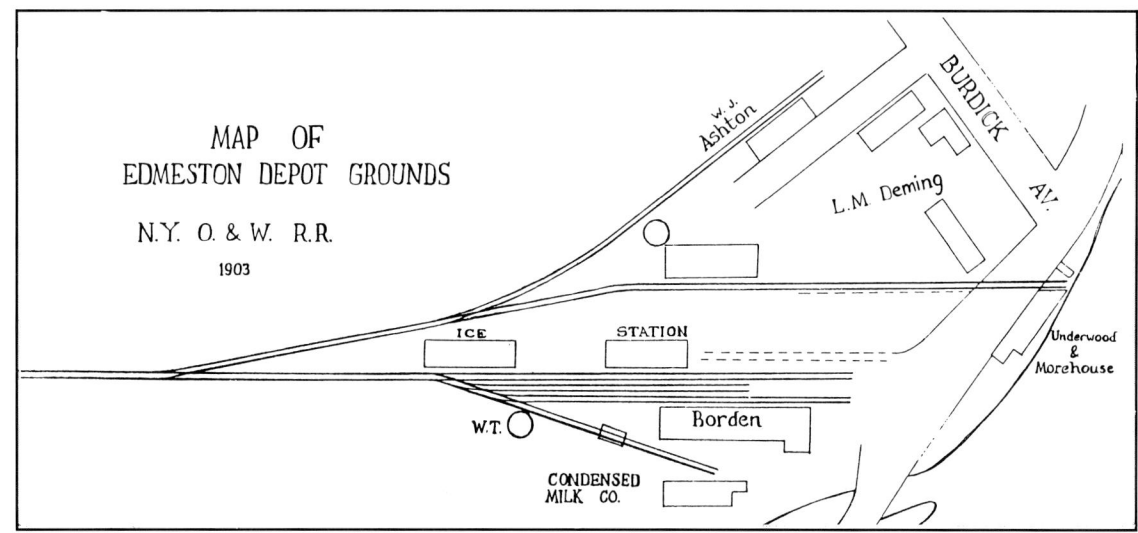

In early days, further expansion of the New Berlin branch northward from Edmeston was anticipated in the press and was very likely contemplated by railroad officials.

While passenger trains ran up the New Berlin branch to Edmeston in the early years of the line, they were gone before 1900. The travelers heading up the Unadilla or Wharton Valley had to avail themselves of the mixed train service or a rider car on the rear of the milk train. The population of both Chenango and Otsego Counties along the valleys was too sparse to support anything more elaborate.

In 1941 the O&W sold the entire New Berlin branch, including the Wharton Valley Railway, to the Unadilla Valley Railway. This company operated the former WV until 1960.

THIS PAGE: A variety of perspectives and changes relative to the Borden's plant at Edmeston is shown in three views. It is evident that the creamery was either rebuilt or replaced while the icehouse behind was unchanged. The trestle, seen in the rear view of the plant, was used to bring ice from a pond fed by Wharton Creek. The first and third view show the county road curving to the left and on south to Ambler, Pittsfield and New Berlin. LEFT: EDMESTON HISTORICAL SOCIETY. BELOW: SALLY DAVIS COLLECTION, COURTESY OF BRUCE TRACY. BOTTOM LEFT: EDMESTON HISTORICAL SOCIETY.

16—Borden's Plant and R. R. Station, Edmeston, N. Y.

No. 75-Borden's, Edmeston N. Y.

Station N.Y.O.&.W.Ry.

Borden Milk Plant, Edmeston, N.Y.

In the 1920's, Bordens sold or leased several country plants to the Dairymen's League. The Edmeston complex was included in the change. At a later date, a third creamery was erected on the site by the League, and it was also served by the O&W and later by the Unadilla Valley Rwy. JOE BUX COLLECTION.

FACING PAGE: An aerial view of the depot area in Edmeston shows many of the neighboring businesses. A sawmill and the Dairymen's League plant, the third creamery on the site, are on the nearside of the tracks. The small shanty south of the water standpipe was the freight agent's office after the station was leased to a feed dealer. Behind the station is the Sheffield Farms creamery and a fuel and agricultural supply dealer. To the left of Sheffield's can be seen the right-of-way for a siding that served the additional building extending beyond the top of the photograph. The ownership and functions of the different buildings changed frequently. EDMESTON HISTORICAL SOCIETY.

TOP RIGHT: Few may have thought at the time that the establishment of a business like Card's Garage in Edmeston held serious consequences for rail transportation. An early version of a pickup truck sits at the left loaded with milk cans and bags of feed, two major components of rail business in rural areas. BRUCE TRACY COLLECTION.

RIGHT: Two trackmen stand near the south end of the Edmeston yard. Among their many labors were filling switch lamps with kerosene, clearing culverts and drainage channels, shoveling snow or ashes as required, and daily inspection of the roadbed and structures within the limits of their section. JOE BUX COLLECTION.

ABOVE AND UPPER LEFT: The first turntable at Edmeston was located east of the main track and near the station. Its contruction was similar to some of the lighter bridges. The construction photograph at the upper left includes men who were building the right-of-way as well as the engine turning facility. A single-stall enginehouse at right permitted simple maintenance and servicing procedures to be done out of the weather. JOE BUX COLLECTION.

FACING PAGE: The second turntable was located farther south and was both longer and heavier to support larger engines. The locomotive had to be properly balanced on the table so that the crew could turn it manually. When snow was deep, sectionmen had to shovel out the shallow pit. LEFT: This photograph shows the large, circular, concrete base of the same turntable as it appears today. It must be a source of wonder and speculation to recent arrivals in the neighborhood. RIGHT: WALTER KIERZKOWSKI COLLECTION. LEFT: AUTHOR'S PHOTOGRAPH.

Unadilla Valley Railway operations on the New Berlin branch virtually duplicated those established by the O&W. Unless an observer read a local paper in the fall of 1941 or saw the small lettering on the tender, he might not have realized the change. Here is an ex-O&W engine rolling along an ex-O&W branch with an ex-O&W caboose on the rear of the train crossing Route 8 north of South New Berlin. We hardly have more than the photographer's word that this is the Unadilla Valley Railway. The gentle change was less disturbing to the rural ways of the valley. JOHN PICKETT.

Chapter 15: Unadilla Valley Railway

The day we first saw the Unadilla morning train moving, almost theatrically, toward West Edmeston it happened that No. 6 was newly shopped and that the white trim of its footboards and the dulled blue of the Russian iron boiler lagging were clearly discernible. Hardly two units of its twelve-car consist were identical; there was a bright-yellow Katy reefer, a black-painted Lackawanna box car, a couple of variously orange fruit cars from the Espee, a brace of milk tanks belonging to Sheffield Farms, a pearl-gray Lehigh & New England cement hopper and, at the end, a little red four-wheel bouncer right out of the Christmas window of Schwarz, the Fifth Avenue toy merchant.

Lucius Beebe, *Mixed Train Daily* (246).

Between the Delaware, Lackawanna & Western at Bridgewater and the New York, Ontario & Western at New Berlin, the Unadilla River quietly flowed by the villages of Unadilla Forks, Leonardsville, West Edmeston, and South Edmeston, a distance of 19 miles. Appeals to both railroads to extend their lines through the valley were unsuccessful, and after some half-hearted attempts, a link to connect the valley communities with the two railroads was begun in 1889. A new corporation was formed that purchased track components and rented a locomotive from the DL&W. Besides the locomotive and track materials, additional arrangements were made with the DL&W that led to close ties between the two companies. The DL&W planned to obtain a greater amount of interchange as a result of this assistance once the line was completed. The new line was called the Utica & Unadilla Valley Railroad.

Construction began at the north end and slowly moved south, so slowly in fact, that only .75-mile of line was built. Construction resumed in 1892 under a new corporation called the Unadilla Valley Railway. This was necessary due to the defective charter under which the UV had been formed. Under the UV name the road reached New Berlin in 1895 and established its connection with the O&W. The completion was marked by the driving of a silver spike at New Berlin on July 7. Inbound freight on the new line ran heavily toward feed, farm supplies, farm animals, coal, and materials for a foundry near Leonardsville, while the outbound business was milk, cheese, and farm produce. Passenger service was basically local in nature, with through service to Utica being provided via the connection with the DL&W's Richfield Springs branch.

The UV's original power was a 4-4-0 and a 4-6-0, the 4-4-0 lasting well into the 1940's. The O&W sold an M-class 2-6-0 to the line in 1915 and it was supplemented with a pair of new 2-6-2's bought in 1919.

The UV's most profitable years occurred between 1900 and World War I. Financial results were mixed from that point up to the time the railroad was sold to the H.E. Salzberg Co. of New York City for

LEFT: *Unadilla Valley No. 4 works the Sheffield Farms milk plant in New Berlin. The UV is known to have leased cars for milk service from other railroads, including the Pennsylvania. The first car at the left does not appear to be from the PRR, O&W or DL&W and leads to speculation that the UV may have also approached car leasing companies for rolling stock.* COURTESY OF CAL'S CLASSICS. FACING PAGE: *A busy timetable for the summer of 1919 shows through passage was possible between Utica and Sidney via the Unadilla Valley. The passenger trains took 55 minutes to cover the 19 miles making for an approximate speed of 20 miles per hour.* AUTHOR'S COLLECTION.

$75,000 in 1936. The Salzbergs operated a number of shortline railroads through the years and they were also dealers in second-hand railroad equipment.

Several important changes took place after Salzberg acquired the UV. Traffic solicitation became a major effort and rates were established that were competitive with trucking. Community and customer relations were improved. These new policies, plus the business boom of the war, resulted in a significant increase in carload traffic. Also, a closer and improved operating relationship with the O&W was instituted and more freight was interchanged through New Berlin.

In October, 1941, the UV purchased the entire New Berlin branch, including the Wharton Valley Railway, from the O&W. Additionally, the deal included the option to buy the 2.33 miles of track from New Berlin Junction to Sidney for $2000 should the O&W abandon it. Salzberg now needed additional motive power and equipment to run the expanded system. O&W 2-6-0 No. 272, a flanger, two cabooses, and the tenders from engines 280 and 281 went to the UV. These tenders were paired with UV's 2-6-2's. Later it bought the smokebox front from O&W 281 to repair the 272. This has caused confusion for UV historians who believed the whole 281 went to the UV. Finally, a snowplow and one additional locomotive were purchased from the O&W. This was the 42, a single-cab 2-6-0 that became UV No.7.

The larger ex-O&W engines were not popular on the original UV route between Bridgewater and New Berlin. No. 272 was probably never used on the north end and No.7 rarely saw that part of the line. The lighter rail was better suited to the smaller locomotives with lighter axle loadings. The UV did install some heavier rail on the north end after the war, but the switch to diesel power about the same time made the rail relay program less critical. A turntable was required at New Berlin Junction after the O&W turned the branch over to the UV. Since New Berlin was the operation and maintenance focal point, engines returned there after each run. Some track and switch changes were probably made at New Berlin Junction to accommodate occasional interchange there between the two roads.

It is not absolutely clear what trackage rights the UV had between New Berlin Junction and Sidney. However, it does appear that the UV did bring interchange cars into the O&W yard. Another story says that the UV ran into Sidney for a little more than a year and stopped when the turntable was installed at New Berlin Junction. There was no longer an operator at the latter location when the line was sold to the UV. Generally accepted operational procedures would have required UV crews to obtain a train order by phone before entering the O&W at New Berlin Junction. This could have been given by the operator at GX tower or the yardmaster at Sidney. With the proper permission, the UV train could proceed south 2.33 miles to the Sidney yard.

In 1947, the UV purchased a pair of General Electric 70-ton diesel-electric locomotives, numbers 100 and 200. Generally referred to as 70-tonners, this type of unit was especially popular with the Salzberg roads and other short lines similar to the

UNADILLA VALLEY RAILWAY

TIME TABLE No. 61.

In Effect Sunday, June 1, 1919. Superseding Time Table of November 4, 1917.

FOR THE GOVERNMENT AND INFORMATION OF EMPLOYES ONLY.
SUBJECT TO CHANGE WITHOUT NOTICE

SOUTH BOUND / NORTH BOUND

	10	8	6	4	2	DISTANCE FROM UTICA	STATIONS	STATION NUMBERS	DISTANCE BETWEEN STATIONS	1	3	5	7	9	
	Passenger Sunday Only	Milk and Passenger Sunday Only	Passenger Daily Except Sunday	Freight and Passenger Daily XX	Milk and Passenger Daily Except Sunday					Passenger Daily Except Sunday	Freight and Passenger Daily XX	Milk and Passenger Daily Except Sunday	Passenger Sunday Only	Milk and Passenger Sunday Only	
	P.M.	A.M.	P.M.	P.M.	A.M.					A.M.	P.M.	P.M.	P.M.	P.M.	
			5.20		6.40		UTICA D.L.&W.R.R.			10.15		9.05	12.10		
READ DOWN	5.30	9.15	6.30	1.30	9.24	18.14	Lv. Bridgewater Arr.	1	18.14	9.10	1.15	6.05	9.10	5.15	READ UP
	5.36	9.24	6.38	1.39	9.37	20.61	River Forks	2	2.47	8.50	1.07	5.45	8.45	5.02	
	5.43	9.45	6.48	2.05	9.55	23.14	Leonardsville	3	2.53	8.43	12.47	5.30	8.38	4.47	
	5.52	10.10	6.57	2.25	10.20	26.79	West Edmeston	4	3.65	8.29	12.22	5.15	8.27	4.32	
	f 6.00	f 10.17	f 7.05	f 2.34	f 10.27	30.04	Sweet's	5	3.25	f 8.21	f 11.58	f 5.00	f 8.19	f 4.18	
	6.10	10.40	7.13	2.51	10.45	32.97	South Edmeston	6	2.93	8.14	11.50	4.45	8.12	4.10	
	6.25	11.15	7.28	3.10	11.15	37.27	Arr. NEW BERLIN Lv.	7	4.30	8.00	11.30	4.30	8.00	4.00	
		1.30		6.43	1.30	62.27	SIDNEY N.Y.O.&W.Ry.			2.10		2.10			
	P.M.	P.M.	P.M.	P.M.	P.M.					A.M.	A.M.	P.M.	A.M.	P.M.	
	Sunday Only	Sunday Only	Daily Except Sunday	Daily XX	Daily Except Sunday					Daily Except Sunday	Daily XX	Daily Except Sunday	Sunday Only	Sunday Only	

f indicates that trains will stop for passengers on signal only.

Trains Nos. 3 and 4 will perform freight service between Bridgewater and New Berlin.

Enginemen must reduce speed to ten (10) miles per hour when passing the crossings at Yaw's Bridge and Main's, and have engines under perfect control. Enginemen and trainmen must use great caution in crossing the highways and roads at Leonardsville Station, keep the bell constantly ringing when moving about the Leonardsville yards, and under no circumstances make a flying switch at Leonardsville south of the Station.

X X Trains Nos. 3 and 4 will not run on Sundays or Holidays.

H. A. BROME, General Manager,
NEW BERLIN.

The railroad's New Berlin station was said to have been raised to avoid flood waters of the nearby Unadilla River. In the top view, a northbound train pulls in as passengers make ready to board and freight is brought to trackside. After purchase of the New Berlin branch, the UV closed the O&W station, moved the agent to Mt. Upton, and used the building shown in these photographs to handle all local freight work. TWO PHOTOGRAPHS: JOE BUX COLLECTION.

UV. By 1950 it was determined that one GE unit was sufficient to handle the business and the other went off to another family property, the Des Moines & Central Iowa. If the need arose, one of the remaining steamers could be fired up for temporary service. In 1956, the last two steam engines, including No. 7 (ex-O&W No. 42), were scrapped. The 7's demise thus preceded that of the O&W by only a year, and it was the last O&W steam locomotive extant.

Business on the UV took a significant downturn in 1956 when the Dairymen's League plant in Mt. Upton closed. This facility was the largest customer on the railroad. The O&W shutdown the following year was another blow, and further discouragement came with the fact that more feed dealers and creameries were switching over to truck transport. The loss of the connection at New Berlin Jct. eliminated the need for the UV to operate south of Mt. Upton and the 6.5 miles of track south of that point was left to rust and weeds. However, the UV still had its original rail connection with the DL&W at Bridgewater.

There is an interesting story that the Salzbergs were planning to buy a section of the O&W main line after the road shutdown. The bankruptcy court had divided the road into segments that were bid upon by scrap dealers and connecting railroads. The Salzbergs were purportedly interested in the Sidney-Norwich section. However, the O&W through that area had very few active receivers or shippers and it is difficult to see why a shortline operator would be attracted to it. The story received support from the fact that Salzberg bought three of the O&W's NW2 diesel switchers from M.S. Kaplan of Chicago in June of 1957 and had them brought to New Berlin. The three engines had been purchased by the O&W in 1948 and were numbered 111, 112, and 113. The 1000 h.p., 124-ton units were substantially more powerful and heavier than the lone 70 tonner that the UV employed. Like the second-hand O&W steam engines before them, the NW2's presented the UV with operating problems and limitations due to their weight. Clearly, neither the UV traffic nor track required or could support such a large unit. The engines must have been purchased either on speculation or for expanded operations. The 113 was painted in the cream and orange standard scheme used by the Salzberg lines but it was not lettered. Despite its unsuitable characteristics, the 113 was occasionally used by the UV as a backup unit after the steam locomotives were scrapped. During its one week's service however, the NW2 broke several rails on the north end. The three engines left the property in March 1959 in a sale to the Chicago, Rock Island & Pacific.

Business continued to deteriorate along the UV. The foundry in Leonardsville closed, and many homes and businesses changed over to fuel oil for heating; so the inbound coal traffic disappeared. The Salzberg interests said that the operation had reached the point where expenses exceeded income and they applied for permission to abandon in 1960. This permission was soon granted, and in November of that year the scrap train, working northward and taking up the rails behind it, reached Bridgewater. The final cars were turned over to the Erie Lackawanna, and the 70-ton GE locomotive migrated northeastward to St. Johnsbury & Lamoille County Railroad in Vermont.

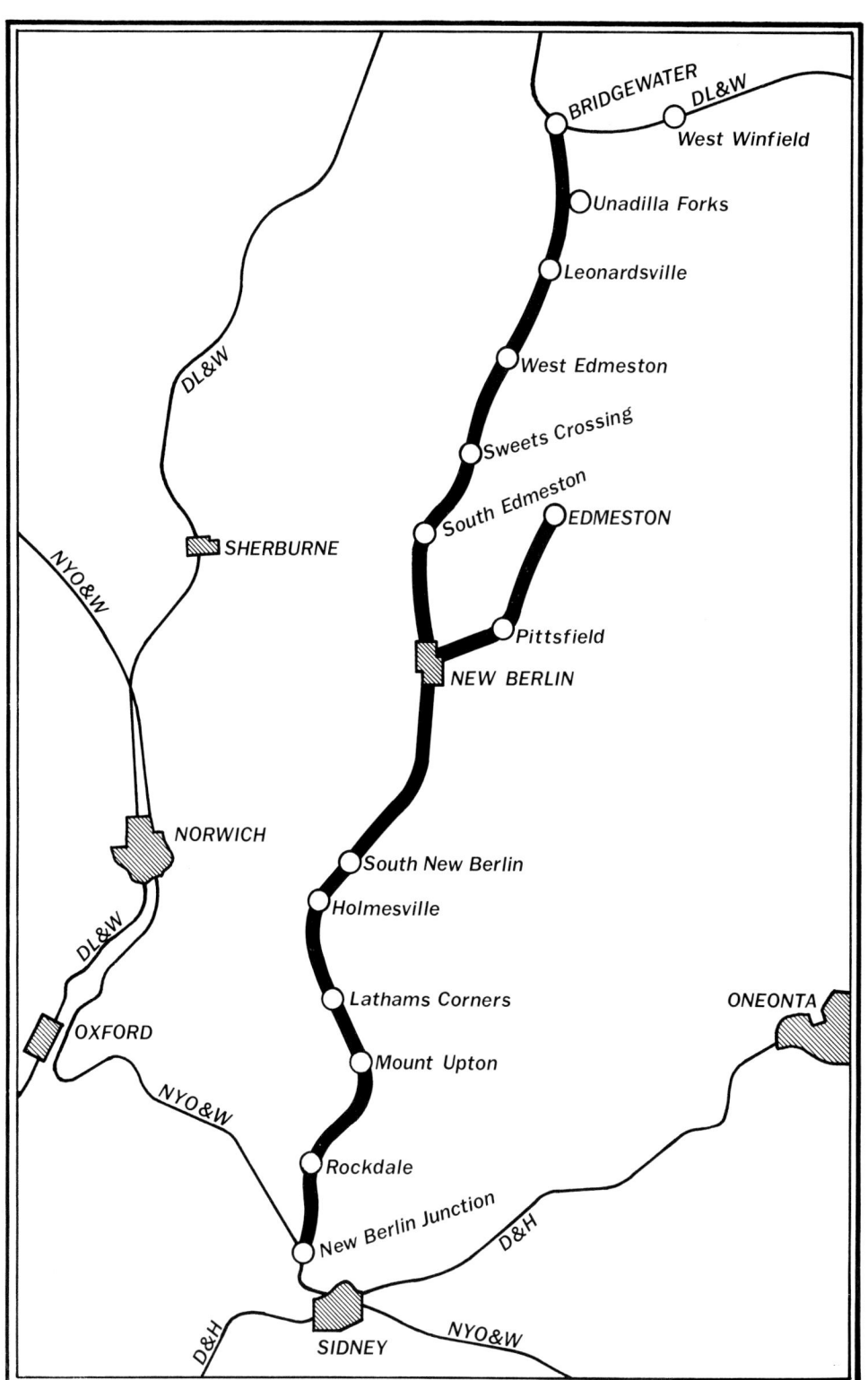

The original Unadilla Valley Railway ran between Bridgewater and New Berlin. The company more than doubled its size when it bought the O&W's New Berlin branch including the Wharton Valley extension between New Berlin and Edmeston. MAP BY CHUCK YUNGKURTH.

The simple, utilitarian No. 1 was named "Pendragon" after Uther Pendragon, the king of the Britons in Arthurian legend. The name also meant high chief or leader in English and Welsh history. It was a proper title for the company's first locomotive. RICHARD REIT COLLECTION.

RIGHT: First No. 6 was built in 1911 and had served on two roads in the south before purchase by the UV. It was one of the last two steam locomotives on the railroad and was scrapped in 1956 along with engine 7, the former O&W No. 42. THEODORE F. GLEICHMANN, JR. COLLECTION.

BELOW: Located off the pleasant shady back streets of New Berlin, the UV enginehouse is surrounded by a hazy atmosphere redolent with coal smoke, steam, hot metal and a host of additional odors unique to railroad shops and steam locomotives. Like most short lines, the UV was reluctant to dispose of locomotive parts that might find one more use. The foreground track leads to the station and the O&W interchange. CAL'S CLASSICS.

LEFT: Still bearing her O&W road number but now lettered for the UV, the 272 was one of the heaviest locomotives used on the UV. The engine was badly damaged in a winter derailment near Rockdale. It returned to service after parts from another O&W engine were used for repairs. WILLIAM S. YOUNG.

BELOW: In 1954, the year of this photograph, the UV still had a steam locomotive on the property for which the coal pile and conveyor at the right were maintained at New Berlin. However the work was being done by a diesel, and the empty yard indicated that even the more modern power had only a limited future as well. In a short six years, the UV would follow the O&W into history. TED GLEICHMANN, JR. COLLECTION.

ABOVE: A wooden baggage car sits at the UV's New Berlin station. Such cars were assigned to express service between Weehauken and New Berlin and ran over the O&W for most of the trip. The Railway Express Agency, essentially the predecessor of today's United Parcel Service, provided much of the nation's express parcel service into the 1960's. HAROLD DEAL PHOTOGRAPH, MIKE HOLDRIDGE COLLECTION.

RIGHT: A last wisp of steam leaves the whistle of engine No. 4 as a UV train enters a rural crossing. A wooden GPEX milk car in service to the Dairymen's League is the head car and will eventually be interchanged to the DL&W or the O&W. CAL'S CLASSICS.

THIS PAGE: Caboose 51 was bought by the UV when the O&W switched to four-axle cabooses which were roomier, generally smoother riding, and could accommodate an entire crew during a layover. Surprisingly, this car still exists and may be restored at Arkville, N.Y. Two later acquisitions from the O&W were the 101 and 103. The UV added the side door to both cars for convenience in handling package and express shipments. The 103 wears the Salzberg colorful cream, orange and black stripe scheme and sits at the New Berlin plant of the Dairymen's League while the engine attends to other tasks on July 31, 1954. CABOOSE 51: CAL's CLASSICS. CARS 101 AND 103: TED GLEICHMANN, JR. COLLECTION.

RIGHT: Steam's replacement on the Unadilla Valley was a pair of General Electric switchers, but it was soon decided that one was adequate for the line. Engine 200 became a familiar sight as it rumbled up and down the valley between Bridgewater, New Berlin Jct., and on up the Wharton Valley to Edmeston. DOUG ELLISON COLLECTION. BELOW: The brightly painted UV 200 meets the austere Lackawanna 955 at Bridgewater for an interchange of cars. MIKE HOLDRIDGE COLLECTION.

ABOVE AND TOP RIGHT: The General Electric engine arrives from the south in the former O&W New Berlin yard just beyond the shadow of the O&W station. DOUG ELLISON COLLECTION. In a winter scene at New Berlin, the 200 heads north on the original UV and passes over the switch that marks the beginning of the Wharton Valley line at the left. MERRITT LLOYD PHOTOGRAPH, MIKE HOLDRIDGE COLLECTION.

RIGHT: A brakeman signals the engineer to couple the orange and cream diesel to a boxcar at Edmeston on August 31, 1956. The once busy terminal of the Wharton Valley was being visited on an infrequent basis by that date. The small building to the right was an O&W section shanty that was converted to an agent's quarters. It was much less expensive to maintain than the big station next to it. TED GLEICHMANN, JR. COLLECTION.

RIGHT: Steam engine No. 6 is about to leave New Berlin for the final time as the diesel hauls it off for the trip to the scrap dealer. The main rods have been removed and all journals and bearing surfaces have been generously lubricated to ensure that the 6 will exit the property peacefully. MERRITT LLOYD PHOTOGRAPH, MIKE HOLDRIDGE COLLECTION.

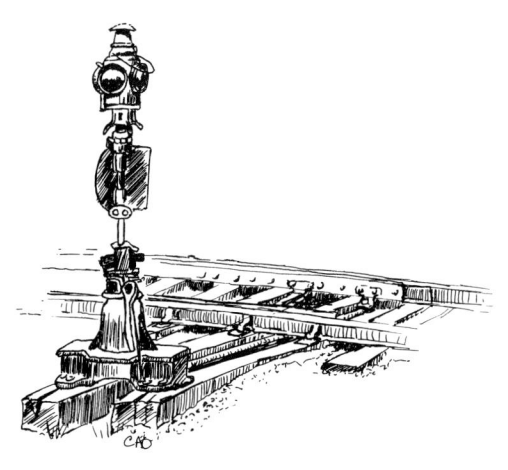

RIGHT: Engine 300 was a 50-ton General Electric unit that was brought to the UV for a period of unsuccessful testing in 1956. It found tasks more suitable to its abilities on another Salzberg property, the Southern New York at Oneonta. MERRITT LLOYD PHOTOGRAPH, MIKE HOLDRIDGE COLLECTION.

Four photographs show ex-O&W diesel No. 113 working the former New Berlin branch between New Berlin and Mt. Upton on December 29, 1958. LEFT AND BOTTOM LEFT: The southbound train stands in cold relief against a wintry Chenango County landscape. Because of the weather, a trackman or two might be riding in the cab and would use shovels and brooms to clean out switches and flangeways at highway crossings. BOTTOM RIGHT: At South New Berlin the crew pulls out of a siding and onto the main track after dropping a car. A pendulum type of warning device known as a 'wig-wag' and probably dating back to O&W days still provides the crossing protection. FACING PAGE: Additional switching will be done at Mt. Upton, where several businesses still depend upon rail service. Since there is no longer an agent here, the telephone and the U. S. Mail are used to conduct business between the agent in New Berlin and all on-line customers. FOUR PHOTOGRAPHS: JIM SHAUGHNESSY.

Because it served the O&W longer than the other cars or possibly because it handled more different assignments, the 804 seems to have been the company's most frequently photographed rail car. Here it is laying over at Summitville while assigned to the Summitville-Kingston run. There can be little doubt that the motorman preferred that side of the run where he operated the car from the quieter rear control compartment. Leaking exhaust gases, clattering valves and noisy machinery filled the forward end according to reminiscences of men who ran motor cars on other lines. The date of the photograph is July, 1933. H. K. VOLLRATH COLLECTION.

Chapter 16: The Gas-Mechanical and Gas-Electric Cars

When he [engineer R. E. Rowe] was assigned to 804, his face seemed to grow darker, and on one most memorable occasion he finally expressed himself, fully and forcibly. When the motor conked out at Randallsville, he collected his tools and dived into the engine compartment. An agonizing period of tinkering and testing brought a murderous scowl to the face of the sweating engineman. At last he erupted from the doorway, flung his wrenches far out into the adjacent field and addressed a few well-chosen (unprintable) words to the motor car and the company that had been so addleheaded as to buy her in the first place. There were, as the public learned to its dismay, rather strong opinions on the subjects.

William F. Helmer, *O&W* (125).

In the employment of motor cars, the O&W may have hoped for one of two possible outcomes. First was that the cars would be a temporary measure to reduce the costs of operating passenger trains until such time as the patronage dropped to the point where the runs could be discontinued. The second possible outcome might have been the public's return to the railroad and its modern equipment with a lack of smoke, irritating cinders, and soot. If the latter were true, perhaps the management thought that the lure of modernity found in this application of the internal combustion engine to railcars might result in whole fleets of such cars providing all local passenger service needs. Not only were passengers switching over to the highways, but mail express and small freight shipments were going that way as well. Certainly the railcar offered a solution to the immediate problem of reducing costs of branch line passenger service. State, county, and municipal governments were improving highways so that all-weather travel was truly possible. The automobile and truck manufacturers were improving their products yearly so that transportation by this mode was becoming more reliable. It would still take several years, however, for dependability, comfort, gas stations, repair facilities, and motels (cabins in the early days) to entice virtually all the intermediate and long-distance passengers away from the trains.

By requiring a smaller train crew, the motor cars reduced labor costs, and this certainly did not make them popular with labor unions. Those motor cars that were bi-directional did not require the time, effort, or facilities needed to turn a steam locomotive or an entire passenger train. Those that were not bi-directional could be turned more easily, with the train arranged for the return trip in one move. Steam locomotive and passenger car requirements were reduced, and this forecast the retirement of older, less efficient locomotives and wooden passenger cars.

Unfortunately, most of the motor cars suffered from a poor public image. Their interiors tended to be spartan—frequently to the point of physical discomfort on some of the longer runs. The public also recognized them for what they were: attempts to reduce costs by providing simple, inexpensive accommodations. Unlike many of the main-line diesel locomotives they gave rise to, few motor cars would be complimented for design aesthetics. Their brutish radiators, flat fronts, and cluttered roofs caught and held the eye of one fascinated by mechanics but assaulted the senses of most travelers. According to those who rode them, the exhaust sounds were often less than rhythmic and indicated frequent misfiring. However, this was not much different from the behavior of many automobile engines of the 1920's and was not unexpected. Derisive terms were frequently applied to them. When one of the motor cars showed up on the Scranton Division, it was referred to as a *peanut grinder*. (When a motor car was introduced on the nearby Jefferson Division of the Erie, a conductor was reported to be so incensed that he refused to collect cash fares from passengers not having tickets.)

Those charged with motor car maintenance, engineers assigned to operate them, and firemen whose skills were not needed, could be highly derogatory of their performance and design. A cold chisel and ten-pound sledge, standard repair equipment on steam locomotives, would solve few of their mechanical problems. Their occasional (occasional might have to be defined) temperamental fits brought more than one old steam engineer close to apoplexy and his passengers along with him. However, the same experiences generally were true wherever the application of a new technology trod upon well-established patterns. Internal combustion arrived, was tried, and eventually conquered the old order.

The O&W purchased a total of four motor cars in a two year period. This was in the mid-1920's when many other railroads had already sampled a variety of these cars and generally reported them as acceptable if not always highly successful. The first railcar to arrive on the O&W came in April or May of 1924 and was numbered 801. Actually it would more

properly be called a rail bus and it bore some resemblance to a stretched Galloping Goose of Rio Grande Southern Railroad fame. It was built by the Sykes Company of Winthrop Harbor, Illinois. Sykes was a minor builder in the railcar business, producing approximately 30 cars between 1923 and 1928. This single car order went to Sykes as the result of a ten-car order placed by the New Haven, which had controlled the O&W's affairs since early in the century.

The 801 weighed twelve tons, which was five tons less than the New Haven's version. It was 43 feet long and seated 38 people, with a baggage compartment at the rear. Power was provided by a 175-h.p.

ABOVE: Fresh out of the construction shop, the O&W's first motor car had an official portrait taken at the St. Louis Car Co. shop in 1925. Although it carried many of the appliances seen on its steam-propelled stable mates, its power-producing compartment was minuscule in comparison to the combined volume of the firebox, boiler and cylinders of something like a Y class 4-8-2. ST. LOUIS CAR COLLECTION, COURTESY OF WASHINGTON UNIVERSITY ARCHIVES.

FACING PAGE: Lacking an O&W plan or diagram for the Sykes car, this one from the New Haven will serve as an acceptable substitute. After comparing this diagram with photographs of New Haven Sykes cars, it seems to be a more accurate representation of the O&W car; but the date, however, indicates that it was part of the original New Haven order. JOE BUX COLLECTION.

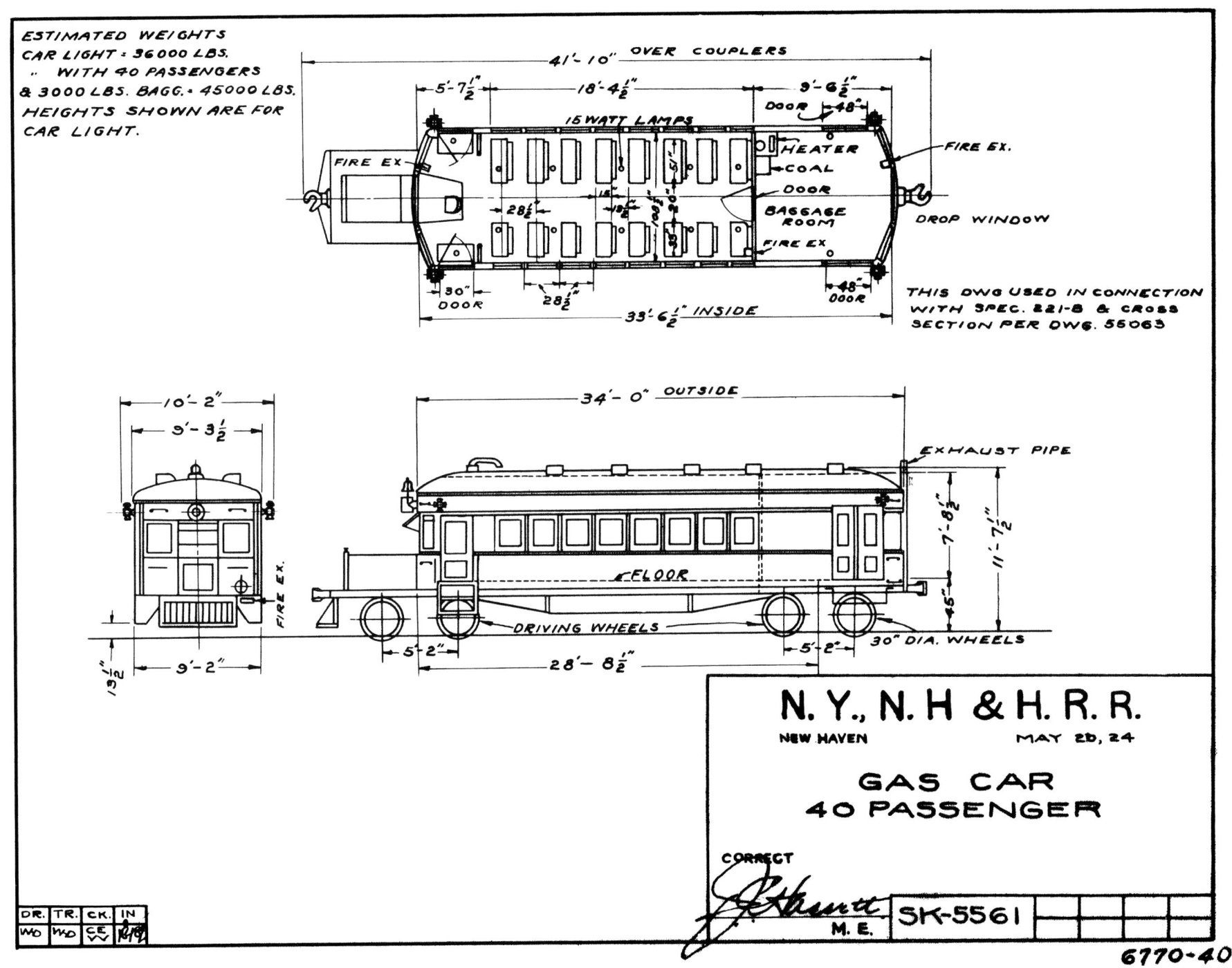

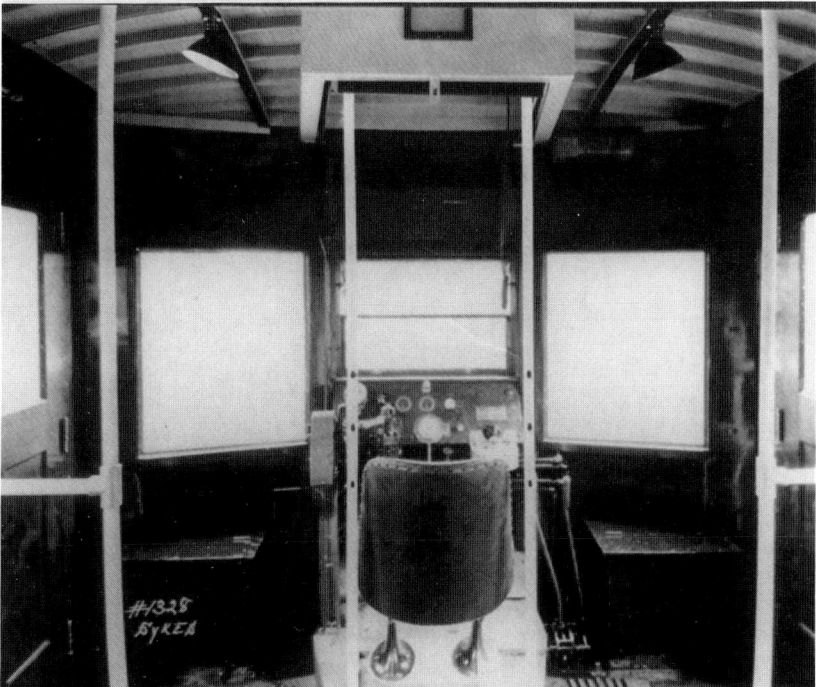

FACING PAGE: *The O&W's single-car order to Sykes was closely connected to a New Haven order for several cars that were only slightly different from the 801. These four views of New Haven 9004 give some idea of the O&W car's appearance.* ST. LOUIS CAR COLLECTION, COURTESY OF WASHINGTON UNIVERSITY ARCHIVES.

RIGHT: *The 801 sat in storage at Middletown while management looked for a buyer or tried to find some further use for the investment. Apparently the New Haven was not interested in adding the car to its own fleet of Sykes units, with which it was reported satisfied. Over the course of time some items, such as the headlight and marker lamps, were removed from the car.* ROBERT F. COLLINS.

six-cylinder Sterling gasoline marine engine. Sterling was a Buffalo, N.Y., manufacturer of engines for truck, bus and marine uses. Marine engines developed the highest horsepower at that time, but they were designed to use large amounts of cooling water, and some compromises were made for rail use. The construction was done at the St. Louis Car Company plant in that city. Sykes apparently did not have its own facility.

A major cause of this company's lack of success was that it built gas-mechanical cars, which were less reliable and more difficult to operate than gas-electric cars. The problem with the direct mechanical drive was that it lacked the flexibility to absorb the shocks of the rail joints, switches, and crossing diamonds. No pneumatic rubber tires cushioned the jolts that traveled right through to the crankshaft and connecting rods. Since these cars were frequently purchased for service on secondary lines where track and roadbed conditions were below main line standards, the greater irregularities tended to aggravate the situation. As General Electric, Electro-Motive, and other manufacturers proved, generators and truck-mounted motors were more adaptable to rail service. There were also the problems of maintaining a clutch and shifting the gears which were present with the mechanical drive system. Those with truck driving experience will recall their own difficulty at times with synchronizing gears.

The 801's drive shaft came back to a gearbox and system of universal joints which drove two other shafts. These were connected to the inner axle of each truck. It was believed to have six forward and two reverse speeds. The car had a coal-burning heater located in the baggage compartment and presumably under the eye of the conductor. The motorman sat behind the middle front window and was not separated from the passengers. The car apparently had air brakes. It was painted maroon with white or yellow lettering and cost $22,449.31.

Assigned to Summitville-Monticello service, the 801 made two round trips per day and recorded a total of 29,895 miles of operation for 1925. O&W President John B. Kerr, in an annual report for the year, said that the first car "having demonstrated its usefulness and economy in operation, three cars of the gasoline-electric type and of greater capacity were ordered, one of which is now in operation on the Monticello branch, and the others will be delivered within the next two months. Their use will work a considerable economy in the cost of passenger train service and at the same time give the public better accommodation than could be otherwise furnished." The 801 was officially retired in 1939 after a period of idleness at Middletown shops. The body sat at Roscoe for a number of years and was then moved to Oneonta, N.Y., for an unsuccessful restoration attempt.

The O&W went to a more proven performer for the remainder of its modest gas car fleet. The J.G. Brill Company of Philadelphia was one of the largest streetcar builders in the country. Brill's history in the railcar business went back to the post-Civil War period when the company produced horsecars for the nation's larger cities. In the first decade of the new century it entered the gas-electric car field as a

LEFT: By 1941, the body of the 801 had been taken to Roscoe and placed at trackside, reportedly for a section house or tool shanty. Sometime in the early 1960's, it was moved to Oneonta, N.Y., for an attempt at restoration; but its frame members and sheet metal had deteriorated too far to justify the project. MALCOLM ROY PHOTOGRAPH, COURTESY OF JOE BUX AND DEPOT ATTIC.

BELOW: This letter and a generic plan from Brill (facing page) marked the O&W's entry into electro-motive propulsion. The plan is general but in the period it was typical for a railroad's officers to specify details that met specific service requirements. O&W SOCIETY COLLECTION.

builder of car bodies for other companies. In the early 1920's Brill built a single gas-mechanical car for the Service Motor Truck Company. This included some new design ideas that made for smoother riding qualities as well as easing the stresses to which various parts of the power train were subjected.

The result of this car's success was a merger between Brill and the Service Motor Truck Company which produced the ability to fabricate complete gas-electric cars. Brill later aligned itself with the Westinghouse Company to produce a full line of gas-electric cars to fill a variety of rail needs. Included in this final phase was the production of many of the largest of the self-propelled rail cars. Brill's biggest competitor in the field was Electro Motive Divisions's predecessor, Electro-Motive Corporation. EMD is a part of General Motors Corporation and is a large manufacturer of diesel-electric locomotives today due to EMC's early lead in diesel-electric propulsion technology.

In 1925 Brill introduced its Model 250, so named because of its Brill-Westinghouse 250-h.p. gasoline engine. At that time it was the most powerful unit in the catalog. The 250-engine-powered cars weighed 44 to 60 tons depending upon options. The O&W's first Brill, the 802, was a 45-ton, 60-foot car that seated 52 passengers. Again the New Haven

THE J. G. BRILL COMPANY

PHILADELPHIA, PA.

CABLE ADDRESSES
"BRILL" PHILADELPHIA
"AXLES" LONDON
"BOGIBRIL" PARIS

22233

July 13th, 1925.

Mr. J. H. Nuelle, Vice-President & Gen. Mgr.,
New York, Ontario & Western Railway Co.,
Middletown, N. Y.

Dear Sir:-

I wish to thank you for your letter of July 10th returning copy of our print No. 18761 which has been marked with your approval.

The engineering work is under way on your car and we will keep you advised as to when it is started in the shop in order that we may have such of your organization here as you may wish.

Yours very truly,

Sales Manager
Automotive Car Division

CJM:AS

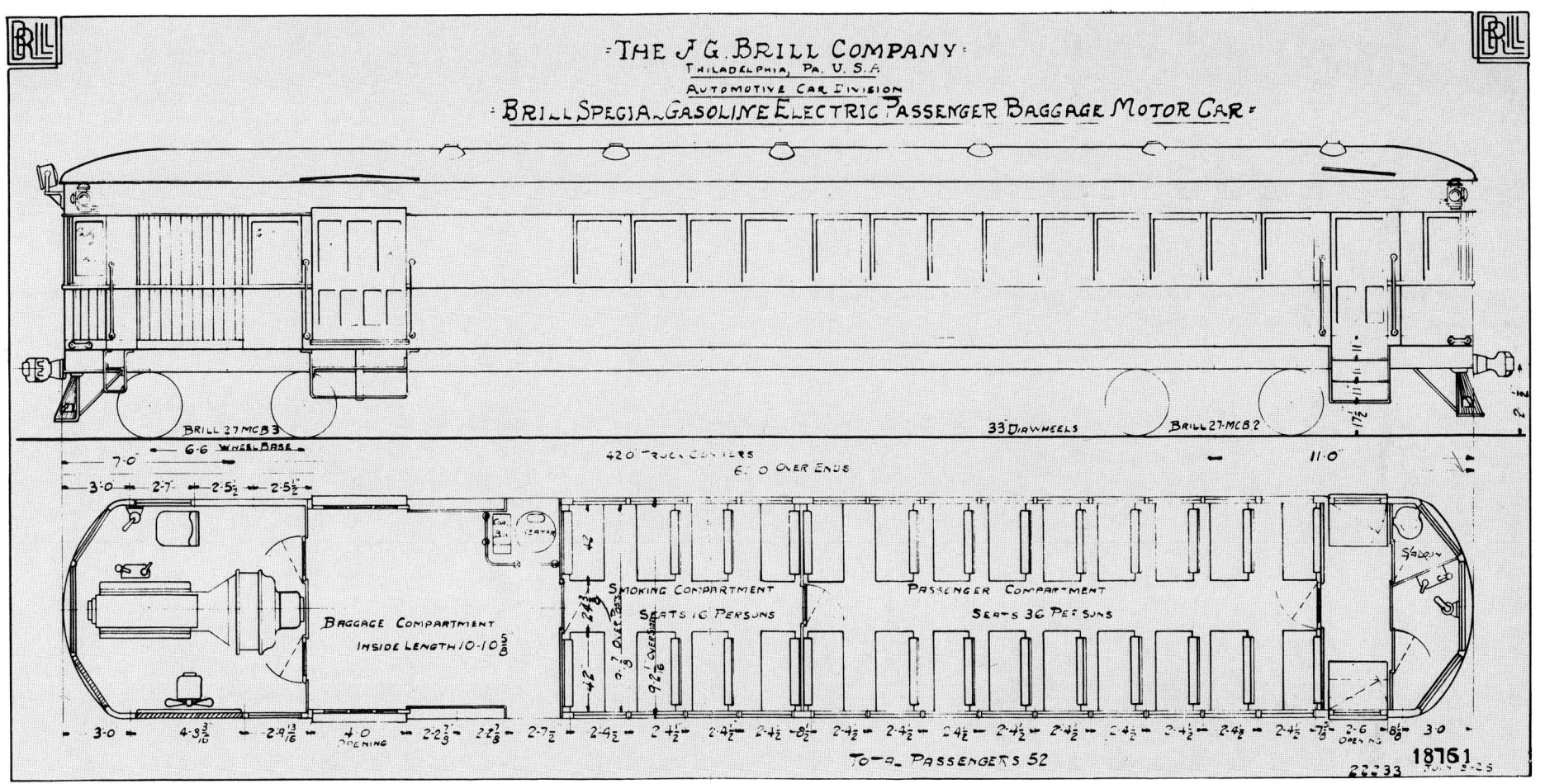

was connected with this purchase. Letters between Brill and the O&W indicate that the car was to follow the floor plan of New Haven 9024, a Brill product of 1924 with a Sykes power plant. The 802's 250-h.p. engine drove a Westinghouse 160-KW generator which supplied current to two 140-h.p. traction motors on the forward truck. The engine compartment had the engineer's controls on one side and the radiator on the opposite side wall. This was unlike EMC and some other builders who placed the radiator on the roof or in the front of the car. Behind the engine was a baggage compartment which also contained a coal-fired hot-water heater. A 16-seat smoking section was next, followed by the 36-seat passenger compartment. Steel partitions with swing-type doors separated all compartments. A small dry-hopper lavatory facility was located in the rear vestibule, opposite the rear operator's compartment. The car was fully bi-directional and carried 150 gallons of fuel. According to one newspaper account, this car was equipped with electro-pneumatic control for multiple unit operations. No written or photographic evidence of such multiple unit operations has appeared up to this time however. The article also stated that the car had a maximum speed of 48 miles per hour.

The interior of the passenger section was finished in mahogany with reversible seats upholstered in dark brown imitation leather. Shades were provided at the side windows and flooring was hard maple.

The 802 cost $38,500 f.o.b. Philadelphia and arrived on the O&W in the second half of 1925. The 802 had not yet been completed when Middletown officials began a second round of correspondence with Brill for two more cars to be delivered in 1926. The 803 and 804 were also Model 250's, but of greater weight and length. They were 55-ton cars with a 73-foot length. The 804 was equipped with a ten-foot railway post office compartment which

ABOVE: Soon to roll through the rural environs of New York State, the 802 takes shape at the Brill plant in Philadelphia. The car rests on shop trucks prior to the installation of engine, generator, control systems, seats, and other components. Cars 802 and 803 had baggage and smoking sections but only the 804 had a postal compartment. BRILL COLLECTION. COURTESY OF THE HISTORICAL SOCIETY OF PENNSYLVANIA.

LEFT: A truck of the 803 bears many similarities to the diesel locomotive truck that was still in the future. The electric traction motors have not yet been installed. Most of the motor weight will ride on the axles through bearing surfaces and a bracket on the bolster will support the rest. BRILL COLLECTION, COURTESY OF THE HISTORICAL SOCIETY OF PENNSYLVANIA.

Interior furnishings of the 802 (top left) and the 803 (top right) were basic as might be expected in view of the rural areas they were to serve. It was surprising to find that 3-2 seating was specified for the 803 and the 804. This arrangement was generally not well received by passengers since it could force a person to sit between two strangers. It was very likely that the double seats on the right filled before those seats on the left. RIGHT: We're looking through the baggage compartment, into the smoking and regular passenger sections of car 803. The heating system at left was a coal-fired, hot water type. The small coal box must have held adequate fuel for one trip, and the baggageman had the responsibility of checking the fire and removing the ashes. THREE PHOTOGRAPHS: BRILL COLLECTION, COURTESY OF THE HISTORICAL SOCIETY OF PENNSYLVANIA.

The difference in lengths of the 802 and the 803 are visible in these two pictures at the Brill plant. Both cars had similar, if not exact, features in many areas. Only the lead truck was powered on the three Brill cars. To the rear of the truck is the fuel tank. Unlike many other railroads, the O&W was fortunate in avoiding accidents that could have resulted in serious gasoline fires. One reason why many railroads preferred diesel power for rail cars was that the fuel was less volatile as well as less expensive. *TWO PHOTOGRAPHS: BRILL COLLECTION, COURTESY OF THE HISTORICAL SOCIETY OF PENNSYLVANIA.*

limited its seating to 69 passengers, whereas the 803 could handle 88 passengers. Like the 801, the Brills were also a maroon color. The order cost $105,000 for both cars, and this was conditioned upon the New Haven's placing an order within six months of a specified date. Apparently both roads got a better deal if they ordered what was essentially the same car. Later that year the New Haven did order five cars that were a few tons lighter but of the same length. An interesting coincidence was that the neighboring Lehigh & New England had purchased a Model 250 just before the 803 and 804 were contracted for.

With four motor cars in service, the railroad managed to roll 157,784 passenger miles out of them in 1926. This represented approximately eleven percent of the total passenger-train miles, not including mixed trains, for that year. In 1927 this rose to 16 percent despite the fact that the total passenger-train miles had decreased. Apparently the road did use a coach as a trailer for one or more of the motor cars since 116 motor trailer miles are reported in the company's annual figures for 1926. This might have been a feasibility test. Nevertheless, from December, 1925, to December, 1934, there was an 80 percent drop in the number of passengers carried. (This figure may vary by a few percent due to a change in the O&W accounting procedure between 1928 and 1929. However, the decrease is clearly staggering.) This was accompanied by a 64 percent drop in the number of passenger-train miles during the same period. The downward trend would continue relatively unabated, and the need for the motor cars diminished.

Besides the Port Jervis and Monticello branches, motor cars were assigned to the Kingston, Delhi, and Utica branches. They also provided the final summer-only second passenger train on the Scranton Division when they worked a Cadosia-Mayfield turn. Mr. Richard Howe, quoted in Chapter Two on milk-train operations on the Scranton Division, recalled making a trip on one of the Brill cars or

ABOVE: The 804 made its debut at an Atlantic City railroad convention in 1926. Railroad and supply industry officials would display their recent projects with pride, hopes of acceptance, and perhaps some sales orders as well. Brill cars sold well enough for the company to gain the number two position as producers of rail cars. Their designs were generally less boxy and cluttered than those of the number one builder, Electro Motive Corporation. COURTESY OF JOE BUX AND DEPOT ATTIC. BELOW: The 804 eventually received a snowplow pilot similar to those applied to the Y-2 class 4-8-2 engines. The location in this photograph is believed to be Kingston. WALTER RICH COLLECTION.

Unfortunately, the photographer did not list the reason for the 803's presence in Middletown. No doubt the cars were used for inspection trips by officials and they also came in for mechanical attention, but nothing in the available records indicates revenue service south of Summitville. CASEY W. SCALES PHOTOGRAPH, COURTESY OF JOE BUX

The O&W chose a unique style of letters and numerals for its passenger equipment; and 804, standing at Sidney, provides a clear example. The road's motor cars were painted maroon with orange lettering. The locomotive-hauled wooden and steel passenger cars had the same style lettering but in yellow or dulux color. WILLIAM SCHRIVER COLLECTION.

The 803 appears to be laying-over on a warm day of undisclosed date and the crew may be lounging inside before beginning or resuming work. Passengers appreciated the lack of soot and cinders in these cars, and if the baggage compartment door was closed, the engine noise should not have been too annoying. CARL OHLSON COLLECTION.

The 804, recognizable by its postal compartment door, pauses in front of the Northern Division headquarters' building and station at Norwich. The car is most likely working the Delhi-Utica Flyer run which called for a Norwich stop about 9:30 A.M. on the northbound side. WALTER RICH COLLECTION.

gasoline trains, as they were sometimes called. His recollection was that the car swayed quite a bit where track maintenance was lacking. He also thought that they did not have a smoking section because his father was shocked when he saw a local young lady smoking in public on the car. These cars also worked the far north end of the main line in the final years of passenger service to Oswego.

On December 12, 1930, the 803 was sold to the New Haven, becoming its 9112. The 802 followed on April 1, 1932, becoming NH 9113; and finally the 804 left on July 24, 1935, to become New Haven 9114. The 803 was similar to the New Haven's early Brill cars, while the 802 was shorter. This may be why the New Haven renumbered and converted it to Inspection Car 9 in 1940. The 804 was modified by removing the partition between the postal and baggage sections to make one large baggage compartment. Along with most of the New Haven's original Brill cars, the three ex-O&W cars continued in service until the mid-1940's.

BELOW: In an age familiar with the music of George Gershwin, the novels of F. Scott Fitzgerald, and the home runs of Babe Ruth, local trains of both the O&W and the D&H crossed paths at Sidney, exchanged a passenger or two, traded some express shipments, and resumed their journeys. The O&W judged the 804 adequate for these tasks; so one car handled postal, baggage and passenger functions. The D&H still required separate cars for each purpose and, with one minor exception, chose to ignore rail motor cars. JOE BUX COLLECTION.

ABOVE: New Haven inspection car 9 is stopped at Canaan, Connecticut, while on a trip over the former Central New England lines. The car, originally O&W 802, became New Haven 9113 for revenue service and in 1940 was finally renumbered 9 for inspection service. For this last service the car was provided with several new features for system-wide self-sufficiency. It was on the New Haven's roster until 1952. L. BEAUJON PHOTOGRAPH. COURTESY OF NEW HAVEN RAILROAD HISTORICAL AND TECHNICAL ASSOCIATION.

Addenda

Addendum A: Arrangements of Milk Train Operations in 1898, 1914 and 1920

The 1898 Employees' Timetable illustrates the milk train arrangements of the period. Number 10, the long milk, left Oneida at 8:15 A.M. and made all stops to Randallsville. The Rome milk train, Number 182, left that city at 7:30 A.M. for an 8:20 A.M. connection at Clinton with train Number 60, which left Utica at 7:00 A.M. The combined train arrived at Randallsville, where it cleared for Number 2 and waited to make the connection with Number 10. With the arrival of this train at Randallsville, the small yard must have been crowded. Numbers 60 and 10 both had to clear Number 2, and there was probably milk from the Pecksport Line to be picked up as well. After getting its increasingly longer train together, Number 10 continued south, picking up the rattling, clanking cans at each stop.

Speed in loading the cans was important, and many a waiting passenger and depot lounger was fascinated by the milk handlers' trick of spinning the cans into the cars. A little before 1:00 P.M., Number 10's milk cars banged across the Delaware & Hudson crossing as the train arrived in Sidney. Milk train Number 174 from the New Berlin branch originated at Edmeston at 9:30 A.M. each morning and arrived in Sidney, after a 32-mile run, a full hour ahead of Number 10. The train continued on to Walton where ten minutes were allowed for the addition of the New Berlin branch milk to Number 10's consist at 2:25 P.M.

Two hours earlier, Number 12, the short milk, originating at Walton, had left town with the production from the local and Delhi branch creameries. A stop at Cadosia allowed for an engine change or servicing, a meal stop or crew change for the engine and trainmen, and the addition of the Scranton Division milk. During the week, this milk was brought north on the morning passenger train, which arrived in Cadosia at 1:15 P.M. This was ten minutes after the arrival of Number 12. On Sundays, the Scranton Division had its own milk train, Number 205, which had a much earlier arrival at Cadosia. Continuing south, milk from the Ellenville branch was brought to Summitville on mixed trains during the week and on a passenger train on Sunday. Number 12 would finally arrive at Cornwall a half hour ahead of Number 10. The two trains were combined here and run to Weehawken as Number 10. If the traffic required, Number 12 would run as an extra to Weehawken.

In 1914, the company's milk agent made a report to the Adams Express Company on the operations of the through milk trains. There had been several changes since 1898. At this later date train Number 14 left Oswego at 8:00 A.M. daily and picked up all milk between that point and Sidney with the exception of milk stops between Randallsville and Norwich. Train 60, which left Rome at 10:00 A.M. daily, covered the Rome and Utica branches and made the main line milk stops between Randallsville and Norwich. At Norwich, Number 60 was combined with Number 14. From Sidney south, Number 14 ran through to Weehawken with an 11:05 P.M. arrival. Number 14 covered 325 miles and Number 60 ran fifty five miles.

Train 10 originated at Edmeston at 11:00 A.M. at this time, and picked up milk into Sidney. It then headed for Weehawken with stops at Cadosia for the Scranton Division milk and at Summitville for the Monticello and Kingston branch milk. Number 10 was due in Weehawken at 9:40 P.M. after covering 200 miles. Number 174 covered 32 miles.

Train Number 12 started at Sidney at 10:40 A.M. daily and did the local work to Cornwall, picking up the Delhi branch milk at Walton, the Delaware & Northern milk at East Branch, and the Middletown & Unionville cars at Middletown. This train was due in Weehawken at 8:55 P.M. after covering 200 miles.

The 1920 Employees' Timetable indicates that Number 10 resumed a Northern Division point of origin, this time at Oswego. Rome and New Berlin branch milk arrangements, except for train numbers, were still the same. Number 12, the short milk, had been extended to Sidney and left there daily at 9:50 A.M. The New Berlin branch milk on Number 510 arrived at Sidney much later, but continued to make the connection with Number 10. Delhi branch and Scranton Division milk was handled by local freights or passenger trains, since no separate trains are indicated in the operating information.

Addendum B: MDT's Milk Tank Trailer Car

In the O&W Society's collection there is a letter from Merchants Despatch Transportation Incorporated, indicating that the NYO&W had an interest in its milk tank trailer cars. As indicated in chapter four, Merchants Despatch was a car builder, owner, and lessor affiliated with the New York Central System. Only three of these rather complex cars are said to have been constructed. They were basically a short piggyback car that had rotating platforms or turntables for two single-axle tank trailers. From a photograph of the car one can surmise that the mechanical complexity of the design must have limited the car's success. Fitch's simpler, easy-to-operate system may well have stifled further development and promotion of Merchants Despatch piggyback cars for milk services.

Addendum C: The Big Three of the Dairy Industry

In 1939, Borden's, The Dairymen's League, and Sheffield Farms controlled one-third of the milk business in the New York City metropolitan area. A dozen large independents like Queensboro, Grand View, Sunshine, and Renkins Dairy Companies controlled another third, and 80 to 100 small independents shared the remaining third. The big three were shipping about 60 percent by rail, the second group 40 percent, and the last group, less than 25 percent.

Borden's

Gail Borden was born in Norwich, N.Y., on November 9, 1801. After a period of moving about the country, he eventually settled in Texas, where he was active in the struggle for Texas independence. Afterward, he experimented with dehydrating and condensing beef into a food product that would not spoil quickly. The idea was successful but not on a commercial basis. In 1856 he got a patent for a vacuum-condensing procedure that could concentrate milk by 80 percent. Although the germ theory of disease was yet unknown, part of Borden's success lay in the fact that he was unknowingly destroying harmful bacteria by his process. He saw a connection between clean barns, clean cattle, and hygienic milk handling.

In 1857 the New York Condensed Milk Company was formed to produce Borden's new product. In 1875 fresh milk was added to the line. In 1892, evaporated milk was introduced, and Borden's began selling fresh milk in Chicago. During the next 25 years, the company continued a program of geographic expansion. In 1902 it bought the American and Canadian holdings of Anglo-Swiss Condensed Milk Company which had plants on the NYO&W. Borden's acquired over a hundred dairy-related companies including J.M. Horton and Reid's Ice Cream. By 1930, Borden's or companies it had acquired were making dry milk, mincemeat, cheese, and casein—a milk derivative used in glue. In 1929 four operating companies were set up. These handled food products, dairy products, ice cream, cheese, and produce products. The company credits itself with the development of instant coffee and special glues used in the manufacture of exterior plywood. Later activities saw Borden's involved in international manufacturing of chemicals, snack foods, cosmetics, and other diversification through acquisitions. At the present time Borden's is still very much in the dairy foods business, but fluid milk is only a small part of its large operations.

Borden's was the largest user of railroad cars in the transportation of milk. It owned and leased a greater variety of designs than any other dairy company. Many of its cars had colorful heralds and lettering. In 1939, this company was shipping 60 percent by rail and 40 percent by truck. Borden's may have stopped shipping milk over the O&W before 1937.

The Dairymen's League

The Dairymen's League, Incorporated, came into being in 1907 as a result of organizational attempts dating back to 1889. The League was a bargaining association designed to get the best possible price for milk produced by its farmer members. After several years of unsuccessful attempts to get higher prices for its milk, the League had its first victory in 1916. Members withheld milk for 14 days and forced dealers to recognize the association and sign contracts with it. By 1920 the Dairymen's League marketing area included New York City, Buffalo, Syracuse, Rochester, Utica, and Elmira in New York along with Erie, Williamsport, Sunbury, Scranton, and Wilkes-Barre in Pennsylvania. At that time the League acquired processing plants to produce fluid milk, butter-powder, and cheese, which resulted in a change from a bargaining association to an operating cooperative. The trade name *Dairylea* was adopted in 1923. In the first decades of this century, the League claimed credit for many firsts in milk production and processing. It was also instrumental in the passage of federal and state legislation that aided dairymen.

Eventually a number of factors, including the handling of milk by bulk tank in the mid-1950's, caused the League to totally eliminate country plants by the late 1970's. Operations expanded into milk-related products such as yogurt, cottage cheese, and ultra-pasteurized products under the new name of Dairylea Cooperative Incorporated. Unlike the other big two in the dairy industry, the Dairymen's League did not own any railroad rolling stock but did lease a variety of cars from General American and National Car Company.

Sheffield Farms

Sheffield Farms traces its history back to 1841 when Thompson W. Decker established a route for the distribution of pure country milk in New York City. Within a few years he was shipping milk into the city by rail from Westchester County. The Slawson brothers followed Decker's lead in 1866 and also distributed country milk in the city. In 1880, L. B. Halsey married the daughter of Mrs. Ann Marie Sheffield and left the law profession to take over management of his mother-in-law's dairy farm at Mahwah, New Jersey. Halsey was interested in improving all aspects of the dairy business. One of his major achievements was setting up the first pasteurizing equipment in this country at Bloomville, New York.

In 1902, five dairy interests, including the previously mentioned pioneers, merged to form Sheffield Farms-Slawson-Decker Company, later shortened to Sheffield Farms. In 1913, the company introduced Sealect milk, a product of strict standards and the highest sanitation possible. Sheffield put in large city plants at Jamaica, Long Island, and Fifty-seventh Street, Manhattan. In 1941, Sheffield had 80 country plants within 400 miles north, 450 miles west, and 150 miles southwest of New York City. This company was the first to produce milk in sealed bottles, introduce vitamin D to milk, and homogenize milk for home use. When Sheffield broadened its business interests the dairy division became known as Sealtest. Sheffield made wide use of both owned and leased rail equipment. In 1939, this company owned 59 rail tank cars and leased 44. Sheffield is no longer in the fluid milk business, but its facility at Norwich, New York, produces ingredients for pharmaceutical use, flavor products, and other items used by the food industry.

Addendum D: Feed Mills and Milling

Prior to the coming of the railroads, farmers had to depend upon raising their own grain for use as animal feed. Corn, oats, barley, and buckwheat were the grains most commonly grown. After harvesting, the grains were brought to a local miller where they would be ground, bagged and brought back to the farm. The farmer would then mix or feed the clear grains at his discretion. There were no scientific formulas to follow unless farmers shared information among themselves. Generally, poultry and dairy cattle were the largest users of such feeds. Later, organized farmer groups, state agricultural and technical schools, feed manufacturers, and various state and federal government agencies brought in scientific methods in the raising of farm animals. This included improved feeds and feeding practices. As a result, an entire new industry—made possible by the railroads—came into existence.

Most of the main line and all of the branches of the New York, Ontario & Western ran through agricultural areas. From its earliest days, the line had a role in supplying the rural communities with the imported necessities to raise crops and animals. Now the railroad made it possible to bring, in large volumes, a variety of high nutrient grains and by-products from several industries that could be mixed to make top quality feeds for more productive farming.

Corn was the main element in feeds. It could be in the form of corn meal, corn oil, hominy feed, brewers' grits, gluten feed, germ meal or any of a great number of cereals. Spent brewery and distillery grains, linseed and cotton seed oil meal, and wheat feeds that included three or four by-products from flour mills were additional ingredients.

Oil seed meals were another component. These came from tropical plants such as coconuts and palm oil seeds from which soap manufacturers had pressed the oils to obtain fats. In the early 1930's, high-protein soybean meal, a new by-product from soybean processing, was added to the milling process.

These by-products were dried and shipped to the feed mills in boxcars that were equipped with grain doors made of wood and installed in the boxcar's doorway by a cooper. This made the car a tight container to prevent loss by the leakage of the lading. They were usually not visible since the car's sliding wood or steel door covered them. Later, grain doors were made of cardboard, which was reinforced with supporting steel straps across the doorway. In spite of these efforts, many cars still leaked meal. This drew pigeons, rats, and other animals to railroad yards where the cars had stood and some of the lading had trickled out.

Covered hopper cars began to come into feed service in the mid-1940's. These cars had several advantages over box cars in the transportation of feed and feed ingredients. They were loaded through weather-tight roof hatches and were primarily unloaded by gravity through hopper doors that did not need cooperage. The load could be dumped into an auger bin between the rails of the feed mill siding. Pounding the car sides with a hammer or some scraping with a hoe through a roof hatch released any lading that stuck to the car sides. Today, feed mills use covered hoppers almost exclusively.

Molasses was also used in making feed. This arrived in tank cars that were equipped with steam heating coils. In cold weather, live steam would be piped into the car to heat the molasses to a flowing temperature. In some cases the local creamery, a ready source of steam, provided this service. Molasses acted as a binder for the dry ingredients and made the feed palatable and appealing to animals.

The great U.S. milling centers such as Buffalo and Minneapolis originated uncounted carloads of grain and grain by-products for feed mills. Miner-Hillard in Wilkes-Barre was a large corn-milling concern that shipped to NYO&W communities. Metropolitan area breweries and distilleries from Kentucky sent their spent, odoriferous, dried grains to agricultural areas around the country. New Jersey's harbor-side industries were a great source of tropical plant residues that were used in feed.

When these carloads of feed elements arrived at a mill, they were unloaded by an auger or bucket elevator. The unloading device led to a system of delivery pipes that ran to the top of the mill. Here each particular ingredient was directed to separate storage bins. When a farmer came in to buy feed, he gave the formula or name of the mix desired. Specific quantities of each component were measured out by weight and put into a mixer for making batches that weighed as much as a ton or more. The finished mix was then put in 100-pound bags for the farmer to take home.

In the early 1950's, bulk delivery of feeds was begun. This eliminated the bagging of each batch and allowed for delivery of feed direct to the farmer's storage facility.

Rising costs of labor and raw materials called for a tighter, more efficient industry. This trend, coupled with a reduction in the number of farms, forced many of the small mill operators out of the business and saw the larger operators consolidating their mixing facilities and outlets.

The feed business was conducted at several levels. There were large, regional concerns such as the Grange League Federation (GLF), Eastern States Milling, and Ralston-Purina; smaller companies such as Camp Milling, Crawford Brothers, and I.L. Richer that served a section of the state; and finally there were local businesses that worked from a single location such as Beardsley and Sisson in South New Berlin, N.Y., or Moses Brothers at Eaton, N.Y.

GLF and Ralston-Purina did their feed milling in large facilities located in Buffalo or other cities close to the ingredient suppliers and volume transportation systems. Bagged and bulk shipments were made to local franchise outlets. Crawford Brothers had its own retail outlets and used the O&W to ship milled feed from its Walton plant to both on- and off-line stores. I.L. Richer did the same but used the DL&W to a greater degree since the line served Norwich mill. Camp Milling did not have its own retail outlet but shipped to independents throughout the northeast.

The retail stores did not limit themselves to feed. They also carried fertilizers, hardware, building materials, coal, oil, and many other items for both home and farm use. Most of these supplies came in by rail.

Feed mills still depend upon rail service today although trucks have taken over part of the business. There have been a number of changes in feed ingredients and processing, and several of the factors mentioned above are no longer true. Large-capacity covered hoppers are used almost exclusively to bring the grains to those mills still served by rail.

Addendum E: Commentary on Arthur Mitchell's August, 1945, ride on the Delhi mixed train

Mr. Mitchell's trip presents some interesting questions for the knowledgeable and curious reader. His reference to a tuscan red combine, brick station, and a wye at Delhi are at odds with a number of sources, both written and photographic.

A pre-1900 annual report states that the railroad had changed the color of its passenger cars from red to dark green. Color photographs also show dark green passenger cars, and it is generally believed that the red paint was only applied to older passenger equipment consigned to work service by the time of his story.

At Delhi, numerous photographs show both the freight and passenger stations to be of wooden construction.

The railroad did change the track arrangements at Delhi several times; there has been no indication of a wye, but there is frequent reference to a turntable. In addition, a newspaper in the collection of the Frisbee Museum in Delhi shows a new F3 being turned on the table in 1948. There might have been a problem with the table or perhaps there was some operational advantage to running the steam locomotive in reverse on the day of Mr. Mitchell's trip. As a rule, officials did not want an engine to operate in reverse if a turning facility was available.

A final note concerns the conductor's invitation to Mr. Mitchell to "ride the steps of the engine." Pilot steps on locomotives were banned by the Federal Railroad Administration because they figured in a number of accidents involving trainmen. Such a casual invitation is hard to imagine in today's litigious and safety-conscious atmosphere.

Addendum F: Track Maps for the main line between Walton and Sidney and the the Delhi branch.
The main line between Walton and Sidney

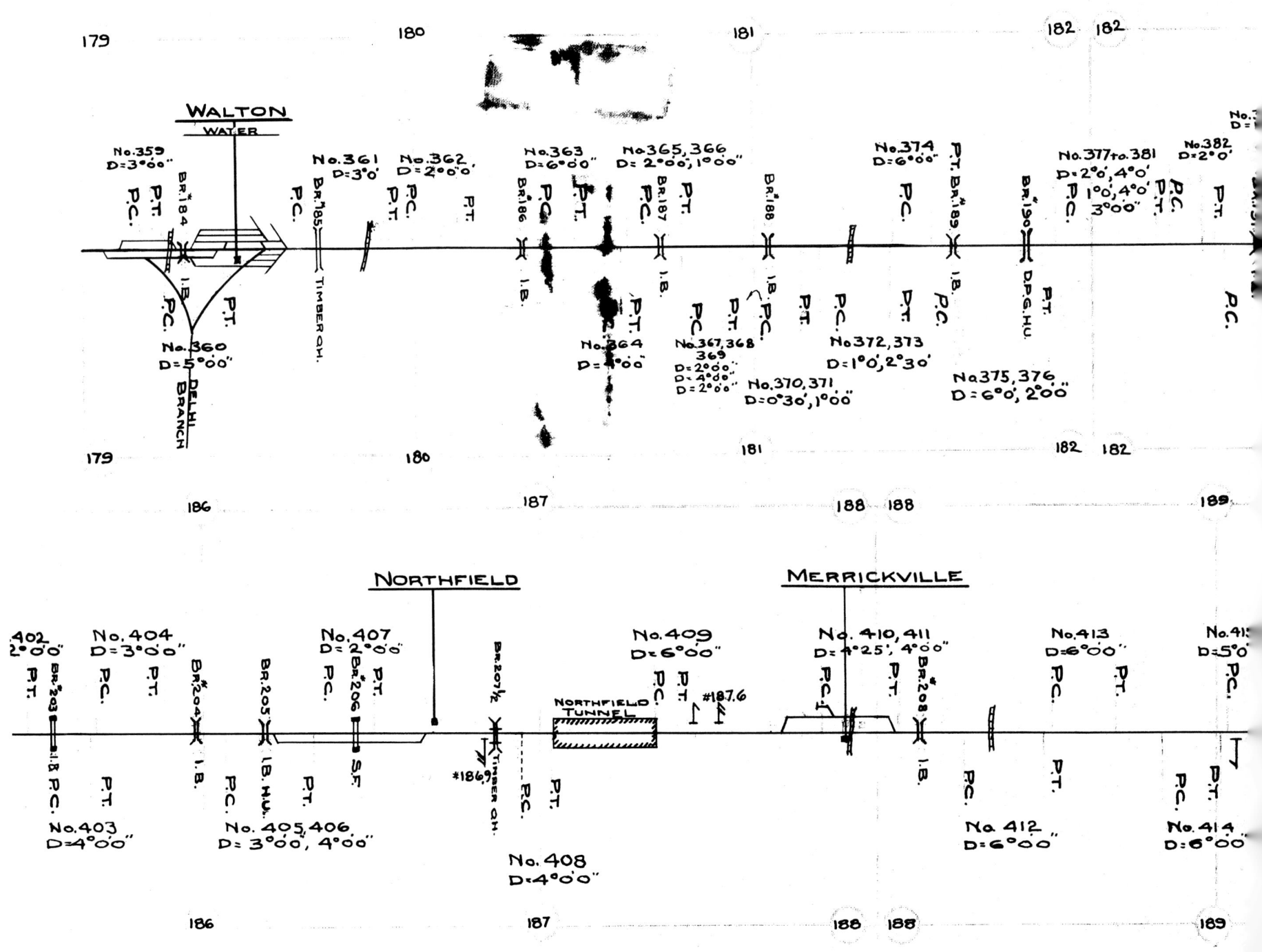

183
184
185
185
No.385
D=3°0'0"
No.388
D=3°0'0"
No.389, 390
D=2°0', 6°00"
No.392, 393
D=6°0', 5°0'0"
No.396, 397
D=2°0', 4°00
No.400
D=3°0'0"
No.402
D=2°0'0"
BR.192
BR.194
BR.199
BR.201
I.B.
S.F.
No.386
D=2°0'0"
No.387
D=2°0'0"
No.391
D=6°0'0"
No.394, 395
D=4°0', 2°0'
No.398
D=4°0'0"
No.399
D=2°0'0"
No.401
D=2°0'0"
No.403
D=4°0'0"
190
191
191
192
FRANKLIN
No.417
No.422
D=6°0'0"
No.423
D=5°0'0"
No.424
D=3°0'0"
No.427
D=1°0'0"
No.429
D=2°0'0"
No.431
D=6°0'0"
BR.209
BR.210
BR.211
BR.212
BR.213
BR.214
BR.215
VIADUCT
No.418
D=2°0'0"
No.419, 420, 421
D=6°12'40", 5°55'10", 6°12'0"
No.425
D=3°0'0"
No.426
D=1°0'0"
No.428
D=2°0'0"
No.430
D=2°0'0"

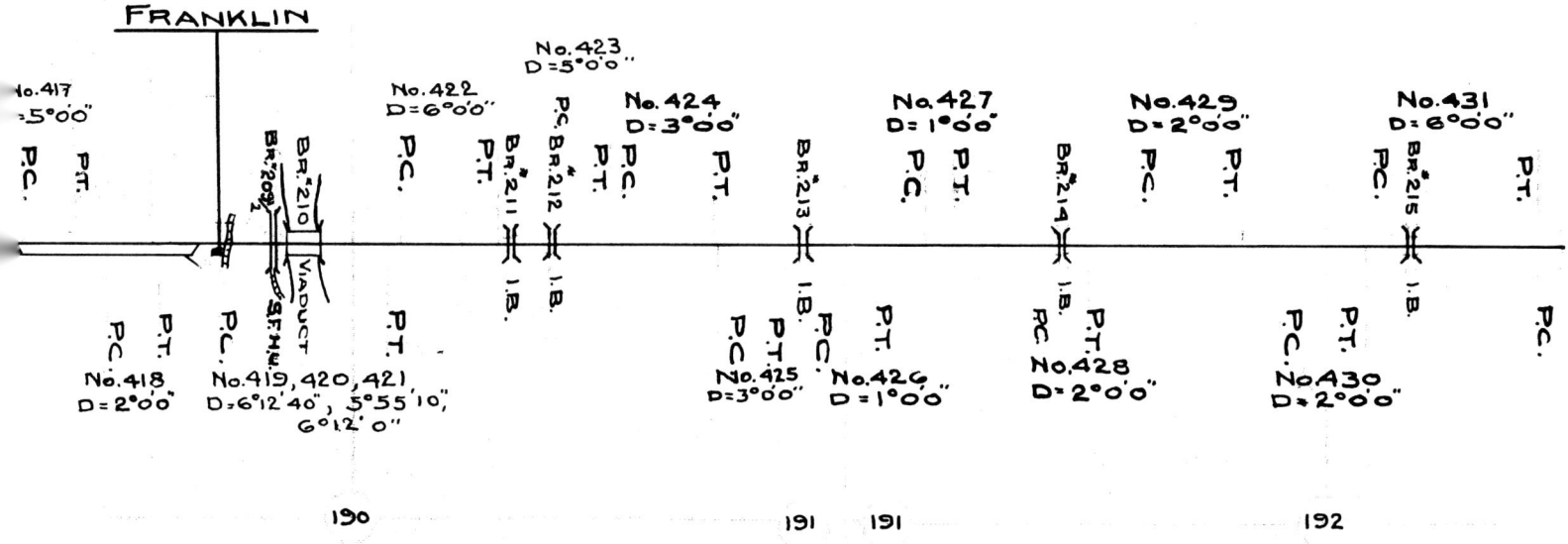

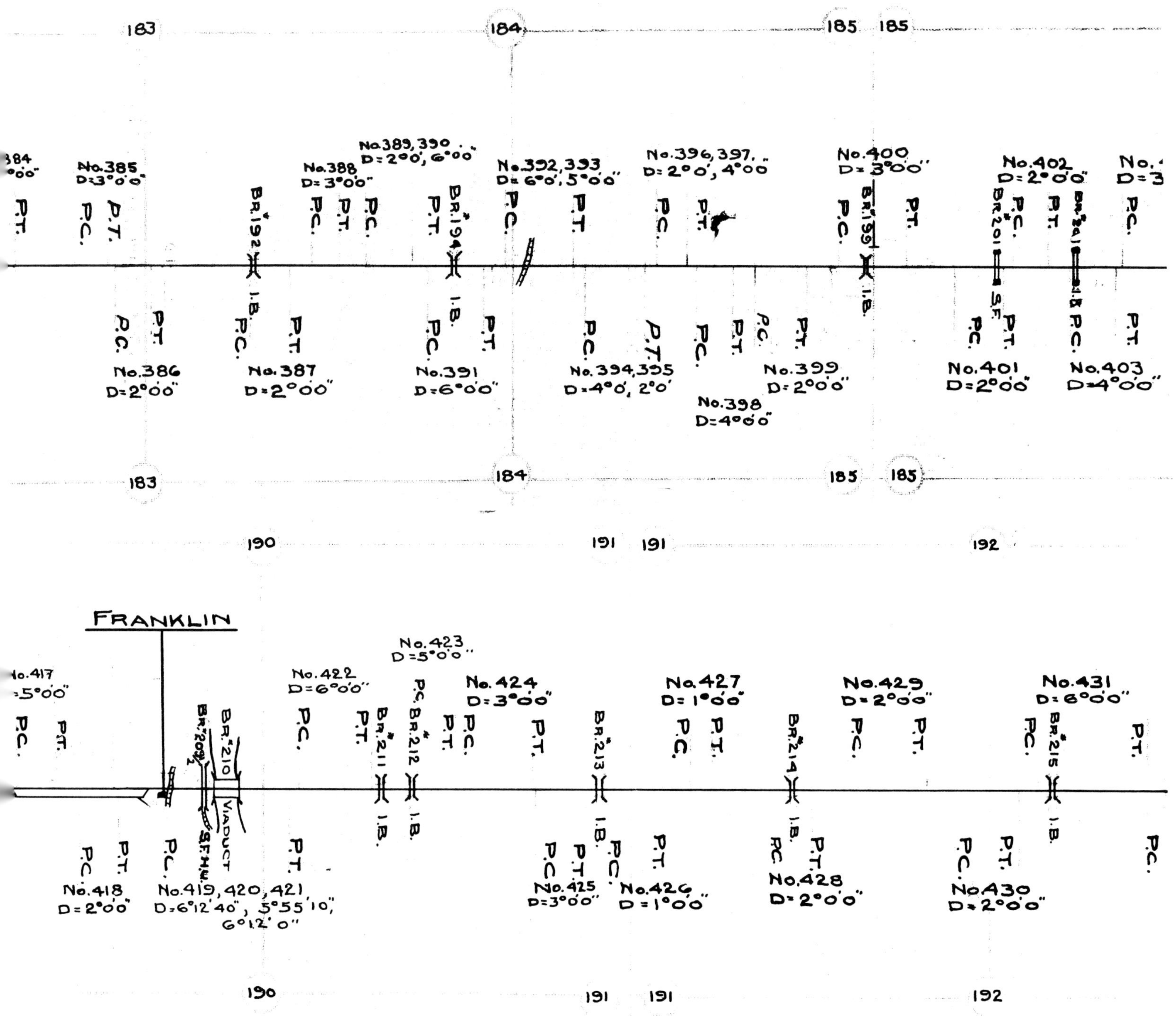

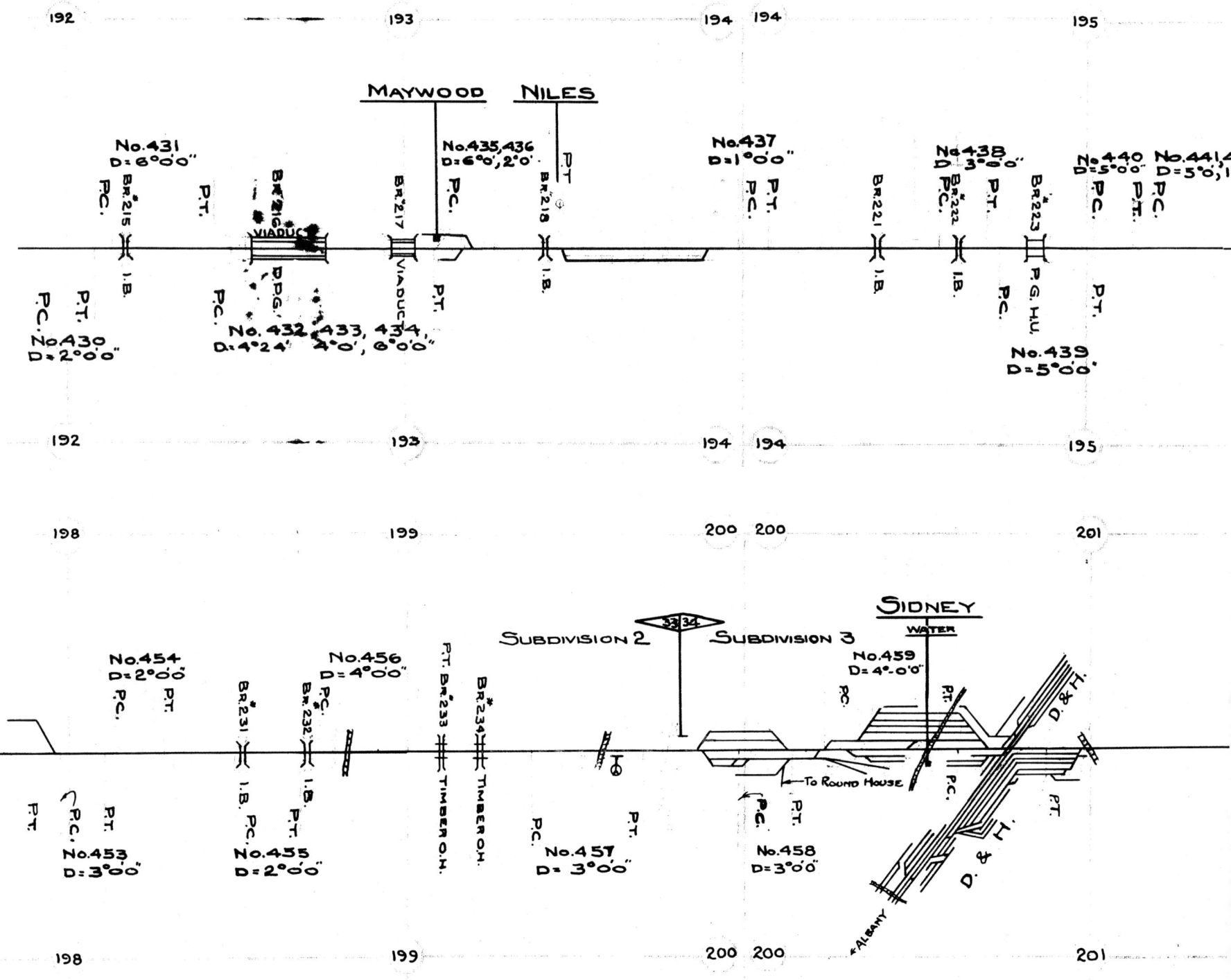

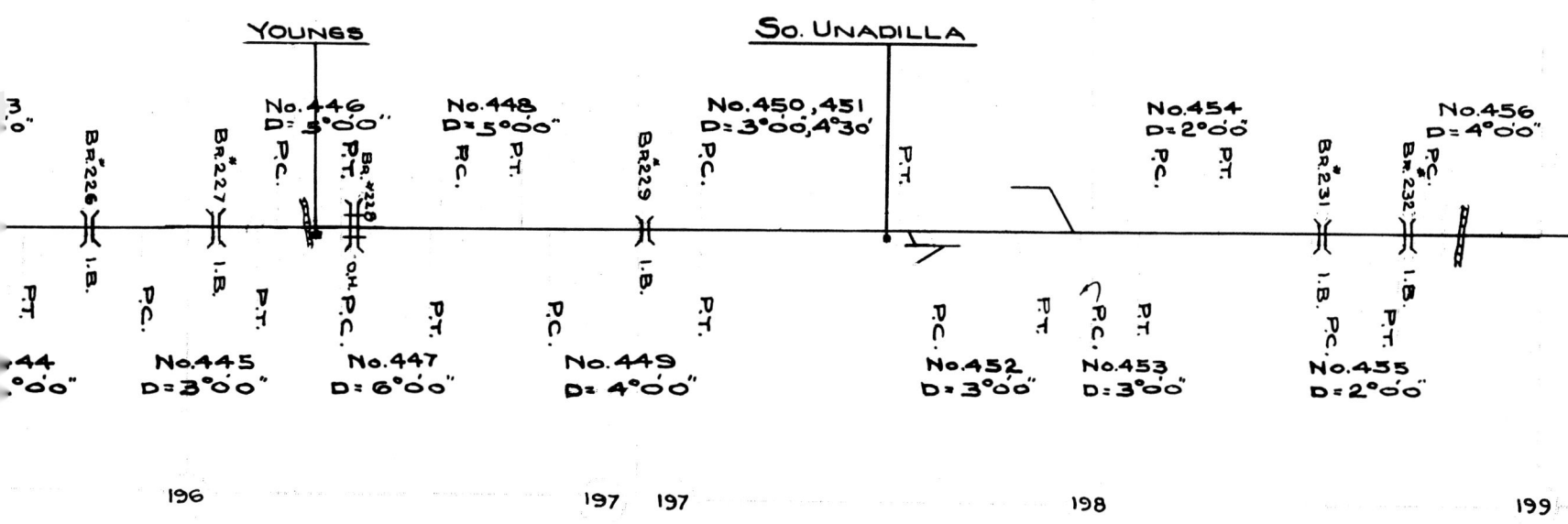

The Delhi branch between Walton and Delhi

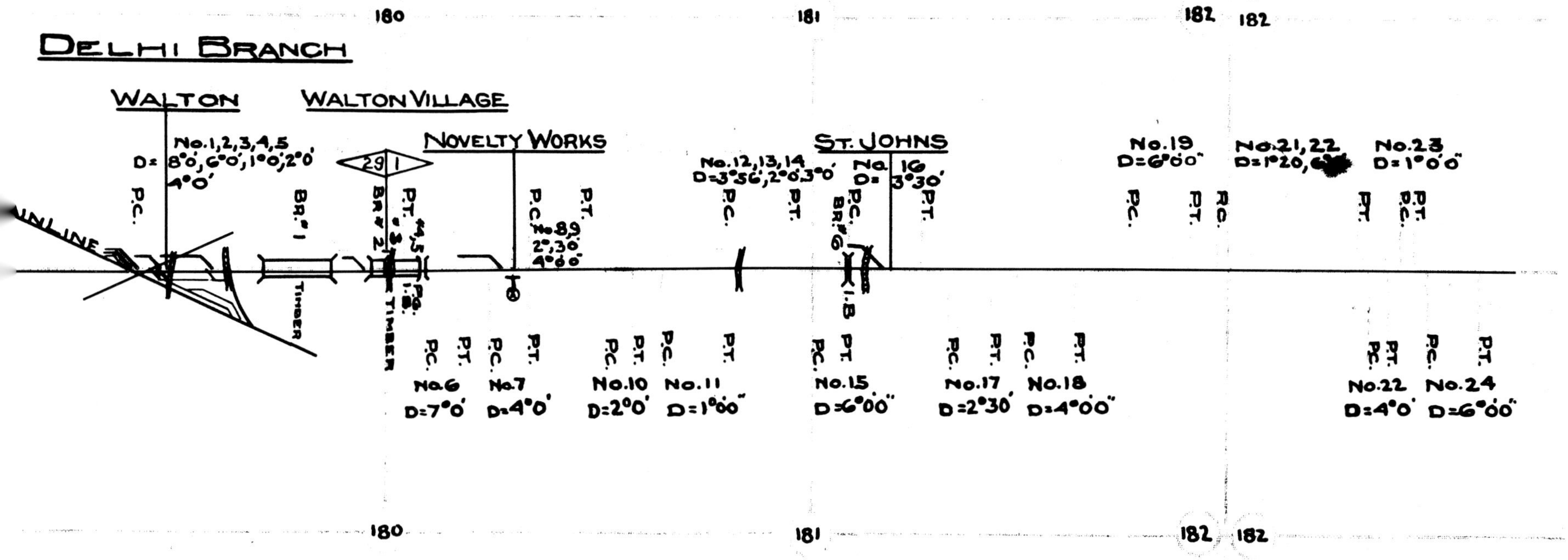

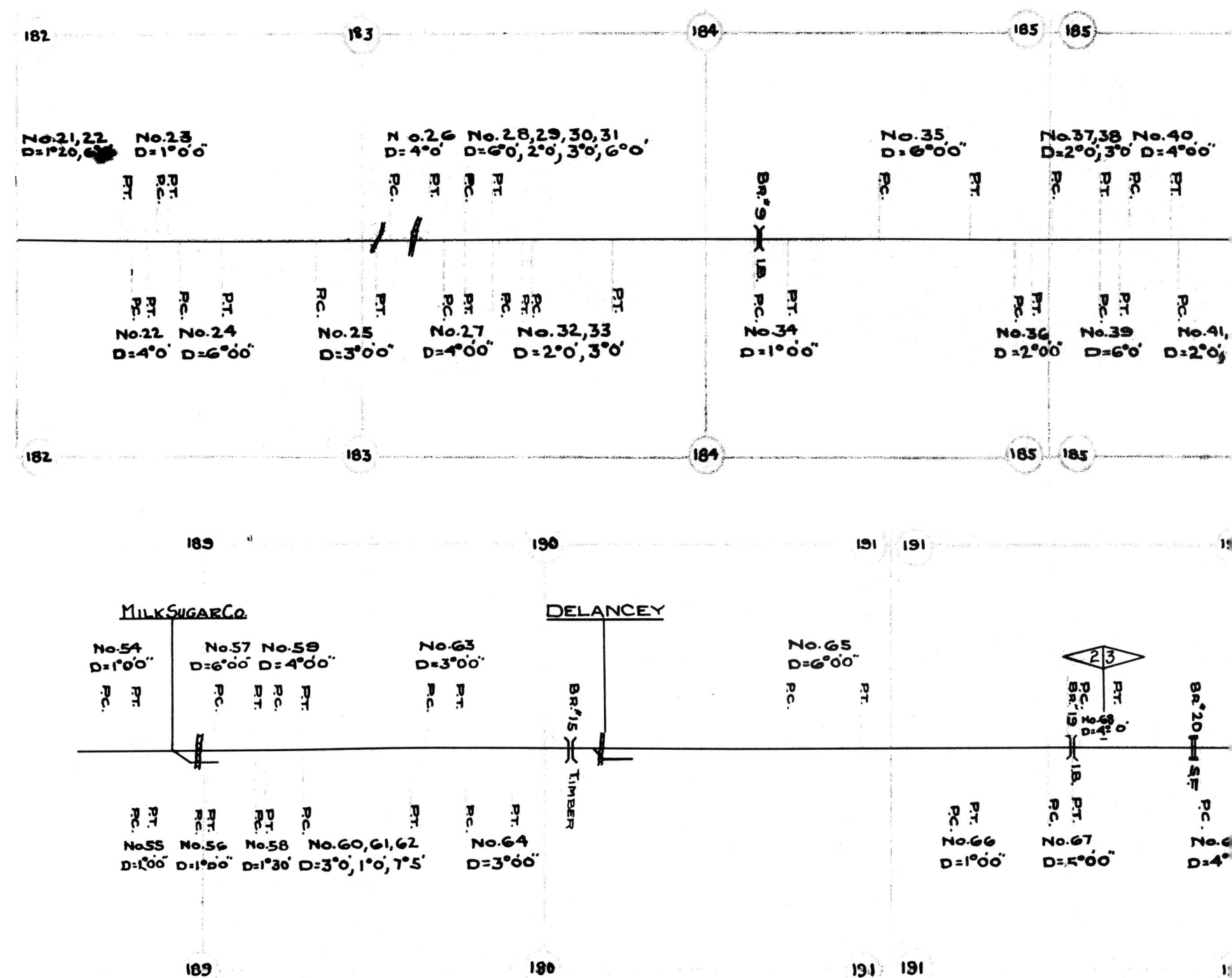

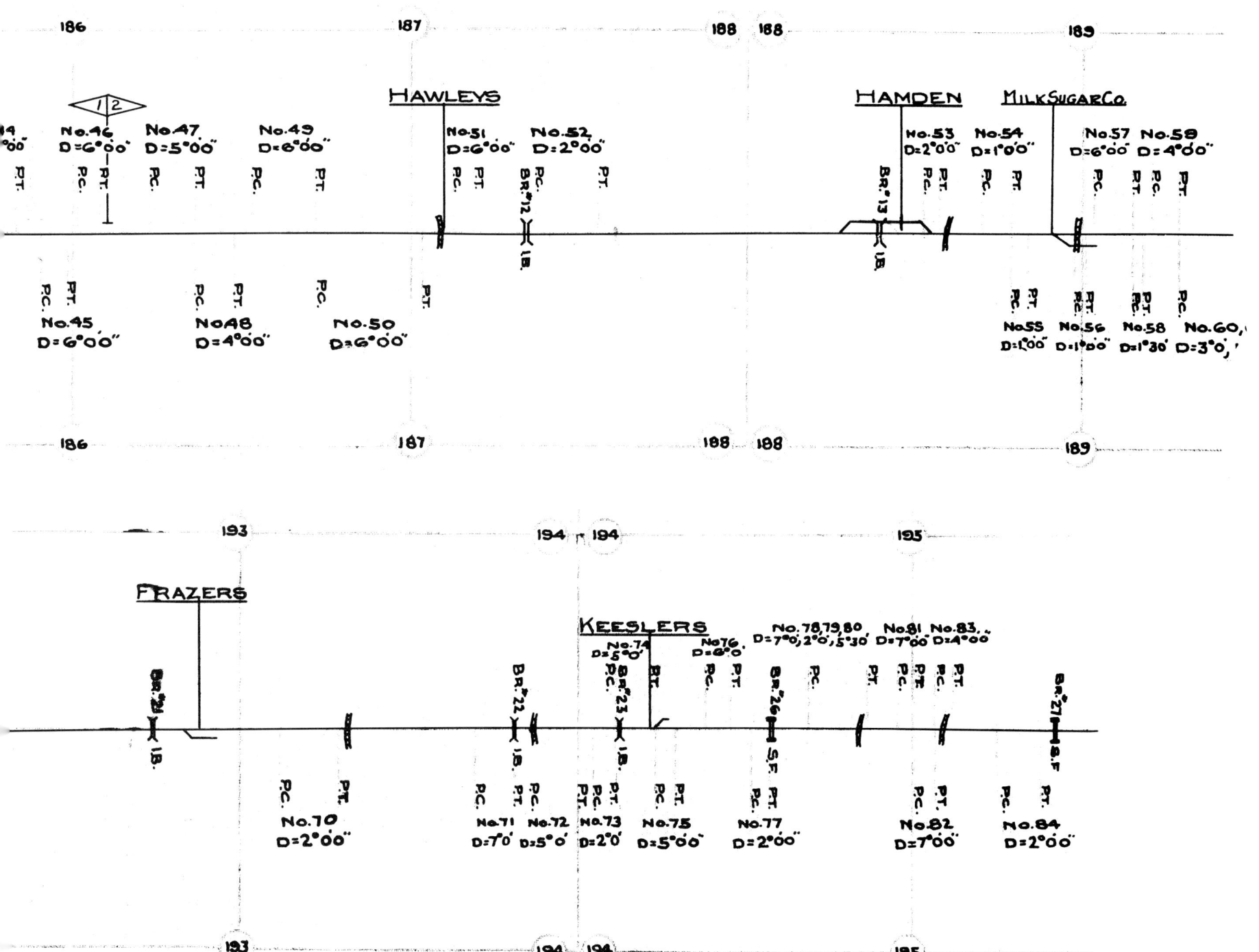

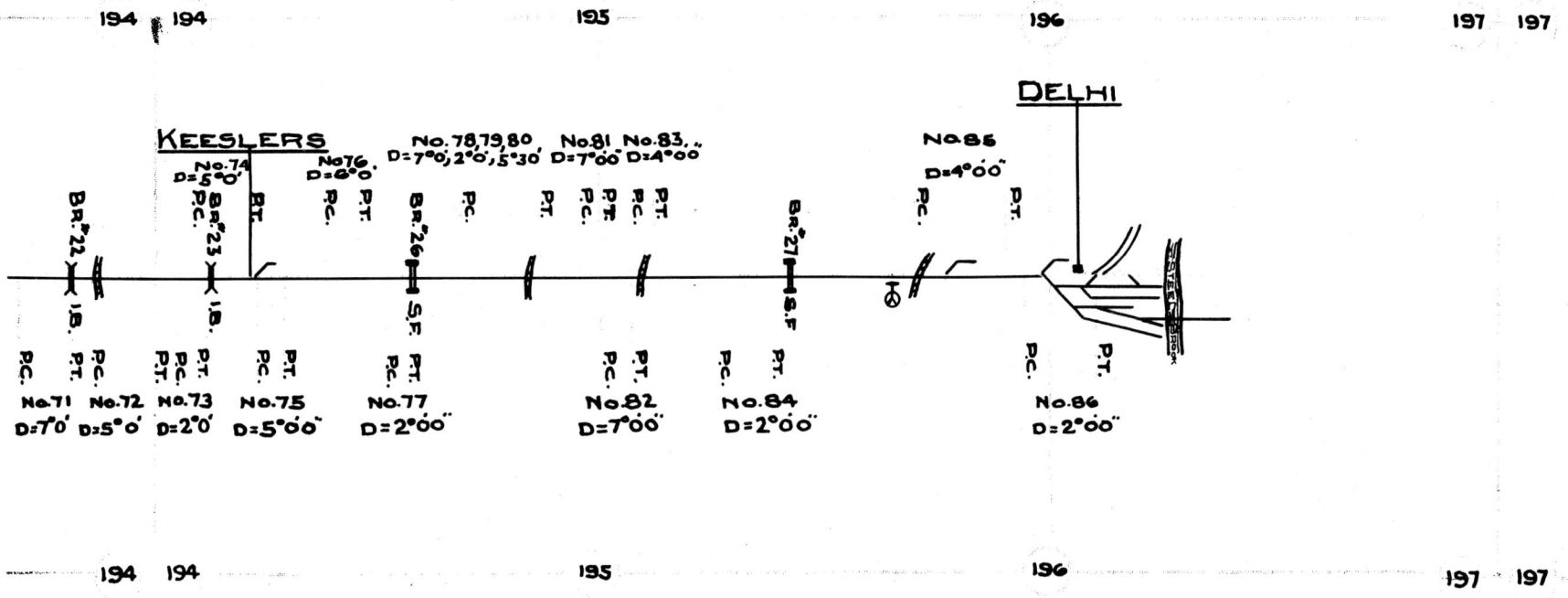

Addendum G: Topographic Maps of the Delhi branch, New Berlin branch, and main line between Walton and New Berlin Junction

The next four pages show complete topographic maps of the geographic area that is the subject of this book. The approximate scale of these maps, as reproduced, is 0.64 inches to one mile.

Map 1, on page 345, shows the NYO&W complete Delhi branch and the main line from Walton to Merrickville.

Map 2, on page 346, shows the NYO&W shows the NYO&W main line from Merrickville through Sidney to New Berlin Junction and the New Berlin branch between New Berlin Junction and Mt. Upton.

Map 3, on page 347, shows the NYO&W New Berlin branch between Mt. Upton and Sage's Corners.

Map 4, on page 348, shows the NYO&W New Berlin branch between Sage's Corners and Edmeston, and the UV line north from New Berlin.

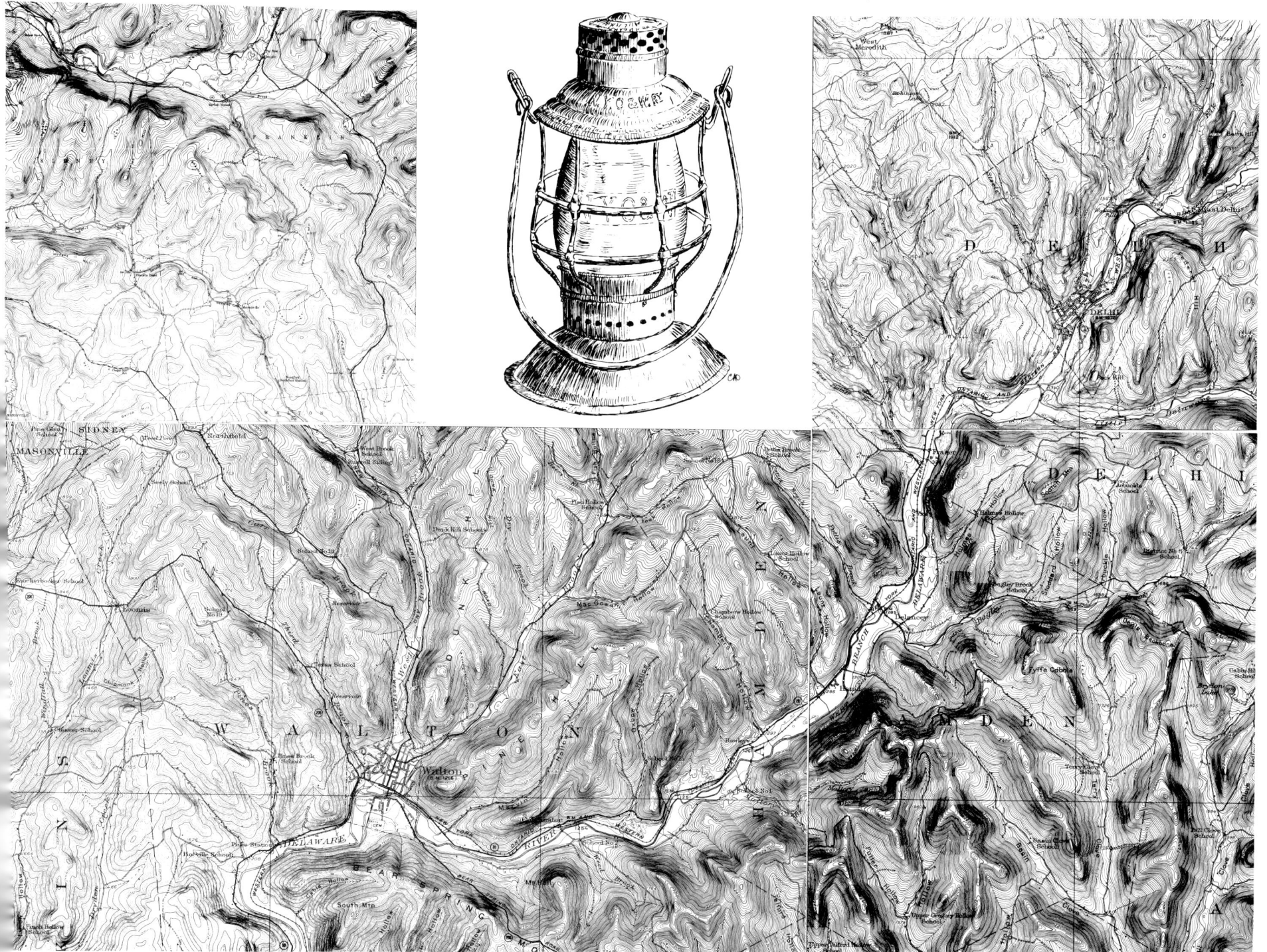

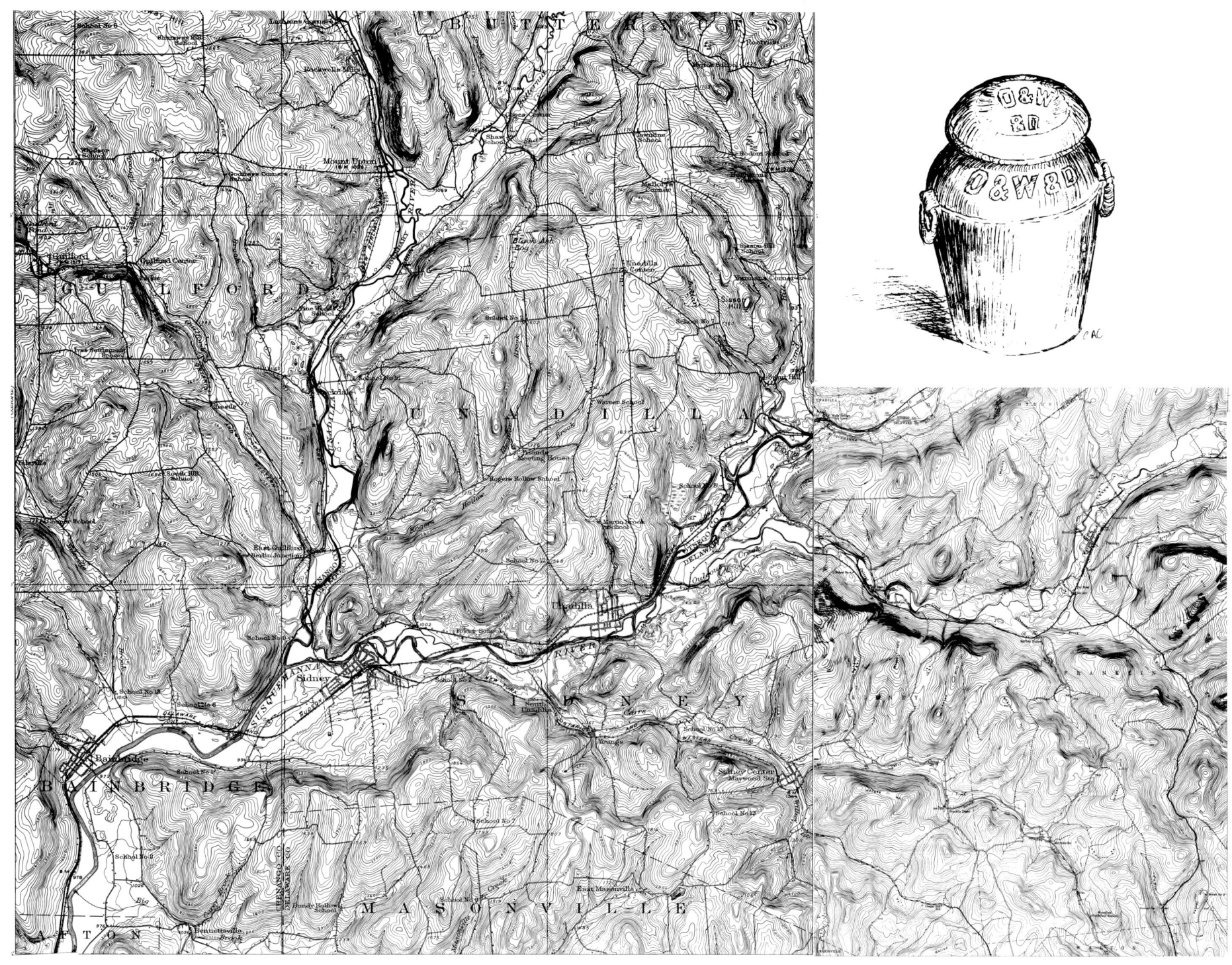

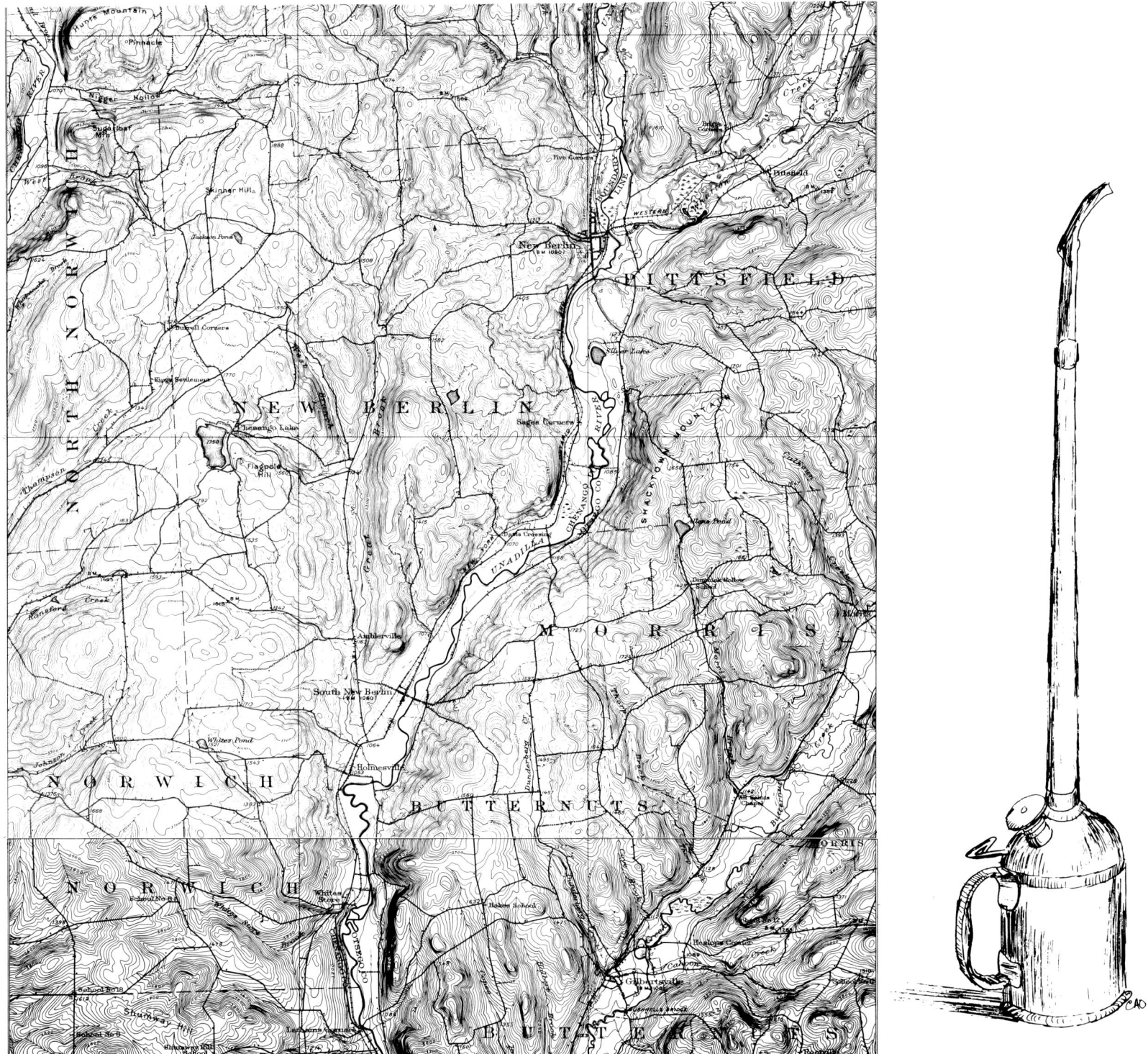

347

Bibliography

Books

Allen, Richard Sanders. *Covered Bridges of the Northeast*. Brattleboro, Vermont: The Stephen Greene Press, 1974.

Archer, Harry D. *The Damn Nuisance*. N.p.: n.p., circa 1971.

Beebe, Lucius. *Mixed Train Daily*. Berkeley, California: Howell-North, 1961.

Beers, F.W. *1869 Atlas of Delaware Co., New York*. 1869, Reprint. New Berlin, New York: Molly Yes Press, 1981.

Beetle, David H. *Along the Oriskany*. Utica, New York: Utica *Observer-Dispatch*, 1947.

Benowski, Frances. *Merrickville and Around*. Walton, New York: The Reporter Co., 1986.

Best, Gerald M. *Minisink Valley Express*. San Marino, California: Golden West, 1956.

_____. *The Ulster and Delaware*. San Marino, California: Golden West, 1972.

Brownell, Mert. *Unadilla Valley*. Deposit, New York: Courier Printing, 1976.

Bux, Joe, and Ed Crist *New York, Ontario & Western Railway, Scranton Division*. Middletown, New York: O&W Historical Society, 1985.

Campbell, K.V. *Sidney Then and Now*. Sidney, New York: Sidney Historical Association, 1972.

Carson, Robert B. *Main Line to Oblivion, The Disintegration of the New York Railroads in the Twentieth Century*. Port Washington, New York: National University Publications, 1971.

Casey, Robert J., and W. A. S. Douglas *Pioneer Railroad*. New York: McGraw-Hill, Inc., 1948.

Crist, Ed, and John Krause *The Final Years*. Fredon, New Jersey: Carstens Publications, 1977.

Delaware County Bicentennial Book Committee, *Delaware County*. Deposit, New York: Valley Offset, 1976.

DeNatale, Douglas, *Two Stones For Every Dirt*. Fleischmanns, New York: Purple Mountain Press, 1987.

DeVine, John F. *Three Centuries In Delaware County*. New York: n.p., 1933.

Edmeston Museum, and Edmeston Rotary Club, eds. *Echoes of the Past*. Edmeston, New York: Bishop Printshop, 1976.

Everts, and Farliss. *History of Otsego County*. 1878, Reprint. Ovid, New York: W.E. Morrison, 1978.

Farrington, Jr., S. Kip. *Railroading from the Rear End*. New York: Coward, McCann Inc., 1946.

_____. *Railroading the Modern Way*, New York: Coward, McCann, Inc., 1951.

_____. *Railroads of Today*. New York: Coward, McCann, Inc., 1949.

Gibson, Donald. *The Unadilla Valley Railroad*. Manuscript in New Berlin, N. Y., library, n.d.

Helmer, William F., *O&W*. Berkeley, California: Howell-North, 1959.

_____. *Rip Van Winkle Railroads*. Berkley, California: Howell-North, 1970.

Henry, Robert Selph. *This Fascinating Railroad Business*. New York: Bobbs-Merrill, 1943.

Hill, Dewey D., and Elliot R. Hughes *Ice Harvesting in Early America*. New Hartford, New York: New Hartford Historical Society, 1977.

Horton, Gertrude Fitch. *The Delaware & Northern and the Towns It Served*. Fleischmanns, New York: Purple Mountain Press, 1989.

Hovemeyer, Pauline. *100 Years in the History of Delhi, New York, 1860-1960*. Delhi, New York: Republican-Express, n.d.

Hungerford, Edward. *The Story of the Rome, Watertown and Ogdensburgh Railroad*. New York: McBride & Co., 1922.

_____. *Ice Harvesting*. Boston, Massachusetts: W.T. Wood & Co., 1904.

Kasson, John F. *Civilizing the Machine: Technology and Republican Values in America*. New York: Grossman, 1976.

Keilty, Edmund. *Doodlebug Country*. Glendale, California: Interurban Press, 1982.

_____. *Interurbans Without Wires*. Burbank, California: Interurban Press, 1979.

Lane, Frank, and Helen, *Walton Yesteryears*. Walton, New York: Reporter Co., 1987.

Lewis, Robert G. *Handbook of American Railroads*. New York: Simmons-Boardman, 1951.

Lucas, Walter Arndt. *The History of the New York, Susquehanna and Western Railroad*. New York: Railroadians of America, 1939.

Marcus, Alan I. and Howard P. Segal *Technology In America, A Brief History*. New York: Harcourt Brace Jovanovich, 1989.

Miller, Donald L. and Richard E. Sharpless *Kingdom of Coal*. Philadelphia: University of Pennsylvania

Press, 1985.

"Motor Cars & Passenger Construction Details (Part 8)" from the 1943 Car Builders Cyclopedia. Reprinted in *Train Shed Cyclopedia No. 86*. Rohnert Park, California: Newton K. Gregg: 1979.

Mott, Edward H. *Between the Ocean and the Lakes*. New York: John S. Collins, 1899.

Mumford, Lewis. *Technics and Civilization*. New York: Harcourt, Brace and Co., 1934.

Munsell, W.W., and Co. *History of Delaware County, New York*. New York: W.W. Munsell and Co., 1880.

Murray, David, ed. *Delaware County, New York, History of the Century, 1797-1897*. Delhi, New York: William Clark, 1898.

Myers, Daniel Frank. *The Wood Chemical Industry in the Delaware Valley*. Middletown, New York: O&W Historical Society, 1986.

Palmer, Richard F. *Butter and Cheese Express*. Sherburne, New York: Chenango County Historical Society, 1974.

Pugh, Fred. *Days Along the Buckwheat & Dandelion*. Brookfield, New York: Worden Press, 1984.

"Rail Motor Cars 1919-1928" from *Car Builders Cyclopedia and Car Builders Dictionary*. Reprinted in Train Shed Cyclopedia No. 30. Rohnert Park, California: Newton K. Gregg: 1975.

Raitt, John E. *Ruts in the Road*. Walton, New York: Reporter Co., 1983.

Reck, Franklin M. *On Time*. N.p.: General Motors Corp., 1948.

Robertson, Archie. *Slow Train to Yesterday*. Boston: Houghton Mifflin, 1945.

Sayer, and Noble. *Guide to the N.Y. Midland R.R., 1873*, Reprint. Middletown, New York: Trumbull Pub., 1971.

Selitzer, Ralph. *The Dairy Industry In America*. New York: Magazines for Industry, 1976.

Shaughnessy, Jim. *Delaware & Hudson*. Berkeley, California: Howell-North, 1967.

Schivelbusch, Wolfgang. *The Railway Journey, The Industrialization of Time and Space in the 19th Century*. Berkley, California: The University of California Press, 1986.

Smith, James H. *History of Chenango and Madison Counties, New York*. Syracuse, New York: D. Mason & Co., 1880.

Smith, James H. *History of Chenango County, 1784-1880*. N.d. Reprint. New Berlin, New York: Molly Yes Press, 1979.

Stilgoe, John R. *Metropolitan Corridor: Railroads and the American Scene*. New Haven, Connecticut: Yale University Press, 1983.

Styran, Roberta M., and Robert R. Taylor *The Welland Canals*. Erin, Ontario: Boston Mills Press, 1987.

Swanberg, J. W. *New Haven Power*. Medina, Ohio: Alvin F. Staufer, 1988.

Unadilla Valley Historical Society, *Unadilla Valley*. Deposit, New York: n.p., 1976.

Wakefield, Manville B. *To the Mountains by Rail*. Grahamsville, New York: Wakefair Press, 1970.

Weller, John L. *The New Haven Railroad*. New York: Hastings House, 1969.

White, John H. *The Great Yellow Fleet*. San Marino, California: Golden West, 1986.

Wilber, Floyd A. *Early Glimpses of New Berlin and Related Areas Nearby*. New Berlin, New York: n.p., 1967.

Periodicals

"Baby Railroad." *Fortune Magazine*. August, 1938: 50-55+.

Best, Gerald M. "History and Motive Power of the New York, Ontario and Western Railroad." *Railway and Locomotive Historical Society Bulletin No. 40*. May 1936: 16-32.

Eighmey, Henry P. "Grass Roots Railroad." *Trains*. May, 1944: 16-19.

"Equipment of the New York, Ontario & Western Railway." *Railroad Model Craftsman*. March, 1963: 20-23.

"From Coal Road to Bridge Route." *Trains*. August, 1949: 36-37.

Gross, H.H. "Shawangunk Barrier." *Railroad Magazine*. September, 1946: 11-43.

Hojnacki, Kenneth L. "The Sykes Seagull rail bus." *Model Railroader*. April, 1983: 115-117.

Kreitner, Ken. "Lament for an Old Woman." *Trains*. February, 1981: 31-32.

"Locomotive Roster of the New York, Ontario & Western." *Railroad Magazine*. May, 1943: 105-109.

Malinoski, Robert R. "NYO&W Scranton Division: March 17, 1933." *Trains*. March, 1987: 44-50.

"The Mighty O&W." *Courier Magazine*. October, 1953: 7-10+.

Neusser, A.V. and Pearce, C.E. "The NYO&W." *Trains*. August, 1942: 20-30.

"Obituary of an Old Woman." *Trains*. July, 1957: 23-30.

"Ontario & Western Sold by Segments." *Short-Line Railroader*. Summer, 1957: 3-5+.

Robinson, Winfield. "Delaware and Northern Railroad." *Railway and Locomotive Historical Society Bulletin* No. 43: 23-29.

Roehm, Peter. "The Old Woman of the Shawangunks, The N.Y.O.&W. Story. (Part 1)" *Jersey Central Lines*, May, 1981: 15-26.

_____. "The Old Woman of the Shawangunks, The N.Y.O.&W. Story. (Part 2)" *Jersey Central Lines*, June, 1981: 29-39.

Short-Line Railroader, No. 33, Summer, 1957: Ed. Wm. S. Young. Cranford, N. J..

White, John H. "An Early Chapter in Freight Handling, Cincinnati and the Container." *Queen City Heritage Magazine*, vol. 43, No. 3 (1985): 32+.

Other Sources

Pratt, George William. "History of the New York, Ontario & Western Railroad." M.A. Diss., Cornell University, 1942.

Slawson, George C. "New York & Oswego Midland Railroad." Manuscript in author's collection, 1942.

Stellwagen, John C. "The New York & Oswego Midland Railroad Company: The Planning Stages." Manuscript, n.d.

Wm. Wyer & Co. "Report on New York, Ontario & Western Railway Company" prepared for Samuel M. Pinsly.

Annual Reports, New York, Ontario & Western Railway: 1880-1953.

N.Y.O.&W. Railway Co., Reorganization Proceedings in the United States District Court for the Southern District of New York. Vols. 1-24.

Much information came from newspaper articles and various reports, letters, and memos in railroad paper collections of the O&W Historical Society and individuals listed in the acknowledgements.

Index

Many subjects are followed by chapters with pages listed in parenthesis. This indicates frequent mention and/or photographs of the subject within those chapters. All page references which are in bold type refer to photographic captions on those pages.

A
Adams Express Co. 280,334
Albany, N.Y. 148, 229, 245, 249
Alexandria, Va. 104, 106, 108
Ambler, N.Y. (chapter 14, 290-303)
Andes, N.Y. 114, 116
Apex, N.Y. 152
Arkville, N.Y. 114. 314
Atlantic City, N.J. **331**
Avery, Ira **289**

B
Bartlett, H.E. 114
Bauman, John 215
Bellows Falls, Vt. 83
Bennett, A.J. 40
Binghamton, N.Y. 229, 238, 245, 249
Bloomingburg, N.Y. 40, 42, 71
Bloomville, N.Y. 115-116, 336
bluestone 175, 225
Boice, George A. 215
Borden, Gail 31, (addendum C, 335)
Boston, Ma. 83
Bovina, N.Y. 116
Bradley, Frank A. **289**
Bradley, Jesse S. 272
Brady, Mark 295
Bridgewater, N.Y. 277, 305-306, 309, **315**

Brill Co. (chapter 16, 320-333)
Burnside, N.Y. 44
bus service 140, 281

C
Cadosia, N.Y. **2**, **4**, **10**, **14**, **16**, 53-54, 147-148, 331, 334
California State Railway Museum 89
Campbell Hall, N.Y. 42
Canaan, Conn. **333**
Canfield, Edward 191
Central Square, N.Y. 41
Chenango Co., N.Y. 269, 297, 318
Chester, N.Y. 39
Chicago, Ill. 335
Churchill's, N.Y. 175
Cincinnati Motor Terminals **100**
Cleveland, Grover 118
Cleveland, Ohio 99
Clinton, N.Y. 334
Colchester, N.Y. (chapter 6, 112-149)
Collins, Jack 54
condensed milk (chapter 1, 18-37; chapter 2, 38-69), 281, **292**
containerization (chapter 5, 98-111)
Cornell, Thomas 114-115
Cornwall, N.Y. 40,241,334
covered bridges 118, **131**, **133**, **141**
creameries (by diary companies)
    Anglo-Swiss Condensed Milk Co. 44, 157, (addendum C, 335)
    Beaker's Creamery **202**
    Borden's 20, **27**, 31, **33**, **36**, 44, **56**, **58**, **61**, **73**, 89, **89**, **90**, **91**, 92, **94**, 95, **96**, **97**, 103, 106, **107**, **109**, **110**, **111**, 116, **117**, 118, 136, **139**, 157, **159**, 211, 215, **218**, 219, **222**, 270, 273, **275**, **276**, **277**, 281-282, 291, **292**, **293**, 295, 297-298, (addendum C, 335)
    Bowman's Dairy Co. **92**

Breakstone's 80, 157
Chenango Farm Products 270
Dairyland Milk & Cream **130**
Dairymen's League 8, 20, 53, **54**, **57**, 80, **82**, 83, **89**, **90**, **91**, 103, 118, 148, 157, 159, 270, **277**, 297, **299**, **300**, 308, **313**, **314**, addendum C, 335)
Delaware County Farmers' Co-op **129**, 148
Eisensteins Creamery 270
Grand View Dairy Co. (addendum C, 335)
Graustein Dairy Co. 83
Great American Cheese Co. 130
Hamden (?) Co-operative Creamery **136**
Harmony Creamery Co. 83
Hohneker Dairy Co. 26, (chapter 5, 98-111)
Jetter Dairy 55
J. M. Horton (addendum C, 335)
McDermot Dairy Co. **30**, **132**
Merridale Dairies 116, 148
Muller Dairies 103
National Sugar Milk Co. 270
Nestle's (chocolate manufacturer) 159
Newark Milk & Cream Co. **35**
New York Condensed Milk Co. 116, (addendum C, 335)
Orange County Milk Assn. 40
Queensboro Dairy Co. (addendum C, 335)
Reid's Ice Cream Co. (addendum C, 335)
Renken's Dairy Co. (addendum C, 335)
Rockdale Creamery **272**, **282**
Sheffield Farms **8**, **11**, 54, 57, **86**, **87**, 90, **92**, 103, 116, 132, 157, **159**, 270, 274, 281, 297, **300**, **306**, (addendum C, 335)
Standard Dairy Co. **26**, **104**
Sunshine Dairy Co. (addendum C, 335)
Supplee-Wills-Jones Milk Co. **96**
Walton Milk & Cream 157
Whiting Milk Co. 83
Wieland Dairy Co. 83, **84-85**

creameries (by town in photograph or plan)
    Bernhards', N.Y. (Bernhards' Bay) **46**
    Burnside, N.Y. **33**, **56**
    Campbell Hall, N.Y. **23**
    Central Square, N.Y. **50**
    Colchester, N.Y. **118**, (plan, 142), (creamery grounds, 143)
    Cooks Falls, N.Y. **45**
    Crystal Run, N.Y. **22**, 23
    Delancey, N.Y. **132**
    Delhi, N.Y. **117**, **129**
    Earlville, N.Y. **26-27**
    Eaton, N.Y. **47**, (plan, 48)
    Edmeston, N.Y. **293**, **298-300**
    Frasers, N.Y. **130**
    Hamden, N.Y. **136**, **139**
    Hawley, N.Y. (plan, 142)
    Kenwood, N.Y. **22**
    Lakewood, Pa. **57**
    Merrickville, N.Y. **202**, **204**
    Morrisville, N.Y. **22**
    Mountaindale, N.Y. (plan, 30)
    Mt. Upton, N.Y. **275-277**
    Munns, N.Y. **26**, **51**, **105**
    New Berlin, N.Y. **292-293**, **306**
    Norwich, N.Y. **27**
    Owego, N.Y. **35**
    Pennelville, N.Y. **31**
    Pleasant Mount, Pa. **54**
    Preston Park, Pa. **50**
    Randallsville, N.Y. **11**
    Rockdale, N.Y. **272**
    Rock Tavern, N.Y. **38**
    Shelburne-Four Corners, N.Y. **26**, **104**
    Sidney, N.Y. **256**
    Sidney Center, N.Y. **217-218**
    Smyrna, N.Y. **30**
    South New Berlin, N.Y. **73**, **282**
    State Bridge, N.Y. (plan, 28-29)
    Valley Mills, N.Y. **5**, **26**
    Walton, N.Y. **159**
    West Brook **176**
    West Monroe, N.Y. **50**
    Winterton, N.Y. (plan, 24-25)
    Youngs, N.Y. **222**
creamery operations (chapter 1, 18-37; chapter 2, 38-69)
Cross & Ferguson 114
Currie, Howard 148

D

Davis Crossing, N.Y. **43**, (chapter 13, 268-289)
Delancey, N.Y. (chapter 6, 112-149)

Delaware County, N.Y. **18**, 40, **43**, **67**, 113-116, 118, 148, 157, 175, 185, 229
Delaware & Hudson Canal Co. 229, 231, 238
Delhi branch 42, (chapter 6, 112-149), 157, 163, 173, 269, 331, 334, 337
Delhi Flyer **117**, 140, **332**
Delhi, N.Y. 40, 73, (chapter 6, 112-149), 151, 153, 173
diagrams, clearance
    Northfield Tunnel clearance for piggyback cars 197
    standard tunnel clearance 191
diagrams, equipment
    motor car (Brill) 327
    motor car (NYNH&H) 323
    O&W wooden milk car 74
diesel locomotives 81, 147-148, 173, 179, 195, 306, 308-309, 326, 337
diesel locomotive photographs
    D&H **249**
    DL&W **107**, **315**
    NYO&W **16-17**, **171-173**, **247**, **250**, **263**
    UV **315-319**
    SNY **317**
Diver, Pat **8**
Ducollon, Bryan **234**
Duluth, Minn. 275
Dumond, Harold **222**

E

East Branch, N.Y. 13, 42, 114
East Guilford, N.Y. (New Berlin Jct.) 261
Eaton, N.Y. **11**, 337
Edgerton, A. C. 114
Edmeston, N.Y. 40, 275, 285, (chapter 14, 290-303), (chapter 15, 304-319), 334
Ellenville, N.Y. 269, 334
Elyria Enameled Products Co. 83, 85
Electro Motive Corp, (chapter 16, 320-333), (see also diesel locomotives and General Motors)
Electro Motive Division (see diesel locomotives and General Motors)
Erie Canal 239
evaporated milk (chapter 1, 18-37)

F

Fallsburgh Tunnel 185
Fargo, N.Y. **60**
farms (photographs) **18**, **20-21**, **37**
feed mills (also feed milling) (addendum D, 336-337)
Firthcliff, N.Y. **15**
Fitch, Benjamin F. 56, (chapter 5, 99-111), 335
Forest City, Pa. 54, 233

Franklin, N.Y. (see also Franklin Depot) 114, 189, 199, 231
Franklin Depot, N.Y. (chapter 10, 198-227)
Frasers, N.Y. (chapter 6, 112-149)
Fruit Growers Express Co. 80, 104, 107-108
Fulton, N.Y. 40-41

G

Gage, William & Jerome 269
General American (chapter 4, 82-97)
    General American Car Co. **84**
    General American Refrigerator Express (GARE) **11**, **12**, **13**, **14**, (chapter 4, 82-97), **82**, 86-87, 89, 94-96, 106, **110**
    General American Transportation Corp. (GATX) (chapter 4, 82-97), 102, 111, 336
    General American Pfaudler Corp. (GPEX) **8**, **9**, **12**, **14**, **17**, **54**, (chapter 4, 82-97), **110**, 111, **246**, **313**
General Electric Co. (chapter 16, 320-333)
General Motors (see also diesel locomotives) 81, 326-327
Gilbert (civil engineer) 269
Gillette, N.Y. 225
Glascote Products, Inc. 104
Goethals, Lt. Col. 274
Goshen, N.Y. 40
graphs
    coal received at Sidney for Northern Division points 239
    forty-quart cans to NYC in 1900 41
    NYO&W milk traffic, 1880-1950 44
Gray, E. E. **289**
Guilford Summit, N.Y. 229, 261
GX interlocking tower (Sidney, N.Y.) 241, **242**, **244**, 306

H

Hamden, N.Y. **42**, (chapter 6, 112-149)
Hamilton, N.Y. **13**
Hancock, N.Y. 54
Harding, Robert 234
Harding, William **4**
Harper, H. Glenn 148
Haver, William R. 291
Hawk, Fred 54
Hawk Mountain Tunnel 185
Hawley, N.Y. **42**, (chapter 6, 112-149)
Hobart, N.Y. 116
Hoboken, N.J. **94**
Hoboken, N.Y. 281, 285, **292**, 295, (see also New Berlin, N.Y.)
Hohneker, Fred (chapter 5, 98-111)
Holmesville, N.Y. (chapter 13, 268-289)
Holstein cattle **18**, **21**
Howe, H.J. **289**
Howe, Richard 53, 331

353

I

Illinois Railway Museum 89, 95
Indiana Harbor, Ind. 108
Interstate Commerce Commission (ICC) 41, 55, 282
ice harvesting 19, (chapter 2, 38-69)
ice houses **22-23**, **26**, (chapter 2, 38-69), **296**

J

Jackson & Sharpe **75**
Jamaica, N.Y. 336
Jersey City, N.J. 39-40, 95, **110**, **111**

K

Kaplan, M.S. 308
Kerr, John B. 325
Kilmer, Mrs. Wanita 211, 215
Kingston, N.Y. 114
Kingston branch 331, 334
Kuhler, Otto 169

L

Lake Ontario 195, 239
Lakewood, Pa. 54, 56, **57**
Lane, Frank & Helene 151
Lanesboro, Pa. 229
Lansingville, N.Y. 118 (see also Delancey, N.Y.)
Latham's Corners, N.Y. (chapter 13, 268-289)
Leonardsville, N.Y. 305, 309
Lewis, Fred 195
Lewis, Ted **196**
Liberty, N.Y. **8**, 40, 89, 152, 175, 291, 295
Littlejohn, DeWitt C. 40, 114, 185
Livingston Manor, N.Y. 40, **70**, **77**
Logan, John **43**
long milk (train) 41
Lord, Jarvis 151
Lyon Brook Bridge **6**

M

Mahwah, N.J. 336
maps (see also plans)
    Colchester creamery grounds 143
    Delhi, N.Y., station grounds 120
    Edmeston, N.Y., depot and grounds 297
    engine classes permitted on various portions of railroad 178
    Franklin Depot, N.Y., grounds 207
    Merrickville, N.Y., station grounds **201**
    milk markets 36
    New Berlin, N.Y., original terminal 285
    Northfield, N.Y., present and proposed routes 192
    Northfield, N.Y., station grounds 180
    Northfield Tunnel profile 190
    oil company siding at New Berlin, N.Y. 283
    O&W/D&H track arrangements at Sidney, N.Y. 252
    Rome, N.Y., sidings 69
    Sidney Center, N.Y. (Maywood), station grounds 212
    Sidney, N.Y., interlocking (crossing with D&H) 243
    Sidney, N.Y., sidings to Bendix Aviation (Scintilla Works) 254
    Sidney, N.Y., yard 252
    South Unadilla, N.Y., station grounds 224
    switchback and tunnel routes at Northfield, N.Y. 185
    traffic density map 288
    Unadilla Valley Rwy. 309
    Walton, N.Y., yard 154
    West Brook, N.Y., station grounds 176
    Youngs, N.Y., station grounds 221
Margaretville, N.Y. 114
Matteson, Charles I. 295
Mayfield, Pa. 14, 55, 331
Maywood, N.Y. (see Sidney Center)
McDonald, Bill **234**
McGarity, James **289**
McNaugh, John 116
Merchants Despatch Transportation Corp. (MDT) 89, **94-96**, (chapter 5, 98-111; addendum B, 335)
Merrick, John 199
Merrickville, N.Y. 189, (chapter 10, 198-227)
Middlemast, Ebenezer 148
Middletown branch 42
Middletown, N.Y. **10**, **12**, **15**, 40, 56, **70**, 72, **81**, 99, 104, 148, 229, 269, **325**, 327, **332**, 334
milk car photographs (can cars only)
    DL&W **75**
    LV **75**
    NYO&W **4**, **7**, **46**, (chapter 3, 70-81), **105**, **162**, **278**, **282**
    NYS&W **75**
milk cooling (chapter 1, 18-37; chapter 2, 38-69), 71, 85
milk platforms **52-53**, 297
milk truckers 31, **33**, 55-56, 81, **94**, 95, (chapter 5, 98-111), 274
milking practice (chapter 1, 18-37)
milling in transit 152
Mitchell, Art 140, (addendum E, 337)
Moffat Tunnel 189
Monticello branch 148, 325, 334
Monticello, N.Y. **68**
Morris, N.Y. 231
motor cars 281, (chapter 16, 320-333)
Motor Terminals (MTIX) (chapter 5, 99-111)
Mountaineer Limited **2**, **8**, **10**, **169**
Mt. Upton, N.Y. 44, 80, 261, 267, (chapter 13, 268-289), 308, **318**
Mumford, T.L. 272
Munnsville, N.Y. **4-5**, **26**, **51**, **67**, **105**
Murphy, John 4
Murray, Robert 118, 131-132

N

National Car Co. (NX) (chapter 5, 98-111), 336
National Dairy Show 83
National Fitch Corp. 104, (chapter 6, 112-149)
Natoli, Tom **289**
Newark, N.J. 107
New Berlin branch 40, 44, 114, 238, 241, (chapter 12, 260-267; chapter 13, 268-289; chapter 14, 290-303), 308, 318, 334
New Berlin Jct., N.Y. 245, (chapter 12, 260-267; chapter 13, 268-289; chapter 14, 290-303), 306, 308-309, 315
New Berlin, N.Y. 31, 40-41, 234, (chapter 13, 268-289; chapter 14, 290-303; chapter 15, 304-319)
New Haven Car Works 72
New York City, N.Y. 39, 40, 53, 113-114, 116, 118, 140, 277, 336
New York Public Service Comm. 55
New York Public Utilities Comm. 222-223
Niagara River 239
Niles, N.Y. (chapter 10, 198-227)
North American Car Co. 80
North Bergen, N.J. 102
North Walton, N.Y. (see also Northfield and Northfield Tunnel) 177, 189
Northern Division 73, 79, 147, 233, 238, 332-334
Northfield, N.Y. 171, (chapter 8, 174-183), 219, 225, 233
Northfield Tunnel 10, 163, 175, **178-183**, (chapter 9, 184-197), 199, 211-212
Norton, Windy **117**
Norwich, N.Y. 40, **67**, 79-80, **105**, 152, 229, 233-234, 238, 272, 277, 288, 308, **332**, 334-337

O

Ogden's, N.Y. 175
Ogden, William Butler 175
Oneida, N.Y. 5, 41, 334
Oneonta, N.Y. 114-115, 175, 279, 317, 325-326
Ontario Express (train) **9**
Orange County, N.Y. **20**, **37**, 39, 40, 113, 116
Orange County Milk Assn. 40
Oswego County, N.Y. 46
Oswego, N.Y. 39, 41, 151, 195, 229, 239, 275, 333-334
Otsego County, N.Y. 291, 297
Oxford, N.Y. 175

P

Panama Canal 274
Parker, N.Y. 44
Pecksport Loop 11, 334

Pecktown, N.Y. 291
Pfaudler Corp. (chapter 4, 82-97)
Philadelphia, Pa. 327-328
Piermont, N.Y. 39-40
Pittsfield, N.Y. 31, (chapter 14, 290-303)
plans, creamery
    Colchester, N.Y. 142
    Eaton, N.Y. 48
    general arrangements 32
    Mountaindale, N.Y. 30
    State Bridge, N.Y. 28
    Winterton, N.Y. 24
plans (ice houses) 25, 66
plans (rolling stock)
    MDT milk car 95
    NX bulk tank flatcar 107
plans (stations and structures)
    Delancey, N.Y. 134
    Delhi, N.Y. 121
    Edmeston, N.Y. 296
    milk platform 52
    Merrickville, N.Y. 203
    Middletown, N.Y., icehouse 66
    New Berlin, N.Y., coal shed 286
    Northfield, N.Y., cross-section of south tunnel portal 194
    Northfield, N.Y., tunnel profile 190
    Sidney Center, N.Y. 216
    Sidney, N.Y., engine house 257
    Sidney, N.Y., front elevation 248
    Walton, N.Y. 166
    Walton, N.Y. (tell-tale) 170
Pleasant Mount, Pa. 53, **54**
Port Jervis & Monticello branch 81, 331
Port Jervis, N.Y. **81**
Powell, A.C. 229
Poyntelle, Pa. 54-55

R

rail cars (see motor cars)
Railroad Enthusiasts **238**
Railroad Model Craftsman 85
Railroadians of America **11**
Railroads
    Albany & Susquehanna 113, 114-115, 219, 229, 231, 238, 272
    Andes & Delhi 116
    Baltimore & Ohio 83, 198
    Boston & Maine 73, 83, 89, 104, 147
    Buffalo & Susquehanna 185
    Central New England 42, **333**
    Central of New Jersey 62
    Central Vermont 95
    Chicago & Northwestern 175
    Chicago, Rock Island & Pacific 309
    Cincinnati, Lawrenceburg & Aurora **100**
    Cooperstown & Charlotte Valley 117
    Delaware & Eastern 42, 14, 116
    Delaware & Hudson 55, 73, 114, 147, 152, 228-229, **230-232**, 233, 238-239, 241, **244-245, 249**, **251**, 256, 259, 275-276, **333**, 334
    Delaware & Northern 13, 42, 114, 141, 334
    Delaware, Lackawanna & Western 27, 55, 81, **94**, 97, **107**, 198, 238, 277, 305, 306, 308, 313, **315**, 337
    Delaware Valley 116
    Delhi & Hudson River 116
    Delhi & Middletown 114-116, **118**
    Denver & Salt Lake 185
    Des Moines & Central Iowa 308
    Ellenville & Kingston 41
    Erie 39, 55, 81, 95, 104, **110**, 113, 175, 198, 229, 238, 322
    Erie Lackawanna 309
    Fitchburg 139
    Gulf, Mobile & Ohio 89
    Jefferson 229
    Lehigh & New England 331
    Lehigh Valley 55, 81, **94**, 104, **111**
    Louisville & Nashville 89
    Middletown & Unionville 334
    Middletown, Unionville & Water Gap 40
    New Jersey Midland 40
    New York Central 41, 73, 89, 103-104, 111, 113, 147, 175, 335
    New York & Erie 39-40, 113, 229
    New York, Kingston & Syracuse 115
    New York, Lake Erie & Western **153**
    New York, New Haven & Hartford **322-324**, 325 327, 331, **333**
    New York, Susquehanna & Western **75**
    New York, West Shore & Buffalo 40, 151
    Pennsylvania 55, **96**, 103-104, 212, 306
    Port Jervis, Monticello & Kingston 41
    Port Jervis, Monticello & New York 41
    Reading 62
    Rio Grande Southern 322
    Rome & Clinton 238-239, 276
    Rome, Watertown & Ogdensburgh 41, 50
    Rondout & Oswego 114-115
    Rutland 104
    Southern New York **317**
    St. Johnsbury & Lamoille County 309
    Utica, Clinton & Binghamton 238-239, 275-276
    Ulster & Delaware 42, 114-116
    Unadilla Valley 41, 247, 261-262, **264**, **267**, 270, 275, 277, 279, 281, 282, 285, 297, 299, (chapter 15, 304-319)
    Utica & Undailla Valley 305
    Wallkill Valley 42
    Wharton Valley 31, 40-41, 261, 275, 279, 281, 285 (chapter 14, 290-303), 306, 309, **316**
Railway Express Agency 280, **313**
Randallsville, N.Y. **11**, **87**, 238-239, 334
Richfield Springs, N.Y. 277, 305
Righter, J.C. 219
Rochester, N.Y. 89
Rock Rift, N.Y. **77**
Rockdale, N.Y. (chapter 13, 268-289), 312
Rockwell, Chester 270, 276
Rockwells Mills (chapter 13, 268-289)
Roosevelt, Theodore R. 118, 276
Rome, N.Y. 69 (map), 239, 334
Root, Bill **117**
Roscoe, N.Y. 114, 148, 151, 173, 325, **326**
Russell's, N.Y. 177

S

Sages Corners, N.Y. (chapter 13, 268-289)
Salzberg, H.E. 277, (chapter 15, 304-319)
Sanford, Cal **117**
Scranton Division 4, 8, 16, 53-54, **57**, 148, 191, 239, 331, 334
Scrutton (locomotive engineer) 272
Selleck, Thaddeus 39
Service Motor Truck Co. 326
Sherburne-Four Corners, N.Y. 102, **104**
Shofkom, Charles W. **237**
short milk (train) 41
Sidney, N.Y. 40-41, 114, 140, 48, 151-152, 177, 185, 189, **198**, 211-212, 223, 225, (chapter 11, 228-259), 261, 267, 269, 270, 272, 275-276, 281, 290, 295, 297, 306, 308, **332**, 334
Sidney Plains, N.Y. (see Sidney)
Sidney Center, N.Y. 175, (chapter 10, 198-225)
South Edmeston, N.Y. 305
South New Berlin, N.Y. (chapter 13, 268-289), **304**, 318, 337
South Unadilla, N.Y. (chapter 10, 198-227)
Southern Division 52, 238
spring houses 19, **20**
Stamford, N.Y. 115
Starlight, Pa. **53**
steam locomotives (by number in photograph)
    O&W steam locomotives
        2 **145**
        4 **234**
        10 **4, 280**
        25 **281**
        33 **284, 289**
        34 **117, 152**
        35 **105, 241**
        41 **290**

42 **237, 240, 246**
44 **4, 240**
53 **250**
68 **234**
71 **112, 206**
76 **117**
77 **5**
115 **234**
128 **233**
135 **160**
145 **227**
146 **234**
165 **160**
177 **158**
205 **165**
214 **160**
220 **14**
225 **11, 87, 105**
226 **10**
227 **164**
241 **7, 236**
242 **165**
244 **8**
245 **15, 164**
246 **68**
251 **162**
255 **196**
273 **79, 215**
275 **160, 161, 177**
278 **123**
284 **171**
301 **77, 237**
304 **246**
310 **217**
311 **171**
316 **177**
322 **13**
323 **10**
324 **170**
401 **12**
405 **2, 8, 169**
408 **15**
410 **9, 15, 168**

O&W steam locomotive photographs that can not be identified by number, by page listing only
5, 6, 13, 79, 129, 136, 139, 145, 147, 162, 174, 181, 204, 209, 211, 226, 235, 244, 259, 262, 270, 278, 303

UV steam locomotives
1 **310**
4 **264, 306, 313**
6 **311, 317**
7 **304**
272 **312**

D&H steam locomotives
249 **602**

Stellwagen, John C. 114
Sterling Co. (chapter 16, 320-333)
St. Louis Car Co. (chapter 16, 320-333)
St. Louis Museum of Transportation 89
Stockbridge Valley, N.Y. **5**
Stratton, E.L. 289
Sullivan County, N.Y. 52, 113
Summitville, N.Y. **12**, 41, **77**, 175, **320**, 325, 332, 334
Susquehanna, Pa. 233
switchbacks 177, (chapter 9, 184-197), 199
Sykes Company (chapter 16, 320-333)

T

Talbot, D.F. 291
town bonding 114, 229, 269
Trunk Line Assoc. 55
tunnel (other than Northfield)
    Moffat 189
tunnel clearance diagram 197
Tweedle's, N.Y. 177

U

Ulster Co. 113
Union Refrigerator Line **78**
Unadilla Forks, N.Y. 305
Unadilla, N.Y. 114, 219
Unadilla Valley Historical Society 267
Underwood brothers 291

Underwood, Homer 291
Utica branch 41, 331
Utica Flyer **112**, **117**, **122**, 140
Utica, N.Y. 140, 231, 238-239, 277, 288, 305, 334

V

Vail, Jacob 40
Valley Mills, N.Y. **5**
Van Buren, L. Ward **289**
Videtto, Mott 232-233

W

Walton, N.Y. **8-9**, 40, 54, **61**, **79**, 80, 114, 118, 140-141, 144-149, (chapter 7, 150-173), 175, 177, 179, 189, 211, 229, 233, 235, 272, 334, 337
Ward, Lary & Babcock 191
Washington, D.C. 148
Weedon, Archer **234**
Weehawken, N.J. 40, 53, 55, 80, 89, 99, 111, 313, 334
Welland Canal 195, 239
West Brook (chapter 8, 174-183)
West Edmeston, N.Y. 305
Westinghouse Co. (chapter 16, 320-333)
White Motor Co. 104
White, Walter 100
Whites Store, N.Y. (chapter 13, 268-289)
Wilkes-Barre, Pa. 245
Williams, R.B. 114
Wilmington, Del. 104
Woodford Valley, N.Y. (also see Northfield, N.Y.) 177
wrecks 44, **77**, **140**, **177**, 179, 183, **226**, **246**, 276-277, **278**, **287**, **293**
Wright, R. E. 148

Y

Youngs, N.Y. (chapter 10, 198-227)
Young's Gap, N.Y. 9, 175
Yungkurth, Chuck 85, 95 (MDT car plan), 107 (NX car plan)

Z

Zig Zag Tunnel (see Northfield Tunnel)